Politics of Citizenship and Migration

Series Editor
Leila Simona Talani
Department of European and International Studies
King's College London
London, UK

The *Politics of Citizenship and Migration* series publishes exciting new research in all areas of migration and citizenship studies. Open to multiple approaches, the series considers interdisciplinary as well political, economic, legal, comparative, empirical, historical, methodological, and theoretical works. Broad in its coverage, the series promotes research on the politics and economics of migration, globalization and migration, citizenship and migration laws and policies, voluntary and forced migration, rights and obligations, demographic change, diasporas, political membership or behavior, public policy, minorities, border and security studies, statelessness, naturalization, integration and citizen-making, and subnational, supranational, global, corporate, or multilevel citizenship. Versatile, the series publishes single and multi-authored monographs, short-form Pivot books, and edited volumes.

For an informal discussion for a book in the series, please contact the series editor Leila Simona Talani (leila.talani@kcl.ac.uk), or Palgrave editor Isobel Cowper-Coles (isobel.cowpercoles@palgrave.com).

This series is indexed in Scopus.

Ebenezer Durojaye • Robert Doya Nanima
Abiola Idowu-Ojo
Gladys Mirugi-Mukundi
Editors

Realising Socio-Economic Rights of Refugees and Asylum Seekers in Africa

Our Lives Matter

palgrave
macmillan

Editors
Ebenezer Durojaye
Socio-Economic Rights Project
Dullah Omar Institute
University of the Western Cape
Cape Town, South Africa

Robert Doya Nanima
Department of Criminal Justice and Procedure, Faculty of Law
University of the Western Cape
Cape Town, South Africa

Abiola Idowu-Ojo
African Commission on Human and Peoples' Rights
Banjul, The Gambia

Gladys Mirugi-Mukundi
Socio-Economic Rights Project
Dullah Omar Institute
University of the Western Cape
Cape Town, South Africa

ISSN 2520-8896 ISSN 2520-890X (electronic)
Politics of Citizenship and Migration
ISBN 978-3-031-16547-4 ISBN 978-3-031-16548-1 (eBook)
https://doi.org/10.1007/978-3-031-16548-1

This Palgrave Macmillan imprint is published by the registered company Springer Nature Switzerland AG.
The registered company address is: Gewerbestrasse 11, 6330 Cham, Switzerland

Paper in this product is recyclable.

Foreword

This brief preface is not intended to reflect the brilliant contributions that come for the first time to address the issue of the realization of the economic and social rights of refugees and asylum seekers in Africa.

Introducing a comprehensive study on the relationship between ESCR and the situation of refugees and asylum seekers in Africa amounts to thoroughly exploring the actions taken by African States in the management of these rights for the benefit of migrant populations such as refugees and asylum seekers.

It is not a question of synthesizing all the reflections contained in this quality work but of questioning first of all the questions on which the effectiveness of the enjoyment of economic, social and cultural rights for refugees and asylum seekers, in their diversity, is based, namely, examining the degree of protection of the latter in international law, highlighting the challenges they face and finally providing recommendations on the approach to be designed for the realization of these rights.

This is why this remarkable atypical work invites multiple readers to place the issue in the wake of the vulnerability of refugees and asylum seekers in Africa, which no longer needs to be demonstrated as it remains at the heart of the very status of the refugee as provided for in the conventional framework.

More specifically, when refugees or asylum seekers leave their country of origin, they are exposed to discriminatory practices that primarily impact their socio-economic situation.

It is worth remembering that any reflection involves challenges on this question; the book rightly fulfills its mission. The challenges are mostly recorded in the nominated expression of the enjoyment of human rights.

However, if the socio-economic rights from which refugees and asylum seekers must benefit correspond to multiple questions, these are not always reconcilable with the interests of African States. What then would be the way forward? Without the political will of the host States, national policies would continue to exclude and discriminate against refugees and asylum seekers from the implementation and effectiveness of socio-economic rights.

African Commission on Human and Peoples Rights, Special Rapporteur on Refugees, Asylum Seekers, Migrants and Internally Displaced Persons, Addis Ababa, Ethiopia

Sahli Fadel Maya

Preface

This book examines the socio-economic rights challenges of refugees and asylum seekers in Africa. It seeks to fill a major gap in literature by providing a nuanced discussion of the barriers to the realisation of the socio-economic rights of refugees and asylum seekers in Africa. It equally aims to provide some concrete recommendations to African governments towards the realisation of the socio-economic rights of refugees and asylum seekers.

The approach involves a legal and normative analysis of the international, regional and national norms relating to the socio-economic rights of refugees and asylum seekers. Beyond examining some general principles on the rights of refugees and asylum seekers, this book also adopts country case studies on the realisation of the socio-economic rights of refugees and asylum seekers. The book draws lessons from selected African countries, to highlight gaps, challenges and good practices with regard to the realisation of the socio-economic rights of refugees and asylum seekers in the region. The book reveals that while many of the countries in Africa have ratified the UN Refugee Convention and its OAU counterpart, the degree of domestication and implementation differs. While some national laws such as in South Africa, have progressively incorporated the provisions of the UN and OAU Refugee Conventions, others such as Nigeria and South Sudan have adopted a half-hearted approach to this.

The book is divided into three parts of 15 chapters. Part I comprises three chapters on general principles on the rights of refugees and asylum seekers. Part II has three chapters that deal with the mechanisms at the regional level for the protection of the rights of refugees and asylum seekers in Africa. Part III contains eight chapters drawing lessons from selected African countries on efforts towards the realisation of the socio-economic rights of refugees and asylum seekers.

The book will be useful to researchers, students, academics, policy makers and international organisations or institutions interested in advancing the rights of refugees and asylum seekers.

Cape Town, South Africa	Ebenezer Durojaye
Cape Town, South Africa	Robert Nanima
Banjul, The Gambia	Abiola Idowu-Ojo
Cape Town, South Africa	Gladys Mirugi-Mukundi

Acknowledgements

We would like to express our gratitude to all the contributors for their patience and commitment throughout the process for the finalisation of this book. Thanks equally go to all the persons that participated in our webinar series on the Socio-Economic Rights of Refugees in Africa. In this regard, we would like to thank our colleagues at the Dullah Omar Institute and the African Commission on Human and People's Rights.

Contents

Notes on Contributors

Joseph Geng Akech is a human rights lawyer and a doctor from the University of Pretoria, South Africa. He has published widely in constitutional law, human rights and governance. His doctoral thesis is entitled "foreign influence and the legitimacy of constitution building in South Sudan."

St. Emmanuel Ayooluwa is Sub-Dean, Faculty of Law, Adekunle Ajasin University, Akungba-Akoko, Ondo State, Nigeria.

Rashri Baboolal-Frank is a senior lecturer, University of Pretoria, Advocate of the High Court of South Africa.

Kennedy Chege is a researcher and a doctoral candidate attached to the Department of Science and Technology and the National Research Foundation SARChI Research Chair, at the Faculty of Law, University of Cape Town.

Musavengana Winston Theodore Chibwana is a research fellow, Institute of Gender and Africa Studies, University of the Free State, South Africa.

Ebenezer Durojaye is a professor and head of the Socio-Economic Rights Project at the Dullah Omar Institute, University of the Western Cape, South Africa. His areas of research include human rights, socio-economic rights, sexual and reproductive health and rights, gender and constitutionalism. He has written extensively in these areas. He is the co-editor of the book *Constitutional Resilience and the COVID-19 Pandemic: Perspectives from Sub-Saharan Africa* (Palgrave Macmillan 2022).

Abiola Idowu-Ojo is a senior legal officer at the African Commission on Human and Peoples Rights, Banjul, The Gambia.

Gerard Emmanuel Kamdem Kamga is Senior Lecturer and Coordinator of the Research and Postgraduate Division, Free State Centre for Human Rights, University of the Free State.

Callixte Kavuro is a postdoctoral research fellow at the Department of Public Law, Stellenbosch University. He obtained his doctoral degree from Stellenbosch University, his master degree from University of Cape Town (UCT), and his undergraduate degree from University of the Western Cape (UWC). He is an admitted advocate of the High Court of South Africa.

Emma Charlene Lubaale is an associate professor, Faculty of Law, Rhodes University.

Julie Lugulu is a lecturer in the Department of Public Law, Kabarak University, Kenya; she is also a doctoral candidate, Dullah Omar Institute for Constitutional Law, Governance and Human Rights, University of the Western Cape, Faculty of Law, South Africa.

Gladys Mirugi-Mukundi is a researcher with the Socio-Economic Rights Project at the Dullah Omar Institute, University of the Western Cape. Her research expertise and interest are in human rights, socio-economic rights, social justice and inclusive societies, women and access to housing, rule of law and corruption. She is the co-editor the ESR Review: Economic and Social Rights in Africa, a quarterly publication that aims to inform and educate policymakers and members of civil society, about key developments relating to socio-economic rights at the national and international levels.

Ferd Moyomba is a lecturer in the Department of Public Law, Mount Kenya University Parklands Law Campus, Kenya. He is also a PhD candidate at the University of Pretoria, Faculty of Law, South Africa.

Angela Nkatha Mutema is a lecturer at Jomo Kenyatta University of Agriculture and Technology, School of law, Nairobi, Kenya. She is an advocate of the High Court of Kenya and a member the International

Commission of Jurists, Kenya Chapter. Her research interests are in international law, and private law with a focus on alternative justice systems.

Robert Doya Nanima is an associate professor in the Department of Criminal Justice and Procedure, Faculty of Law, University of the Western Cape. He is also attached to the Dullah Omar Institute, as a research fellow. He continues to conduct research in the areas of children's rights, public law, criminal law and socio-economic rights.

James Tinotenda Ndemera is a doctoral researcher at Rhodes University, South Africa.

Bright Nkrumah is an assistant professor in the Department of Ecology and Environmental Studies, The Water School, Florida Gulf Coast University. He received his DPhil from the Center for Human Rights, University of Pretoria and has published extensively on political contestation, minority rights, food (in)security, urban agriculture and democratisation.

Olubayo Oluduro is Professor of Law at the Adekunle Ajasin University, Akungba-Akoko, Ondo State, Nigeria. He was formerly the Dean, Faculty of Law at the Adekunle Ajasin University and currently, the Director, Linkages and International Programmes Office (LIPO) at the Adekunle Ajasin University, Nigeria. He is the author of *Oil Exploitation and Human Rights Violations in Nigeria's Oil Producing Communities*, Intersentia Publishers, Cambridge—Antwerp—Portland, 2014. He has published extensively both in local and international refereed journals on a wide range of legal and interdisciplinary subjects, particularly in the field of Environmental Law and Human Rights. He has also consulted widely on Environmental Law, Health and Human Rights issues.

CHAPTER 1

Socio-Economic Rights for Refugees and Asylum Seekers Under International Law

Ebenezer Durojaye, Robert Doya Nanima, Abiola Idowu-Ojo, and Gladys Mirugi-Mukundi

X, a refugee woman, experienced challenges when she was pregnant and suffered a miscarriage. When her water broke, she was rushed to the hospital with blood already dripping down her legs. Despite this condition, the health care workers at the hospital refused to assist her as she was undocumented. Consequently, people had to contribute money for her to

E. Durojaye (✉) • G. Mirugi-Mukundi
Socio-Economic Rights Project, Dullah Omar Institute, University of the Western Cape, Cape Town, South Africa
e-mail: edurojaye@uwc.ac.za; gmirugimukundi@uwc.ac.za

R. D. Nanima
Department of Criminal Justice and Procedure, Faculty of Law, University of the Western Cape, Cape Town, South Africa
e-mail: rnanima@uwc.ac.za

A. Idowu-Ojo
African Commission on Human and Peoples' Rights, Banjul, The Gambia
e-mail: Idowu-Ojoa@africa-union.org

E. Durojaye et al. (eds.), *Realising Socio-Economic Rights of Refugees and Asylum Seekers in Africa*, Politics of Citizenship and Migration, https://doi.org/10.1007/978-3-031-16548-1_1

see a private doctor where she was properly attended to. This incident occurred during the time she had an appointment with the Department of Home Affairs for her permit.[1] This unpalatable experience would seem to be the lot of many refugees and asylum seekers in the region.

The United Nations High Commissioner for Human Rights has pointed out that: '[B]eing a refugee means more than being an alien. It means living in exile and depending on others for such basic needs as food, clothing and shelter'.[2]

Across the world, and Africa in particular, refugees and asylum seekers continue to face serious challenges regarding their human rights. They are sometimes treated with contempt and subjected to various forms of inhuman and degrading treatment. According to the UNCHR, an estimated 80 million people worldwide experience one form of displacement or another. Of this figure, about 43 million are refugees, four million are asylum seekers and 46 million are internally displaced persons.[3] Developing countries are host to approximately 85 per cent of refugees and asylum seekers.[4] In Africa, Uganda, with approximately 1.4 million refugees and asylum seekers, hosts the largest number in the region.[5]

Although the experiences of refugees and asylum seekers are not homogenous, they face similar challenges with regard to living a dignified life in their host countries. Tension often exists between refugees and asylum seekers and citizens of host states. This often turns violent and leads to refugees and asylum seekers being unable to secure jobs or earn a living. More importantly, the realisation of their socio-economic rights is grossly undermined by many host countries.

According to the 1951 UN Convention Relating to the Status of Refugees (UN Refugee Convention), a 'refugee' is:

> [A person who] owing to a well-founded fear of being persecuted for reasons of race, religion, nationality, membership of a particular social group or political opinion, is outside the country of his nationality and is unable or,

[1] J Freedman et al. 'Sexual and reproductive health of asylum seeking and refugee women in South Africa: understanding the determinants of vulnerability' (2020) 28 (1) *Sexual and Reproductive Health Matters* 324–334.

[2] OHCHR 'Fact Sheet 20: Human rights and refugees' (July 1993).

[3] See UNCHR 'Refugee data finder' https://www.unhcr.org/refugee-statistics/ (accessed 29 June 2022).

[4] As above.

[5] As above.

> owing to such fear, is unwilling to avail himself of the protection of that country, or who, not having a nationality and being outside the country of his former residence, is unable or, owing to such fear, is unwilling to return to it.[6]

The Organisation of African Unity Refugee Convention Governing the Specific Aspects of Refugee Problems in Africa of 1969 (OAU Refugee Convention) provides a broader definition of a refugee, which offers protection to a wider group of persons. It includes the definition above and adds that a refugee is also:

> [E]very person who, owing to external aggression, occupation, foreign domination or events seriously disturbing public order in either part or the whole of his country of origin or nationality, is compelled to leave his place of habitual residence in order to seek refuge in another place outside his country of origin or nationality.[7]

On the other hand, an asylum seeker is someone who has fled his/her country for another country due to persecution or serious human rights violations. He/she has applied for a refugee status but is still waiting for the outcome of his/her application.

From these definitions, it is clear that refugees and asylum seekers differ from economic migrants, who willingly leave their country to seek opportunities in another country. The main difference is the voluntariness on the part of economic migrants as compared to refugees and asylum seekers who are forced to leave their countries. Another important point to make regarding the definitions is that the OAU Refugee Convention serves as an important complement to the UN Convention on Refugees. It should be noted that many African countries are parties to both the UN Convention and the OAU Refugee Convention.

While international law affords refugees and asylum seekers the enjoyment of their human rights, including socio-economic rights, in reality states have only paid lip service to these rights. As a continent grappling with conflicts and insurrections, the number of refugees and asylum seekers in Africa has increased considerably over the years. It is estimated that

[6] Art 1(A) of the UN General Assembly, Convention Relating to the Status of Refugees, 28 July 1951, United Nations, Treaty Series, vol. 189, p 137.

[7] Article 1 of the OAU, Convention Governing the Specific Aspects of Refugee Problems in Africa (OAU Convention), 10 September 1969, 1001 UNTS 45.

more than 32 million Africans are internally displaced persons (IDPs), refugees or asylum seekers—this figure is up from 29 million a year ago.[8] Of these 32 million forcibly displaced persons, three-quarters are internally displaced (24 million IDPs).[9] The UN Refugee Convention is the first international instrument to provide protection to refugees and asylum seekers. It outlines a number of protections for refugees and asylum seekers. Beyond providing a definition for a 'refugee' and an 'asylum seeker' respectively, it urges states to ensure that the rights and dignity of refugees and asylum seekers are guaranteed. The Convention prohibits states from turning away a refugee under the principle of non-refoulement. More importantly, the Convention urges states in some respects to accord to refugees the same treatment as they do to non-citizens in the same circumstances, or to non-citizens generally.[10] States ought to treat refugees and asylum seekers as they would treat other non-nationals insofar as moveable and immovable property rights are concerned. This should also apply to other rights related to the acquisition of property, including leases and other contracts.[11] In addition, states are to apply the same favourable treatment afforded to nationals' access to housing to refugees and asylum seekers. The Convention also requires that refugees' rights to employment and social security be protected.[12]

In addition to the protection provided by the Refugee Convention, the International Covenant on Economic, Social and Cultural Rights (ICESCR)[13] contains extensive provisions to protect the socio-economic rights of all individuals, including refugees and asylum seekers. The Committee on Economic, Social and Cultural Rights (CESCR) has noted on several occasions that the socio-economic rights guarantee in the Covenant must be accorded to everyone, especially vulnerable and marginalised groups such as women, children, refugees and asylum seekers. More importantly, the CESCR has noted that refugees and asylum seekers are more likely to face discrimination in the enjoyment of their ICESCR

[8] Reliefweb '32 Million Africans forcibly displaced by conflict and repression' (18 June 2021), https://reliefweb.int/report/world/32-million-africans-forcibly-displaced-conflict-and-repression (accessed 7 November 2021).

[9] As above.

[10] Article 7 of the UN Refugee Convention.

[11] Article 13 of the UN Refugee Convention.

[12] See, for instance, article 24 of the UN Refugee Convention. See discussion on social security in Chap. 3 by Chege.

[13] UN General Assembly, International Covenant on Economic, Social and Cultural Rights, 16 December 1966, United Nations, Treaty Series, vol. 993, p 3.

rights and has urged states to take appropriate measures to address this challenge.[14]

At the regional level, the OAU Refugee Convention provides broader protection for a person seeking refugee status as far as it includes asylum seekers. States are to apply the provisions of the OAU Refugee Convention to all refugees irrespective of race, gender, religion or political opinion.[15] The OAU Refugee Convention imposes duties on refugees and asylum seekers by providing that they are to abide by the laws of the host state and ensuring that they do not engage in any acts to destabilise the host state. The Convention does not explicitly guarantee the socio-economic rights of refugees and asylum seekers, nor does it adopt a rights-based approach.[16] However, the existing provisions on socio-economic rights in regional human rights instruments such as the African Charter on Human and Peoples' Rights (African Charter),[17] the Protocol to the African Charter on the Rights of Women (Maputo Protocol)[18] and the African Charter on the Rights and Welfare of the Child (ACRWC),[19] appear to apply to refugees and asylum seekers in the region.

It should be noted that article 12(3) of the African Charter recognises the rights of every individual to seek and obtain asylum in other countries. The African Commission on Human and Peoples' Rights (African Commission) has affirmed the human rights of refugees and asylum seekers in general and socio-economic rights in particular.[20] Some of the

[14] See, for instance, UN Committee on Economic, Social and Cultural Rights (CESCR), General Comment 14: The Right to the Highest Attainable Standard of Health (Art 12 of the Covenant), 11 August 2000, E/C.12/2000/4; and UN Committee on Economic, Social and Cultural Rights (CESCR), General Comment 20: Non-discrimination in economic, social and cultural rights (art 2, para 2, of the International Covenant on Economic, Social and Cultural Rights), 2 July 2009, E/C.12/GC/20.

[15] African Union, Convention for the Protection and Assistance of Internally Displaced Persons in Africa (Kampala Convention), 23 October 2009. Adopted in 2009 and entered into force on 6 December 2012.

[16] See G Bekker 'The protection of asylum seekers and refugees within the African human rights system' (2013) 13 *African Human Rights Law Journal* 1.

[17] OAU, African Charter on Human and Peoples' Rights (Banjul Charter), 27 June 1981, CAB/LEG/67/3 rev. 5, 21 ILM 58 (1982).

[18] African Union, Protocol to the African Charter on Human and People's Rights on the Rights of Women in Africa, 11 July 2003.

[19] OAU, African Charter on the Rights and Welfare of the Child, 11 July 1990, CAB/LEG/24.9/49 (1990) (ACRWC).

[20] ACHPR, Resolution 470 on the Protection of Refuges, Asylum seekers and Migrants in the fight against the COVID-19 pandemic in Africa, adopted 3 December 2020.

decisions of the African Commission have reiterated the obligations of states to ensure the protection of the rights of refugees and asylum seekers, including their socio-economic rights.[21] Further, while examining states reports, the African Commission has made useful recommendations to states on how to safeguard the human rights of refugees and asylum seekers.[22]

The African Committee of Experts on the Rights and Welfare of the Child was established and mandated to promote and protect the rights of the child in Africa.[23] It is instructive to note that the African Charter on the Rights and Welfare of the Child provides for the protection of refugees and asylum seekers.[24] At its core, the same protection accorded to refugees is extended to internally displaced children.[25] The African Committee on the Rights and Welfare of the Child also uses a child rights-based approach in enforcing the human rights protection of the child.[26] This includes the application of the best interests' principle, right to life, survival and development, non-discrimination and participation of the child.[27] The African Committee of Experts engages with states through the use of state party reports and the issuance of concluding observations thereon, investigative missions and cooperation with other stakeholders in the promotion and protection of the rights of the child.[28]

Notably, the Kampala Convention relating to Internally Displaced Persons (IDPs)[29] is equally relevant for the purpose of this book. Its relevance stems from the fact that IDPs tend to experience similar challenges to refugees and asylum seekers.

In addition to the binding instruments, efforts have been made by the African Union (AU) to develop a continental policy framework to address

[21] See, for instance, *Rencontre Africaine pour la Défense des Droits de l'Homme v Zambia* (2000) AHRLR 321 (ACHPR 1996); see also *Sudan Human Rights Organisation v Sudan* (2009) AHRLR 153 (ACHPR 2009), which deals with the socio-economic rights of refugees.

[22] See, for instance, para 26 of the ACHPR, Concluding Observations and Recommendations – South Africa: First Periodic Report 1999–2001, 38th ordinary session of the African Commission, 21 November to 5 December 2005, Banjul, The Gambia.

[23] See art 36 of the ACRWC.

[24] See art 23 of the ACRWC.

[25] As above.

[26] See arts 3, 4, 5 and 7 of the ACRWC.

[27] As above.

[28] See arts 42–45 of the ACRWC.

[29] The Kampala Convention (n 15).

the challenges faced by migrants, including refugees and asylum seekers. The AU has adopted the Migration Policy Framework for the region.[30] This comprehensive document captures the various challenges of migrants, including refugees and asylum seekers. It proposes detailed and useful recommendations to address the various challenges experienced by migrants, refugees, asylum seekers and internally displaced persons.

Despite the developments at the regional level, the recognition of the socio-economic rights of refugees and asylum seekers remains a major challenge at the national level in Africa. Refugees and asylum seekers continue to face discriminatory practices and are deprived of their socio-economic rights by host states. This may be attributed to factors such as the non-domestication of international norms and standards on the rights of refugees and asylum seekers, lack of appropriate legislation to address the needs of refugees and asylum seekers, hostility and xenophobic tendencies by host states, and lack of political will by host states to implement existing standards on the rights of refugees and asylum seekers. The situation was compounded by the outbreak of Covid-19, which rendered refugees and asylum seekers more vulnerable to the negative consequences of the pandemic.[31] This has resulted in the poor realisation of the socio-economic rights of refugees and asylum seekers on the continent. Against this backdrop, this book seeks to discuss the various barriers to the realisation of socio-economic rights of refugees and asylum seekers, and opportunities that exist to overcome these barriers.

This volume has several unique selling points:

1. It is a first of its kind study to comprehensively address the socio-economic rights challenges faced by refugees and asylum seekers in Africa.
2. Practices in African countries are assessed against international frameworks on the importance of upholding the rights of refugees and asylum seekers.
3. It is the product of a unique collaboration between established and emerging African scholars about a serious and topical issue affecting

[30] See the African Union 'Migration Policy Framework for Africa and Plan of Action (2018–2030)' (2018).

[31] L Guadagno 'Migrants and the COVID-19 pandemic: An initial analysis' WHO Migration Research Series 60 (2020) 5; see also International Commission of Jurists 'Living like people who die slowly: The need for right to health compliant COVID-19 responses' (2020) 42.

the region. This also provided the rare opportunity for the two groups of scholars to work together with a view to finding lasting solutions to a serious challenge confronting not only the region, but the international community as a whole.

4. The volume focuses on the socio-economic rights challenges of refugees and asylum seekers and examines the commitment of African governments to promote and protect these rights. It also offers lessons from across the region on how to address the socio-economic rights challenges of refugees and asylum seekers with a view to ensuring that 'no one is left behind'.

1 Framework and Approach of This Book

This book is significant because it is one of the few volumes to examine the socio-economic rights challenges of refugees and asylum seekers in Africa. While some books have explored the socio-economic rights of refugees in general, none have focused on the obligations of African states to enforce the socio-economic rights of refugees and asylum seekers. The authors argue that virtually all African countries have ratified at least one human rights instrument that recognises the socio-economic rights of people, including those of refugees and asylum seekers. Thus, African governments are obligated to ensure the realisation of these rights to refugees and asylum seekers.

It should be noted that despite the growing importance of socio-economic rights, some states are still sceptical in enforcing these rights. This is due to the argument that these rights are not justiciable. This scepticism is often reinforced by arguments of commentators that socio-economic rights should not be a subject of legal adjudication. Chief among these commentators is Lon Fuller, who argues that subjecting socio-economic rights to court intervention may lead to unanticipated outcomes beyond the control of the court.[32] This is because these rights are complex and uncertain. He likens the adjudication of socio-economic rights to a spider's web: if one strand of the web is cut, this will affect the other strands.[33] In other words, the adjudication of socio-economic rights may lead to multiplier effects far beyond the control of the court.

[32] LL Fuller 'The forms and limits of adjudication' (1978) *Harvard Law Review* 353–409.
[33] As above.

Other commentators have echoed Fuller's argument by contending that to permit courts to intervene in socio-economic rights will undermine the principle of the separation of powers.[34] It has also been argued that courts are not the best institutions to make decisions involving the allocation of resources, as judges lack the competence to deal with budgetary matters.[35] It should be noted that the CESCR has attempted to clarify the nature of states' obligations regarding the implementation of socio-economic rights. In its General Comment 3 on states obligations, the CESCR noted that states are expected to take appropriate measures within their resources to ensure the realisation of socio-economic rights for everyone, including refugees and asylum seekers.[36] The CESCR noted that while it may not be possible to realise the enjoyment of socio-economic rights immediately in all cases, states should be seen to be taking steps towards realising these rights.[37] The CESCR stated that the failure to take steps to realise these rights will amount to retrogressive measures. More importantly, the CESCR opines that the extent of a state's resources is not as important as how judiciously it has utilised the resources available to it.[38]

There are counter arguments to the non-justiciability of socio-economic rights. Some commentators have argued that civil and political rights are as problematic to enforce as socio-economic rights, and that both sets of rights require substantial resources to be fully implemented.[39] It is further argued that while the principle of separation of powers is important, this should be complemented by the doctrine of checks and balances, which requires the judiciary to assess the constitutionality of the actions of other

[34] See, for instance, J Cottrell and Y Ghai 'The role of the courts in implementing economic, social and cultural rights' in Y Ghai and J Cottrell (eds.) *Economic, social and cultural rights in practice - The role of judges in implementing economic, social and cultural rights* (2004) 61.

[35] See Thabo, M. T., & Odeku, K. O. (2021). Separation of powers, checks and balances and judicial exercise of selfrestraint: an analysis of case law. Obiter, 42(3), 547–560 generally.

[36] CESCR General Comment No. 3: The Nature of States Parties' Obligations E/*1991/23.*

[37] As above.

[38] As above.

[39] See, for instance, C Ngang Judicial enforcement of socio-economic rights in South Africa and the separation of powers objection: The obligation to take 'other measures' (2014) 14 *Africa Human Rights Law Journal* 655. See also A An-Naim, To affirm the full human *rights* standing of *economic, social* and cultural *rights* in Y Ghai and J *Cottrell* (eds.) *Economic, social and cultural rights in practice - The role of judges in implementing economic, social and cultural rights* (2004).

arms of government.[40] In the *Treatment Action Campaign case*, the South African Constitutional Court affirmed the powers of the courts to hear socio-economic rights cases and that they have the role of ensuring that other arms of government act in line with their constitutional mandate. [41]

Furthermore, advocates of socio-economic rights have argued that all rights are universal, interdependent and inter-related.[42] Therefore, it is superficial to classify socio-economic rights as aspirational rights that are unenforceable, while civil and political rights are deemed enforceable.[43] A similar position was taken in Vienna during the International Human Rights Conference when the international community declared that all human rights intersect with one another.[44] Affirming this position, the CESCR, in its General Comment 14, for example, noted that the enjoyment of the right to health intersects with other rights such as dignity, equality and non-discrimination, privacy, life, and freedom from torture and inhuman and degrading treatment.[45] Inspired by this reasoning, the African Commission on Human and Peoples' Rights in some of its jurisprudence has affirmed that the violation of the right to health undermines the rights to life, dignity, equality, housing and food.[46] This appears to negate any doubt about the enforceability of socio-economic rights.

[40] J Cottrell and Y Ghai 'The role of the courts in implementing economic, social and cultural rights' in Y Ghai and J Cottrell (eds.) *Economic, social and cultural rights in practice - The role of judges in implementing economic, social and cultural rights* (2004) 61.

[41] *Minister of Health and Others v. Treatment Action Campaign* 2002 (5) SA 721 (CC), 2002 (10) BCLR 1033 (CC).

[42] See, for instance, M Ssenyonjo 'Reflections on state obligations, with respect to economic, social and cultural rights in international human rights law' (2011) 15 (6) *International Journal of Human Rights* 969–1012.

[43] As above, see also C Scott and P Macklem, 'Constitutional ropes of sand or justiciable guarantees? Social Rights in a New South African Constitution' (1992) 141 *University of Pennsylvania Law Review*; see also D Chirwa and L Chenwi, 'The Protection of Economic, Social and Cultural Rights in Africa' in D Chirwa and L Chenwi (eds.), The Protection of Economic, Social and Cultural Rights in Africa: International, Regional and National Perspectives.

[44] UN General Assembly, *Vienna Declaration and Programme of Action*, 12 July 1993, A/CONF.157/23.

[45] General Comment 14 para 14.

[46] See, for instance, *Social and Economic Rights Action Center (SERAC) and Another v Government of Nigeria* Communication 155/96 decided at the 30th ordinary Session of the African Commission held from 13 to 27 October 2001, Banjul, The Gambia; see also *Free Legal Assistance Group and Others v. Zaire*, Communication. No. 25/89, 47/90, 56/91, 100/93. *Sudan Human Rights Organisation & Another v Sudan* (2009) AHRLR 153 (ACHPR 2009).

Indeed, a recent decision of the South African High Court has found that the exclusion of asylum seekers from social palliatives to cushion the negative effects of the Covid-19 pandemic was irrational and unconstitutional.[47] The Court held that the policy of the government undermines the rights to equality and dignity of the asylum seekers.[48] In *Union of Refugee Women and Others v Director: Private Security Industry Regulatory Authority and Others*,[49] the South African Constitutional Court held that 'Refugees are indisputably the most vulnerable group in our society and their plight calls for compassion'. These are important decisions affirming equal rights to social protection for refugees and asylum seekers. The message underlying the decisions of the courts is that refugees and asylum seekers are human beings deserving of equal treatment. It also conveys the message that the exclusion of certain categories of people from benefiting from the government's social security programme on the basis of nationality is discriminatory and therefore unacceptable.

However, in reality challenges remain to the enforceability of these rights, particularly in the context of migrants. Therefore, there is a need to adopt programmes and policy founded on the principle of equality in addressing the needs of refugees and asylum seekers in society. States' intervention to meet the needs of refugees and asylum seekers must not be based on charity or privilege. Rather it must be rights-based and conform to the principles of equality and non-discrimination.

Although many African countries do not specifically recognise socio-economic rights in their constitutions and are therefore unable to realise these rights for their people, the circumstances of refugees and asylum seekers tend to be more precarious. This is because they may be excluded from programmes or policies adopted by the host governments to meet the needs of their citizens. An example of this relates to the devastating impact of the Covid-19 pandemic and efforts by governments to mitigate this impact on the people. Most of the responses by African governments to Covid-19 by way of provision of palliatives excluded refugees and

[47] See *Scalabrini Centre of Cape Town and Another v Minister of Social Development and Others* (22808/2020) [2020] ZAGPPHC 308.

[48] As above.

[49] *Union of Refugee Women v Director: Private Security Industry Regulatory Authority* 2007 (4) BCLR 339 (CC).

asylum seekers as beneficiaries.[50] The UN Special Rapporteur on migrants in one of his reports has lamented the lack of basic amenities and human rights challenges experienced by refugees and asylum seekers during the Covid-19 pandemic.[51] This affirms the point that refugees and asylum seekers are often treated as 'outsiders' by host countries and their socio-economic rights are trampled on.[52] To date, no book has captured the various challenges to socio-economic rights and the right to live a dignified life which refugees and asylum seekers experience daily. Thus, this book seeks to fill this major gap by providing a nuanced discussion of the barriers to the realisation of the socio-economic rights of refugees and asylum seekers in Africa. It equally aims to provide some concrete recommendations to African governments towards the realisation of the socio-economic rights of refugees and asylum seekers.

Our approach involves a legal and normative analysis of the international, regional and national norms relating to the socio-economic rights of refugees and asylum seekers. Beyond examining some general principles on the rights of refugees and asylum seekers, this book also provides country case studies on the realisation of the socio-economic rights of refugees and asylum seekers. The notion of equality and non-discrimination in the context of the socio-economic rights of refugees and asylum seekers is the conceptual framework that runs through this book. Whether in the denial of access to healthcare services, food, employment, social security or a dignified living, the bottom line has always been their non-recognition as human beings worthy of protection. In this regard, the book draws lessons from selected African countries to highlight gaps, challenges and good practices with regard to the realisation of the socio-economic rights of refugees and asylum seekers in the region.

The book reveals that while many of the countries in Africa have ratified the UN Refugee Convention and its OAU counterpart, the degree of domestication and implementation differs amongst countries. While some national laws such as in South Africa have progressively incorporated the

[50] C Ferdinand 'Unspoken inequality: How COVID-19 has exacerbated existing vulnerabilities of asylum-seekers, refugees, and undocumented migrants in South Africa' (2020) 19 *International Journal of Equity in Health* 1.

[51] Felipe González Morales (Special Rapporteur on the Human Rights of Migrants), *One and a Half Years After: The Impact of COVID-19 on the Human Rights of Migrants*, U.N. Doc. *A/76/257* (July 30, 2021).

[52] As above.

provisions of the UN and OAU Refugee Conventions, others such as Nigeria and South Sudan have adopted a half-hearted approach to this.

2 Comparison with Other Books

There are a number of books that address the plights of refugees and asylum seekers internationally. Most of these publications focus on the human rights of refugees and asylum seekers generally, and the few that focus on their socio-economic rights do not address comprehensively the challenges of refugees and asylum seekers in Africa. As mentioned earlier, Africa not only serves as a host to refugees and asylum seekers, but also serves as a provider. The pervading high level of poverty, lack of service delivery and corrosive corruption, coupled with the devastating impact of Covid-19, have deepened inequality in the region. Refugees and asylum seekers are disproportionately affected by this situation. This makes it imperative to contextualise the challenges in the realisation of the socio-economic rights of refugees and asylum seekers in the region.

In her book *International Refugee Law and Socio-Economic Rights* (Cambridge 2007), Michelle Foster provides a critical discussion of the safeguards existing under international law to guarantee the socio-economic rights of refugees and asylum seekers. The book proposes a nuanced and progressive interpretation of the UN Refugee Convention to advance the socio-economic rights of refugees. It argues that such an interpretation must align with the clarifications provided by international human rights treaties. However, this book differs from ours in the sense that its focus is on the international law regime to protect the socio-economic rights of refugees, but it does not engage in country case studies in Africa. Our book focuses mainly on the socio-economic rights challenges of refugees and asylum seekers across Africa. It provides nuanced analyses of the challenges involved in the realisation of refugees' and asylum seekers' rights and offers useful recommendations in this regard.

A much earlier book by James Hathaway titled *The Rights of Refugees under International Law* (Cambridge University Press 2005) presents the first comprehensive analysis of the human rights of refugees as set by the UN Refugee Convention. It raises some critical questions relating to the rights of refugees, such as whether refugees should be allowed to enjoy freedom of movement, to work, to access public welfare programmes, or to be reunited with family members. Hathaway links the standards of the UN Refugee Convention to key norms of international human rights law, and applies his analysis to the world's most difficult protection challenges. While this book makes an important contribution to the rights of refugees and asylum seekers, its focus is on international law and it does not give adequate attention to the socio-economic rights challenges of refugees in Africa. Moreover, it does not consider the norms and standards relevant to advancing the socio-economic rights of refugees in the region. Our book provides important discussions on the norms and standards for the realisation of the socio-economic rights of refugees and asylum seekers in Africa and the role of human rights bodies in safeguarding these rights.

An edited volume by Fatima Khan and Tal Schreier titled *Refugee Law in South Africa* (Juta 2014) provides an overview of some of the challenges facing refugees and asylum seekers in South Africa. However, only one chapter of the book is dedicated to considering the socio-economic rights challenges of refugees and asylum seekers in South Africa. Aside from the fact that the book only focuses on South Africa, the discussion on the socio-economic rights of refugees and asylum seekers is minimal. Our book therefore provides a more detailed discussion from a continental perspective of the challenges relating to the socio-economic rights of refugees and asylum seekers.

In *Regional Approaches to the Protection of Asylum Seekers* (Routledge 2015), an edited volume by Ademola Abass and Francesca Ippolito (eds.), the editors, using a comparative approach, examine the challenges asylum seekers face across the regions of the world. The book is a collection of chapters that explore the different challenges facing asylum seekers and the reforms towards addressing them. The aim of the book is threefold. First, it seeks to provide an understanding of the existing legal regimes at the regional level to address the challenges faced by asylum seekers. Second, it explores the role of regional institutions including courts and other bodies as well as national human rights institutions in the protection of asylum seekers. Third, the book also emphasises the important contribution made by Latin America to the protection of asylum seekers and lessons other regions may learn from this. However, the book only features one chapter on the protection of asylum seekers in Africa. To the extent that the focus is on regional approaches and mainly on the rights of asylum seekers, it differs greatly from our book. Our book not only focuses exclusively on Africa, but also addresses the socio-economic rights of refugees and asylum seekers in the region. In this volume the chapters address crucial socio-economic rights of refugees and asylum seekers. While we do not aim to address all the socio-economic rights affecting refugees and asylum seekers, our focus is on the rights to food, health, work, education and social security. Host states have often denied these rights to refugees and asylum seekers, and the situation was exacerbated by the Covid-19 pandemic.

3 Chapters in the Book

The book is divided into three parts encompassing a total of 15 chapters.

Part I comprises three chapters on general principles on the rights of refugees and asylum seekers. Part II has three chapters that deal with the mechanisms at the regional level for the protection of the rights of refugees and asylum seekers in Africa. Part III contains eight chapters drawing lessons from selected African countries on efforts towards the realisation of the socio-economic rights of refugees and asylum seekers.

3.1 Part I: General Principles on Refugees and Asylum Seekers

In Chap. 2, Durojaye et al. provide an overview of the protection of the socio-economic rights of refugees and asylum seekers under international and regional human rights law. They examine various instruments such as the International Covenant on Economic, Social and Cultural Rights, and the UN Refugee Convention. In addition, they examine African regional human rights instruments with regard to the realisation of the socio-economic rights of refugees and asylum seekers, such as the African Charter on Human and Peoples' Rights, the African Charter on the Rights and Welfare of the Child, the Protocol to the African Charter on Human and Peoples' Rights on the Rights of Women (Maputo Protocol), and the OAU Refugee Convention. The chapter equally evaluates the approach of the African Commission on Human and Peoples' Rights to the socio-economic rights of refugees and asylum seekers.

In Chap. 3, Kavuro looks at the link between the right to human dignity and the realisation of the rights of refugees in Africa. He argues that the humanitarian approach to refugee protection serves to inhibit their access to socio-economic rights and benefits, as the means to restore dignity and normalcy to their lives. Viewing the protection through the lens of citizenship and national sovereignty, he illustrates the challenges concerning the realisation of socio-economic rights of refugees in Africa and the impact of those challenges on the protection of their dignity, health and well-being. He observes that these challenges are reinforced by the absence of refugees' voices in the democratic processes or political fora where citizens express their unhappiness or concerns.

In Chap. 4, Chege evaluates the right to social protection for refugees and asylum seekers in Africa in the Covid-19 era. He commences by outlining the normative legal framework for the right to social protection for refugees and asylum seekers in Africa. His discussion covers the key international, regional and domestic legal instruments that enshrine and protect this right. He then highlights the challenges experienced in terms of the realisation of the rights for refugees and asylum seekers on the African continent during the Covid-19 era. Drawing from experiences of refugees and asylum seekers in South Africa, he explores the opportunities for the realisation of social protection for refugees and asylum seekers.

3.2 Part II: Mechanism for the Protection of the Rights of Refugees and Asylum Seekers

In Chap. 5, Nkrumah evaluates the potential role of the African Court on Human and Peoples' Rights in promoting the socio-economic rights of migrants. He seeks to address the central research question of how the African Court can contribute towards alleviating the socio-economic hardships of RAS. He argues that the African Court could improve the socio-economic conditions of migrants by advocating for their inclusion in the conventional social security structure of host states. However, he argues that the optimism around the African Court's intervention is likely to wane unless it takes bold steps in overcoming the normative and institutional constraints that hinder its effectiveness towards developing a timely jurisprudence on social security.

In Chap. 6, Nanima contextualises the socio-economic rights of the refugee child from the perspective of the African Charter on the Rights and Welfare of the Child and the interpretation provided by the African Committee of Experts on the Rights and Welfare of the Child. He argues that it is critical that the refugee child in Africa is at the centre of the various initiatives that arise. He makes mention of the position of the refugee regime in international law, followed by an evaluation of the normative guidance under the African Children's Charter. He engages the emerging jurisprudence to show the extent to which the African Children's Committee has lived up to the task of promoting the rights of the refugee child in Africa.

In Chap. 7, Musavengana extends the conversation to transnational child rights civil society networks (TCRNs) and how they may address the socio-economic rights of child refugees. He identifies that TCRNs broadly address cross-border child rights violations, and argues that they have a pertinent role in addressing common child rights issues within their regions, based on global and regional child rights instruments. Using a constructivist approach, he argues for potential engagements between the TCRNs and the African Children's Committee with a view to realise socio-economic rights of refugee children in Africa.

3.3 Part III: Country Case Studies

In Chap. 8, Kamga and Rashri appraise the protection of the rights of refugees in South Africa using the concepts of the rule of law and the principle of non-refoulement. Following a detailed analysis of the international refugee protection system, they review how the principle has been applied in South Africa. They then offer recommendations to the South African government on how to improve the protection of the socio-economic rights of refugees and asylum seekers.

In Chap. 9, Lubaale confronts the multiple layers of vulnerability concerning the maternal health rights of refugee women in Uganda. Using the decision in *Center for Health, Human Rights and Development (CEHURD) v Attorney General* as a case study, he discusses the challenges to the realisation of the right to health of refugee women in Uganda. He locates maternal health rights of refugees within the broader international human rights law framework and offers recommendations to address the challenges.

In Chap. 10, Kamga visits the tensions between national security and refugee protection within the context of the Boko Haram insurgency in the Lake Chad Basin. He reviews the existing tensions between issues of national security, human rights and refugee protection in the Lake Chad region in general and in Cameroon in particular. He extends the conversation to the implications of the violation of key human rights instruments regarding international refugee protection, the possible degradation of diplomatic relations, and escalation of tension between countries. He concludes by noting the role of states party to international refugee instruments and the need to protect socio-economic rights.

In Chap. 11, Akech looks at the prospects and challenges in the legal protection of socio-economic rights of internally displaced persons, refugees and asylum seekers in South Sudan. He argues that while South Sudan has ratified necessary legal frameworks for the protection of IDPs and refugees, implementation remains a key challenge. With a footing on access to socio-economic rights and services, he examines the situation of refugees and asylum seekers and how legal frameworks may be used to ensure the realisation of socio-economic rights.

In Chap. 12, Ndemera investigates Zimbabwe's refugee encampment policy on the enjoyment of socio-economic rights of refugees. He investigates how the Refugee Encampment Policy presents an encumbrance to the socio-economic rights of refugees in Zimbabwe, and argues that it presents resultant challenges in the realisation of socio-economic rights. He adds that the policy stifles the implementation of international law on socio-economic rights. He then provides recommendations aimed at increasing integration as a means for enhancing socio-economic rights for refugees in Zimbabwe.

In Chap. 13, Lugulu and Moyomba evaluate the enjoyment of the right to work by refugees and asylum seekers in Kenya. The thematic approach to this right is engrained in a discussion of international laws on refugees and socio-economic rights. The authors explore the relationship between refugee law and human rights laws and the challenges faced by refugees and asylum seekers with regard to socio-economic rights. With the use of domestic case law, they delve into the role of the courts in the promotion and protection of refugees' rights.

In Chap. 14, Mutema examines the factual and legislative aspects surrounding the realisation of socio-economic rights of refugees in Malawi. She poses hypothetical questions around the normative status of the enjoyment of socio-economic rights by refugees in Malawi, their involvement in gainful economic activities, and the directives from government. She evaluates international, regional and national law and the courts' approaches to the enjoyment of socio-economic rights. Her engagement of various court decisions creates traction for conclusion and recommendations.

In Chap. 15, Oluduro and Ayooluwasi critique the realisation of socio-economic rights of refugees and asylum seekers in Nigeria. They offer statistics on the numbers of registered refugees in Nigeria and argue that various issues relating to them would seem to flow into Nigeria from Cameroon. They identify the enjoyment of socio-economic rights as one of the challenges and examine the extent to which these rights are realised.

They add that Nigeria may strengthen the protection of the socio-economic rights of refugees through institutional frameworks.

This book will serve as an important resource to researchers, policy makers, academics, international institutions, civil society groups, law students and political science students and regional and sub-regional institutions. It will stimulate debate and provide a useful resource to anyone interested in the discussion of the realisation of the socio-economic rights of refugees and asylum seekers.

Bibliography

Books

Abass, A & Ippolito, F (eds) *Regional approaches to the protection of asylum seekers* (Routledge 2015)

Fraser, M *International refugee law and socio-economic rights* (Cambridge 2007)

Hathaway, J *Rights of refugees under international law* (Cambridge University Press 2005)

Khan, K & Schreier, T *Refugee law in South Africa* (Juta 2014)

Journal Articles

Bekker, G 'The protection of asylum seekers and refugees within the African human rights system' (2013) 13 *African Human Rights Law Journal* 1

Ferdinand, C 'Unspoken inequality: How COVID-19 has exacerbated existing vulnerabilities of asylum-seekers, refugees, and undocumented migrants in South Africa' (2020) 19 *International Journal of Equity in Health* 1

Case Law

Rencontre Africaine pour la Défense des Droits de l'Homme v Zambia (2000) AHRLR 321 (ACHPR 1996)

Papers/Reports

Guadagno, L 'Migrants and the COVID-19 pandemic: An initial analysis' WHO Migration Research Series 60 (2020)

International Commission of Jurists 'Living like people who die slowly: The need for right to health compliant COVID-19 responses' (2020)

ACHPR

ACHPR, Concluding Observations and Recommendations – South Africa: First Periodic Report 1999-2001, 38th ordinary session of the African Commission, 21 November to 5 December 2005, Banjul, The Gambia

ACHPR, Resolution 470 on the Protection of Refuges, Asylum seekers and Migrants in the fight against the COVID-19 pandemic in Africa, adopted 3 December 2020

AU Documents

AU, African Charter on the Rights and Welfare of the Child, 11 July 1990, CAB/LEG/24.9/49 (1990)

AU, Convention for the Protection and Assistance of Internally Displaced Persons in Africa (Kampala Convention), 23 October 2009. Adopted in 2009 entered into force in 6 December 2012

AU 'Migration Policy Framework for Africa and Plan of Action (2018-2030)' (2018)

African Union, Protocol to the African Charter on Human and People's Rights on the Rights of Women in Africa, 11 July 2003

OAU, African Charter on Human and Peoples' Rights (Banjul Charter), 27 June 1981, CAB/LEG/67/3 rev. 5, 21 ILM 58 (1982)

OAU, Convention Governing the Specific Aspects of Refugee Problems in Africa (OAU Convention), 10 September 1969, 1001 UNTS 45

UN Documents

OHCHR 'Fact Sheet 20: Human rights and refugees' (July 1993)

UN Committee on Economic, Social and Cultural Rights (CESCR), General Comment 14: The Right to the Highest Attainable Standard of Health (Art 12 of the Covenant), 11 August 2000, E/C.12/2000/4

UN Committee on Economic, Social and Cultural Rights (CESCR), General Comment 20: Non-discrimination in economic, social and cultural rights (art 2, para 2, of the International Covenant on Economic, Social and Cultural Rights), 2 July 2009, E/C.12/GC/20

UN General Assembly, Convention Relating to the Status of Refugees, 28 July 1951, United Nations, Treaty Series, vol. 189, p 137

UN General Assembly, International Covenant on Economic, Social and Cultural Rights, 16 December 1966, United Nations, Treaty Series, vol. 993, p 3

Internet Sources

Reliefweb '32 Million Africans forcibly displaced by conflict and repression' (18 June 2021) https://reliefweb.int/report/world/32-million-africans-forcibly-displaced-conflict-and-repression (accessed 7 November 2021)

UNCHR 'Refugee data finder' https://www.unhcr.org/refugee-statistics/ (accessed 29 June 2022)

CHAPTER 2

The Relevance of and Challenges in the Enjoyment of Socio-Economic Rights of Refugees and Asylum Seekers in Africa

Ebenezer Durojaye, Robert Doya Nanima, Abiola Idowu-Ojo, and Gladys Mirugi-Mukundi

1 Introduction

The United Nations High Commission for Refugees indicates that up to 82.4 million people across the globe have been displaced, that 26.6 million are refugees and asylum seekers, and that 30 million are from Africa.[1]

[1] UNHCR 'Figures at a glance' (2021) https://www.unhcr.org/figures-at-a-glance.html (accessed 9 January 2022).

E. Durojaye (✉) • G. Mirugi-Mukundi
Socio-Economic Rights Project, Dullah Omar Institute, University of the Western Cape, Cape Town, South Africa
e-mail: edurojaye@uwc.ac.za; gmirugimukundi@uwc.ac.za

E. Durojaye et al. (eds.), *Realising Socio-Economic Rights of Refugees and Asylum Seekers in Africa*, Politics of Citizenship and Migration, https://doi.org/10.1007/978-3-031-16548-1_2

This number has been rising since 1951 and continues to do so.[2]

Consonant with the introduction in the preceding chapter, this chapter provides an overview of the relevance of addressing socio-economic rights (SERs) of refugees and asylum seekers in the international and regional human rights legal framework. By design, it looks at critical aspects of the plight of refugees and asylum seekers, such as the indivisibility of rights, and the need to deliberately enhance the rights of refugees and asylum seekers. The authors question the mode of measuring progress and emphasise the importance of using African solutions to African problems. The chapter also grapples with the challenges that stifle the realisation of socio-economic rights of refugees and asylum seekers. The lack of a universal consensus on the tools for the realisation of socio-economic rights is discussed and the challenges in situational, geographical and legal-administrative settings are presented.

2 The Relevance of Addressing the Socio-Economic Rights of Refugees and Asylum Seekers in International Law

There is a wealth of normative and jurisprudential guidance relating to socio-economic rights in international law. This guidance emerges from both binding and non-binding treaties and declarations, consensus statements, and various initiatives such as the Sustainable Development Goals and the African Union Agenda 2063. There are also directions as to how these instruments and initiatives apply to SERs for refugees and asylum seekers. The evaluation of these international and regional instruments and their monitoring mechanisms can aid in the realisation of SERs of refugees and asylum seekers and is a step in the right direction. There has to be a measurement of the final effect of the normative and jurisprudential guidance on the actual enjoyment of SERs.

[2] M Hussein and M Haddad 'Visualising 70 years of refugee journeys' *Al Jazeera* 20 June 2021 https://www.aljazeera.com/news/2021/6/20/infographic-world-refugee-day-journey (accessed 9 January 2021).

R. D. Nanima (✉)
Department of Criminal Justice and Procedure, Faculty of Law, University of the Western Cape, Cape Town, South Africa
e-mail: rnanima@uwc.ac.za

A. Idowu-Ojo
African Commission on Human and Peoples' Rights, Banjul, The Gambia
e-mail: Idowu-Ojoa@africa-union.org

The focus on the SERs of refugees in international and regional law engages the ways (or methods) in which to enforce such rights. This is especially important where national systems have failed to afford protection to refugees. A look at how the monitoring mechanisms deal with such issues is important if one is to realise SERs in both a vertical and horizontal nexus. As noted in Chap. 1, there are various international and regional standards in instruments concerning the promotion and protection of SERs. While building on the foregoing chapter, this chapter takes an important step further to ascertain the relevance of international law in the promotion and protection of SERs. To this end, the relevance lies in ascertaining (1) how the treaty gives effect to SERs and (2) how the monitoring body has developed jurisprudence to this end.

2.1 *Indivisibility of Rights*

The indivisibility of rights is an indication that the protection of civil and political rights has a bearing on SERs. By default, the International Covenant on Civil and Political Rights (ICCPR) offers normative guidance regarding the realisation of these rights. It recognises that the enjoyment of civil and political freedom can only be achieved where one enjoys both civil and political rights, as well as SERs.[3] Furthermore, it recognises that the right to self-determination is intertwined with the duality of free determination of political status and the pursuit of economic, social and cultural development.[4]

The obligation on the state to respect and ensure the enjoyment of all the rights in the ICCPR includes the consideration of the socio-contexts of rights-bearers.[5] At its core, the state's obligation cannot be severed from the enjoyment of the SERs. Where the socio-origins point to the existence of vulnerabilities such as that an individual is a child, a woman, a refugee or an asylum seeker, this should inform the steps that the state should take in the realisation of all rights. This obligation is non-derogable as far as it extends to instances where a state is faced with emergencies that threaten its existence.[6]

[3] Fourth preambular paragraph, ICCPR.

[4] Article 1.1 of the ICCPR.

[5] Article 2.1 of the ICCPR.

[6] Article 4.1 of the ICCPR on derogation. It is true that there are some limitations, but generally, the obligation on the state has to be upheld.

2.2 Enhancing Deliberate Protection of Refugees and Asylum Seekers

The emphasis on SERs by the International Covenant on Economic, Social and Cultural Rights (ICESCR) and its monitoring body, the Committee on Economic Social and Culture Rights (CESCR), provides both normative and jurisprudential guidance on the need for protection in a vertical and horizontal continuum.[7] The ICESCR provides for various socio-economic rights such as the right of all peoples to self-determination,[8] the right to work,[9] and the right to just and favourable conditions of work.[10] Other specific rights include the right to form and join trade unions and other trade union rights,[11] the right to social security and social insurance,[12] and rights for families, mothers and children (inculcating aspects of vulnerable groups).[13] A discussion of these rights is provided in Chap. 1 and does not warrant repetition in this chapter.[14] The relevance of the realisation of the SERs for refugees and asylum seekers lies in how the ICESCR guides duty bearers in the use of critical principles such as progressive realisation,[15] for all persons regardless of their status and the areas they occupy, as, for instance, refugees and asylum seekers.[16]

[7] Article 1.2 of the ICESCR. See also the statement by the CESCR, Duties of states towards refugees and migrants under the International Covenant on Economic, Social and Cultural Rights, 13 March 2017, UN Doc E/C.12/2017/1 (2017) para 1. The statement was adopted by the CESCR at its sixtieth session, held from 20 to 24 February 2017.

[8] Article 1.

[9] Article 6.

[10] Article 7.

[11] Article 8.

[12] Article 9.

[13] Article 10.

[14] Article 11. Other rights include the right to health, Article 12, and the right to education, Articles 13 and 14.

[15] Article 2 of the ICESCR.

[16] While Article 2(1) requires each State Party to undertake steps to the maximum of its available resources to achieve the progressive realisation of the rights recognised in the ICESCR, both International Human Rights Law and International Criminal Law place a duty on non-state actors to ensure the enjoyment of all rights of individuals where they control territory like a state.

2.3 Need for Measurement of Actual Protection of Socio-Economic Rights

Measurements are often based on statistics on subjects or a given phenomenon. Critical initiatives such as the Sustainable Development Goals require specific targets to inform the extent to which the goals are realised. To this end, the Voluntary National Reviews become instrumental in assessing the extent to which specific progress has been made towards a special target by a state. As a point of departure, the need for a form of measurement that establishes the extent to which the SERs of refugees and asylum seekers have been realised comes to the fore. It is important that this measurement is not only targeted at refugees and asylum seekers in peaceful contexts, but also across an array of conflict-stricken areas and territories that host refugees and asylum seekers. There is a need to measure the extent to which states realise SERs and their discretion in doing so in peaceful and conflict-ridden host communities. The aforementioned need calls for this study. The ICESCR grants discretion to developing countries to determine non-nationals' (such as immigrants, refugees and asylum seekers) extent of enjoyment of SERs.[17]

The Limburg Principles contextualise the concept of progressive realisation and thus add clarity to the enjoyment of SERs. This obligation to progressively realise SERs requires states parties to take expeditious actions to fulfil their obligations under the ICESCR.[18] While some obligations such as non-discrimination and the enjoyment of the right to basic education require immediate realisation, progressive realisation is dependent on the effective use of available resources.[19] The ICESCR's Committee on Economic Social and Cultural Rights (CESCR) recognises the challenges

[17] This is in line with the requirement of progressive realisation that requires that discretion must be exercised subject to the enjoyment of human rights and the national economy.

[18] UN Commission on Human Rights, Note verbale dated 5 December 1986 from the Permanent Mission of the Netherlands to the United Nations Office at Geneva addressed to the Centre for Human Rights (Limburg Principles), 8 January 1987, E/CN.4/1987/17, para 22.

[19] The Limburg Principles (n 22) para 24. For a detailed engagement on the progressive realisation of SERs, see UN Committee on Economic, Social and Cultural Rights (CESCR), General Comment 3: The Nature of States Parties' Obligations (Art 2, Para 1 of the Covenant), 14 December 1990, E/1991/23.

faced by refugees, migrants and especially undocumented migrants. The CESCR's recognition of the status of legal refugees is a reminder of state obligations under the ICESCR.[20]

2.4 *Need for Evaluation of African Solutions to African Problems*

Despite the international law on the protection of SERs, the need to evaluate the position on the continental scene is critical to gauging the value of Africa's treaties. For instance, the African Charter on Human and Peoples' Rights (ACHPR) provides both normative and jurisprudential guidance on matters concerning the enjoyment of socio-economic rights in Africa.[21] The African Union Organisations are silent about the distinction that is made between civil and political rights on the one hand and SERs on the other, when it comes to the justiciability and/or implementation of these rights. Furthermore, there are specific group rights such as the right to self-determination, free disposal of wealth and natural resources, economic, social and cultural development, national and international peace and security, and a general satisfactory environment.[22] The African Commission on Human and Peoples' Rights provides for the justiciability of SERs.[23]

The African Charter on the Rights and Welfare of the Child (ACRWC, African Children's Charter)[24] also offers normative guidance on the promotion and protection of the rights of the child. It makes no distinction between the SERs and civil and political rights. Rather, it calls on states parties to use all necessary means, such as legislative, administrative, financial, educational and social, to realise both civil and political rights as well as SERs.[25] The value of the African Children's Charter lies in the use of a child-centred approach underpinned by the four principles of the best interests of the child, namely, participation, non-discrimination, the right to survival, and development.[26] In addition, it builds on the lived realities

[20] Duties of States towards refugees and migrants under the International Covenant on Economic, Social and Cultural Rights (n 8) para 11.

[21] African Charter (n 5).

[22] Articles 19–24.

[23] Ssenyonjo (n 22) 366–375.

[24] African Children's Charter (n 6).

[25] As above, Article 2.

[26] Articles 4–6 of the African Children's Charter.

of the child in Africa. It takes account of the challenges of refugees, internally displaced children, children in conflict situations (or children affected by armed conflict), child marriages and harmful child practices.[27] Importantly, the African Children's Charter makes provision for the protection of a child refugee and extends the same protection to the internally displaced child.[28] This approach provides normative guidance for the protection of children's rights in various contexts including in communities of peace, armed conflict zones and during periods of transition (when they live as refugees and asylum seekers).

The OAU Convention Governing Specific Aspects of Refugees in Africa (OAU Refugee Convention) is a major regional instrument that offers an opportunity for states to use a continental-contextual understanding of refugees. Its relevance has to be measured by the added value it provides in the promotion and protection of SERs of refugees. For instance, this instrument uses various principles such as (1) a wider definition of a refugee, (2) the principle of non-refoulement and (3) the right to asylum as an individual. In addition, other normative contexts include (4) the concept of burden-sharing, (5) aspects of temporary or interim protection, (6) the protection of an asylum seeker as a rights-holder and (7) voluntary repatriation.[29] The greatest shortfall of the OAU Refugee Convention is, however, the exclusion of internally displaced persons (IDPs).[30] It may be argued that an IDP does not fall within the category of a person who has moved away from the protection of a state due to a well-founded fear. It becomes complex for the internally displaced person who has not moved from the territories of specific states. First, it is important to state that concerning the well-founded fear requirement, the proof is often not readily available due to the process of Refugee Status Determination.[31]

[27] Nanima gives a detailed account of SERs of refugee children in Chap. 6 in this volume. See BD Mezmur 'Happy 18th Birthday to the African Children's Rights Charter: Not counting its days but making its days count' (2017) 1 *Africa Human Rights Yearbook* 125.

[28] Article 23.

[29] For a detailed engagement of these principles that compare and contrast this position with the position in the Refugee Convention, see T Maluwa and A Katz 'Who is a refugee?: Twenty-five years of domestic implementation and judicial interpretation of the 1969 OAU and 1951 UN Refugee Conventions in post-apartheid South Africa' (2020) 27 *Indiana Journal of Global Legal Studies* 129.

[30] See the discussions in T Maluwa 'International law in post-colonial Africa' in T Maluwa *International law in post-colonial Africa* (1999) 180.

[31] HE Cameron *Refugee law's fact-finding crisis: Truth, risk, and the wrong mistake* (2018) 33. Carr (n 39).

While some countries may wish to make the determination quickly, others are still at liberty to undertake extensive, demanding and fact-finding tasks.[32] This leads to a subjective rather than an objective approach to protecting refugees and a possible denial of protection.[33] The acclaimed complementary role of the OAU Refugee Convention to the Refugee Convention must be tested against the extent to which it supports the protection of the SERs of refugees and asylum seekers in all environments.[34] This instrument provides a definition which considers the environmental context of the refugee and reduces his or her burden to prove the existence of a well-founded fear. Some critical points are worth noting in addition to this.

3 Challenges to the Realisation of SERs of Refugees in Africa

Numerous challenges affect refugees and asylum seekers, including poverty, lack of social security, poor legislation and lack of government will.[35] It is important that the challenges are considered in the context of continental and national perspectives. This chapter acknowledges the chapters in the book which present the challenges that refugees and asylum seekers face. To avoid a repetition of the aspects covered elsewhere in the book, this chapter attempts to highlight the challenges across the spectrum.

[32] Anderson, A, Foster, M, Lambert, H and McAdam, J 'A well-founded fear of being persecuted...but when?' (2020) 42 *Sydney Law Review* 155.

[33] JC Hathaway and WS Hicks 'Is there a subjective element in the Refugee Convention's requirement of well-founded fear?' (2005) 26 *Michigan Journal of International Law* 505. Various cases reflect the need for both an objective and subjective approach to the recognition of a refugee. See *Saleh v US Dep't of Justice* 962 F.2d 234, 239 (2d Cir. 1992); *Canada (Att'y Gen.) v. Ward* [1993] 2 SCR 689, 691; *Regina v. Sec'y of State for the Home Dep't* [1988] AC 958 (HL) (appeal taken from QB) (UK); *Re Minister for Immigration & Multicultural Affairs* [2001] HCA 22 (Austl); *Zgnat'ev v Minister for Justice, Equality & Law Reform* [2001] IEHC 70 (Ir); *Luu the Truong v Chairman of the Refugee Status Review Bd* [2001] HCAL 3261, 45 (HK).

[34] Article I, para 1 of the OAU Refugee Convention reproduces the UN Refugee Convention definition.

[35] Various chapters in the book deal with national and supranational systems and the challenges in the enforcement of SERs. See Chaps. 3, 4, 5, 6, 9 and 11 for the subjective and contextual challenges.

3.1 *Lack of Universal Consensus on the Immediate Realisation of SERs*

Firstly, the lack of a universal consensus on the immediate realisation of SERs affects their perceived enjoyment. While the ICESCR and other associated treaties provide for the progressive realisation of rights, African treaties generally call for immediate realisation of rights. For instance, the ACHPR offers normative guidance on the enjoyment of SERs in the context of immediate realisation.[36] A similar position is evident in the ACRWC, which calls on states parties to take all necessary steps, including administrative and legislative, to ensure that all the rights in the African Children's Charter are enjoyed.[37] The question of whether or not Africa has the ability to meet its onerous obligations must be answered in the negative as the continent is fettered by significant challenges such as poverty and lack of structures to ensure the promotion and protection of the said rights.[38] One might argue that there have been many normative developments and jurisprudential guidance such as the Draft Principles and Guidelines on Economic, Social and Cultural Rights in the African Charter on Human and Peoples' Rights (ACHPR).[39] The translation of the normative to actual, measurable enjoyment remains critical to the fulfilment of SERs of all persons including refugees.

Steps to translate the normative to the narrative are evident in some of the working methods of the human rights bodies. To this end, the African Commission has a Special Rapporteur on Refugees, Asylum Seekers and

[36] The ACHPR, Article 1. See also Mbazira C 'Enforcing the economic, social and cultural rights in the African Charter on Human and Peoples' Rights: twenty years of redundancy, progression and significant strides' (2006) 6 (2) *African Human Rights Law Journal* 333–357.

[37] ACRWC, Article 1. See Nanima RD 'Evaluating the role of the African Committee of Experts on the Rights and Welfare of the Child in the COVID-19 era: Visualising the African child in 2050' (2021) 21(1) *African Human Rights Law Journal* 52–73.

[38] Mbazira C 'Enforcing the economic, social and cultural rights in the African Charter on Human and Peoples' Rights: twenty years of redundancy, progression and significant strides (2006) 6 (2) *African Human Rights Law Journal* 333–357.

[39] See also the Draft Principles and Guidelines, adopted by the African Commission at the 48th session, in November 2010 www.achpr.org/english/other/Draft_guideline_ESCR/Draft_Pcpl%20&%20Guidelines.pdf (accessed 6 July 2022).

Internally Displaced Persons,[40] who is tasked to engage in issues concerning refugees, asylum seekers and internally displaced persons in Africa.[41] This is a step in the right direction to lobby with states parties on the realisation of the (socio-economic) rights of refugees, asylum seekers and internally displaced persons.[42] The lack of regional consensus on the immediate realisation of the SERs of refugees and asylum seekers affects and stifles the progress being made towards such enjoyment.[43] With regard to the African Committee of Experts on the Rights and Welfare of the Child (ACERWC), recent jurisprudential guidance shows that there have been developments through the use of General Comments, and that the African Children's Committee engages the Child Rights-Based approach with regard to SERs and refugees. For instance, due to the principle of the right to life, survival and development, the registration of child deaths is important in refugee settlements or internally displaced persons camps.[44] Similarly, due to the need to end child marriages, the African Children's Committee reiterates that states parties should protect children who are asylum seekers, refugees, migrants, returnees or internally displaced persons against all forms of violence, and that they must take measures that aid the physical, psychological, social and legal protection of the child.[45] It is required that both holistic and robust approaches are used to ensure the protection of the right to life, survival and development as precursors to the realisation of SERs through good governance, targeted policies and adequate provi-

[40] The mandate of the Special Rapporteur was established at the 35th ordinary session of the African Commission on Human and Peoples' Rights, in Banjul, The Gambia, 21 May to 4 June 2004. Resolution 72 was adopted at the subsequent 36th ordinary session in Dakar, Senegal, 23 November to 7 December 2004. The detailed mandate of the Special Rapporteur is available at https://www.achpr.org/specialmechanisms/detail?id=5 (accessed 6 July 2022).

[41] Resolution 72, adopted at the subsequent 36th ordinary session in Dakar, Senegal, 23 November to 7 December 2004.

[42] Resolution 72 (above).

[43] Some of the activities include the passing of a letter of appreciation to the Republic of Kenya for granting citizenship to over 1600 refugees, a declaration on the commemoration of World Refugee Day in 2017, and a statement on the status of refugees, asylum seekers, internally displaced persons and migrants in Africa on the commemoration of International Migrants Day. A lot more could be done to harness such guidance at the continental level with state involvement in this noble cause.

[44] General Comment on Article 6 of the African Charter on the Rights and Welfare of the Child, para 20.

[45] In the Joint General Comment by the ACHPR and the ACERWC on ending child marriages, para 58.

sion of the required services.[46] In addition, General Comment 5 on States Party Obligations calls for system strengthening in the implementation of article 1 on states party obligations.[47]

The African Children's Committee has handed down several decisions that deal with SERs.[48] In the *Nubian Children's case* and the case against *Mauritania* aspects of SERs are underscored. In the *Kenyan Nubian Children's case*, the African Children's Committee held that the decision by the government not to grant this group citizenship led to statelessness that affected the children's realisation of SERs such as access to education and healthcare.[49] It reiterated the need to grant citizenship to a child as a precursor to the enjoyment of SERs.[50] In *Minority Rights Group International and SOS Enclaves on behalf of Said Ould Salem and Yarg Ould Salem v Mauritania*,[51] the Committee found that based on the use of due diligence, the respondent state failed to prevent and protect children from the dangers of slavery.[52] Consequently, it failed to provide the enjoyment of SERs such as the right to education.[53] It is argued that such jurisprudential developments offer critical opportunities for states to implement Resolutions, Recommendations and Decisions relevant to refugees, asylum seekers, returnees and other persons of concern under their respective mandates, adopted by both the African Children's Committee and the African Commission.[54]

[46] ACERWC General Comment 5 on State Party Obligations under the African Charter on the Rights and Welfare of the Child (Article 1) and systems strengthening for child protection (2018) para 4.3 https://www.africanchildforum.org/clr/General%20Comments%20Docs/2018%20updates/ACERWC/legal_instruments_acgc_gc_5_en.pdf (accessed 7 January 2022).

[47] As above.

[48] See the list of communications at acerwc.africa/table_of_communications (accessed 15 July 2022).

[49] *Institute for Human Rights and Development in Africa (IHRDA) and Open Society Justice Initiative on behalf of Children of Nubian descent in Kenya v The Government of Kenya* Decision 002/Com/002/2009 para 46.

[50] As above.

[51] *Mauritania* para 6.

[52] Related to the principle of protection discussed above. See *Vertido v Philippines*, Committee on the Elimination of Discrimination against Women, para 8.4, 1 September 2010, UN Doc CEDAW/C/46/D/18/2008 (2010).

[53] Report of the Special Rapporteur on Violence against Women: Its causes and consequences, Yakin Ertürk: Intersections between culture and violence against women (2007) para 37.

[54] Paragraph 5.

3.2 *Situational, Geographical and Administrative Challenges*

At the national level, there are various limitations, the most critical being emergencies. The Covid-19 pandemic has heralded the hardships that refugees and asylum seekers have to surmount to enjoy socio-economic rights. Some countries employ the encampment models that keep refugees and asylum seekers in refugee camps.[55] Others that have an integration model for refugees and asylum seekers still reflect the challenges of refugees and asylum seekers such as the expiry of permits during the pandemic, and the lack of legal documentation.[56] Consider a hypothetical situation where refugees arrive in a host state after March 2020, and cannot apply for asylum status. The lack of a legal status means that refugees and asylum seekers will struggle to access services such as education and health services.[57] Of critical importance is the delays caused by administrative blockages that often treat refugees and asylum seekers as 'insignificant others' without regard for their right to equality, human dignity and non-discrimination.[58] For instance, it is documented that the conclusion of an application for recognition as a refugee in South Africa takes up to a year or longer.[59] Other intricate challenges that are covered at a national level include low-quality staff,[60] corruption and administrative challenges,[61] lack of legal knowledge on the part of the refugees and asylum seekers,[62] the inability of the national asylum system to seamlessly deal with all migrant applications,[63] and the perception that asylum seekers are threats to national security.[64]

[55] For the experience in Kenya, see Nanima, R. D. (2017). An evaluation of Kenya's parallel legal regime on refugees, and the courts' guarantee of their rights. *Law, Democracy & Development*, *21*(1), 42–67.

[56] T Washinyira 'Refugees struggle to renew their asylum documents with Home Affairs online system' (4 February 2022) https://www.groundup.org.za/article/refugees-struggle-with-home-affairs-online-system/ (accessed 2 April 2022).

[57] See a detailed discussion in Chaps. 4 and 5. See also Human Rights Watch (2005) 'Living on the Margins Inadequate Protection for Refugees and Asylum Seekers in Johannesburg' https://www.hrw.org/report/2005/11/16/living-margins/inadequate-protection-refugees-and-asylum-seekers-johannesburg (accessed 7 April 2023).

[58] Human Rights Watch (as above).

[59] Human Rights Watch (as above).

[60] Human Rights Watch (as above).

[61] Human Rights Watch (as above).

[62] Human Rights Watch (as above).

[63] Human Rights Watch (as above).

[64] As above.

4 Towards a Balancing of Rights Between Citizens and Non-citizens

In any state there is always a tension between the extensive degree to which citizens enjoy their rights and the limited levels of enjoyment of rights afforded to non-citizens. Equality before and protection by the law becomes increasingly illusory for non-citizens, even in constitutional democracies. This poses the rhetorical question: Should there be a balance in the enjoyment of rights on account of one's status as a citizen? If so, what should be the yardstick while maintaining the right to equality and what is the common denominator? The answers to these questions in the context of the enjoyment of SERs of refugees and asylum seekers offer insights. Before these are discussed, however, it is important to elaborate on the concept of equality as understood in international law.

It is important to ascertain how equality serves the purpose of ensuring that both citizens and non-citizens can benefit from the enjoyment of rights in a state. To answer this question, we consider the normative guidance from international law and how this is translated in the national sphere. This subsequent discussion is informed by the fact that the right to equality underscores the indivisibility of rights as far as it becomes the bedrock from which socio-economic rights are not only enjoyed but seen to be enjoyed. As mentioned earlier, the right to equality is provided for in various international instruments. The most notable instrument is the International Covenant on Civil and Political Rights (The ICCPR). The ICCPR considers equality in three basic ways: first, in the context of equality before courts and tribunals and the right to a fair trial;[65] second, equality of rights between men and women,[66] and third, in the bounds of protection of the family, the right to marriage and equality of spouses.[67] By design, it is important to supersede this limited approach and rather look at equality from the context of the right as an enabler to the enjoyment of all rights in the ICCPR. The right to equality as understood in the ICCPR should be extended to the degree that it enables the enjoyment of SERs.

From a normative perspective, the ICCPR provides for the right to life, which encapsulates the concept of the totality of livelihood of an individual. This means that the enjoyment of the right to life and the quality

[65] The ICCPR, article 14.
[66] Article 3.
[67] Article 23.

thereof extends to the need for the state to ensure the enjoyment of the SERs.[68] It is also interesting to note that since the right to life is to be enjoyed by all human beings, it inevitably includes refugees and asylum seekers. The question at this stage is to what extent the provision of the right to life can be supported by the right to equality in the jurisprudential spaces. The Human Rights Committee (HRC) has informed states that the enjoyment of the right to life requires that special measures of protection are taken especially for persons in vulnerable situations as a result of specific threats or pre-existing patterns of violence.[69] It is interesting that among the vulnerable groups that are mentioned are children, displaced persons, asylum seekers and refugees.[70] In addition, the HRC calls for the protection of the right to life where there is deprivation of liberty or limited movement such as in camps for refugees and internally displaced persons.[71]

It should be noted further that the duty to ensure the enjoyment of the right to life inculcates the obligation on states to take appropriate measures to deal with general conditions in society that may prevent the enjoyment of life with dignity.[72] To this end, some of the measures that require the enjoyment of a good-quality life include invoking the enjoyment of SERs such as access to food,[73] water, shelter, healthcare,[74] sanitation and housing. Measures aimed at fighting stigmatisation of vulnerable groups and promoting deliberate education programmes point to the use of equality as the common denominator in ensuring the enjoyment of SERs.

[68] Article 6.

[69] The HRC General Comment on Article 6 of the ICCPR on the Right to Life, CCPR/C/GC/36, para 23. See also the Inter-American Court of Human Rights, *Barrios Family v. Venezuela*, judgment of 24 November 2011, para 124.

[70] General Comment (above) para 23. See also CCPR/C/HND/CO/1, para. 9 and Concluding Observations on the Report of the Republic of Kenya, CCPR/C/KEN/CO/3, para. 12.

[71] This was raised in the HRC General Comment (above) para 25 and in the Report to the HRC of Kosovo, Serbia and Montenegro; CCPR/C/UNK/CO/1, para. 14.

[72] The HRC General Comment (above) paras 8 and 26. See also Human Rights Committee, general comment No. 6, para. 5; CCPR/C/79/Add.105, para. 12.

[73] CCPR/CO/72/PRK, para. 12.

[74] Toussaint v. Canada (CCPR/C/123/D/2348/2014), para. 11.3. See also the HRC General Comment (above) paras 8, 25, 26, 40 and 54 on the enjoyment of the right to health in different circumstances.

5 Conclusion

This chapter has provided an overview of the protection of the socio-economic rights of refugees and asylum seekers under international and regional human rights law. As a point of departure, it has evaluated the relevance of addressing issues concerning SERs of refugees and asylum seekers, the challenges in realising their rights, and the need to balance these in the context of both citizens and non-citizens. It is apparent that several critical notions inform the relevance of addressing SERs of the mentioned vulnerable groups. This relevance is punctuated by the indivisibility of rights, and the need for deliberate protection of these vulnerable groups. The relevance extends to the need to measure success towards such protection and an evaluation of the use of tailored solutions to African challenges. The challenges to the realisation of SERs of refugees and asylum seekers oscillate around the lack of a universal consensus on their immediate realisation coupled with situational, geographical and administrative challenges. It is realised that a balancing of the rights of citizens and non-citizens in the enjoyment of SERs can be best achieved with the use of the broad right to equality as it intersects with the informed enjoyment of both civil and political rights on the one hand and SERs on the other.

Bibliography

Books

Cameron, HE *Refugee law's fact-finding crisis: Truth, risk, and the wrong mistake* (Cambridge University Press 2018a)

D'orsi, C *Asylum-seeker and refugee protection in Sub-saharan Africa: The peregrination of a persecuted human being in search of a safe haven* (Routledge 2015)

Cameron, HE *Refugee law's fact-finding crisis: Truth, risk, and the wrong mistake* (Cambridge University Press 2018b)

Jackson, IC *The refugee concept in group situations* (Martinus Nijhoff 1999)

Ouguergouz, F *The African Charter on Human and Peoples' Rights: A comprehensive agenda for human dignity and sustainable democracy* (Martinus Nijhoff 2003)

Chapters in Books

Maluwa, T 'International law in post-colonial Africa' in Maluwa, T *International law in post-colonial Africa* (Brill 1999)

Simeon, JC 'What is the future of non-refoulement in international refugee law?' in Juss, SS (ed.) *Research handbook on international refugee law* (Edward Elgar Publishing 2019)

Yusuf, AA 'The public law of Africa and international law: Broadening the scope of application of international rules and enriching them for intra-Africa purposes' in Jalloh, CC & Elias, O (eds.) *Shielding humanity: Essays in international law in honour of judge Abdul G Koroma* (Brill 2015)

Journal Articles

Alice, E 'Refugee Status Determination in Africa' (2006) 14 *African Journal of International and Comparative Law* 221

Anais, T 'The threshold of Africa: OAU and UN Definitions in South African asylum practice' (2002) 15 *Journal of Refugee Studies* 409

Anderson, A; Foster, M; Lambert, H & McAdam, J 'A well-founded fear of being persecuted... but when?' (2020) 42 *Sydney Law Review* 155

Carr, BA 'We don't need to see them cry: Eliminating the subjective apprehension element of the well-founded fear analysis for child refugee applicants' (2005) 33 *Pepperdine Law Review* 535

Cox, TN 'Well-founded fear of being persecuted: The sources and application of a criterion of refugee status' (1984) 10 *Brook Journal of International Law*

Hansungule, M 'The suspension of the SADC Tribunal' (2013) 35 *Strategic Review for Southern Africa* 135

Hathaway, JC & Hicks, WS 'Is there a subjective element in the refugee convention's requirement of well-founded fear?' (2004) 26 *Michigan Journal of International Law* 505

Kapindu, RE 'No return to persecution or danger: Judicial application of the principle of non-refoulement in refugee law in South Africa and Malawi' (2020) 10 *Constitutional Court Review*107

Maluwa, T & Katz, A 'Who is a refugee?: Twenty-five years of domestic implementation and judicial interpretation of the 1969 OAU and 1951 UN Refugee Conventions in post-apartheid South Africa' (2020) 27 *Indiana Journal of Global Legal Studies* 129

Mezmur, BD 'Happy 18th Birthday to the African Children's Rights Charter: Not Counting Its Days but Making Its Days Count' (2017) 1 *Africa Human Rights Yearbook* 125

Nathan, L 'The disbanding of the SADC Tribunal: A cautionary tale' (2013) 35 *Human Rights Quarterly* 870

Medard, RR 'Some reflections on the OAU Convention on Refugees: Some pending issues' (1983) 16 *Comparative and International Law Journal of South Africa* 155

Liebenberg, S 'The international covenant on economic, social and cultural rights and its implications for South Africa' (1995) 11 *South African Journal on Human Rights* 359

Ssenyonjo, M 'Analysing the economic, social and cultural rights jurisprudence of the African commission: 30 years since the adoption of the African Charter' (2011) 29 *Netherlands Quarterly of Human Rights* 358

Wood, T 'Who is a refugee in Africa? A principled framework for interpreting and applying Africa's expanded refugee definition' (2019) 31 *International Journal of Refugee Law* 290

Cases

Annette Pagnoulle (on behalf of Abdoulaye Mazou) v Cameroon Communication 39/90 (1997), 10th Activity Report

Canada (Att'y Gen) v Ward [1993] 2 SCR 689

Free Legal Assistance Group, Lawyers' Committee for Human Rights, Union Interafricaine des Droits de l'Homme, Les Témoins de Jehovah v Zaire Communications 25/89, 47/90, 56/91, 100/93 (1996), 9th Activity Report

Institute for Human Rights and Development in Africa (IHRDA) and Open Society Justice Initiative on behalf of Children of Nubian descent in Kenya v The Government of Kenya Decision: No 002/Com/002/2009

Interights, Institute for Human Rights and Development in Africa, and Association Mauritanienne des Droits de l'Homme v Islamic Republic of Mauritania Communication 373/2009 (formerly 242/2001), (2010), 28th Activity Report

John K. Modise v Botswana Communication 97/93 (2000), 14th Activity Report

Kevin Mgwanga Gumne et al v Cameroon Communication 266/2003, (2009), 26th Activity Report, Annex IV

Luu the Truong v Chairman of the Refugee Status Review Bd [2001] HCAL 3261, 45 (HK)

Malawi African Association and Others vs Mauritania Communications 54/91, 61/91, 98/93, 164/97 à 196/97 and 210/98 (2000), 13th Activity Report.

Re Minister for Immigr. and Multicultural Aff., Ex parte Miah [2001] HCA 22

Re Minister for Immigration & Multicultural Affairs [2001] HCA 22 (Austl.)

Regina v Sec'y of State for the Home Dep't [1988] AC 958 (HL) (appeal taken from QB) (UK)

Saleh v US Dep't of Justice 962 F.2d 234, 239 (2d Cir. 1992)
The Social and Economic Rights Action Center and the Center for Economic and Social Rights v Nigeria (SERAC case) Communication 155/96, (2001), 15th Activity Report, Annex V
Union Inter Africaine des Droits de l'Homme Communication 159/96 (1997), 11th Activity Report
Vertido v Philippines, Committee on the Elimination of Discrimination Against Women, 1 September 2010, UN Doc CEDAW/C/46/D/18/2008
Zgnat'ev v Minister for Justice, Equality & Law Reform [2001] IEHC 70 (Ir)

AU and African Committee Documents

African Charter on Human and Peoples Rights, OAU Doc. CAB/LEG/67/3 rev. 5, 21 ILM 58 (1982)
African Charter on the Rights and Welfare of the Child, 11 July 1990, CAB/LEG/24.9/49 (1990)
ACERWC General Comment 5 on State Party Obligations under the African Charter on the Rights and Welfare of the Child (Article 1) and systems strengthening for child protection (2018)
Concluding Recommendations by the African Committee of Experts on the Rights and Welfare of the Child (ACERWC) on the Republic of South Africa initial report on the status of implementation of the African Charter on the Rights and Welfare of the Child
Concluding Recommendations by the African Committee of Experts on the Rights and Welfare of the Child (ACERWC) on the Republic of Mozambique's report on the status of implementation of the African Charter on the Rights and Welfare of the Child
General Comment on art 6 of the African Charter on the Rights and Welfare of the Child
Guidelines for National Periodic Reports, in Second Annual Activity Report of the African Commission on Human and Peoples Rights 1988–1989, ACHPR/RPT/2nd, Annex XII;

UN Documents

General Comment 3: The nature of States parties' obligations (art 2, para 1, of the Covenant) adopted at the 5th session (1990) of the Committee on Economic, Social and Cultural Rights, UN CECSR Document E/1991/23
Report of the Special Rapporteur on Violence against Women: Its causes and consequences, Yakin Ertürk: Intersections between culture and violence against women (2007)

Resolution 72, adopted at the subsequent 36th Ordinary session in Dakar, Senegal, 23 November - 7 December 2004

Resolution on Economic, Social And Cultural Rights in Africa, ACHPR/Res.73(XXXVI)04, (2004)

Statement by the Committee on Economic, Social and Cultural Rights, UN Committee on Economic, Social and Cultural Rights (CESCR), Duties of States towards refugees and migrants under the International Covenant on Economic, Social and Cultural Rights, 13 March 2017, E/C.12/2017/1, (adopted by the CESCR at sixtieth session, held from 20 to 24 February 2017)

The Limburg Principles On The Implementation Of The International Covenant On Economic, Social And Cultural Rights [UN doc. E/CN.4/1987/17

UN Committee on Economic, Social and Cultural Rights (CESCR), Duties of States towards refugees and migrants under the International Covenant on Economic, Social and Cultural Rights, 13 March 2017, E/C.12/2017/1

UN General Assembly, Convention Relating to the Status of Refugees, 28 July 1951, United Nations, Treaty Series, vol. 189, p 137

UN General Assembly, International Covenant on Economic, Social and Cultural Rights, 16 December 1966, United Nations, Treaty Series, vol. 993, p 3

Internet Sources

Advisory Opinion of the African Commission on Human and Peoples' Rights on the United Nations Declaration on the Rights of Indigenous Peoples, https://www.achpr.org/public/Document/file/Any/un_advisory_opinion_idp_eng.pdf

Declaration by the Special Rapporteur on Refugees, Asylum-Seekers, Displaced Persons and Migrants in Africa on the occasion of the World Refugee Day, 2017 https://www.achpr.org/news/viewdetail?id=32

Draft Principles and Guidelines, adopted by the African Commission at the 48th session, in November 2010, www.achpr.org/english/other/Draft_guideline_ESCR/Draft_Pcpl%20&%20Guidelines.pdf

Hussein, & Haddad, M 'Visualising 70 years of refugee journeys' *Al Jazeera* 20 June 2021 https://www.aljazeera.com/news/2021/6/20/infographic-world-refugee-day-journey

Memorandum of Understanding between ACHPR and UNHCR, https://www.achpr.org/presspublic/publication?id=23

Statement by the Special Rapporteur on Refugees, Asylum Seekers, Internally Displaced Persons and Migrants in Africa on the occasion of the Celebration of the International Migrants Day https://www.achpr.org/news/viewdetail?id=42

Statement by the Special Rapporteur on Refugees, Asylum Seekers, Internally Displaced Persons and Migrants in Africa on the occasion of World Refugee Day 2015, https://www.achpr.org/news/viewdetail?id=97

Statement by the Special Rapporteur on Refugees, Asylum Seekers, Internally Displaced Persons and Migrants in Africa on the occasion of the Celebration of the International Migrants Day, https://www.achpr.org/news/viewdetail?id=43

Statement on Letter of Appreciation to the Republic of Kenya, https://www.achpr.org/news/viewdetail?id=217

UNHCR Global Trends 2020 (2021) Figures at a glance. Available https://www.unhcr.org/figures-at-a-glance.html

CHAPTER 3

The Right of Access to Social Protection for Refugees and Asylum Seekers in Africa in the Covid-19 Era

Kennedy Chege

1 Introduction

Countries across the world responded to the spread of the Coronavirus (Covid-19) pandemic by instituting lockdown measures to contain transmission. With respect to the African continent, which is the focus of this chapter, these measures had enormous consequences for economies and, in turn, for populations. Multitudes of people lost their livelihoods, as the Covid-19 pandemic exposed a myriad of shortcomings in numerous countries, such as the lack of access to basic socio-economic services and limited social protection measures (e.g. healthcare, housing, education), job losses, and the high risk of debt distress in African economies. Additionally, in respect of countries that already had social protection systems in place, the pandemic exposed the inadequacies of these systems, as they struggled

K. Chege (✉)
Faculty of Law, University of Cape Town, Cape Town, South Africa

E. Durojaye et al. (eds.), *Realising Socio-Economic Rights of Refugees and Asylum Seekers in Africa*, Politics of Citizenship and Migration, https://doi.org/10.1007/978-3-031-16548-1_3

to provide a buffer against abject poverty or a safety net for their most vulnerable populations.[1]

According to a policy brief by the United Nations Department of Economic and Social Affairs (UN DESA), there is an increasing awareness among African countries that to address the adverse effects of the pandemic, as well as to ensure preparedness for future catastrophes, they need to introduce, scale up or expand, adapt or reform social protection programmes and measures.[2] Africa continues to have the lowest social protection coverage in the world,[3] meaning that most African countries do not have social protection systems for their own nationals, let alone for non-nationals, including refugees and asylum seekers. The UN's International Labour Organization (ILO) estimates that only approximately 17 per cent of the total population of the continent receive at least one social protection benefit, compared to a global average of about 47 per cent who receive such benefits, meaning that about 1.2 billion Africans lack access to any social protection coverage.[4]

Refugees and asylum seekers hosted by countries that already had such systems in place continue to be disproportionately affected.[5] These vulnerable groups tend to be excluded from the social protection schemes adopted by governments, in addition to the challenges that they already experienced in accessing their socio-economic rights prior to the pandemic.[6]

The right of access to social protection is recognised and protected in international law. Examples of such international instruments are the UNs' Universal Declaration of Human Rights (UDHR),[7] and the UN's

[1] Y Assefa et al. 'Analysis of the COVID-19 pandemic: Lessons towards a more effective response to public health emergencies' (2022) 18 *Globalization and Health* 10.

[2] United Nations Department of Economic and Social Affairs (UN DESA) 'Social policy and social protection measures to build Africa better post-COVID-19' *Policy Brief No. 93* (March 2021), 2.

[3] As above.

[4] International Labour Organization (ILO) 'World Social Protection Report 2020–22' ILO Flagship Report (2021) 19.

[5] M Marchi et al. 'Experience of discrimination during COVID-19 pandemic: The impact of public health measures and psychological distress among refugees and other migrants in Europe' (2022) 22 *BMC Public Health* 942.

[6] MG Breglia and FC Rosati 'Policy brief: Developmental social protection for refugees in the aftermath of Covid-19' Task Force 10: Migration (September 2021) 3.

[7] UN General Assembly, Universal Declaration of Human Rights, 10 December 1948, 217 A (III) (UDHR), articles 22 and 25(1).

1951 Convention Relating to the Status of Refugees (1951 Refugee Convention).[8] These instruments exist among other international and regional norms which relate to the rights of refugees and asylum seekers, and are explained briefly here.

There is currently no single globally accepted definition of 'social protection', which is often used synonymously with the term 'social security', as definitions tend to vary across countries.[9] This chapter views the term 'social protection' as a set of policies and initiatives, programmes and interventions by the public sector that are aimed at cushioning people, especially vulnerable groups, against poverty and social exclusion. Social protection encompasses social assistance (non-contributory benefits),[10] social insurance (contributory benefits), as well as labour market interventions.[11]

Furthermore, the discussion in this chapter incorporates the contemporary idea that social protection could be perceived through the lens of an 'adequate standard of living', a theme that in recent years has received significant attention in the general discourse regarding this right.[12] In terms of this idea, social security is a means towards a decent standard of living,[13] which possibly justifies its extension to circumstances where there is an existing source of income that may have been insufficient to meet a defined standard of living. This conception is contrary to the traditional view that the provision of social security is confined to instances where there is a complete lack of income. For example, according to Eide, in the context of the right to food, the right to property is the basis for the improvement of the standard of living because the land is used for

[8] UN General Assembly, Convention Relating to the Status of Refugees (1951 Refugee Convention), 28 July 1951, United Nations, Treaty Series, vol. 189, p 137, articles 23 and 24(1)(b).

[9] As above.

[10] I Currie and J de Waal *The Bill of Rights Handbook* (2013) 592.

[11] United Nations High Commissioner for Refugees (UNHCR) 'Social protection and the global compact on refugees' (13 July 2018) https://www.unhcr.org/5b4f46817.pdf (accessed 31 March 2022).

[12] UN General Assembly, International Covenant on Economic, Social and Cultural Rights (CESCR), 16 December 1966, United Nations, Treaty Series, vol. 993, p 3; see also South African Human Rights Commission (SAHRC) '3rd Economic and Social Rights Report' (1999/2000) 12.

[13] SAHRC (n 12) 12.

subsistence farming.[14] In the absence of property, one is forced to rely on the right to work as a means of improving one's standard of living.[15] However, in the event that neither property nor work provides sufficient income for an adequate standard of living, the right of access to social security provides the fall-back option.[16] This principle is encapsulated under article 11(1) of the International Covenant on Economic, Social and Cultural Rights (ICESCR).[17] Therefore, even in circumstances where the right of access to social security is not expressly stated in legal and policy frameworks, this right could still be given effect through the recognition of related rights. The ICESCR is regarded in international law as the most fundamental instrument relating to socio-economic rights.

Although there is an acknowledgement of the right of access to social protection for refugees and asylum seekers in international, regional and domestic norms/instruments, provision for this right by states is often dependent on one's citizenship status. This leads to the exclusion of non-nationals, including refugees and asylum seekers, regardless of their legal status in their host countries. Hathaway, a leading scholar of international refugee law, states that 'the entitlements owed to the refugee depend on the level of attachment of the refugee to the host state'.[18] In addition, there are a myriad of other barriers such as maladministration and bureaucratic factors that hinder refugees and asylum seekers from accessing social protection, as will be explained in Sects. 4 and 5 of this chapter, in the context of selected African countries which are regarded as among the top refugee-hosting countries on the continent. These countries are Uganda, Ethiopia and South Africa.

It is against this backdrop that this chapter commences by briefly outlining the normative legal framework for the right of access to social protection for refugees and asylum seekers in Africa. This discussion references some of the key international and regional legal instruments that enshrine and protect this right. The discussion provides the basis for arguing for its extension, as a legally enforceable right, to vulnerable groups such as refugees and asylum seekers throughout Africa. The chapter proceeds to

[14] A Eide 'The right to adequate food and to be free from hunger: Updated study on the right to food, submitted by Mr. Asbjørn Eide in accordance with Sub-Commission decision 1998/106' UN Doc E/CN.4/Sub.2/1999/12 (28 June 1999) 95.

[15] As above.

[16] As above.

[17] CESCR (n 12), article 11(1).

[18] JC Hathaway *The rights of refugees under international law* (2005) 123.

address when and how socio-economic rights such as the right of access to social protection are realised within the African context.

The various responses by governments to mitigate the adverse effects of the Covid-19 pandemic on their populations in the selected countries are addressed. More importantly, the section analyses the impact that these responses had, and continue to have, on the ability of refugees and asylum seekers to access social protection services. A greater emphasis is placed on the situation in South Africa, because apart from being a top refugee-hosting country on the continent, lauded for possessing a progressive, well-established and mature social protection system, information on South Africa's social protection system is well documented and more easily accessible as compared to many other countries. An effective response to the socio-economic challenges posed by the Covid-19 pandemic ought to consider the economic and health impact of the pandemic on refugees and asylum seekers.

The above considerations result in the highlighting of some of the barriers/challenges experienced in terms of the realisation of the right of access to social protection for refugees and asylum seekers on the African continent during the Covid-19 era. Similarly, this discussion also uses country-specific examples, with a greater focus on South Africa for the reasons provided above. Following the discussion, this chapter proposes several interventions and recommendations for the effective realisation of the right of access to social protection for refugees and asylum seekers on the continent.

2 Key International and Regional Norms for the Right of Access to Social Protection for Refugees and Asylum Seekers in Africa

The rights to social protection and an adequate standard of living are enshrined in several international human rights instruments. Immigrant and refugee rights have long been an issue of critical importance globally. The 1951 Refugee Convention acknowledges that the issue of refugees is a matter of international concern and must be addressed in the context of international cooperation and burden-sharing.[19] Across the world and on the African continent in particular, refugees and asylum seekers continue

[19] 1951 Refugee Convention (n 9).

to face challenges to the recognition and enforcement of their human rights. They often experience difficulties in accessing employment opportunities, education, basic healthcare services, and other forms of social and economic rights/social protection generally, especially in developing countries that face challenges in providing these rights to their own nationals.[20] The Covid-19 pandemic has further exposed the vulnerability and marginalisation of these groups across Africa.

2.1 International and Regional Standards

International law accords refugees and asylum seekers the enjoyment of their human rights, including the right of access to social protection, through a network of legal instruments that create obligations upon countries to respect, protect, facilitate and fulfil these rights. These norms form the basis of an international framework for the observance of socio-economic rights, including the right of access to social protection. However, despite the guarantee of these socio-economic rights, countries often fall short of protecting and safeguarding them. For example, undocumented refugees and asylum seekers tend to be excluded from social protection schemes that could facilitate access to health and social services, especially during the Covid-19 pandemic.[21] The pandemic has exposed the urgent need to ensure that these vulnerable groups are included in the national healthcare and social protection schemes of countries, as the role of social protection is widely recognised as key in countries' responses to humanitarian crises and catastrophes.

In 2020, for instance, especially in developing countries, social protection responses to the pandemic and its adverse consequences were adopted and reaffirmed as strategies or tools to increase resilience and support people in mitigating the socio-economic effects of Covid-19.[22] However, there remains limited documentation and reporting regarding the extent to which migrant populations either benefited or did not benefit from

[20] Human Rights Watch 'Living on the Margins: Inadequate protection for refugees and asylum seekers in Johannesburg' (2005) 17 *Human Rights Watch* 1 at 52.

[21] J Bornman and J Oatway 'South Africa: Migrants excluded from government food aid' *AllAfrica* 13 May 2020 https://allafrica.com/stories/202005130663.html (accessed 12 April 2022).

[22] M Andrade, L Sato and M Hammad 'Improving social protection for migrants, refugees and asylum seekers in Egypt: An overview of international practices' UNICEF Research Report 57 (2021) 31.

emergency social protection measures. Access to these measures is thought to be very limited, owing to the legal and practical barriers that these vulnerable groups face in accessing social protection systems.[23] The lack of documentation for refugees and asylum seekers is potentially the biggest factor that inhibits their access to social protection measures.

This section of the chapter examines some of the key international, regional and domestic legal instruments that enshrine and protect the right of access to social protection for refugees and asylum seekers in Africa. It provides a synopsis of the most fundamental legal and policy tools for the right of access to social protection for refugees and asylum seekers. A human rights-based approach is taken which acknowledges that refugee law and international human rights law are intrinsically linked and closely intertwined.[24] The section also recognises that social protection constitutes an essential human right that can protect migrants, refugees and asylum seekers by increasing their chances of contributing positively to the economy and society. A human rights-based approach towards social protection also ensures that refugees and asylum seekers are treated with dignity, equality and respect.

The different legal and policy instruments outlined in this chapter are imperative to providing the legal underpinnings and the assessment of the degrees to which the right of access to social protection for refugees and asylum seekers is recognised, both internationally and within the African continent. The summary of the legal norms does not purport to constitute a closed list of the relevant legal and policy instruments.

The various international and regional refugee and human rights conventions underlie the principles of non-discrimination/equal treatment and dignity. Therefore, states parties to human rights treaties and conventions are obligated to progressively safeguard all economic, cultural and social rights, including the rights of access to social protection, to all individuals within their territories, irrespective of their legal status in their destination/host countries. These instruments prescribe specific protections for disadvantaged and vulnerable individuals and groups.

Some of the most significant international and regional legal and policy tools and instruments are discussed, to the extent that they recognise and protect the right of access to social protection, particularly for vulnerable

[23] As above.

[24] International Justice Resource Center 'Asylum & the rights of refugees' https://ijrcenter.org/refugee-law/ (accessed 12 April 2022).

populations. A broad and detailed discussion of the international, regional and domestic norms on the rights of refugees and asylum seekers is provided in chap. 1 of this book.

2.1.1 UN 1951 Refugee Convention

The 1951 Refugee Convention (the 1951 Convention), which has hitherto been ratified by approximately 150 states globally, and its 1967 Protocol relating to the Status of Refugees (1967 Protocol), constitute the seminal law relating to international refugee protection today.[25] They also provide the most comprehensive and legally binding codification of the rights of refugees. Nearly all the countries of Africa have signed and ratified this 1951 Convention, albeit with reservations with respect to certain countries such as Botswana.[26]

The 1951 Convention provides the definition of a 'refugee' under article 1(A)(2) and outlines minimum standards for their treatment.[27] This Convention is underpinned by several fundamental principles, including non-discrimination and the principle of *non-refoulement*, which is enshrined in article 33 thereof.[28] The principle of *non-refoulement* requires that a refugee may not be expelled or returned (*refouled*) against their will to a territory where they face threats to their life or freedoms.[29] Therefore, these principles must be applied without discrimination based on race, sex, age, religion, disability, country of origin or other prohibited grounds of discrimination. This principle is universally regarded as a human right and is expressly provided for in domestic, regional and international human rights treaties such as article 3 of the UN Convention against Torture and Other Cruel, Inhuman or Degrading Treatment or Punishment of 1984.[30]

The non-discriminatory feature of the 1951 Convention, manifested through both articles 23 and 24 concerning the right of access to social

[25] 1951 Refugee Convention (n 9); UN General Assembly, Protocol Relating to the Status of Refugees, 31 January 1967, United Nations, Treaty Series, vol 606, p 267 (1967 Protocol).

[26] E Macharia-Mokabi and J Pfumorodze 'Advancing refugee protection in Botswana through improved refugee status determination' (2013) 13 *African Human Rights Law Journal* 152 at 154.

[27] 1951 Refugee Convention (n 9). (n 9), article 1(A)(2).

[28] 1951 Refugee Convention (n 9). (n 9), article 33.

[29] As above.

[30] UN General Assembly, Convention against Torture and Other Cruel, Inhuman or Degrading Treatment or Punishment, 10 December 1984, United Nations, Treaty Series, vol. 1465, p 85, article 3.

protection, is the most important principle for the purposes of this chapter. Article 24(1)(b) specifically outlines what constitutes social security, namely 'legal provisions in respect of employment injury, occupational diseases, maternity, sickness, disability, old age, death, unemployment, family responsibilities and any other contingency which, according to national laws or regulations, is covered by a social security scheme'.[31] This provision obligates states to accord refugees the same treatment as applied to their nationals regarding the aforementioned. Article 23 also provides that states parties should accord refugees the same treatment as their nationals with regard to the provision of public relief and assistance.[32] This provision is similar to article 20 of the 1951 Convention, which calls for the same treatment of refugees as the general population of a state, where a rationing system exists.[33] Article 24 further mandates states parties, with few exceptions, to accord refugees the same treatment as nationals with regard to social security guarantees.[34] The application of the principle of parity entails the outlining of the conditions under which social protection should be afforded to refugees.[35] Article 17 is also significant, as it stipulates that refugees must be afforded the 'most favourable treatment accorded to nationals of a foreign country in the same circumstances, as regards the right to engage in wage-earning employment'.[36]

2.1.2 Organisation of African Unity (OAU) Convention

The OAU Convention[37] constitutes a key instrument for regulating refugee protection in Africa. At a symposium by the OAU and the United Nations High Commissioner for Refugees (UNHCR) in 1994, it was reaffirmed that this Convention constitutes the cornerstone of refugee protection in Africa.[38] The OAU Convention complements the above-mentioned 1951 Convention and its 1967 Protocol. However, unlike the

[31] 1951 Refugee Convention (n 8), article 24(1)(b)..

[32] 1951 Refugee Convention (n 8), article 23.

[33] 1951 Refugee Convention (n 8), article 20.

[34] 1951 Refugee Convention (n 8), article 24.

[35] As above.

[36] 1951 Refugee Convention (n 8), article 17.

[37] OAU, Convention Governing the Specific Aspects of Refugee Problems in Africa (OAU Convention), 10 September 1969, 1001 UNTS 45.

[38] UNHCR 'Recommendations of the OAU/UNHCR symposium on refugees and forced population displacements in Africa' (21 September 1994) https://www.unhcr.org/excom/scip/3ae68ccc14/recommendations-oauunhcr-symposium-refugees-forced-population-displacements.html (accessed 14 June 2022).

1951 Convention, the OAU Convention does not contain any express provisions relating to social protection for refugees across the African continent.

Nevertheless, article 5(3) of the OAU Convention regulates the voluntary return/repatriation of refugees to their countries of origin.[39] It obligates countries of origin to facilitate their resettlement and grant them the full rights and privileges that it grants its nationals.[40] This non-discriminatory feature of the provision provides the basis for extending the right of access to social protection to refugees upon repatriation to their countries of origin.

2.1.3 Universal Declaration on Human Rights (UDHR)

The UDHR was adopted by the UN General Assembly in 1948 and is regarded as the foundational document in international human rights law.[41] Article 22 of the UDHR enshrines access to social security by stipulating that everyone has the right to social security.[42] It also imposes a positive duty on states to make efforts, including cooperating with other states, to ensure the realisation of the economic, social and cultural rights of everyone.[43]

Additionally, article 25(1) recognises the right of everyone to a standard of living that is adequate for their health and well-being, and that of their families, including necessary social services.[44] This provision further established the right to security 'in the event of unemployment, sickness, disability, widowhood, old age or other lack of livelihood in circumstances beyond his control'.[45] This recognition of the right of access to social protection is a manifestation of the internationally recognised equality of treatment/non-discrimination principle of international human rights law. This allows the extension of the legal coverage of social protection to refugees and asylum seekers by law, across countries.

The ILO acknowledges that often when countries enact laws that recognise this principle of non-discrimination, a narrow definition of migrants, refugees and asylum seekers, which refers to their legal status, can hinder

[39] OAU Convention (n 37), article 5(3).
[40] OAU Convention (n 37), article 5(3).
[41] UDHR (n 7).
[42] UDHR (n 7), article 22.
[43] As above.
[44] UDHR (n 7), article 25(1).
[45] As above.

their effective coverage and especially that of the most vulnerable populations.[46] Therefore, human rights violations disproportionately affect migrants, refugees and asylum seekers when the law does not explicitly protect them.

2.1.4 *Social Security (Minimum Standards) Convention*

The most widely cited international instrument regarding social security is the standards defined and developed by the ILO.[47] The ILO perceives social security as public benefits offered for the purpose of compensating for certain types of risks that are contained in its Social Security (Minimum Standards) Convention of 1952.[48] This Convention is considered to embody the internationally accepted definition of the principle of social security. It identifies nine forms of social security as follows: medical care, sickness benefit, unemployment benefit, old-age benefit, employment injury benefit, family benefit, maternity benefit, availability benefit and survivor's benefit.[49]

This Minimum Standards Convention is fundamental, as it regulates and provides guidelines for the development and implementation of social security systems for countries. It sets out, into a single, comprehensive and legally binding instrument, the minimum standards for each of the identified forms of social security. Importantly, the Minimum Standards Convention introduces the idea of a minimum general level that is compatible with human dignity, which states must attain in their socio-economic development. Through this Convention, the ILO recognises the essential role that social security plays in achieving economic development and the upliftment of the most marginalised and vulnerable segments of the population, as well as effectively managing crises.

2.1.5 *ILO's Social Protection Floors Recommendation, 2012*

The ILO's Social Protection Floors Recommendation, 2012 (No 202) is significant, as it complements conventions and other recommendations of the ILO, including the Minimum Standards Convention discussed

[46] UNICEF 'Improving social protection for migrants, refugees and asylum seekers: An overview of international practices' Research Report (2021) 4.

[47] International Labour Organization (ILO), Convention Concerning Minimum Standards of Social Security, 28 June 1952, C102 (Social Security Convention). See SAHRC (n 8) 11–12.

[48] SAHRC (n 12) 12.

[49] Social Security Convention (n 47).

above.[50] This Recommendation guides member states when developing comprehensive social security systems and extending social security coverage by prioritising the establishment of national floors of social protection that are accessible to all indigent segments of the population.[51] Social protection floors consist of nationally defined sets of basic social security guarantees, which ensure universal access to essential healthcare and income security to prevent or alleviate poverty, vulnerability and social exclusion.[52]

The Preamble of Recommendation No 202 reaffirms that 'the right to social security is a human right', and commits to the principle of universality of protection, based on social solidarity.[53] Article 6 stipulates that Members should provide the basic social security guarantees referred to in the Recommendation, to at least all residents and children, as defined in national laws and regulations.[54] It further mandates countries to deliver a minimum level of protection for all, particularly the poor and most vulnerable segments of society. This provision implies that the guarantees of the social protection floor, enshrined under article 5 thereof, apply to migrants and refugees.[55] These guarantees include access to essential healthcare that meets the criteria of availability, accessibility, acceptability and quality, and basic income security at a nationally defined minimum level.[56]

2.2 *Key Regional Instruments*

In Africa, social protection has emerged as one of the priority areas in its development agenda, as encapsulated in the African Union's Agenda 2063 action plan.[57] Article 19 of the recent Protocol to the Treaty Establishing the African Economic Community Relating to Free Movement of Persons, Right of Residence and Right of Establishment[58] specifically recognises

[50] International Labour Organization (ILO), Recommendation Concerning National Floors of Social Protection, 14 June 2012, R202.

[51] As above.

[52] Recommendation Concerning National Floors of Social Protection (n 50).

[53] Recommendation Concerning National Floors of Social Protection (n 50), article 3(a).

[54] Recommendation Concerning National Floors of Social Protection (n 50), article 6.

[55] G Koehler 'Refugees and their rights' (2020) http://www.icsw.org/index.php/news/85-refugees-and-their-rights (accessed 15 June 2022).

[56] Recommendation Concerning National Floors of Social Protection (n 50), article 5.

[57] AU 'Second continental report on the implementation of Agenda 2063' (2022).

[58] AU, Protocol to the Treaty Establishing the African Economic Community Relating to Free Movement of Persons, Right of Residence and Right of Establishment, 2018 (2018 Protocol).

the need for social security benefits to be extended to non-nationals in a member state.

Despite the broad recognition, both continent-wide and region-specific legal and policy instruments generally lack comprehensive provisions regarding the right of access to social protection for refugees and asylum seekers. The absence of such provisions plays a major role in refugees' and asylum seekers' failure to receive social protection. Countries are seemingly not obligated to provide these services, or cannot commit to providing them to refugees and asylum seekers, if there is no legislative basis for the provision of social protection to refugees and asylum seekers.

Similarly, the African Charter on Human and Peoples' Rights (Banjul Charter) does not contain any express provisions which recognise the right of access to social protection. However, articles 16 (relating to the right to health) and 18(4) (special measures of protection for the elderly and disabled populations) may be interpreted as incorporating the right of access to social protection.[59] Article 2 of this Charter stipulates that everyone is entitled to the enjoyment of the rights and freedoms recognised therein, without distinction of any kind, including distinctions based on their status.[60] Therefore, this provision includes refugees and asylum seekers as persons who are entitled to the rights and freedoms guaranteed in the Charter, including the above rights under articles 16 and 18(4) of the Charter.

Apart from the above legal norms, there are multiple other international, regional and domestic legal and policy instruments that contain provisions relating to the socio-economic rights of refugees and asylum seekers, including the right of access to social protection for these groups. These norms include the UN's Global Compact on Refugees (GCR);[61] the UN's Sustainable Development Goals;[62] and the recently adopted Protocol to the African Charter on Human and Peoples' Rights on the

[59] OAU, African Charter on Human and Peoples' Rights (Banjul Charter), 27 June 1981, CAB/LEG/67/3 rev. 5, 21 ILM 58 (1982), articles 16 and 18(4).

[60] Article 2 of the Banjul Charter (n 59), article 2.

[61] United Nations (UN) 'The global compact on refugees' (9 February 2018) https://www.un.org/pga/72/wp-content/uploads/sites/51/2018/02/Global-Compact-on-Refugees-9-Feb.002.pdf (accessed 21 March 2022).

[62] Food and Agriculture Organization of the United Nations (FAO) 'Sustainable Development Goals: 17 Goals to transform our world' https://www.fao.org/3/CA3121EN/ca3121en.pdf (accessed 4 April 2022).

Rights of Citizens to Social Protection and Social Security.[63] There are numerous other instruments in addition to the aforementioned. The following section addresses the various situations when and how socio-economic rights such as the right of access to social protection services are realised on the continent.

3 When and How Are Socio-Economic Rights, Such as the Right of Access to Social Protection, Realised?

As highlighted in the previous section, the right of access to social protection is firmly grounded in international human rights law. Hathaway contends that the right to non-discrimination may be the only legal guarantee that refugees and asylum seekers need in a host country, and proceeds to state that 'any unequal treatment must be properly justified according to consistently applied and acceptable criteria'.[64] Based on this contention, refugees and asylum seekers should have the right of access to social protection, as is the case with nationals within countries, by virtue of host countries having ratified international and regional human rights and refugee law.

A World Health Organization (WHO) study in 2020 confirmed that the Covid-19 pandemic has had a highly negative impact on the living and working conditions of refugees and migrants.[65] These circumstances justify the need for social protection measures to be implemented by host countries to protect these vulnerable groups, as it is the responsibility of the host governments where refugees are located to protect them during crises such as Covid-19. In 2020, the UNHCR's key focus was on advocating for the inclusion of refugees in the national response plans to the pandemic, thus further implying that these groups at the time were

[63] AU, Fifth Draft: Protocol to the African Charter on Human and Peoples' Rights on the Rights of Citizens to Social Protection and Social Security; African Commission on Human and Peoples' Rights 'High level continental seminar on the right to health and social protection in Africa - Key conclusions and recommendations' (10 December 2021) https://www.achpr.org/news/viewdetail?id=229 (accessed 14 June 2022).

[64] Hathaway (n 18) 123.

[65] WHO 'Migrants and refugees say COVID-19 has dramatically worsened their lives' (18 December 2020) https://www.who.int/news-room/feature-stories/detail/migrants-and-refugees-say-covid-19-has-dramatically-worsened-their-lives (accessed 12 April 2022).

excluded from the different social protection measures of countries across the world.[66]

Although the realisation of socio-economic rights is mainly a political process reliant on the commitment by a state to prioritise such rights, it does not only depend on the state. It also depends on civil society's and humanitarian groups' ability to mobilise and pressure/lobby (e.g. through activism) states to ensure that they are committed to achieving these rights for everyone. It further depends upon other state institutions and actors such as the judiciary and organs of the state, and other relevant national and international stakeholders. With a multiplicity of actors, there is a need for coordination between them to ensure that social protection systems achieve their intended objectives.

Socio-economic rights such as the right of access to social protection are realised when active steps are taken to ensure that people are able to fulfil their basic needs by having access to social protection services, adequate healthcare, housing, education and employment opportunities, among other basic rights. In most African countries today, socio-economic rights are enshrined in constitutions and further embedded in other laws and policies. Similar to the discussion above regarding the recognition of these socio-economic rights in international norms and instruments, their full realisation in domestic settings across the African continent is currently lacking. The reasons provided by scholars for this failure include the following: insufficient resources coupled with unequal distribution of wealth; corruption; weak governance structures; maladministration; the lack of political will; and ineffective implementation mechanisms. These are among the factors that will be explained below.

Additionally, the extent to which socio-economic rights are realised varies across countries on the continent, since it is influenced by several factors. These factors include the different levels of economic development that would influence a country's ability to provide social protection services, and accountability mechanisms—countries with strong democratic institutions, civil society organisations, and measures to ensure checks and balances are more likely to be effective in realising socio-economic rights for their people. The presence of effective legal systems

[66] UNHCR 'Refugee health challenges remain high amid COVID-19' (1 July 2021) https://www.unhcr.org/en-us/news/press/2021/7/60dda08e4/refugee-health-challenges-remain-high-amid-covid-19.html (accessed 12 April 2022).

and political will of a state are also fundamental factors that influence a country's provision of social protection services.

To properly assess the barriers/challenges that refugees and asylum seekers faced in accessing the right of access to social protection across Africa during the Covid-19 pandemic, it is imperative to explore the measures that governments took to alleviate the burden of the pandemic on their people and how such measures have affected refugees and asylum seekers. The following section provides contextual applications of the realisation of the right of access to social protection. It approaches the inquiry from the perspective of government responses in Uganda, Ethiopia and South Africa, which constitute top refugee-hosting countries, not only on the continent but globally.

4 Realising the Right of Access to Social Protection for Refugees and Asylum Seekers in the Covid-19 Era: Selected Country Case Studies

Although Africa continues to have the lowest social protection coverage because of several factors, significant progress has been made over the past two decades to extend these services, particularly to the poorest and most vulnerable segments of the population. Due to the Covid-19 pandemic, African leaders have realised the need to scale up or adapt social protection programmes to meet the challenges brought about by the pandemic as well as to ensure preparedness for unprecedented future events.[67]

According to the ILO, in response to the pandemic, 51 of the 55 countries on the continent announced over 227 social protection measures between February and November 2020,[68] including the following: cash transfers (Kenya, South Africa and Zimbabwe implemented cash transfer programmes to support vulnerable households); food assistance (governments across the continent introduced food assistance programmes to provide relief to vulnerable households); wage subsidies (governments in South Africa, Mauritius, Ghana and Rwanda introduced wage subsidies to employers whose businesses were affected); and tax relief (governments implemented certain tax relief measures to support businesses and households affected by the pandemic).[69]

[67] UN DESA (n 2), 5.
[68] UN DESA (n 2), 2.
[69] UN DESA (n 2), 2–3.

Additionally, governments mainly in West and Central Africa including Côte d'Ivoire, the Democratic Republic of Congo (DRC), Gabon and Senegal, as well as in North Africa (Morocco) and Southern Africa (South Africa, Botswana, Mauritius and Lesotho), established special funds and ring-fenced resources to addresses the effects of the pandemic.[70] Apart from government seed money, these special funds were mainly financed through tax-deductible donations from the private sector.[71] Despite these efforts, a 2021 study from Human Rights Watch revealed that in Ghana, Kenya, Nigeria and Uganda, the programmes that were introduced or expanded reached only a fraction of households that required support during the pandemic.[72]

Although the experiences of refugees and asylum seekers are not homogeneous between countries, it is certain that they face similar challenges regarding living a dignified life within their host countries. This section of the chapter highlights some of the social protection measures that were adopted by governments in three major refugee-hosting countries on the continent to alleviate the adverse effects of the Covid-19 pandemic. The countries discussed next are Uganda, Ethiopia and South Africa.

4.1 Uganda

Uganda is currently Africa's largest refugee-hosting country. At the end of March 2023, the size of its refugee population was reported be 1,532,168.[73] Uganda is renowned for possessing a progressive refugee policy that meets international refugee protection standards, and is anchored in its Refugees Act of 2006,[74] and the 2010 Refugee Regulations.[75] This legal framework affords refugees various rights and freedoms, including freedom of movement, and the right to work, own property, establish a business and access socio-economic services, including healthcare and education.

[70] As above.

[71] UN DESA (n 2), 5.

[72] Human Rights Watch 'Africa: Covid-19 Aid Falling Short' 12 October 2021 https://www.hrw.org/news/2021/10/12/africa-covid-19-aid-falling-short (accessed 12 April 2023).

[73] UNHCR 'Uganda Comprehensive Refugee Response Portal' 31 March 2023 https://data.unhcr.org/en/country/uga (accessed 3 April 2023).

[74] Act 21 of 2006.

[75] Refugees Regulations, No. 9 of 2010.

Uganda has been praised for its generally inclusive response to the pandemic, including its efforts to protect and safeguard the interests of refugees and asylum seekers. Some of the measures that were instituted during the pandemic include the following: the government of Uganda provided cash transfers to refugees through the Social Assistance Grants for Empowerment programme; the World Food Programme (WFP) and other humanitarian organisations provided food assistance to refugees; and refugees were provided access to free healthcare services, including testing and treatment for Covid-19.[76]

Despite the progressive legal and policy framework for refugees in Uganda and the government's efforts to protect refugees, attempts by the government and other stakeholders such as humanitarian organisations to provide basic services to refugees continue to be affected by multiple challenges, including insufficient funding. Hence, social protection programmes for refugees in Uganda tend to be underfunded,[77] thus leaving significant gaps in provision and assistance. The complexity of refugee assistance and the involvement of multiple domestic and international actors (e.g. the government, UN agencies and other humanitarian organisations) have also been reported to cause a lack of coordination, resulting in the inefficient use of resources and duplication of services.[78] Also, as a result of inadequate infrastructure across Uganda, refugees and asylum seekers may struggle to access basic socio-economic services such as healthcare and education.

4.2 Ethiopia

Like Uganda, Ethiopia comprises one of the largest hosting countries for refugees and asylum seekers on the continent. It hosts over 900,000 refugees, mainly from neighbouring countries, including South Sudan, Somalia, Eritrea and Sudan. One of the main social protection services for refugees in Ethiopia is the provision of food assistance. The government,

[76] UNHCR 'Food Security Dashboard: Uganda Refugee Response Plan (RRP) 2020–2021' 14 January 2022 https://data2.unhcr.org/en/documents/details/90440 (accessed 26 March 2023).

[77] Evan Easton-Calabria 'Uganda has a remarkable history of hosting refugees, but its efforts are underfunded' 26 August 2021 https://theconversation.com/uganda-has-a-remarkable-history-of-hosting-refugees-but-its-efforts-are-underfunded-166706 (accessed 3 March 2022).

[78] As above.

in collaboration with international humanitarian organisations such as the WFP, provides monthly food rations to refugees.[79] Ethiopia has also implemented various other social protection services for refugees, focusing on basic needs such as food, health and education, as well as legal services.

In response to the adverse effects of the Covid-19 pandemic in Ethiopia, by October 2020, only 13 per cent of households had received some form of government assistance.[80] It is noteworthy that the proportion of the poorest households receiving government assistance (i.e. 18 per cent) was higher than the national-level proportion,[81] thus indicating the government's efforts to prioritise and target the poor. Food assistance was the most common form of government assistance to households, as most received cash and food/cash for work assistance through the government's flagship social protection programme, the Productive Safety Net Programme (PSNP).[82]

The PSNP constitutes the largest and probably most well-known social protection programme across Sub-Saharan Africa. It has since 2005 provided food and cash assistance to the poorest households across Ethiopia. Although the Ethiopian government targeted low-income families for assistance, the scale of assistance to the poorest and most vulnerable segments of society was insufficient.[83] The PSNP is reported to have hitherto had a modest impact in terms of improving food security and alleviating poverty in the country.[84]

Similarly, a major challenge that the social protection system of Ethiopia faces is inadequate funding,[85] as resources for social protection programmes that are geared towards refugees in Ethiopia are often limited.

[79] UNHCR 'WFP, UNHCR, RRS appeal for funding to continue feeding over 750,000 refugees in Ethiopia' 9 August 2022 https://www.unhcr.org/africa/news/news-releases/wfp-unhcr-rrs-appeal-funding-continue-feeding-over-750-000-refugees-ethiopia (accessed 3 March 2022).

[80] A Deshpande et al. 'Social assistance in Ethiopia during COVID-19' 28 May 2021 https://www.brookings.edu/blog/future-development/2021/05/28/social-assistance-in-ethiopia-during-covid-19/ (accessed 3 March 2022).

[81] As above.

[82] As above.

[83] AS Deshpande et al. 'Coverage of social assistance in Ethiopia during the COVID-19 pandemic: a time-to-event analysis' (2022) *BMJ Global Health* 8.

[84] As above.

[85] UNHCR 'Ethiopia Country Refugee Response Plan 2020–2021' 23 January 2020 https://reliefweb.int/report/ethiopia/ethiopia-country-refugee-response-plan-2020-2021 (accessed 3 April 2023).

The government therefore relies on funding from international organisations and other donors,[86] which may be uncertain or insufficient to provide adequate social protection for refugees in the country. Another challenge to the social protection system of Ethiopia is the limited coverage for refugees as a result of factors such as lack of information on the availability of social protection, and other bureaucratic barriers.

4.3 South Africa

South Africa has for a long time been a preferred destination for migrants, refugees and asylum seekers from other regions of the continent, largely as a result of its commitment to upholding human rights as well as the rights of refugees and asylum seekers.[87] The country ratified both the 1951 Refugee Convention and the OAU Convention, which provide that refugees must be treated in the same way as the citizens of the host country. It subsequently domesticated these Conventions by enacting its Refugee Act of 1998, which is modelled upon the 1951 Refugee Convention and provides the specific framework, that is, policies and the law relating to refugees, for the country.[88]

Along with other socio-economic rights such as the rights to healthcare services, food and water, South Africa has a constitutional duty to extend the right to social protection to 'everyone', subject to the availability of resources. Section 27(1)(c) of its Constitution stipulates that: 'Everyone has the right to have access to … social security, including, if they are unable to support themselves and their dependents, appropriate social assistance'.[89] Section 27(2) in turn provides that: 'The state must take reasonable legislative and other measures, within its available resources, to achieve the progressive realisation of each of these rights'.[90] Section 28(1)(c) further grants every child the right to basic social services.[91] These socio-economic rights are to be viewed through the overarching founding

[86] As above.

[87] FC Mukumbang et al. 'Unspoken inequality: How COVID-19 has exacerbated existing vulnerabilities of asylum-seekers, refugees, and undocumented migrants in South Africa' (2020) 19 *International Journal for Equity in Health* 141.

[88] Act 130 of 1998 (Refugee Act).

[89] Constitution of the Republic of South Africa (Constitution), Section 27(1)(c).

[90] Constitution (n 89), section 27(2).

[91] Constitution (n 89), section 28(1)(c).

values of the Constitution, encapsulated in section 1(a), namely equality, human dignity, and the advancement of human rights and freedoms.[92]

With regard to the meaning of the word 'everyone' under section 27(1)(c) above, the Constitutional Court in the landmark *Khosa v Minister of Social Development* decision found that it is a term of general import, with unrestricted meaning, which means what it conveys.[93] By referring to section 7(1) of the Constitution and by adopting a purposive interpretation, the Court concluded that the word 'everyone' includes 'all people in our country'.[94] This case related to an application by Mozambican citizens living in South Africa as permanent residents, for an order confirming the constitutional invalidity of certain provisions of the Social Assistance Act 59 of 1992 that disqualified persons who are not South African citizens from receiving certain welfare grants. The Court held that excluding permanent residents from the social assistance scheme merely because they lack citizenship is unreasonable according to section 27(2) of the Constitution, as it infringes upon their rights to human dignity and equality.[95]

The *Khosa* judgement is particularly relevant to the discussion in this chapter, as the Court dealt with a specific vulnerable group and their unequal treatment by the state in the provision of social protection benefits. It follows from the finding that the unequal treatment of different groups of people, such as refugees and asylum seekers, in a social protection system would be deemed to be unfair and unreasonable in the country, as it precludes them from the equal enjoyment of their constitutionally guaranteed rights. As a result, this decision opened the door for marginalised and vulnerable groups such as refugees and asylum seekers to be included in the social protection system of South Africa.

When South Africa transitioned to democracy in 1994, the ruling African National Congress government sought to close the large inequality gaps that had been created by the previous apartheid discriminatory policies.[96] This closure provided the impetus behind the development of the country's social protection system, which is today considered to be the

[92] Constitution (n 89), sections 1(a).

[93] *Khosa v Minister of Social Development; Mahlaule v Minister of Social Development* 2004 (6) SA 505 (CC) para 111 (*Khosa* case).

[94] The *Khosa* case (n 93) para 47.

[95] The *Khosa* case (n 93) para 85.

[96] J Seekings and N Nattrass *Class, race, and inequality in South Africa* (2005) 45.

most developed across the continent.[97] Therefore, in light of the above constitutional provisions, the South African government took measures to develop a social protection system for the country. However, as will be shown here, as a result of multiple factors, this system does not extend to 'everyone', since vulnerable groups such as refugees and asylum seekers continue to be excluded. Consequently, the country is yet to live up to its constitutional obligations to extend such benefits to these historically marginalised groups.

Additionally, the South African government enacted the Refugee Act to protect refugees in the country. Section 27(b) states that refugees enjoy full legal protection, which includes the enjoyment of the rights set out in the Bill of Rights of the Constitution.[98] Despite not being expressly mentioned, this provision incorporates the right to social protection, following section 27(1)(c) of the Constitution. The discussion here delves into the exclusion of refugees and asylum seekers from receiving this right to social security that is safeguarded in legislation, including by the supreme Constitution of South Africa, particularly during the Covid-19 period. As a result, this exclusion implies that the country has thus far failed to fulfil its obligations to provide refugees and asylum seekers with the social protection benefits equal to everyone, including marginalised and vulnerable groups.

When the effects of the Covid-19 pandemic began to be felt in South Africa at the beginning of 2020, the government responded, using a combination of existing social protection programmes, unemployment insurance and additional programmes to support the most vulnerable and affected groups.[99] It utilised a largely cash-based approach, consisting of unemployment benefits for formal sector workers, and cash transfers to vulnerable individuals, informal workers and beneficiaries of existing grants.[100] The Business Relief Fund, which amounted to R500 billion and was offered to 100 per cent South African-owned businesses that were adversely affected by the pandemic and that possessed at least 70 per cent

[97] J Seekings *The social question in pre-apartheid South Africa: Religion and the state* (2020) 201.

[98] Refugee Act (n 88), section 27(b).

[99] L Gronbach et al. 'Social protection in the COVID-19 pandemic: Lessons from South Africa' CGD Policy Paper 252 (February 2022) 3.

[100] As above.

South African employees,[101] was one of the additional programmes that were instituted to address the adverse effects of the pandemic. Evidently, this programme automatically excluded businesses that were owned by refugees and asylum seekers from benefiting from the Fund, since they were not eligible under the above criteria.

More importantly, another additional programme by the South African government was the special Covid-19 Social Relief of Distress Grant (SRD grant).[102] This grant was launched with the intention of reaching vulnerable populations that were previously not covered by the existing social protection systems.[103] At the time, it was estimated that there were approximately 266,694 refugees and asylum seekers in the country.[104] These vulnerable groups faced significant barriers to accessing social protection systems, most being legal, administrative and structural in nature. For example, initially, asylum seekers and special permit holders were excluded as beneficiaries of the SRD grant, following directives by the Minister that the grant would only be provided to South African citizens, permanent residents and registered refugees.[105] Also, applicants for this grant had to provide their personal information, including their identification (ID) numbers or their Department of Home Affairs' (DHA) refugee permit number.[106] Such requirements posed fundamental challenges to refugees' and asylum seekers' ability to access this grant.

ID numbers are only issued to citizens and permanent residents. The DHA refugee permit numbers requirement therefore did not consider the plight of undocumented refugees. This exclusion was despite the fact that undocumented refugees and asylum seekers are vulnerable populations, as they were not eligible for the other social grants that were open to citizens, permanent residents and registered/documented refugees. The continued exclusion of refugees and asylum seekers further exacerbated the

[101] N Noyoo 'South Africa's social policy response to COVID-19: Relief measures in an unequal society' CRC 1342 Covid-19 Social Policy Response Series 21 (2021) 6.

[102] Noyoo (n 101) 3.

[103] As above.

[104] F Khan and M Kolabhai 'Bureaucratic barriers to social protection for refugees and asylum seekers during the COVID-19 disaster in South Africa' (2021) 7 *AHMR African Human Mobility Review* 74 at 78.

[105] Disaster Management Act: Directions Regarding Measures to Address, Prevent and Combat the Spread of COVID-19 Relating to the Freshwater and Marine Fishing Sectors (GN 538 of 2020, GG 43324, 14 May 2020).

[106] Khan and M Kolabhai (n 104) 85.

problem, since these marginalised groups were already facing multiple barriers to accessing social protection prior to the pandemic and continued to be disproportionately affected.

It was only pursuant to legal intervention in June 2020 by the Scalabrini Centre of Cape Town that the legal right of access to the SRD grant was extended to asylum seekers.[107] The Court in this case held that the Minister's Directions mentioned above were unlawful, unconstitutional and invalid to the extent that they excluded asylum seekers and special permit holders from the Covid-19 grant. This apparent victory for asylum seekers was seemingly short-lived, as there were further challenges in the exercising of the rights of asylum seekers, specifically relating to documentation. The DHA, which administers the asylum system, has historically made it difficult for refugees and asylum seekers to access legal documentation through their stringent administrative procedures that have led to serious backlogs in asylum appeals, and a 96 per cent rejection rate of applications.[108]

Furthermore, when the pandemic struck in 2020, the DHA closed its offices to refugees and asylum seekers. Many of their permits and legal documentation expired during the lockdown.[109] The closure of these offices also meant that those who arrived in the country after March 2020 had no way of applying for asylum status. Without the requisite legal documentation, refugees and asylum seekers struggle to access basic services, enrol their children in schools and open bank accounts. They are also vulnerable to arrest and deportation, exploitation by employers and unscrupulous police officers extorting bribes, among other hurdles.

The following constitute some of the key barriers/challenges to the realisation of the right of access to social protection for refugees and asylum seekers in South Africa, as a case study example. This discussion recognises that the challenges that refugees and asylum seekers face in South Africa are not independent of an already failing system where even South African nationals, particularly within the historically racially segregated

[107] *Scalabrini Centre Cape Town and Another v Minister of Social Development and Others* 2021 (1) SA 553 (GP).

[108] Amnesty International 'South Africa: Failing asylum system is exacerbating xenophobia' (29 October 2019) https://www.amnesty.org/en/latest/news/2019/10/south-africa-failing-asylum-system-is-exacerbating-xenophobia/ (accessed 19 March 2022).

[109] T Washinyira 'Refugees struggle to renew their asylum documents with Home Affairs online system' (4 February 2022) https://www.groundup.org.za/article/refugees-struggle-with-home-affairs-online-system/ (accessed 2 April 2022).

areas,[110] do not benefit from social protection services such as healthcare, education, shelter and employment. The structural barriers which refugees and asylum seekers face are part of the inequality, unequal development, marginalisation and exclusion that large sections of South Africans face, years after the end of the apartheid era.

5 Barriers to the Effective Realisation of the Right of Access to Social Protection for Refugees and Asylum Seekers

The Covid-19 pandemic has made it more difficult for refugees and asylum seekers to access social protection and other forms of aid. This section of the chapter outlines a non-exhaustive list of the major challenges/ barriers to the realisation of the right of access to social protection for refugees and asylum seekers. The section draws on the context of several countries, especially South Africa.

5.1 Insufficient Social Protection Coverage and Resource Constraints

At the core of the realisation of the right to social protection are the issues of the availability of resources and political will. The ILO estimates that the financing gap for the provision of social protection benefits across Africa amounts to less than 10 per cent of countries' GDPs.[111] There is thus a general lack of public expenditure allocated to social protection. This poses a major barrier for refugees and asylum seekers in terms of the progressive development of social protection.

Secondly, in respect of healthcare, which is especially crucial in light of the global pandemic, a recent report on the state of universal health coverage in Africa indicated that only 48 per cent of the population receive the healthcare services that they need.[112] Access to healthcare in Africa for refugees and asylum seekers has been a challenge for a long time, and the

[110] L Patel 'South Africa's social welfare system faces deepening challenges' *The Conversation* 16 March 2016 https://theconversation.com/south-africas-social-welfare-system-faces-deepening-challenges-55962 (accessed 2 April 2022).

[111] ILO (n 4) 58.

[112] Africa Health Agenda International Conference 'The state of universal health coverage in Africa: Report of the AHAIC Commission' (2021) 6.

situation was even more dire during the pandemic. Countries had limited healthcare facilities even before the pandemic and refugees were severely affected. Covid-19 has exacerbated these barriers. Dr. Tedros Adhanom Ghebreyesus (WHO Director-General) previously asserted that '[r]efugees and migrants live and work in often harsh conditions with inadequate access to health, housing, water, sanitation and other basic services'.[113] His call to action was evident in the following statement: 'It is vital for all countries to reduce barriers that prevent refugees and migrants from obtaining health care and to include them in national health policies'.[114]

Some of the reasons which explain the low coverage in social protection include the following: limited financial resources; a lack of political will to implement and expand social protection coverage to every section of the population; and the dominance of the informal sector on the continent, thus making it difficult to implement contributory social security schemes.[115] Also, national legislation may either expressly or implicitly exclude refugees or asylum seekers from specific permits and other benefits such as the SRD grant in the context of South Africa as mentioned earlier. Domestic legislation may establish less favourable conditions for these vulnerable groups under countries' existing social protection systems.

Additionally, the majority of informal workers on the African continent are often not covered by any form of social protection, particularly contributory systems, namely social insurance,[116] as they do not work for registered employers. This contributes to the overall low coverage rates. In terms of resource constraints, international organisations such as the ILO, the WFP and the UNHCR have in the past highlighted major shortfalls in funding that is needed to meet the needs of refugees and asylum seekers in Eastern Africa and throughout the continent.[117] As a result of a lack of resources on the part of host countries, as well as limited support from developed countries, there have been further reductions in existing services offered to refugees and asylum seekers. These challenges are prevalent in many countries including Uganda, Kenya, Rwanda, the DRC,

[113] WHO (n 65).

[114] As above.

[115] ILO (n 4) 19.

[116] S Devereux 'Social protection responses to COVID-19 in Africa' (2021) 21 *Global Social Policy* 421 at 422.

[117] UN, 'UN agencies appeal for $266 million to feed refugees in eastern Africa' *UN News* 2 March 2021 https://news.un.org/en/story/2021/03/1086122 (accessed 28 March 2022).

Somalia and Tanzania.[118] In Rwanda, for example, refugees in camps received $7.72 (7600 Rwandan francs) per month to purchase food from local markets during the Covid-19 lockdown after there was a 25 per cent cut in funding.[119]

5.2 *Administrative Delays*

Although South Africa's laws concerning refugees and asylum seekers are renowned for being among the most progressive in the world, they are often difficult to implement and the relevant procedures are fettered by long delays.[120] For a long time, refugees and asylum seekers have lamented the delays they face with the processing of their applications at Refugee Reception Offices (RROs), with the waiting periods taking up to a year, or longer.[121] These delays are mostly attributed to insufficient staff and inadequate equipment (e.g. malfunctioning computers).[122] Such difficulties give rise to a significant number of refugees and asylum seekers remaining undocumented and therefore unable to acquire rights, including the right of access to social protection. Possessing legal documentation or obtaining a legal status is essential, as it allows these vulnerable groups to legally claim the various socio-economic, political and civil rights that are due to them, including the right of access to social protection services.

Moreover, the long delays in processing claims are concerning for refugees and asylum seekers due to the precarious legal situation and living conditions in which many find themselves during the period of waiting. They are prone to being denied access to education or job opportunities because of the lack of recognition from both public and private sector authorities. These are some of the challenges they face when they do not have the requisite documentation.[123] The Supreme Court of Appeal pronounced on this issue in *Minister of Home Affairs v Watchenuka*.[124]

The Court in the *Watchenuka* case found that, based on the delays in the processing of their applications, the general exclusion (without

[118] Devereux (n 118) 428.

[119] E Manirambona et al. 'Impact of the COVID-19 pandemic on the food rations of refugees in Rwanda' (2021) 20 *International Journal for Equity in Health* 107.

[120] Human Rights Watch (n 20) 2.

[121] Human Rights Watch (n 20) 1.

[122] Human Rights Watch (n 20) 10.

[123] Human Rights Watch (n 20) 22.

[124] *Minister of Home Affairs v Watchenuka* [2004] 1 All SA 21 (SCA) (*Watchenuka* case).

guidelines or case-by-case considerations) of asylum seekers from, for example, the right to education and employment violates their constitutional right to human dignity.[125] Consequently, excluding refugees and asylum seekers from socio-economic programmes, without offering them humanitarian assistance, violates the Bill of Rights. Despite this finding by the Court, however, asylum seekers continue to be excluded from accessing socio-economic rights, including social protection, whilst their applications are pending.[126]

5.3 *Inefficiency and Corruption*

Research from 2021 in Kenya and Nigeria revealed that corruption prevents the limited available social assistance programmes from reaching the most vulnerable segments of the population. In Kenya, Human Rights Watch found evidence that local officials and politicians involved in administering the social protection system ignored eligibility criteria and directed cash transfers and other benefits to their relatives and friends.[127] Such incidents of corruption were also reported in several other African countries throughout the pandemic period, especially in 2020 and 2021.[128]

In South Africa, apart from the administrative delays encountered at RROs, another structural barrier for refugees and asylum seekers relates to the conduct of the relevant government officials/refugee reception officers. These officers have in the past been accused of prejudice, improper conduct and unprofessionalism.[129] There is also a lack of knowledge about refugee and asylum seeker rights among public service providers.[130] This leads to the refusal of services to and abuse of refugees and asylum seekers by officials. Public sector services tend to focus almost exclusively on citizens, and therefore officials may consider refugees and asylum seekers, at best, as a marginal group, and at worst, as competitors for the scarce public resources available. Tension often exists between refugees and asylum seekers on the one hand, and citizens of host countries on the other.[131]

[125] The *Watchenuka* case.

[126] Human Rights Watch (n 20) 22.

[127] Human Rights Watch (n 72).

[128] As above.

[129] Human Rights Watch (n 20) 12.

[130] Human Rights Watch (n 20) 22.

[131] SS Nambuya, J Okumu and R Pagnucco 'Refugee socio-cultural integration and peaceful co-existence in Uganda' (2018) 2 *The Journal of Social Encounters* 81.

These tensions cause refugees and asylum seekers to be treated with contempt at times by the relevant authorities. Refugees and asylum seekers are thus subjected to inhuman and degrading treatment.

Corruption in the RROs is cited by researchers as a significant barrier to refugees' and asylum seekers' access to refugee status determination procedures and protection.[132] Corruption in the DHA could be attributed to issues of capacity limitations, and internal organisational problems, which have far-reaching implications for service delivery in the department. Moreover, insufficient training of RRO officials is also part of the problem.[133]

5.4 *Failure to Formalise the National Asylum System*

Apart from the above, the failure to formalise the national asylum system, which is responsible for the documentation of applicants for refugee status and adjudication of appeals, has contributed to capacity constraints.[134] These constraints are evidenced by the rampant backlogs that leave many applicants without the requisite documentation.[135] The backlogs are worsened by the fact that appeals are adjudicated by a single Refugee Appeal Board for the whole country, which sits only twice or three times per year.[136] There is generally a lack of clear, easily accessible rules regarding the asylum process. This poses a further challenge to their legal protection. Khan and Kolanhai assert that these 'inefficiencies in the asylum documentation and identification system amount to breaches of international, constitutional, and statutory law obligations'.[137]

As a result of the abovementioned structural and bureaucratic barriers, refugees and asylum seekers on the continent are unable to access the same pandemic-related assistance from their respective governments. The concluding section of this chapter provides several recommendations and

[132] K Siegfried 'South Africa's flawed asylum system' *The New Humanitarian* 30 April 2013 https://www.thenewhumanitarian.org/analysis/2013/04/30/south-africa-s-flawed-asylum-system (accessed 7 April 2022).

[133] As above.

[134] S Masuku 'How South Africa is denying refugees their rights: what needs to change' *The Conversation* 12 May 2020 https://theconversation.com/how-south-africa-is-denying--refugees-their-rights-what-needs-to-change-135692 (accessed 7 April 2022).

[135] As above.

[136] As above.

[137] Khan and Kolabhai (n 104) 75.

opportunities to overcome these barriers to the progressive realisation of the right of access to social protection for refugees and asylum seekers across Africa.

6 Recommendations and Opportunities to Overcome the Barriers to Realising the Right of Access to Social Protection for Refugees and Asylum Seekers Across Africa

In light of the discussion above, this chapter proposes several recommendations and opportunities for the effective realisation of the right of access to social protection for refugees and asylum seekers. First, states across the African continent urgently need to establish, strengthen or extend comprehensive, adequate, sustainable and rights-based social protection systems for refugees and asylum seekers within their jurisdiction. Such initiatives would ensure that these social protection systems are inclusive of refugees and asylum seekers.

To address the various obstacles faced by these vulnerable groups in accessing social protection benefits such as healthcare, countries could implement several policy options including ratifying and implementing the relevant international conventions and recommendations such as the GCR, as a first step towards incorporating the principles and standards established therein into domestic law; and introducing complementary measures to address the administrative, practical and organisational obstacles faced by migrant workers. These policy measures recognise that to be effective, social protection needs strong national legal frameworks, which confer civil and socio-economic rights to refugees and asylum seekers.

Countries could also leverage pre-existing social protection programmes, such as short-term emergency programmes that were instituted to address the adverse effects of the pandemic, to build on and expand them into permanent social protection programmes in the respective countries. These programmes should target the most vulnerable sections of the population, including refugees and asylum seekers. Empirical evidence across the continent indicates that social protection measures are most effective when they are targeted at the most vulnerable sections of the population.

In addition, refugee host countries ought to address the systemic deficiencies within the relevant departments responsible for providing refugees and asylum seekers with the requisite documentation to allow them to access their rights to social protection services within the states, such as access to housing, healthcare and employment. Countries such as South Africa also need to streamline their asylum application systems and refugee application and appeal processes. Improving the technical capacity of the government officials in the system should also be prioritised to improve the efficiency of the different procedures and to address existing backlogs in the system that cause administrative delays.

Lastly, to resolve resource constraints, apart from countries prioritising the allocation of funds for social protection programmes in their national budgets and reallocation of public expenditure, there needs to be more international cooperation between countries, which is in line with the objectives of the GCR as well as other international norms.[138] There is, however, growing acknowledgement that meeting and safeguarding the rights of refugees and asylum seekers to health, education and social protection is a shared responsibility among all countries in the world.[139] Despite this acknowledgement, however, progress in fulfilling these rights has been slow, mainly because of the unduly heavy burdens placed on a few developing countries in Africa. There is an urgent need for the international community to expedite the implementation of policies such as the GCR, which, among other features, advocate for strengthened international cooperation and solidarity with refugees and affected host countries.

7 Conclusion

The premise of this chapter is that despite the utility of social protection increasingly gaining universal recognition, it is evident that as a result of a myriad of factors, this right remains out of reach for vulnerable groups such as refugees and asylum seekers, especially within the African continent. This chapter has shown that the right of access to social protection constitutes a universal human right that unequivocally applies to refugees and asylum seekers. This discussion provides the basis for arguing for its extension, as a legally enforceable right, to vulnerable groups.

The discussion transitions to an analysis of the impact of the various responses by governments to mitigate the adverse effects of the pandemic

[138] OAU Convention (n 37), article 2(4).

[139] P Lutz et al. 'Responsibility-sharing in refugee protection: Lessons from climate governance' (2021) 65 *International Studies Quarterly* 476.

on the ability of refugees and asylum seekers to access social protection services across Africa. In this regard, it relies on the situation in three major refugee-hosting countries on the continent, namely Uganda, Ethiopia and South Africa. It continues to highlight some of the barriers/ challenges experienced in terms of the realisation of the right of access to social protection for refugees and asylum seekers on the African continent during the Covid-19 era. Lastly, the chapter proposes several recommendations for the effective realisation of the right of access to social protection for refugees and asylum seekers.

Acknowledgment The author wishes to acknowledge the research assistance and support of Tatenda Kaponda (Children's Rights Project Assistant at the Scalabrini Centre of Cape Town), with gratitude.

Bibliography

Books

Currie, I & de Waal, J *The Bill of Rights Handbook* (2013).
Hathaway, JC *The rights of refugees under international law* (Cambridge University Press 2005).
Seekings J & Nattrass, N *Class, Race, and Inequality in South Africa* (2005).
J Seekings *The social question in pre-apartheid South Africa: Religion and the state* (2020).

Journal Articles

Assefa, Y; Gilks, CF; Reid, S; Van de Pas, R; Gete, DG & Van Damme, W 'Analysis of the COVID-19 pandemic: lessons towards a more effective response to public health emergencies' (2022) *Globalization and Health*.
Deshpande, AS *et al.* 'Coverage of social assistance in Ethiopia during the COVID-19 pandemic: a time-to-event analysis' (2022) *BMJ Global Health* 8.
Devereux, S 'Social protection responses to COVID-19 in Africa' (2021) 21 *Global Social Policy* 421.
Eide, A *The right to an adequate standard of living including the right to food* (1999).
Human Rights Watch 'Living on the Margins: Inadequate protection for refugees and asylum seekers in Johannesburg' (2005) *Human Rights Watch* Vol. 17, No. 15(A).
Khan, F & Kolabhai, M 'Bureaucratic Barriers to Social Protection for Refugees and Asylum Seekers during the COVID-19 Disaster in South Africa' (2021) 7 *AHMR African Human Mobility Review*.

Lutz, P; Stünzi, A & Manser-Egli, S 'Responsibility-sharing in refugee protection: Lessons from climate governance' (2021) 65 *International Studies Quarterly* 476.

M.G Breglia & FC Rosati "*Policy Brief: Developmental Social Protection for Refugees in the Aftermath of COVID-19*".

Macharia-Mokabi, E & Pfumorodze, J 'Advancing refugee protection in Botswana through improved refugee status determination' (2013) *African Human Rights Law Journal (AHRLJ)*.

Manirambona, E; Uwizeyimana, T; Uwiringiyimana, E & Reddy, H 'Impact of the COVID-19 pandemic on the food rations of refugees in Rwanda' (2021) 20 *International Journal for Equity in Health*.

Marchi, M; Magarini, FM; Chiarenza, A; Galeazzi, GM; Paloma, V; Garrido, R; Ioannidi, E; Vassilikou, K; de Matos, MG; Gaspar, T; Guedes, FB; Primdahl, NL; Skovdal, M; Murphy, R; 'Experience of discrimination during COVID-19 pandemic: the impact of public health measures and psychological distress among refugees and other migrants in Europe' (2022) *BMC Public Health*.

Mukumbang, FC, Ambe AN & Adebiyi BO 'Unspoken Inequality: how COVID-19 has exacerbated existing vulnerabilities of asylum-seekers, refugees, and undocumented migrants in South Africa' (2020)19 *International Journal for Equity in Health*.

Nambuya, SS, Okumu, J & Pagnucco, R 'Refugee socio-cultural integration and peaceful co-existence in Uganda' (2018) 2 *The Journal of Social Encounters*.

Noyoo, N '*South Africa's social policy response to COVID-19: Relief measures in an unequal society*', Social Policy Response Series, 21 (2021).

Papers/Reports

Africa Health Agenda International Conference 'The state of universal health coverage in Africa: Report of the AHAIC Commission' (2021).

Gronbach, L; Seekings, J & Megannon, V '*Social Protection in the COVID-19 Pandemic: Lessons from South Africa*' Policy Paper.

International Labour Organization (ILO) 'World Social Protection Report 2020–22' ILO Flagship Report (2021).

South African Human Rights Commission (SAHRC) '3rd Economic and Social Rights Report' (1999/2000).

United Nations Department of Economic and Social Affairs (UN DESA) "Social policy and social protection measures to build Africa better post-COVID-19" *Policy Brief No. 93* (March 2021).

UNICEF 'Improving social protection for migrants, refugees and asylum seekers: An overview of international practices' Research Report (2021).

Case Law

Khosa v Minister of Social Development; Mahlaule v Minister of Social Development 2004 (6) SA 505 (CC).

Minister of Home Affairs and Others v Watchenuka and Another [2004] 1 All SA 21 (SCA).

Scalabrini Centre Cape Town and Another v Minister of Social Development and Others 2021 (1) SA 553 (GP).

Legislation

Constitution of the Republic of South Africa, 1996.

Disaster Management Act: Directions Regarding Measures to Address, Prevent and Combat the Spread of COVID-19 Relating to the Freshwater and Marine Fishing Sectors (G.N. Notice 538 of 2020). (South Africa).

Refugee Act 130 of 1998 (South Africa).

Refugees Act 21 of 2006 (Uganda).

Refugees Regulations, No. 9 of 2010 (Uganda).

AU Documents

African Union (AU) 'Second continental report on the implementation of Agenda 2063' (2022).

Fifth Draft: Protocol to the African Charter on Human and Peoples' Rights on the Rights of Citizens to Social Protection and Social Security.

Organisation of African Unity (OAU), African Charter on Human and Peoples' Rights (Banjul Charter), 27 June 1981, CAB/LEG/67/3 rev. 5, 21 ILM 58 (1982).

OAU's Convention Governing the Specific Aspects of Refugee Problems in Africa (1969 OAU Convention).

UN Documents

Convention Relating to the Status of Refugees (1951 Refugee Convention).

International Labour Organization (ILO), Convention Concerning Minimum Standards of Social Security, 28 June 1952, C102 (Social Security Convention).

ILO, Recommendation Concerning National Floors of Social Protection, 14 June 2012, R202.

UN Committee on Economic, Social and Cultural Rights (CESCR), General Comment 19: The right to social security (Art 9 of the Covenant), 4 February 2008, E/C.12/GC/19.

UN General Assembly, Protocol Relating to the Status of Refugees, 31 January 1967, United Nations, Treaty Series, vol 606, p 267 (1967 Protocol).

UN General Assembly, Universal Declaration of Human Rights, 10 December 1948, 217 A (III) (UDHR).

UN General Assembly, Convention Against Torture and Other Cruel, Inhuman or Degrading Treatment or Punishment, 10 December 1984, United Nations, Treaty Series, vol 1465.

Internet Reports

Andrade, M; Sato, L & Hammad, M '*Improving social protection for migrants, refugees and asylum seekers in Egypt: An overview of international practices*' Unicef Research Report No. 57 (2021).

United Nations High Commissioner for Refugees (UNHCR) 'Social protection and the global compact on refugees' (13 July 2018) https://www.unhcr.org/5b4f46817.pdf (accessed 31 March 2022).

UNHCR 'Ethiopia Country Refugee Response Plan 2020-2021' 23 January 2020 https://reliefweb.int/report/ethiopia/ethiopia-country-refugee-response-plan-2020-2021 (accessed 3 April 2023a).

UNHCR 'Food Security Dashboard: Uganda Refugee Response Plan (RRP) 2020-2021' 14 January 2022a https://data2.unhcr.org/en/documents/details/90440 (accessed 26 March 2023).

UN, 'The global compact on refugees' 09 February 2018 https://www.un.org/pga/72/wp-content/uploads/sites/51/2018/02/Global-Compact-on-Refugees-9-Feb.002.pdf (accessed 21 March 2022).

Internet Sources

African Commission on Human and Peoples' Rights 'High level continental seminar on the right to health and social protection in Africa - Key conclusions and recommendations' (10 December 2021) https://www.achpr.org/news/viewdetail?id=229 (accessed 14 June 2022).

Amnesty International 'South Africa: Failing asylum system is exacerbating xenophobia' (29 October 2019) https://www.amnesty.org/en/latest/news/2019/10/south-africa-failing-asylum-system-is-exacerbating-xenophobia/ (accessed 19 March 2022).

Deshpande, A *et al.* 'Social assistance in Ethiopia during COVID-19' 28 May 2021 https://www.brookings.edu/blog/future-development/2021/05/28/social-assistance-in-ethiopia-during-covid-19/ (accessed 3 March 2022).

Easton-Calabria, E 'Uganda has a remarkable history of hosting refugees, but its efforts are underfunded' 26 August 2021 https://theconversation.com/

uganda-has-a-remarkable-history-of-hosting-refugees-but-its-efforts-are-underfunded-166706 (accessed 3 March 2022).
Food and Agriculture Organization of the United Nations (FAO) 'Sustainable Development Goals: 17 Goals to Transform our World' https://www.fao.org/3/CA3121EN/ca3121en.pdf (accessed 4 April 2022).
G Koehler 'Refugees and their rights' 2020 http://www.icsw.org/index.php/news/85-refugees-and-their-rights (accessed 15 June 2022).
Human Rights Watch 'Africa: Covid-19 Aid Falling Short' 12 October 2021 https://www.hrw.org/news/2021/10/12/africa-covid-19-aid-falling-short (accessed 12 April 2023).
International Justice Resource Center (IJRC) 'Asylum & the Rights of Refugees' https://ijrcenter.org/refugee-law/ (accessed 12 April 2022).
J Bornman & J Oatway 'South Africa: migrants excluded from government food aid' 13 May 2020 https://allafrica.com/stories/202005130663.html (accessed 12 April 2022).
Masuku, S 'How South Africa is denying refugees their rights: what needs to change' *The Conversation* 12 May 2020 https://theconversation.com/how-south-africa-is-denying-refugees-their-rights-what-needs-to-change-135692 (accessed 7 April 2022).
Patel, L 'South Africa's social welfare system faces deepening challenges' *The Conversation* 16 March 2016 https://theconversation.com/south-africas-social-welfare-system-faces-deepening-challenges-55962 (accessed 2 April 2022).
Siegfried, K 'South Africa's flawed asylum system' *The New Humanitarian* 30 April 2013 https://www.thenewhumanitarian.org/analysis/2013/04/30/south-africa-s-flawed-asylum-system (accessed 7 April 2022).
UNHCR 'Refugee health challenges remain high amid COVID-19' 1 July 2021 https://www.unhcr.org/en-us/news/press/2021/7/60dda08e4/refugee-health-challenges-remain-high-amid-covid-19.html (accessed 12 April 2022).
UNHCR 'Recommendations of the OAU/UNHCR symposium on refugees and forced population displacements in Africa' 21 September 1994 https://www.unhcr.org/excom/scip/3ae68ccc14/recommendations-oauunhcr-symposium-refugees-forced-population-displacements.html (accessed 14 June 2022).
UNHCR 'Uganda Comprehensive Refugee Response Portal' 31 March 2023b https://data.unhcr.org/en/country/uga (accessed 3 April 2023).
UNHCR 'WFP, UNHCR, RRS appeal for funding to continue feeding over 750,000 refugees in Ethiopia' 09 August 2022b https://www.unhcr.org/africa/news/news-releases/wfp-unhcr-rrs-appeal-funding-continue-feeding-over-750-000-refugees-ethiopia (accessed 3 March 2022).

UN, 'UN agencies appeal for $266 million to feed refugees in eastern Africa' *UN News* 2 March 2021 https://news.un.org/en/story/2021/03/1086122 (accessed 28 March 2022).

Washinyira, T 'Refugees struggle to renew their asylum documents with Home Affairs online system' (4 February 2022) https://www.groundup.org.za/article/refugees-struggle-with-home-affairs-online-system/ (accessed 2 April 2022).

WHO 'Migrants and refugees say COVID-19 has dramatically worsened their lives' (18 December 2020) https://www.who.int/news-room/feature-stories/detail/migrants-and-refugees-say-covid-19-has-dramatically-worsened-their-lives (accessed 12 April 2022).

CHAPTER 4

Human Dignity and the Realisation of Socio-Economic Rights of Refugees in Africa

Callixte Kavuro

1 Introduction

Protecting human dignity is the benchmark against which the observance of both human rights and refugee rights is largely measured, monitored and analysed. Respect for human and refugee rights means that the dignity of individuals cannot be assailed as it demands that individuals not be treated with contempt, be dehumanised, or be subjected to inhuman and degrading treatment.[1] Moreover, international and national legal orders

[1] Human dignity requires people and authorities to 'acknowledge the value and worth of all individual members of the society'. See I Currie and J de Waal *The Bill of Rights Handbook* 6 ed. (2017) 251.

C. Kavuro (✉)
Department of Public Law, Stellenbosch University, Stellenbosch, South Africa

E. Durojaye et al. (eds.), *Realising Socio-Economic Rights of Refugees and Asylum Seekers in Africa*, Politics of Citizenship and Migration, https://doi.org/10.1007/978-3-031-16548-1_4

are constructed on this conviction.[2] The need to protect human dignity became central to the international legal order after the two world wars. After World War I, the family of nations understood that principles of peace, security, and fair and humane treatment could diminish human suffering and thus contribute to economic development.[3] Owing to greater human suffering caused by World War II, the international order was, as a result, grounded in principles of equality and human dignity.[4] These principles are recognised as sources of human rights law.[5]

Principles of human rights law apply to refugees and asylum seekers in terms of the 1951 Convention Relating to the Status of Refugees (Refugee Convention). Under this Refugee Convention, the United Nations (UN) created 'special' protection for refugees in line with the principle of equality in rights and dignity. This is more evident in principles of non-discrimination and socio-economic inclusion, which underpin the protection of the dignity of refugees. The Refugee Convention remains an essential instrument that prescribes guidelines to develop and frame national refugee policies for its effective implementation.[6]

The inclusive approach to socio-economic protection is advocated on humanitarian grounds and on the demands made to host states to 'do everything within their power to prevent [the social and humanitarian] problem from becoming a cause of tension between States'.[7] The Organisation of African Unity (OAU), now the African Union (AU), shares this view and adopted the Convention Governing the Specific Aspects of Refugee Problems in Africa (AU Refugee Convention) in 1969.

[2] Human dignity is viewed as a source of a person's innate rights to freedom and physical integrity, from which international human rights flow and from which the post-Second World War constitutionalism flows or is associated. See Currie and de Waal (n 1) 250–251.

[3] C Kavuro 'Refugees' access to socio-economic rights: Favourable treatment for the protection of human dignity' PhD thesis, Stellenbosch University, 2018 at 94.

[4] Preamble to United Nations, Charter of the United Nations, 24 October 1945, 1 UNTS XVI.

[5] H Klug 'The dignity clause of the Montana Constitution: May foreign jurisprudence lead the way to an expanded interpretation?' (2003) 64 *Montana Law Review* 133 at 135.

[6] *United States v Aguilar* 883 F.2d 662 (9th Cir 1989), Cert denied, 498 US 1046 (1991). See also *Beharry v Reno* 183 F.Supp.2d 584 (2002). International conventions are generally treated as self-executing if they are enforceable in courts once signed and ratified. Such treaties do not have the force of domestic law before they are given effect to by national legislation.

[7] Preamble to UN General Assembly, Convention Relating to the Status of Refugees, 28 July 1951, United Nations, Treaty Series, vol. 189, p 137.

The AU also recognised 'the need for an essentially humanitarian approach towards solving the problems of refugees'. Emphatically and tacitly, the AU recognised that humane treatment is a principled mechanism through which refugees' misery and suffering can be alleviated and through which a better life and future can be provided to them.[8] However, under both the Refugee Convention and the AU Refugee Convention, human dignity is not explicitly recognised as a right. Yet, this does not mean it lacks importance. It is fundamental, as deprivation of access to socio-economic rights means being deprived of opportunities to lead a dignified life or to be uplifted from degrading circumstances, and deprived of opportunities to progress, develop and prosper.[9]

Against this background, the chapter discusses the challenges to the realisation of the socio-economic rights of refugees and asylum seekers in Africa, and explores the opportunities that exist to realise these rights. It will be concluded that principles and theories such as citizenship, social contract, national sovereignty and humanitarian protection severely impact refugees' and asylum seekers' right of access to socio-economic rights. This, in turn, reduces the effective protection of their human dignity.

2 Human Dignity and Its African Context

2.1 Philosophical Understanding of Human Dignity

The idea that every person is entitled to respect for their inherent dignity owes much to theological thought, which linked dignity to the inherent value of each human being.[10] Theologians understood 'dignity' to be inherent in human nature and closely related to the ideals of equality and freedom. These three precepts are believed to be rooted in the creation of

[8] See C Kavuro 'The value of human dignity in the refugee protection' (2019) 5(1) *African Human Mobility Review* 1516.

[9] S Liebenberg 'The value of freedom in interpreting socio-economic rights' (2008) 1 *Acta Juridica* 149 at 154; M Pieterse 'Eating socio-economic rights: The usefulness of rights talk in alleviating social hardship revisited' (2007) 29 *Human Rights Quarterly* 796; A Sen *Development as freedom* (1999) 38; and M Nussbaum *Creating capabilities: The human development approach* (2011) 34.

[10] H Botha 'Human dignity in comparative perspective' (2009) 20 *Stellenbosch Law Review* 171 at 189.

man in the image and likeness of God.[11] This thinking influenced developments in international law in the early twentieth century relating to the fair and humane treatment of all human beings.

Theologians were of the view that a human being is endowed with a soul, reason and conscience that enable them to think, deliberate and make free choices. On this basis, they presumed that a human being may not irrationally and unreasonably engage in evil acts towards other human beings, oppress them, or treat them in a degrading or cruel manner. Within this view, persecution, oppression, ill-treatment and xenophobia are considered immoral acts that impair the value, essence or dignity of an individual. This is so because everyone is conscientiously obliged to treat other people as 'we would have them treat us'[12] and to love them equally as God loves us.[13] Here, inherent human dignity is justified on the conceptual grounds of freedom, equality, humanity and mutual respect. Of concern is that the medieval theological thinking had shortcomings in some respects as it held onto non-egalitarian notions of human dignity. For instance, it did not view the widely divergent—and unequal—positions of men and women as inconsistent with human dignity.

Nonetheless, in modern theological thought, the ideas of human dignity typically require respect for every human being's free will, and for every individual's right to create their own happiness, pursue their own destiny and realise their own human fulfilment.[14] Human dignity is perceived to be rooted in the natural, human capacity to reason and 'to shape [ourselves] to a range of possibilities not available to other creatures'.[15] As human beings, refugees should not entirely be deprived of the basic avenues or opportunities to shape themselves to a range of possibilities available to citizens.

[11] J Donnelly 'Human dignity and human rights' Research Project on Human Dignity, Swiss Initiative to Commemorate the 60th Anniversary of the UDHR, Protecting Dignity: An Agenda for Human Rights (2009) at 18; and RD Glensy 'The right to dignity' (2011) 34 *Columbia Human Rights Law Review* 65 at 74–75.

[12] P Lee and RP George 'The nature and basis of human dignity' (2008) 21 *Ratio Juris* 173.

[13] D D'Souza *What's so great about Christianity* (2007) 67–82.

[14] A Vaišvila 'Human dignity and the right to dignity in terms of legal personalism (from conception of static dignity to conception of dynamic dignity)' (2009) 3 *Jurisprudence* 111 at 120.

[15] M Rosen *Dignity: Its history and meaning* (2012) 15.

The moral philosopher Immanuel Kant advocated for the notion of equal opportunities and maintained that every human being should live their life in accordance with ends that they freely chose.[16] Human beings are regarded as autonomous agents who can define their own destiny independently. Kant stated that every individual has inherent moral worth.[17] This philosophical notion of human dignity implies that refugees cannot be treated as things or as instruments of the will of the citizens of the country that hosts them. Refugees' highest value—as human beings—demands their host countries to accord to them effective protection that will safeguard their inherent moral human worth.

2.2 *African Context of Human Dignity*

As noted in the introduction, the need to protect the human dignity or the inherent moral human worth of every person forms the basis of affording socio-economic rights to refugees in terms of the Refugee Convention. Entitling refugees to dignified treatment is also a matter concerning the AU Refugee Convention, which complements the Refugee Convention. Human dignity is therefore implied in the notions on which the AU Refugee Convention is constructed. These notions include solving the refugee problems; alleviation of misery and suffering; and African spirit and solidarity.[18] The treatment envisaged by the AU Refugee Convention derives from and must be understood in terms of the African philosophical concept of ***ubuntu***, which means 'to be humane towards others'.[19] The notion of ***ubuntu*** will therefore dictate that the national refugee regimes should be structured in a manner that gives effect to the Refugee Convention and the AU Refugee Convention as infused by the principle of equality in rights and dignity. Being humane towards others implies giving a warm welcome to others and assisting them—individually and collectively—to create their own happiness, pursue their own destiny, and

[16] D Wallace 'Jacques Maritain and Alasdair MacIntyre: The person, the common good and human rights' in B Sweetman (ed.) *The failure of modernism: The Cartesian legacy and contemporary pluralism* (1999) 127, 131.

[17] I Kant *Groundwork for the metaphysics of morals* (2002) 53.

[18] Preamble of the OAU, Convention Governing the Specific Aspects of Refugee Problems in Africa (AU Convention), 10 September 1969, 1001 UNTS 45.

[19] C Kavuro 'Refugee rights in South Africa: Addressing social injustices in government financial assistance schemes' (2015) 5 *Journal of Sustainable Development Law Policy* 176 at 176.

realise their own human fulfilment. In this way, refugees should be assisted to uplift themselves from human suffering and misery and to have, at least, a dignified basic standard of living.

In the light of the above, the AU Refugee Convention recognises the need to create conditions in terms of which refugees can achieve improved lives and futures and so attain a fully dignified life.[20] The protection of refugees must be based on and informed by African values such as equal treatment, mutual respect, mutual concern, equal dignity, unity and solidarity, compassion, and mercy, as well as by the idea that a person enjoys humanity through others.[21] These African values should infuse the protection of refugees' basic needs for them to attain a dignified standard of living comparable with that of others or those around them. If they are denied socio-economic opportunities to advance themselves, refugees will remain trapped in poverty and accordingly remain a burden on the state purse. Surviving on long-term humanitarian relief and assistance will defeat their desire to achieve an adequate standard of living. Such assistance will result in denigrating their inherent moral worth as they are denied the freedom to live their lives in accordance with ends that they freely chose. The provision of socio-economic assistance will not always be considered a dignified approach, especially in those circumstances where the assistance is only for survival and not enough to promote self-sufficiency or self-reliance.

3 Socio-Economic Rights for Refugees and Asylum Seekers

As noted, the widest possible protection of refugees' and asylum seekers' dignity is based on effective and favourable access to socio-economic rights and benefits available in their host country. Particularly, the Refugee Convention provides for several socio-economic rights that must be extended to refugees by a host state. Generally, these rights accrue to refugees simply by virtue of being guaranteed by human rights law. According to the preamble of the International Covenant on Economic, Social and Cultural Rights, access to socio-economic rights serves to promote universal respect for, and observance of, human rights and freedoms. The

[20] Paragraph 1 of the Preamble of the AU Refugee Convention.
[21] Kavuro (n 19) 188–189.

inherent dignity of the human person is severely affected in circumstances where they do not have access to these rights.

On the African continent, the AU Refugee Convention and the AU Convention for the Protection and Assistance of Internally Displaced Peoples (Kampala Convention) are the key regional frameworks for the protection of refugees, asylum seekers and internally displaced persons (IDPs). The latter framework is concerned with individuals who were forced to leave their homes because of instability and tension in African states or natural disasters, but who have not yet crossed the border to seek asylum in another country.[22] In contrast, refugees are individuals who have crossed the border to seek asylum in another country.[23] There are, however, two categories of refugees: recognised refugees (*de jure* refugees) and asylum seekers (de facto refugees). The term 'asylum seeker' is therefore used to refer to someone physically present in the country in which they are seeking asylum and whose application for asylum is still considered and not yet finalised by the host state.[24] The difference between the legal positions of recognised refugees and asylum seekers hinges on the fact that recognised refugees are those asylum seekers whose applications have been approved and who have formally been granted asylum or refugee status. More importantly, the chapter is not concerned with the IDPs who seek physical safety and security within the territory of their home country and can therefore assert their rights as citizens.

Refugee rights are further analysed from the perspective that access to socio-economic rights and associated benefits is further entrenched under the African Charter, which recognises that 'fundamental human rights stem from attributes of human beings which justifies their national and

[22] Article 1(k) of the African Union Convention for the Protection and Assistance of Internally Displaced Persons in Africa (Kampala Convention), 23 October 2009 defines the term IDP to mean 'persons or groups of persons who have been forced or obliged to flee or to leave their homes or places of habitual residence, in particular as a result of or in order to avoid the effects of armed conflict, situations of generalized violence, violations of human rights or natural or human-made disasters, and who have not crossed an internationally recognised State border'.

[23] The definition of refugee is provided for in Chap. 1. By definition, the term refugee generally refers to someone who has left their country of origin to seek a safe haven in another country (and the protection of that country) and is unable and unwilling to return to their country of origin due to a serious threat to their life or freedom. See the UNHCR *A guide to international refugee protection and building asylum systems* (2017) 17.

[24] As above.

international protection'.[25] This approach to the protection of human rights implies that the socio-economic rights of refugees should be protected because these rights also stem from attributes of being human. Enjoyment of socio-economic rights is therefore seen as essential for the right to development and for guaranteeing the freedom of enjoying civil rights such as the right to life, equality and human dignity.[26] The Kampala Convention recognises that member states of the AU have adopted democratic practices and adhere to the principles of non-discrimination, equality and equal protection of the law under the African Charter, as well as under other regional and human rights law instruments.[27] In the light of this and firmly based on the protection of worth and dignity of the human person, the host states have the responsibility to protect the rights of refugees. According to the United Nations High Commissioner for Refugees (UNHCR), the host states must 'play a primary role in providing refugees with protection and assistance'.[28] State responsibilities include the provision of physical, humanitarian, social and economic protection that will facilitate refugees to become self-reliant and fully integrated into the economy.[29] This view is further affirmed by Kate Jastram and Marilyn Achiron, who maintain that the protection of refugees is the primary responsibility of the country hosting them.[30] Such primary responsibility must be discharged through the implementation of the national refugee legislation the host country has adopted.

The salient question is: Which refugees should be assisted to become self-reliant or be allowed to have access to socio-economic programmes for full integration in the host society? To respond to this question, it should first be borne in mind that all categories of refugees do not enjoy the same rights. In this section, our focus is on refugees in camps and those outside of camps. The latter usually reside in cities and are known as 'urban refugees', who must be given exceptional treatment. The issue of 'exceptionalism' arises in situations where refugees must be assisted in the

[25] Preamble.

[26] As above.

[27] As above.

[28] UNHCR Policy on Refugee Protection and Solutions in Urban Areas: September 2009 (2009 UNHCR Policy) para 27.

[29] UNHCR Comprehensive Policy on Urban Refugees, 25 March 1997 (1997 UNHCR Policy) para 9.

[30] K Jastram and M Achiro *Refugee protection: A guide to international refugee law* (2001) 5.

refugee camps following the encampment policy of the host state. These two groups are not found in countries where there are no refugee camps or which apply a non-encampment policy, such as South Africa. In many African countries, asylum seekers are welcomed and accommodated in refugee camps. There is a need to afford exceptional treatment to those who leave the refugee camps to take up residence in an urban area.[31] Whilst living in refugee camps, refugees cannot pursue their dreams or engage in economic activities meaningful to their lives. The humanitarian approach of welcoming and accommodating refugees in a refugee camp obscures their rights to economic development as they cannot claim inclusion in the daily activities of citizens. This remains the case even though refugee camps are viewed as generous, benevolent and compassionate towards refugees. The reality is that refugee camps complicate the realisation of African countries' visions, aspirations, commitments and responsibilities to provide refugees with a better future.

4 Challenges in the Realisation of Socio-Economic Rights

4.1 Threats to National Security

African countries are classified as developing countries. Under the CESCR,[32] developing countries are, with due regard to their economies, allowed to determine to what extent they would guarantee socio-economic rights and benefits.[33] The determination is done based on the precepts of available resources, progressive realisation, and international cooperation and assistance.[34] In terms of the protection of refugees, the extent to which *de jure* and *de facto* refugees will have access to socio-economic rights and benefits for the protection of their dignity is entrenched in the national legislation that determines the nature and scope of the protection to be afforded to them, taking into account the aforementioned precepts. Effective protection could be realised if every African country adopts legal tools and mechanisms for solving the problems of refugees that are not

[31] 2009 UNHCR Policy (n 28) para 14.

[32] UN General Assembly, International Covenant on Economic, Social and Cultural Rights, 16 December 1966, United Nations, Treaty Series, vol. 993, p 3.

[33] Article 2(3).

[34] Article 2(1).

only in line with the AU Refugee Convention, but also with the available resources.[35] These mechanisms are rarely adopted as refugees are no longer viewed as people in the greatest need of humanitarian assistance, but rather as individuals who pose intolerable threats to national peace. They are viewed as economic burdens on the countries that have generously welcomed them and granted them asylum.[36] African countries have developed ill-sentiments and xenophobic attitudes towards refugees because they are considered as 'symptomatic of the tragedy of the ethnic conflict, social disintegration and political anarchy'.[37] This implies that they are treated with contempt.

This problem began in the 1980s when countries shifted from viewing refugees as victims of insecurity and people in the greatest need of humanitarian assistance to viewing them as a threat to national security.[38] According to Eduard Mogire, refugees can jeopardise national security through crimes, terrorism and subversive activities. He further maintains that they can pose cultural, social or economic threats.[39] These security issues influenced governments to change the way they perceived refugees and to consider their protection as a matter of high international politics in the context of domestic and international peace, stability and development.[40] Asylum is granted after assessing whether an asylum seeker has a well-founded fear of persecution, but also whether their physical presence does not constitute a threat to national security.[41] Owing to the scarce resources available, refugees in urban areas are viewed as a threat to citizens' livelihoods, and this view prompted countries to move from a hospitality policy to a hostility policy that is characterised by a denial of asylum, detention and forced expulsion of refugees.[42] Hostility policies result from the counter-terrorism and national security measures undertaken by states and governments to protect the interests of citizens.[43]

[35] Organisation of African Unity (OAU), Addis Ababa Document on Refugees and Forced Population Displacements in Africa, 10 September 1994 para 3.

[36] As above.

[37] Addis Ababa Document (n 35) para 5.

[38] E Mogire 'Refugee realities: Refugee rights versus state security in Kenya and Tanzania' (2009) 26 *Transformation* 15 at 16.

[39] As above.

[40] As above.

[41] As above.

[42] Mogire (n 38) 17.

[43] Office of United Nations High Commissioner for Human Rights (OHCHR), Fact sheet 32: Human rights, terrorism and counter-terrorism (July 2008) 18.

4.2 Treatment of Refugees as Economic Migrants

To avoid competition between refugees and citizens, African countries tend to accommodate refugees in camps with the intent to exclude them from socio-economic protection. Urban refugees are politically defined as economic migrants, who do not deserve refugee protection. Viewed from the AU Refugee Convention, whether political or economic refugees, they should be protected. The AU Refugee Convention obligates African states to protect individuals who are compelled to leave their homes to seek asylum in other African countries due to events which seriously disturbed public order in part or the whole of their country of origin or nationality.[44] These events include the ravages of colonialism and international economic forces, such as economic globalisation[45] or economic sanctions.[46]

In addition to the political unrest that many African countries experience, events associated with national economic challenges also contribute to widespread poverty and widening socio-economic inequalities.[47] Poverty compels individuals to leave their home countries. Put succinctly, many African countries have become impoverished to such an extent that they can no longer conduct the critical functions of government, including delivery of sufficient services, such as social assistance, employment, social security, healthcare, education and housing.[48] Economic challenges lead to dislocations in socio-economic structures, making it difficult to deliver public services to poor citizens. African nations' extreme poverty, coupled with dislocations in socio-economic structures, is a factor that contributes in one way or another to people fleeing their home countries, on the one hand, and to the exclusion of refugees from social, economic

[44] Article 1(2) of the AU Refugee Convention.

[45] See the Preamble of the Constitutive Act of the African Union, 11 July 2000, which recognises that the socio-economic and political changes and development are challenged by globalisation.

[46] There are 25 active sanctions programmes in 11 African countries, with hundreds of individuals, entities and companies designated under these programmes. See H Mossberg 'Beyond carrots, better sticks: Measuring and improving the effectiveness of sanctions in Africa' *The Sentry* (October 2019) https://cdn.thesentry.org/wp-content/uploads/2019/10/SanctionsEffectiveness_TheSentry_Oct2019-web.pdf (accessed 20 March 2020).

[47] Addis Ababa Document (n 35) para 9.

[48] As above.

and development programmes, on the other.[49] African countries experience severe economic hardships or distress and, therefore, to prevent the issue of citizens and refugees competing for limited national resources, the states apply exclusionary policies to refugees. They claim that they have no financial capacity to cope with the influx of asylum seekers.[50] African states further justify the exclusion of refugees on the basis that technical, financial and material support—through international solidarity and cooperation—to lighten the burden of protection of refugees has decreased significantly.[51] This is known as 'donor fatigue' towards funding the protection of refugees in Africa, where the problem of asylum-seeking is growing without prospects of finding durable solutions. Exclusion of refugees from economic protection on the grounds that they are economic migrants is unjustified and unsupported. People in Africa, who are compelled to leave their home countries for economic reasons, fall in the ambit of the definition of 'refugee',[52] as discussed in greater detail next.

4.3 Wide Definition of the Term 'Refugee'

Numerous factors cause people to leave their home country to seek asylum, but the term 'refugee' is, under the Refugee Convention, not interpreted to mean those individuals who flee their home governments due to economic reasons. This is because the concept of 'asylum' is conceived in political terms, and thus a strong tradition is maintained of distinguishing between economic refugees and political refugees. The definition of the concept of asylum or the term refugee is widened by the AU Refugee Convention to include safety and security challenges caused by events disturbing or disrupting public order. The application of the wide definition is controversial. The exclusion of refugees from socio-economic programmes can be attributed to the controversial broad definition. Redson Kapindu contends that the wide definition of the term refugee should be interpreted and applied in a more general sense to refer to all Africans who are forced to leave their home countries because their livelihood, liberty and dignity are seriously threatened—whether by political persecution,

[49] Addis Ababa Document (n 35) paras 9,28.

[50] Addis Ababa Document (n 35) para 13.

[51] Addis Ababa Document (n 35) para 14.

[52] R Kapindu 'Towards a more effective guarantee of socio-economic rights for refugees in Southern Africa' PhD thesis, University of Witwatersrand (2014) 19–20, 50.

extreme poverty, environmental degradation, drought, famine, generalised violence, armed conflict or any other reasons.[53] From this point of view, the principle of refugee protection cannot be limited to political reasons. Events disturbing or disrupting public order in the context of the AU Refugee Convention may include crises of humanitarian concern.[54]

Considering the above, the AU Refugee Convention seeks to protect two groups of refugees, namely, political and humanitarian refugees. Kapindu therefore defines 'political refugees' as those individuals who

> are forced to flee from their own countries by reason of wrongful rights-violating conduct by the state; or similar conduct by non-state actors but the acquiescence of the state authorities; and they seek substitute state protection and political community membership in other countries.[55]

Kapinda furthermore defines 'humanitarian refugees' as individuals who

> are compelled to flee their country of origin due to various factors that threaten to seriously harm their lives; but which are neither directly or indirectly attributable to wrongful state conduct.[56]

Despite these two groups of refugees, African countries, according to Michelle Foster, tend to apply political conditions set forth under the Refugee Convention and overlook those humanitarian conditions under the AU Refugee Convention, thereby depriving humanitarian refugees of protection.[57] In contemporary politics, the humanitarian refugees are termed 'economic migrants', who are viewed as undesirable people or illegal foreigners to be traced, arrested and deported. The issue of economic migrants is usually raised to justify the exclusion of refugees from socio-economic designs, and is used to call for the public support of such an exclusionary approach. Economic migrants fall within the protection of immigration law frameworks. Because they are considered as people who will impose a substantial financial burden on the state, they are classified as undesirable people. For instance, South Africa's Immigration Act 13 of

[53] ME Price *Rethinking asylum: History, purpose and limits* (2009) 17.

[54] Kapindu (n 52) 19–20, 50.

[55] Kapindu (n 52) viii.

[56] As above.

[57] M Foster *International refugee law and socio-economic rights: Refuge from deprivation* (2007) 2–5.

2002 defines an 'undesirable person' to include, but is not limited to, 'anyone who is or is likely to become a public charge',[58] while such individuals are classified as 'prohibited persons' under section 14(b) of Zimbabwe's Immigration Act 22 of 2001 and section 39(2)(c) of Namibia's Immigration Control Act 17 of 1993. They are 'inadmissible persons' under section 11(5) of Rwanda's Immigration and Emigration Act 57 of 2018 and section 33(2)(c) of the Kenya Citizenship and Immigration Act 172 of 2011. This sketches a clear picture that economic refugees are viewed as undesirable persons or prohibited persons who cannot be admitted into the country. They are individuals who are forced to leave their home country on the grounds of poverty, famine or economic deprivation.

4.4 *Politically Based Xenophobic Behaviours*

Viewing refugees as people who compete with citizens for access to scarce resources leads to xenophobic violence, which has become a global phenomenon. Xenophobic violence usually erupts in a country going through economic and political transitions.[59] It is fuelled by political statements that tend to blame refugees for the social ills of the country which inhibit economic growth at individual and community level, even though those social ills existed before their arrival.[60] Xenophobic behaviours are largely developed due to the perception that refugees constitute a threat or danger to the citizens' well-being.[61]

The need to drive away refugees cannot be divorced from the wide definition of the term refugee, which results in an overwhelming increase of individuals falling within the ambit of the term. This overwhelming increase led to the development of compassion fatigue of African nations who, as a result, sought to deviate from their responsibilities through the adoption of national legislation, which does not conform to the spirit and objects of international refugee law.[62] Deviating from their responsibility to protect refugees sends a message to society that refugees are undesirable people, which, in turn, creates tension between citizens and refugees.

[58] Section 30.

[59] DC Ukwandu 'Reflections on xenophobic violence in South Africa: What happens to a dream deferred?' (2017) 9 *African Journal of Public Affairs* 43 at 50.

[60] As above.

[61] As above.

[62] Addis Ababa Document (n 35) paras 15–16.

The deviation further deprives them of the right to equality in human rights and deepens and exacerbates their human suffering.

The political discussions which portray refugees as 'bogus' often lead citizens to an understanding that it is their civil responsibility to protect their national interests. Citizens thus resort to xenophobic violence to drive undesirable foreign nationals (i.e. refugees, asylum seekers and other vulnerable migrants) out of the country. Xenophobic violence has been used as a mechanism to express citizens' unhappiness when the government attempts to include refugees in welfare schemes.[63] Owing to widespread resentment for including refugees in economic development, measures are frequently taken to review the immigration and refugee laws and policies in a way that mirrors or provides tacit support for anti-refugee sentiments, through introducing measures that restrict asylum seekers' access to the country, and measures that limit refugees' access to economic empowerment.[64] For example, South Africa has revised its non-encampment policy to confine asylum seekers to refugee holding facilities and to allow recognised refugees to integrate in its society.[65] These measures derive from the understanding that the majority of citizens continue to live in impoverished conditions and thus easily feel that asylum seekers are greatly benefitting from the fruits of their democracy. Encampment policy is usually employed as a tool to restrict access to national resources.

4.5 The Theory of Social Contract

The theory of social contract inhibits or obscures the universal application of the truth-claims that all human beings are created equal and, as such, all human beings—citizens and non-citizens alike—are entitled to all human rights and freedoms on an equal basis.[66] The theory maintains that the society and its government or authority is established based on the will of its own people, who, in turn, claim the sovereignty of the established government from the family of nations.[67] Through the will of the people,

[63] R Black 'Immigration and social justice: Towards a progressive European immigration policy' (1996) 21 *Transactions of the Institute of British Geographers* 64 at 64.

[64] As above.

[65] S 22(8)–(9) of the Refugees Act as amended by the Refugees Act 11 of 2017.

[66] C Kavuro 'Exploring the full legal protection of refugees and its limitations with reference to natural and positive law' (2018) 39 *Obiter* 17 at 26.

[67] ME Muhammad 'Social contract theories of Hobbes, Locke and Rousseau: An extrapolation of point of harmony and tensions' (2020) 2 *Educational Resurgence Journal* 123 at 123–128.

which is expressed through democratic processes, citizens of the sovereign nation, as a political community, assume political power to determine the rights of those who are not members of their political community. This is an accepted principle of international law that

> every sovereign nation has the power, as inherent in sovereignty, and essential to self-preservation, to forbid the entrance of foreigners within its dominions, or to admit them only in such cases and upon such conditions as it may see fit to prescribe.[68]

It is clear from this principle that citizens, as a political community, enjoy the power to decide who should be admitted into their territory and what rights those admitted, for example, visitors, workers or refugees, should enjoy. This includes the power to decide whether they can accede to an international human rights treaty or whether they can exercise the right to reservations regarding certain provisions of that treaty. Within this understanding, human rights can only apply to non-citizens if a sovereign nation has signed and ratified human rights treaties or if the principle of reciprocity applies.

Challenges of protecting refugees arise from the fact that the responsibility to protect them is accepted by the host country on condition that all sovereign nations will act in concert in a true spirit of international solidarity and cooperation to protect them.[69] In this way, some would see refugee protection as part of the social contract, or at least part of the global social contract. In terms of the social contract, the host state decides on the rights and treatment of refugees and other foreign nationals. In so doing, the host state must comply with the global social contract that sets out standards of treatment of all human beings. To self-preserve and to protect national resources, African countries adopt measures of confining refugees to refugee camps until it is safe for them to return to their home countries.

African countries tend to shy away from assuming the responsibilities of refugees' home countries to protect. Because it is believed that each and every human being is a citizen of a particular sovereign nation, it is also

[68] *Minister of Home Affairs v Watchenuka* [2004] 1 All SA 21 (SCA) para 29, referring to the decision of *Nishimura Ekiu v The United States* 142 US 651 at 659.

[69] Recommendation D of the Refugee Convention, read in tandem with art 2(4) of the AU Refugee Convention.

believed that each sovereign government arranges and allocates rights and freedoms based on the notion of citizenship to protect and promote its citizens' moral worth. Based on this premise, there is nothing wrong with discriminating against non-citizens who are the responsibility of another government to protect. In practice, refugees can only be allowed to integrate into local communities and enjoy access to all public services if the option of voluntary return is no longer available. The integration into the community is therefore regarded as a durable solution to refugee problems.

The principles of refugee protection work under the presupposition that refugees are citizens of foreign countries. Politically, they remain vulnerable to the decisions taken by citizens through the representatives.

Prioritising the protection of citizens over refugees was accepted by the United Nations Ad Hoc Committee on Refugees and Stateless Persons (Ad Hoc Committee). The acceptance is evident from what follows:

> Every state protects its nationals. Its protective influence extends beyond its frontiers. The mere fact that a person possesses a nationality, ie that he is linked to a state by a bond of allegiance, brings him within the orbit of the law, and determines his legal status, in short it secures him a standing which the stateless person, not being a member of any national community does not enjoy.[70]

Refugees are not stateless persons, but they cannot enjoy the protection of the home government that they have fled. If they are admitted in a host country, they should adhere to the laws of the host country and discharge their obligations as prescribed by the laws of the host country. Refugees find themselves in a position of exercising due diligence when engaging with the host government. Yet, the humanitarian conditions in which refugees find themselves in their host countries appeal to citizens to manifest a suitable degree of benevolence and compassion for them.[71] The moral issue of compassion is significant because there are no international mechanisms available to enforce the Refugee Convention and the AU Refugee Convention, and no international body to perform duties under the global social contract within national territorial boundaries. Of concern is that the refugee conventions (unlike human rights conventions) do not create

[70] United Nations Ad Hoc Committee on Refugees and Stateless Persons *A study of statelessness* 1 August 1949, UN Doc E/1112; E/1112/Add.1 (1949) 23.

[71] *Union of Refugee Women v The Director, The Private Security Industry Regulatory Authority* 2007 (4) SA 395 (CC) para 127.

an enforcement mechanism, but rather a body that supervises or monitors the implementation of refugee protection at a national level. The body, which is the United Nations High Commissioner for Refugees (UNHCR), has no enforcement power to hold a government accountable. It follows that refugees have no choice but to accept the conditions created by the host government to be admitted and live while waiting for the situation in their home country to change. Asylum is offered on a temporary basis as refugees are expected to return and contribute to building their home country, and not the country of asylum.

4.6 *Implications of the Exclusion from Political Rights*

Refugee conventions are silent on political rights. It therefore comes as no surprise that freedom of association,[72] entrenched in the Refugee Convention, is limited to joining or creating non-political and non-profit organisations. Although refugees flee their home countries for political reasons, they are not allowed to engage in the political activities of either their host country or their home country. The International Covenant on Civil and Political Rights restricts political rights in the sense of conducting public affairs, directly or through freely chosen representatives; voting and being elected in general elections; and equality in access to public services to citizens.[73] The same approach is adopted by the African Charter on Human and Peoples' Rights with the exception of vesting equal access to public services in everyone.[74] By its very nature, refugee protection is historically humanitarian and is thus enforced within humanitarian parameters. Refugee problems are essentially viewed as temporary, unique and humanitarian. These views result in the exclusion of refugees from engaging in serious political discussions of what caused them to flee their home country or the treatment they should be afforded by their host society. This political exclusion makes it difficult for them to engage or participate in the governance affairs or democratic processes of the host country. The absence of their voice in political realms weakens their protection.

From a political perspective, refugees are usually viewed as outsiders since they do not belong to a political community to which authorities

[72] Article 15 of the Refugee Convention.
[73] Article 25.
[74] Article 13.

have to account.[75] The conceptual discourses of not belonging to a political community result in conditions where they are admitted, recognised and treated without involving them in decision-making processes. Through political participation, the political community decides on the rights of refugees. It is through political platforms, where the voices of refugees are absent, that matters of priority are discussed. Here, harsh decisions may be taken to expel refugees from the country or to confine them to places where they will not have access to any governmental or public services. Refugees are vulnerable because they are not part of an electoral constituency which votes political representatives into power and to whom such representatives are accountable.[76] The absence of a political voice has an impact on refugees' right to human dignity as they cannot make autonomous choices about their future. They must conform and live up to decisions made by the citizens. It is indeed through political fora that citizens' sentiments are expressed; citizens participate in decision-making processes; the government explains its actions and directions, and the rights and benefits are claimed.[77] In this regard, refugees must understand that because asylum was offered to them for compassionate and humanitarian reasons, they must be politically passive. This reminds refugees that they are not political beings of the host community who will be heard. They only live in a host community due to its compassion. Refugees are politically voiceless despite the fact that they enjoy political rights enshrined in the Covenant on Civil and Political Rights and the African Charter. These instruments afford them rights such as the right to freedom of expression[78] and the right to protest.[79] The absence of political participation implies that they lack political muscle that could have been used as a mechanism to advance or claim their rights. As a result, the quest for access to public services to advance full integration into host communities is suppressed. Their economic vulnerabilities and political marginalisation are sustained.

[75] P Vale 'Migration, xenophobia and security-making in post-apartheid South Africa' (2002) 29 *Politikon: South African Journal of Political Studies* 7 at 8.

[76] Kavuro (n 66) 35.

[77] J Rawls *A theory of justice* (1999) 195.

[78] Article 19 of the Covenant and art 9 of the African Charter.

[79] Article 21 of the Covenant and art 11 of the African Charter.

4.7 *Claims for Equality in Rights and Dignity Through Protests*

As noted, it is difficult for refugees to claim the actual entitlement of their basic rights through democratic processes and through political fora. The political rights available to refugees such as the right to freedom of expression, the right to peaceful demonstration, and freedom of association do not offer a strong foundation to claim their right to have access to life-saving services or to express their discontent about their treatment or to hold the government to account.[80] The Rwandan and South African cases highlight the vulnerability of refugees in asserting their rights through demonstrations. In Rwanda, when refugees took to the streets to voice their unhappiness about the reduction of humanitarian assistance, the army and police were deployed. As a result, these refugees were fatally shot.[81] Others were maimed and wounded. Those who survived military attacks were arbitrarily arrested and faced charges in connection with the protests.[82] In South Africa, the protests of refugees are treated with contempt and are responded to by excessive use of force.[83] Because refugees are, in many African countries, confined to refugee camps, they rarely protest against the host government. Their protests are usually directed to organisations providing them with humanitarian assistance and relief. They can only protest against the government if there are serious issues threatening their lives. This, for example, occurred in Moria camp, Greece, when refugee shelters caught fire,[84] and Mae La camp, when the government imposed restrictions on travel permits in order to align their travelling with the COVID-19 regulations.[85]

[80] B Amisi and R Ballard 'In the absence of citizenship: Congolese refugee struggle and organisation in South Africa' (2005) University of KwaZulu Natal at 1–32.

[81] Amnesty International 'Investigate killings of Congolese refugees by Rwandan police' (2019) https://www.amnesty.org/en/wp-content/uploads/2021/05/AFR4798662019ENGLISH.pdf (accessed on 26 March 2021).

[82] Muhammad (n 67).

[83] L Chutel 'South African police use force to disperse refugee sit-in after 3 weeks' *The New York Times* 30 October 2019 https://www.nytimes.com/2019/10/30/world/africa/south-africa-protests.html (accessed 27 March 2021).

[84] Both refugees and migrants were demanding proper housing elsewhere. See 'Moria migrants and Greek islanders protest over new camp' *BBC News* 11 September 2020 https://www.bbc.com/news/world-europe-54125761 (accessed 23 March 2022).

[85] 'Anger over "pay for travel permits" led to protests and riot in Mae La Refugee Camp – Live ammunition fired' *Karen News* 15 December 2021 https://karennews.org/2021/12/anger-over-pay-for-travel-permits-led-to-protests-and-riot-in-mae-la-refugee-camp-live--ammunition-fired/ (accessed 24 March 2022).

Though refugees can make use of the right to demonstrate or protest in the context of direct democracy to remind the government about their rights or assert their place in the host society, they lack political muscle to compel the government to change its discriminatory policies to more generous ones.[86] The absence of political power aggravates their already existing vulnerable situations. Succinctly put, the principle of political exclusion of refugees in democratic processes renders them invisible in the collective efforts to advance the general interests of the host society.[87] In many African countries, access to socio-economic integration for dignified treatment is exceptionally inhibited by their confinement to refugee camps, where their basic humanitarian needs are attended to by humanitarian organisations. The complexities of refugees asserting their equality in rights and dignity are indicative of how they are left to the mercy of the host society. Refugees have no power to object to conditions of treatment decided upon by the host society. Such conditions are not open for negotiation.

Conditions remain concerning offering humanitarian assistance to refugees if and when they are confined to refugee camps. Accordingly, beyond the context of the need to respond to the refugee humanitarian situations, protection of refugees in camps takes place in the incarceration context, as this deprives them of the right to make choices about their lives.[88] Refugees cannot leave the camp without permission. They are deprived of the right to move freely in the host country and engage in economic activities. Without freedom of movement and without the freedom to act in accordance with their rationally autonomous choices, they are reduced to a prison-like situation. A humanitarian approach to refugee protection in camps has a greater impact on their human dignity as they are deprived of liberties of social, economic and political participation enjoyed by citizens and other foreign nationals.

[86] *Larbi-Odam v Member of the Executive Council for Education (North-West Province)* 1998 (1) SA 745 (CC) para 19; and *Minister of Home Affairs v Somali Association of South Africa, Eastern Cape* 2015 (3) SA 545 (SCA) para 37.

[87] Kavuro (n 66) 36.

[88] K McKonnachie 'Camps of containment: A genealogy of the refugee camp' (2016) *Humanity* 397 at 398.

4.8 *Justifications for Refugee Camps*

Most African countries house refugees in refugee camps. These camps are based in Chad, Uganda, the Democratic Republic of the Congo, Sudan, South Sudan, Ghana, Kenya, Algeria, Libya, Malawi, Tanzania, Burundi, Ethiopia, Zambia, Djibouti, Namibia, Guinea, Cameroon, Rwanda, Burkina Faso, Liberia, Mauritania, Tunisia, Benin, Niger, Zimbabwe and Mozambique. In these countries, asylum seekers are compelled to remain in refugee camps and can only leave the camps provided that they are no longer in need of humanitarian and social assistance and that they can support themselves. They cannot leave the camp on the basis that they are formally recognised as refugees. Because they tend to leave their camps illegally, this means they are not assisted. The rationale behind confining refugees to the camps is justified on three grounds, namely the temporary nature of the protection; the provision of safety and security; and how well coordinated the humanitarian assistance is.[89]

Traditionally, those seeking asylum are not expected to stay for long as the host country expects them to return home as soon as there is a change in the political situations in their home country. For this reason, they are provided with temporary safety and security in a refugee camp until the political situation in their country allows them to repatriate voluntarily.[90] According to the UNHCR, refugee camps are therefore defined as 'temporary facilities built to provide immediate protection and assistance to people who have been forced to flee their homes due to war, persecution or violence'.[91] In refugee camps, refugees receive emergency, humanitarian and social relief and assistance, administered by humanitarian organisations in collaboration with local authorities.[92] They remain here until one of the three durable solutions is found, that is, repatriation, local integration or resettlement in a country other than the host or home country.[93] Likewise, refugee camps exist until refugees repatriate or an alternative durable solution to their refugee problems is found.[94]

[89] UNHCR 'Refugee camps' https://www.unrefugees.org/refugee-facts/camps/ (accessed 17 March 2021).

[90] Article 5 of the AU Refugee Convention, read with art 1C of the Refugee Convention.

[91] UNHCR (n 89).

[92] UNHCR *Handbook for Emergencies* 3 ed. (2007) para 75.

[93] Article 8 of the Statute of the Office of the United Nations High Commissioner for Refugees (adopted on 14 December 1950) UNGA Res 428 (V).

[94] McKonnachie (n 88) 398.

In essence, refugee camps are detrimental to refugees' liberty simply because refugee camps are akin to prisons. They appear to separate refugees from members of the host society, to deny them access to public services, and to deprive them of political and economic engagement.[95] Of concern are those events in which refugee situations are prolonged or protracted. Those trapped in protracted refugee situations will languish in camps without hope of pursuing their dreams and leading a dignified life in line with intellectual and financial capacities. If the refugee problem is protracted, they lose hope of a better future. They are deprived of their dignity as they cannot act in accordance with their rational and reasonable will and choice.

5 Conclusion

Various principles and theories inhibit the realisation of human dignity for refugees. Many principles and theories bestow power on the host state to decide conditions upon which refugees will be accepted on its territory. Yet, the temporary nature of asylum negatively affects the claims that socio-economic development or empowerment should be extended to include refugees. As discussed, refugee problems are considered temporary and the confinement of refugees to camps is understood to be momentary. They are expected to return home soon unless their refugee situation is protracted. The assumption of return in the near future may be the reason why so little (or nothing) is done to empower refugees economically in such a way that they can develop a sense of autonomy and self-confidence in their host communities, or in such a way that they can be politically empowered to act individually and collectively to change their existing socio-economic conditions or the existing relationships with the host authorities. They are excluded from political fora and democratic processes that could have assisted them to change or improve their relationships with institutions, and from discourses that unfairly exclude them from socio-economic development and from engaging meaningfully in the economy of their host country. Hannah Arendt aptly described this barrier to enjoyment of socio-economic rights and benefits as follows: 'fundamental deprivation of human rights is manifested first and above all in the deprivation of a place in the world (a political space) which makes

[95] UNHCR (n 92) para 75.

opinions significant and actions effective'.[96] This view depicts the special vulnerability of refugees in the political community.

Protection of refugees should therefore not only be limited to humanitarian relief and social assistance. As vulnerable and poor people, they should be assisted to become self-reliant and self-supportive. A notable improvement in socio-economic conditions is realised if individuals enjoy the ability to hold others to account in a political context. However, holding government accountable, through judicial processes, appears to have no impact on vulnerable refugee conditions as the government disregards judicial decisions. The South African Supreme Court of Appeal noted this with concern when it stated that although refugees are amongst those who are most in need of protection, they 'do not have powerful political constituencies and their problems, more often than not, are ignored by government'.[97] The Court further acknowledged that approaching a court to review government decisions or to assert their rights flowing from their refugee status 'appear[s] to have done little to make their problem visible and to cause the relevant authorities to comply with their obligations'.[98] Accordingly, one cannot hesitate to conclude that the absence of political engagement with the state works to deprive refugees of their socio-economic rights and benefits, and to treat the refugee population like children, who cannot make decisions about their lives or who must sit and wait for the supply of food for their survival. The humanitarian approach deprives them of their dignity as they cannot rely on their intellectual abilities, skills or talents to advance themselves.

Throughout this chapter, it has been demonstrated that refugees are treated as if they are incapable of thinking, reasoning and acting to ameliorate their situations, or of acting for their own sake, or incapable of making autonomous choices. Refugees are essentially deprived of the opportunity to make choices about pursuing their own life goals, visions and dreams. The denial of socio-economic empowerment opportunities and exclusion from political spaces aggravate the denial of autonomous choices, which leads to refugees being treated as second-class citizens. For refugees, this treatment comes with distress, caused by the scarcity of resources and opportunities with which to change their conditions, and

[96] H Arendt *The origins of totalitarianism* (1979) 296.

[97] *Minister of Home Affairs v Somali Association of South Africa, Eastern Cape* (n 86) para 37.

[98] *Larbi-Odam* (n 86) para 37.

creates feelings of shame and humiliation. This situation falls squarely within the ambit of objectification.[99] Michael Sayler describes objectification as being 'treated as a thing instead of an autonomous self' and as

> a form of humiliation [that] may lead to the collapse of one's interpersonal world, resulting in a kind of vertigo and a combination of unexpected exposure, loss of trust, and confusion.[100]

This aptly captures the conditions in which refugees find themselves. And this situation is exacerbated when they are confined to refugee camps. People who are unable to fend for themselves are viewed as a financial burden on the host communities. The difficulties refugees experience in gaining access to national resources eventually collapses their interpersonal world as they surrender their lives to the mercy of the host community for survival.

Bibliography

Books

Arendt, H *The origins of totalitarianism* (Harcourt Brace Jovanovich, 1979)
Currie, I & De Waal, J *The Bill of Rights Handbook* 6 ed (Juta, 2017)
D'Souza, D *What's so great about Christianity* (Regnery Publishing, 2007)
Foster, M *International refugee law and socio-economic rights: Refuge from deprivation* (Cambridge University Press, 2007)
Jastram, K & Achiro, M *Refugee protection: A guide to international refugee law* (Inter-Parliamentary Union, 2001)
Kant, I *Groundwork for the metaphysics of morals* (Yale University Press, 2002)
Nussbaum, MC *Creating capabilities: The human development approach* (Harvard University Press, 2011)
Price, ME *Rethinking asylum: History, purpose and limits* (Cambridge University Press, 2009)
Rawls, J *A theory of justice* (Oxford University Press, 1999)
Rosen, M *Dignity: Its history and meaning* (Harvard University Press, 2012)
Sen, A *Development as freedom* (Oxford University Press, 1999)

[99] MD Sayler 'Humiliation and the poor: A study of the management of meaning' PhD thesis, Fielding Graduate Institute, 2004 at 13.
[100] As above.

UNHCR *A guide to international refugee protection and building asylum systems* (UNHCR, 2017)
UNHCR *Handbook for emergencies* 3 ed (UNHCR, 2007)

Chapters in Books

Wallace, D 'Jacques Maritain and Alasdair MacIntyre: The person, the common good and human rights' in Sweetman, B (ed) *The failure of modernism: The Cartesian legacy and contemporary pluralism* (American Maritain Association, 1999)

Journal Articles

Black, R 'Immigration and social justice: Towards a progressive European immigration policy' (1996) 21 *Transactions of the Institute of British Geographers* 64
Botha, H 'Human dignity in comparative perspective' (2009) 20 *Stellenbosch Law Review* 171
Donnelly, J 'Human dignity and human rights' (2009) *Agenda for Human Rights* 1
Glensy, RD 'The right to dignity' (2011) 34 *Columbia Human Rights Law Review* 65
Kavuro C 'Exploring the full legal protection of refugees and its limitations with reference to natural and positive law' (2018a) 39 *Obiter* 17
Kavuro, C 'Refugee rights in South Africa: Addressing social injustices in government financial assistance schemes' (2015) 5 *Journal of Sustainable Development Law Policy* 176
Kavuro, C 'The value of human dignity in the refugee protection' (2019) 5(1) *African Human Mobility Review* 1510
Klug, H 'The dignity clause of the Montana Constitution: May foreign jurisprudence lead the way to an expanded interpretation?' (2003) 64 *Montana Law Review* 133
Lee, P & George, RP 'The nature and basis of human dignity' (2008) 21 *Ratio Juris* 173
Liebenberg, S 'The value of freedom in interpreting socio-economic rights' (2008) 1 *Acta Juridica* 149
McKonnachie, K 'Camps of containment: A genealogy of the refugee camp' (2016) *Humanity* 397
Mogire, E 'Refugee realities: Refugee rights versus state security in Kenya and Tanzania' (2009) 26 *Transformation* 15
Muhammad, ME 'Social contract theories of Hobbes, Locke and Rousseau: An extrapolation of point of harmony and tensions' (2020) 2 *Educational Resurgence Journal* 123

Pieterse, M 'Eating socio-economic rights: The usefulness of rights talk in alleviating social hardship revisited' (2007) 29 *Human Rights Quarterly* 796

Ukwandu, DC 'Reflections on xenophobic violence in South Africa what happens to a dream deferred?' (2017) 9 *African Journal of Public Affairs* 43

Vaišvila, A 'Human dignity and the right to dignity in terms of legal personalism (from conception of static dignity to conception of dynamic dignity)' (2009) 3 *Jurisprudence* 111

Vale, P 'Migration, xenophobia and security-making in post-apartheid South Africa' (2010) 29 *Politikon: South African Journal of Political Studies* 7

Theses and Dissertations

Kapindu, R 'Towards a more effective guarantee of socio-economic rights for refugees in Southern Africa' PhD thesis, University of Witwatersrand, 2014

Kavuro, C 'Refugees' access to socio-economic rights: Favourable treatment for the protection of human dignity' PhD thesis, Stellenbosch University, 2018b

Sayler, MD 'Humiliation and the poor: A study of the management of meaning' PhD thesis, Fielding Graduate Institute, 2004

AU Documents

African Union, African Union Convention for the Protection and Assistance of Internally Displaced Persons in Africa (Kampala Convention), 23 October 2009

Organisation of African Unity (OAU), African Charter on Human and Peoples' Rights (Banjul Charter), 27 June 1981, CAB/LEG/67/3 rev 5, 21 ILM 58 (1982)

Organisation of African Unity (OAU), Constitutive Act of the African Union, 1 July 2000

Organisation of African Unity (OAU), Convention Governing the Specific Aspects of Refugee Problems in Africa (OAU Convention), 10 September 1969, 1001 UNTS 45

UN Documents

United Nations, Charter of the United Nations, 24 October 1945, 1 UNTS XVI

UN General Assembly, Convention Relating to the Status of Refugees, 28 July 1951, United Nations, Treaty Series, vol 189, p 137

UN General Assembly, International Covenant on Economic, Social and Cultural Rights, 16 December 1966a, United Nations, Treaty Series, vol 993, p 3

UN General Assembly, International Covenant on Civil and Political Rights, 16 December 1966b, United Nations, Treaty Series, vol 999, p 171

UN General Assembly, Statute of the Office of the United Nations High Commissioner for Refugees, 14 December 1950, A/RES/428(V)

Reports/Papers

Amisi, B & Ballard, R 'In the absence of citizenship: Congolese refugee struggle and organisation in South Africa' (2005) University of KwaZulu Natal 1
Office of United Nations High Commissioner for Human Rights (OHCHR), Fact sheet 32: 'Human rights, terrorism and counter-terrorism (July 2008)
Organisation of African Unity (OAU), Addis Ababa Document on Refugees and Forced Population Displacements in Africa, 10 September 1994
UNHCR Policy on Refugee Protection and Solutions in Urban Areas, published in September 2009
UNHCR Comprehensive policy on urban refugees 25 March 1997
United Nations Ad Hoc Committee on Refugees and Stateless Persons 'A study of statelessness' (1949)

South African Case Law

Larbi-Odam v Member of the Executive Council for Education (North-West Province) 1998 (1) SA 745 (CC)
Minister of Home Affairs v Somali Association of South Africa, Eastern Cape 2015 (3) SA 545 (SCA)
Minister of Home Affairs v Watchenuka [2004] 1 All SA 21 (SCA)
Union of Refugee Women v The Director, The Private Security Industry Regulatory Authority 2007 (4) SA 395 (CC)

Foreign Case Law

Beharry v Reno 183 F.Supp.2d 584 (2002)
Nishimura Ekiu v The United States 142 US 651
United States v Aguilar, 883 F.2d 662 (9th Cir 1989), Cert denied, 498 US 1046 (1991)

Internet Sources

Amnesty International 'Investigate killings of Congolese refugees by Rwandan police' (2019) https://www.amnesty.org/en/wp-content/uploads/2021/05/AFR4798662019ENGLISH.pdf (accessed 26 March 2021)
'Anger over "pay for travel permits" led to protests and riot in Mae La Refugee Camp – Live ammunition fired' *Karen News* 15 December 2021 https://karen-

news.org/2021/12/anger-over-pay-for-travel-permits-led-to-protests-and-riot-in-mae-la-refugee-camp-live-ammunition-fired/ (accessed 24 March 2022)

Chutel, L 'South African police use force to disperse refugee sit-in after 3 weeks' *The New York Times* 30 October 2019 https://www.nytimes.com/2019/10/30/world/africa/south-africa-protests.html (accessed 27 March 2021)

'Moria migrants and Greek islanders protest over new camp' *BBC* 11 September 2020 https://www.bbc.com/news/world-europe-54125761 (accessed 23 March 2022)

Mossberg, H 'Beyond carrots, better sticks: Measuring and improving the effectiveness of sanctions in Africa' *The Sentry* October 2019 https://cdn.thesentry.org/wp-content/uploads/2019/10/SanctionsEffectiveness_TheSentry_Oct2019-web.pdf (accessed 20 March 2020)

UNHCR 'Refugee camps' https://www.unrefugees.org/refugee-facts/camps/ (accessed 17 March 2021)

CHAPTER 5

The Role of the African Court on Human and Peoples' Rights in Promoting the Socio-Economic Rights of Migrants

Bright Nkrumah

1 Introduction

In the light of the massive number of migrants fleeing their countries in post-colonial Africa, it became imperative to adopt an instrument that recognises the local challenges of African migrants (especially refugees and asylum seekers, RAS). Consequently, the Organisation of the African Union adopted the 1969 OAU Convention Governing the Specific Aspects of Refugee Problems in Africa (1969 OAU Refugee Convention) as a guiding principle for countries willing to host these destitute migrants,.[1] The instrument, in essence, contains provisions that regulate the conduct of RAS in the host state, while imposing obligations on the

[1] OAU, Convention Governing the Specific Aspects of Refugee Problems in Africa (OAU Convention), 10 September 1969, 1001 UNTS 45.

B. Nkrumah (✉)
Department of Ecology & Environmental Studies, The Water School, Florida Gulf Coast University, Fort Myers, FL, USA

E. Durojaye et al. (eds.), *Realising Socio-Economic Rights of Refugees and Asylum Seekers in Africa*, Politics of Citizenship and Migration, https://doi.org/10.1007/978-3-031-16548-1_5

latter to refrain from maltreating RAS. An important facet of the 1969 OAU Refugee Convention worth highlighting is its expansion on the 1951 Convention's definition of refugees. Article 1(2) of the 1969 Convention defines a refugee as any person

> who, owing to external aggression, occupation, foreign domination or events seriously disturbing public order in either part or the whole of his country of origin or nationality, is compelled to leave his place of habitual residence to seek refuge in another place outside his country of origin or nationality.

Thus, unlike its predecessor, the OAU Convention includes persons fleeing their home countries due to internal strife or instability. The OAU Convention, therefore, goes a step further by linking the refugee definition with the real root causes of massive refugee influxes across the continent.

Approximately a decade after the entry into force of the 1969 OAU Refugee Convention, the African Charter on Human and People's Rights (African Charter) was adopted.[2] The adoption of the African Charter in 1981 could be seen as the watershed moment for the launch of the African human rights system as an overarching mechanism for safeguarding the continent's population from large-scale abuse and deprivation. To ensure compliance with its provisions, the African Charter calls for the establishment of the African Commission on Human and Peoples' Rights (African Commission) to exercise an oversight role of their domestication at the national level. While the African Commission was empowered to receive complaints and conduct independent investigations into alleged deprivations of these entitlements, this mandate was watered down by its quasi-judicial mandate, limiting its ability to make binding decisions. An important addition to the human rights architecture was the establishment of the African Court on Human and Peoples' Rights (African Court) and the African Committee of Experts on the Rights and Welfare of the Child (African Children's Committee) to complement the African Commission in the advancement of human rights across the continent. The complementary role occurs in the realm of the African Court and the

[2] OAU, African Charter on Human and Peoples' Rights (Banjul Charter), 27 June 1981, CAB/LEG/67/3 rev 5, 21 ILM 58 (1982).

African Children's Committee's mandate to hand down binding decisions that could boost the protective role of the African Commission.[3]

It is against this backdrop that this chapter surveys the prospect of the African Court in concretising the socio-economic rights of RAS in the African region. It has four substantive sections, excluding the present introduction. The next section examines the lived experiences of RAS in the region. The third section surveys the socio-economic rights of RAS as entrenched in key normative frameworks. The fourth section considers the practical challenges which might be faced by RAS in seeking to use the corridors of the African Court as a step towards prompting host states to allocate some of their resources to their sustenance. The fifth section advances compelling arguments for judicial activism. The final section makes the case for an activist African Court as a means of empowering disempowered RAS.

2 Lived Experiences of Refugees and Asylum Seekers

At present, six African states have emerged as major destination countries for refugees and asylum seekers (RAS).[4] The migration to these jurisdictions may be tied to three separate, but somewhat related, reasons, namely: (1) relative stable political regime; (2) economic prospects; and (3) proximity to troubled countries. By 2021, clashes among Fulani herdsmen and assaults by Boko Haram insurgents had forced nearly 717,000 people from the Central Africa Republic and Nigeria to seek refuge in neighbouring Chad and Cameroon.[5] At the Horn of Africa, Uganda hosted approximately 386,000 refugees in 2021, making it a hotspot for resettlement.[6] Within that same year, Ethiopia was home to one of the largest refugee

[3] B Nkrumah 'The potential of the African human rights system in addressing poverty' in E Durojaye and G Mirugi-Mukundi (eds.) *Exploring the link between poverty and human rights in Africa* (2020) 228.

[4] UN 'Migration dynamics, refugees and internally displaced persons in Africa' (2021) https://www.un.org/en/academic-impact/migration-dynamics-refugees-and-internally-displaced-persons-africa (accessed 15 March 2022).

[5] As above.

[6] E Easton-Calabria 'Uganda has a remarkable history of hosting refugees, but its efforts are underfunded' *The Conversation* 26 August 2021 https://theconversation.com/uganda-has-a-remarkable-history-of-hosting-refugees-but-its-efforts-are-underfunded-166706 (accessed 25 February 2023).

populations of approximately 740,000 individuals from South Sudan, Sudan Eritrea and Somalia.[7] One caveat that is important to note in this respect is that the unprecedented influx of RAS has placed enormous pressure on the resources of these host states. This pressure has compromised the abilities of the host governments to successfully meet their constitutional obligations of improving the living standards of their citizens.

Against this backdrop, the policy response to RAS' socio-economic integration is bifurcated. On the one hand, Ethiopia and Uganda provide RAS with employment opportunities, as well as land for farming and housing.[8] South Africa, on the other hand, makes a more generous offer of granting access to essential needs, including self-settlement, medical treatment, study and work.[9]

It is important to add that access to the benefits mentioned above is grounded on one's recognition as RAS, either by submitting an asylum application or such application being approved by the relevant department.[10] Consequently, these benefits remain a pipedream for many RAS as bureaucratic inertia delays the processing of their asylum applications, or applications are wrongfully declined due to insufficient evidence to support their claim.[11] In the case of the latter, one is instructed to leave the host country within a short period of time, often without support for one's journey back home.[12] In the face of glaring atrocities and widespread deprivation in their home country, many unsuccessful RAS applicants opt to remain undocumented for years, and thus are unable to access resources and services that their (privileged) documented compatriots have access to.[13] In other words, non-recognition of an individual as an RAS deprives

[7] As above.

[8] S Momodu 'Africa most affected by refugee crisis' (2017) 30 *Africa Renewal* 28.

[9] These gains have somewhat attracted more economic migrants to the shores of South Africa, particularly from neighbouring countries such as Zimbabwe, Malawi, Lesotho and Swaziland. See SL Gordon 'Welcoming refugees in the rainbow nation: Contemporary attitudes towards refugees in South Africa' (2016) 35 *African Geographical Review* 3.

[10] D Fassin, M Wilhelm-Solomon and A Segatti 'Asylum as a form of life: The politics and experience of indeterminacy in South Africa' (2017) 58 *Current Anthropology* 160.

[11] I Moyo 'On borders and the liminality of undocumented Zimbabwean migrants in South Africa' (2020) 18 *Journal of Immigrant & Refugee Studies* 60 at 63.

[12] RE Kapindu 'No return to persecution or danger: Judicial application of the principle of *non-refoulement* in refugee law in South Africa and Malawi' (2020) 10 *Constitutional Court Review* 107 at 117.

[13] M Moagi et al. 'Mozambican immigrants to South Africa: Their xenophobia and discrimination experiences' (2018) 28 *Journal of Psychology in Africa* 196 at 198.

them of access to essential needs including land, education, employment and life-saving treatment.[14] Nonetheless, in instances where an individual has been favourably recognised as an RAS, the difficulty in renewing their documents often hinders their prospect of securing long-term employment, even if they satisfy the basic educational or professional criteria.[15]

Still, as has been witnessed across the globe, the ramifications of the novel Coronavirus pandemic (Covid-19) have further eroded the coping strategies of RAS on three levels.[16] First, the processing of asylum applications was halted by some countries as processing centres were shut down. Thus, while new arrivals cannot submit their applications, there is no channel for the renewal of one's asylum permit.[17] An expired permit reduces one to the status of undocumented migrant, thereby eroding one's entitlement.

RAS, in essence, continue to face twelve bleak socio-economic setbacks in contemporary times: (1) a disproportionate percentage cannot secure employment in informal sectors due to the limited validity of their permits; (2) those with expired permits cannot renew their employment contracts or can be retrenched for lack of documentation; (3) the studies of some students have arguably been terminated for permit expiration; (4) ailing people or expectant mothers might be unable to access medical treatment due to their legal status; (5) many in informal trade have been forced to stop trading due to lockdown restrictions, thereby cutting off their financial stream; (6) exclusion from government's economic support programmes; (7) withdrawal from schools due to illegal residential status; (8) eviction or non-renewal of rental contracts on the basis of expired permits; (9) inaccessibility to medical treatment in government hospitals due to outdated permits; (10) rendered disqualified or retrenched from the (in)formal sectors based on illegal status; (11) unable to access food and other essentials from blocked bank accounts due to illegal status; (12)

[14] F Maphosa and C Ntau 'Undocumented migrants as *homo sacer*: Cases from Botswana and South Africa' (2021) 56 *Journal of Asian and African Studies* 872.

[15] F Khan and M Lee 'Policy shifts in the asylum process in South Africa resulting in hidden refugees and asylum seekers' (2018) 4 *African Human Mobility Review* 1205 at 1210.

[16] A detailed discussion of the impact of the Covid-19 pandemic is beyond the scope of this chapter.

[17] FC Mukumbang, AN Ambe and BO Adebiyi 'Unspoken inequality: How COVID-19 has exacerbated existing vulnerabilities of asylum-seekers, refugees, and undocumented migrants in South Africa' (2020) 19 *International Journal for Equity in Health* 1 at 4.

and 30 per cent reduction in food assistance for East African RAS.[18] In sum, these challenges have culminated in the depletion of household savings to access medical care, food and rent. It is against this backdrop that one ought to understand the socio-economic rights of RAS in Africa.

3 The Right to Rights: Socio-Economic Rights of RAS

The 1951 UN Refugee Convention may be cited as the main instrument that inspired the legal protection of RAS in Africa. The document contains several groundbreaking provisions, particularly in advancing the socio-economic well-being of migrants. In addition to article 17 that accords this subpopulation the liberty to engage in wage-earning jobs, articles 20 to 24 oblige states parties to treat RAS equally as nationals with regard to the rationing system, housing, public education, public relief and social security.

As complementary to the 1951 UN Convention, the OAU Convention adopts an overarching construction of the term 'refugee'. To be exact, article 1(2) of the latter classifies this group as persons fleeing their country of nationality or origin in light of 'aggression' or 'events seriously disturbing public order'. While the instrument does not specifically invoke socio-economic rights as grounds for advancing migrants' access to essential needs, it nonetheless indirectly imposes obligations on receiving states. Specifically, articles 2(1) and (2) urge states parties to receive RAS and 'use their best endeavours...to secure [their] settlement'.

Drawing from the OAU Convention, the right of RAS was subsequently expanded upon in the African Charter. The rights to dignity, integrity, life and non-discrimination under the African Charter theoretically and in practice apply to all within a particular jurisdiction, whether national or non-national.[19] The African Charter contains several unique elements, including the interrelatedness of rights and duties of states towards 'every individual' and 'all peoples', regardless of one's residence

[18] R Zurayk 'Pandemic and food security: A view from the Global South' (2020) 9 *Journal of Agriculture, Food Systems, and Community Development* 17; Humanitarian Aid 'Refugees at risk of hunger and malnutrition, as relief hit in Eastern Africa' (2020) https://news.un.org/en/story/2020/08/1071062 (accessed 25 February 2023).

[19] *Rencontre Africaine pour la Défense des Droits de l'Homme v Zambia* (2000) AHRLR 321 (ACHPR 1996) para 35. See arts 3–5.

status.[20] Accordingly, RAS have been accorded considerable socio-economic rights under the African Charter, with explicit provisions in the areas of equality, life, dignity, education, work, health and security.[21] Since the African Charter provides blanket protection for all Africans without consideration of the unique challenges faced by vulnerable groups, three human rights instruments have subsequently emerged to address the plight of children and women RAS. The significance of specific legal frameworks for these subpopulations cannot be overemphasised as a disproportionate percentage of RAS tend to be women and children.

The first of these instruments is the 1990 OAU African Charter on the Rights and Welfare of the Child (OAU Children's Charter).[22] One of the golden threads running through the instrument is that children granted RAS status or seeking asylum ought to be sustained by the host state through the provision of the necessary socio-economic assistance. The OAU Children's Charter has two main features: it codifies children as possessors of basic rights; and creates avenues for children to claim these rights. Indeed, the OAU Children's Charter was born out of the conviction that its forerunner, the UN Convention on the Rights of the Child, did not sufficiently articulate the economic and socio-cultural realities of the African child.[23] Still, it ought to be acknowledged that the two treaties complement rather than oppose each other.

At the regional level, the OAU Children's Charter may be perceived as the most progressive instrument in safeguarding the rights of the child, including unaccompanied children or children whose parents or guardians are RAS. As an illustration, the OAU Children's Charter proffers the attainment of economic and social rights beyond the conventional confines of 'progressive realisation'. The notion of progressive realisation may have two strands, namely, prioritisation and timing. The first implies that states have the right to set priorities or determine which socio-economic needs ought to be prioritised in light of the (limited) resources of the state.[24] The second implies that these priorities ought to be achieved

[20] See arts 2, 3, 19 and 20.

[21] Articles 3–6; 15–18.

[22] OAU, African Charter on the Rights and Welfare of the Child, 11 July 1990, CAB/LEG/24.9/49 (1990).

[23] UN General Assembly, Convention on the Rights of the Child, 20 November 1989, United Nations, Treaty Series, vol. 1577, p 3.

[24] B Nkrumah *Seeking the right to food: Food activism in South Africa* (2021) 54.

within a specific or reasonable period.[25] Still, under this broad brush or rubric of progressive realisation, there is no benchmark with which to determine whether these priorities are the best options, or what duration can be considered as reasonable.[26] Moreover, the OAU Children's Charter is devoid of any claw-back or inbuilt limitation clause. The instrument thus boldly expresses the rights of all children to health, healthcare, education, freedom from exploitation, leisure, recreation, and cultural activities without any reservation.[27]

By avoiding any ideological differences between the two sets of rights mentioned above, articles 11 and 14 of the treaty recognise the inherent rights to life of the child, the right to education and the right to health. Considering their vulnerability, article 23(1) of the OAU Children's Charter further enjoins member states to undertake the necessary measures to ensure that (un)accompanied children enjoy all the fundamental rights set out in relevant human rights instruments. Interestingly, in a stark departure from article 1 of the 1969 OAU Refugee Convention, article 23(4) of the OAU Children's Charter calls upon states parties to receive and assist (unaccompanied) children who have fled their home countries due to 'natural disaster, internal armed conflicts, civil strife, breakdown of *economic* and *social order* or howsoever caused'.[28] This provision implies that in stark contrast to persecution as the main grounds for seeking refuge, the OAU Children's Children's Charter expands upon this criterion by adding economic hardships as grounds for seeking the protection of another state.[29] This provision is indeed innovative as economic migration has characterised the contemporary movement of Africans, particularly due to deplorable socio-economic conditions in their home countries.

On the question of advancing the rights of women RAS, the 2003 Protocol to the African Charter on Human and Peoples' Rights on the

[25] G de Beco 'The interplay between human rights and development the other way round: The emerging use of quantitative tools for measuring the progressive realisation of economic, social and cultural rights' (2010) 4 *Human Rights & International Legal Discourse* 265 at 276.

[26] B Nkrumah 'Food Protest in South Africa: "Them belly full, but we hungry"' (2018) 19 *ESR Review* 4.

[27] See arts XI, XIII, XIV and XV.

[28] Own emphasis.

[29] M Foster *International refugee law and socio-economic rights: Refuge from deprivation* (2007) 27.

Rights of Women in Africa (Maputo Protocol) sets out a well-defined provision urging African states to reconsider the place of all women in their societies.[30] The cardinal tenet of the instrument is the advancement of the welfare of women through the creation of innovative provisions such as the adoption and operationalisation of positive action to enhance the well-being, integrity and security of every woman. Two aspects of the Maputo Protocol are particularly revealing. First, articles 4, 10 and 11 explicitly catalogue the socio-economic rights of women. Since a considerable number of women RAS are susceptible to exploitation, the Maputo Protocol is emphatic when addressing their socio-economic needs. Without an explicit reference to (non)nationals, it enjoins states parties to ensure that all women have economic and social welfare rights; health and reproductive rights; nutritious and adequate food; adequate housing; and a sustainable environment and development.[31] Second, article 27 of the Maputo Protocol lists the African Court as the mechanism responsible for clarifying contentions relating to its operationalisation. Thus, the only independent judicial oversight of the Maputo Protocol and its forerunner, the African Charter, is the African Court. Having said that, one must not lose sight of the genuine or formidable barriers ahead which could plague the African Court in enforcing the human rights obligations of host states towards RAS. It is against this backdrop that the next section turns to assess the feasibility or practical constraints which might militate against the African Court in enhancing access to food, water, education, health and social security for RAS across the continent.

4 Constraints to the Advancement of Socio-Economic Rights

On 9 June 1998, African leaders adopted the Protocol to the African Charter on the Establishment of an African Court on Human and Peoples' Rights (Court Protocol). Upon entry into force on 25 January 2004, the African Court was established to complement the protective role of the African Commission. Advocates and critics of the African Court will agree that a human rights court is only useful if it serves as a genuine platform where the vulnerable population can be vindicated of the abuse suffered or

[30] AU, Protocol to the African Charter on Human and People's Rights on the Rights of Women in Africa, 11 July 2003.

[31] Articles 13–19.

rights violated. To that end, the Court Protocol enjoins the African Court to perform three key functions: (1) to clarify a relevant section of the African Charter by providing legal opinions on relevant provisions; (2) in instances where victims face grave danger in light of the (in)actions of the state, it is obliged to grant provisional measures to forestall the perpetuation of further abuses against the victim; and (3) to remedy human rights abuses, including providing reparations for victims of abuses. Reparations may be construed as compensation for a debt of injustice.[32] Yet, since these forms of remedies foster an adversarial relationship between perpetrators (in this case the state) and victims, article 27(1) of the Court Protocol also entreats conflicting parties to consider the prospects of amicable settlement of disputes. In reverting to the primary rationale of this section, the possibility of the African Court improving the socio-economic rights of RAS could only be surveyed through the channels by which one could approach the monitoring body.

At the risk of oversimplification, RAS or relevant NGOs may approach the African Court on three grounds: (1) file a complaint alleging that a delay in the renewal of permits constitutes a prima facie breach of their rights to education, employment and health; (2) request an advisory opinion on the right to basic entitlements in the host state; and, most importantly, or (3) asylum seekers could file a complaint alleging targeted exclusion from national social security interventions. As an illustration, at the height of South Africa's Covid-19 lockdown restrictions, the state instituted a R350 (nearly $25) monthly grant to ameliorate the economic hardships faced by millions of South Africans and permanent residents due to the pandemic.[33] Similar favouritism or partial social assistance has been recorded in Kenya, Ethiopia and Uganda where food parcels were more likely to be distributed to nationals who were less affected by the pandemic.[34] Although it seeks to assist the unemployed, it excludes asylum seekers from the list of eligible applicants. Without any source of income, asylum seekers and their dependants are placed in dire economic situations in terms of accessing basic needs, such as paying monthly rent and electricity and water bills, or simple groceries such as mealie meal, bread or sugar.

[32] H McGary 'Reconciliation and reparations' (2010) 41 *Metaphilosophy* 546 at 547.

[33] H Bhorat, M Oosthuizen and B Stanwix 'Social assistance amidst the COVID-19 epidemic in South Africa: A policy assessment' (2021) 89 *South African Journal of Economics* 63 at 66.

[34] S Devereux 'Social protection responses to COVID-19 in Africa' (2021) 21 *Global Social Policy* 421.

Taking a leaf from its protective mandate, the African Court could be seen as having the noble ambition to propel the social security of RAS.[35] But before RAS and interested NGOs even conceive the thought of utilising the services of the Court, they ought to be cognisant of the benchmarks as set out in the Court's Protocol. These benchmarks, which the section refers to as a 'checklist conundrum', while instituted by the AU to entice states to accept the jurisdiction, equally paralyse the prospect of potential applicants in accessing the Court's supranationalised justice. A few of these conundrums are particularly revealing, and are discussed next.

4.1 Exhaustion of Domestic Remedies (EDRs)

At the outset, RAS ought to frame their deprivation in the context of a violation or an infringement as conceived within the text of the national constitution of the host country, and more broadly in the African Charter and other relevant human rights instruments.[36] Nonetheless, since a disproportionate percentage of this sub-group lacks the relevant legal background, or financial resources to hire a lawyer, they are unable to satisfy this benchmark. Given that they are unable to frame and ultimately submit their complaint to local courts, their deprivation remains unnoticed or unreported. Moreover, the geographic location of local courts and the prolonged nature of judicial reviews imply that exhaustion of domestic remedies (EDRs) could be burdensome for individuals who lack the necessities to get by in life. In other words, the rubric of EDRs might be a major deterrent for an individual or a group with insufficient resources to afford a lawyer who might litigate on their behalf at the (sub)national levels to satisfy this benchmark.[37]

4.2 Limited Jurisdiction of the African Court

Before approaching the African Court with an application, RAS or relevant NGOs ought to satisfy themselves that the host state has ratified the

[35] TG Daly and M Wiebusch 'The African Court on Human and Peoples' Rights: Mapping resistance against a young court' (2018) 14 *International Journal of Law in Context* 294 at 305.

[36] As above.

[37] C Okoloise 'Circumventing obstacles to the implementation of recommendations by the African Commission on Human and Peoples' Rights' (2018) 18 *African Human Rights Law Journal* 27 at 36.

Court Protocol. Disappointingly, after more than two decades following its adoption, the instrument has been ratified by thirty states parties only.[38] This implies that almost half of the member states of the AU have still not accepted the competence of the African Court. This casts doubt over the legitimacy of the institution. Also, the high number of non-ratifications by states somewhat indicates the unwillingness of African states to provide leeway for those within their borders to seek supranational intervention if domestic institutions are unable to grant social justice. Consequently, a disproportionate number of nearly 900,000 Eritrean, Somaliland and South Sudanese RAS facing deprivations in Ethiopia are unable to approach the African Court as the country has not accepted the competence of the Court.[39] Although this development is worrying, there is still an iota of hope as notable refugee host states such as Kenya, South Africa and Uganda are parties to the Court Protocol.

4.3 *Limitation Clause Under Article 34(6) of the Court Protocol*

All things considered, the biggest blow to the African Court's jurisdiction lies with the third section of the benchmark, which is the submission of a declaration. In instances where the above two thresholds are met, submission of an application may take two channels, direct or indirect access. Direct access implies that individuals and NGOs with observer status before the African Commission may directly submit a complaint against a states party if that states party has submitted a declaration allowing direct access to the African Court. Specifically, article 5(3) of the Court Protocol stipulates that the 'Court may entitle relevant [NGOs] with observer

[38] States which have still not ratified include Angola, Botswana, the CAR, Cape Verde, Djibouti, the DRC, Egypt, Equatorial Guinea, Eritrea, Ethiopia, Guinea-Bissau, Guinea, Liberia, Madagascar, Morocco, Namibia, Seychelles, Sierra Leone, Somalia, South Sudan, Sao Tome and Principe, Sudan, Swaziland, Zambia, and Zimbabwe; See AU 'List of countries which have signed, ratified/acceded to the Protocol to the African Charter on Human and Peoples' Rights on the Establishment of an African Court on Human and Peoples' Rights' (2017) https://au.int/sites/default/files/treaties/36393-sl-protocol_to_the_african_charter_on_human_and_peoplesrights_on_the_estab.pdf (accessed 25 February 2023).

[39] UNHCR 'Ethiopia refugee crisis explained' (2019) https://www.unrefugees.org/news/ethiopia-refugee-crisis-explained/ (accessed 25 February 2023).

status before the Commission, and individuals to institute cases directly before it, per article 34(6) of this Protocol'. But what is the import of this provision? In answering this discursive question without equivocation, article 34(6) of the Court Protocol stipulates that the 'Court shall not receive any petition under article 5(3) involving a States Party which has not made such a declaration'.

One might speculate that the object of article 34(6) is to safeguard the African Court from being paralysed by an overwhelming caseload or to entice states to get on board. Regardless of the underlying motivation, however, it appears that this clause has outlived its usefulness, as a disproportionate percentage of states have still not acceded. By March 2021, only seven states had made such a declaration, thereby paving the way for NGOs and individuals in these seven states to directly approach the African Court.[40] It is disheartening to note that most of the destination countries with high volumes of RAS have not made such a declaration. It was against this backdrop that the applicant in *Falana v AU* enquired whether the failure of the state to make such a declaration was a breach of the African Charter, and in particular the right to a fair trial under article 7.[41] The applicant further questioned whether the AU, as a supranational entity, could enjoin its members to pursue a certain course of action, specifically submitting an article 34(6) declaration.

In a brief response, the African Court summarily dismissed the application on two grounds. First, on procedural grounds, it stated that it lacks personal jurisdiction as the AU, cited as the respondent, has not ratified the Court Protocol. Thus, as the AU is not a states party to the Court Protocol, such an application cannot be entertained by the African Court. Second, as an organisation, the AU does not have the legal mandate to oblige its members to enter into treaties or legal agreements, as such decisions are the prerogative of sovereign states. This position was reaffirmed by the African Court when Rwanda withdrew its declaration on 1 March 2016.[42] To that end, RAS or related NGOs have limited prospects of directly using the Court as the forum to advance their access to basic commodities.

[40] These are Benin, Burkina Faso, Côte d'Ivoire, Ghana, Malawi, Mali and Tanzania.

[41] *Falana v African Union*, App 1/2011, Judgement (26 June 2012).

[42] *Inbabire Victoire Umuhoza v Rwanda*, App 3/2014, ruling on 3 June 2016.

4.4 *Criticism Against the African Commission's Indirect Access to the African Court*

In the face of insufficient declarations, the available option for RAS and relevant NGOs lies in indirect access to the African Court.[43] This channel is grounded in the Rules of Procedure (RoP) of the African Commission on Human and Peoples' Rights. In terms of Rule 118 of the RoP, the African Commission may seek the assistance of the African Court in enforcing compliance with its recommendations, particularly in instances where a states party is uncooperative. Thus, in the instance where a states party to the African Charter has not made the declaration, RAS and related NGOs can submit a communication to the African Commission which it could then decide on, or refer to the African Court for consideration. This approach could trigger three contentious views. The first view is that refugee activists, on the one hand, could argue that Rule 118 opens a flood gate for RAS in states parties that have not yet made the declaration. The second is that critics, on the other hand, may argue that regular use of Rule 118 may negate the immunity enjoyed by non-declaratory states, as it provides a diversion for applicants to circumvent the claw-back clause under article 34(6). The third view is that legal pundits might postulate that frequent referrals might compromise the competence of the African Commission as an autonomous body, capable of interpreting and applying the African Charter.

4.5 *Exclusion of the African Children's Committee from Accessing the African Court*

Ironically, article 5 of the Court's Protocol excludes the African Children's Committee from the list of institutions that may approach the African Court for the legal interpretation of the African Charter or related regional instruments. Thus, although the African Children's Committee is on a par with the African Commission as an oversight body, the former cannot be used as an indirect route to the African Court. It is quite puzzling, to say the least, why the drafters of the Court's Protocol adopted different views on access to the African Court, given the protective mandate of the two monitoring bodies. Simply put, why would they pave the way for the

[43] F Viljoen 'Understanding and overcoming challenges in accessing the African Court on Human and Peoples' Rights' (2018) 67 *International & Comparative Law Quarterly* 63.

African Commission to be able to seek the intervention of a supranational entity like the African Court while excluding the African Children's Committee, for the protection of children? Providing similar leverage to the African Children's Committee will bridge the fragmentation and reinforce the complementary role among the three monitoring bodies. The exclusion of the African Children's Committee brings to bear two main concerns: (1) the drafters of the Court Protocol block the possibility of unaccompanied children or underage RAS from using the African Children's Committee to directly access the African Court. This is mostly in cases where the concerned state has not submitted article 34(6) declaration obliging the Court to receive application from individuals or public interest litigators; and (2) while the African Court could make reference to and adjudicate on applications relating to the Children's Charter, the African Children's Committee on its own cannot refer a case under consideration to the African Court for further action. It is, however, fair to note that the African Children's Committee's exclusion from article 5 was not deliberate on the part of the drafters, as the Court Protocol precedes the establishment of the African Children's Committee.[44] While this fact is understandable, there is still a sense of urgency for the Court Protocol to be revised to give the African Children's Committee direct access to the Court on matters affecting children.

4.6 *Long Delays in Finalising Communications*

As is typical of many (quasi)judicial bodies, the consideration of communications by the African Commission is often delayed by large volumes of backlogs and repeated adjournment of sessions. The prolonged delays not only deprive the authors of enjoying their rights to a speedy trial, but may serve as a disincentive for RAS to consider the prospect of pursuing their case before the African Court. This reluctance is justified, as the undue delay at the African Commission could be replicated at the African Court, as the state concerned is likely to request a renewed assessment of the procedural and substantive facts of the case. Also, given that the African Court is a new institution, it may conduct a review of the facts as extensively as presented by the African Commission and respondent. Thus, on

[44] AU 'ACERWC 2015–2019 strategic plan' 40 https://au.int/sites/default/files/pages/32903-file-acerwc_strategic_plan_2015-2019.pdf (accessed 25 February 2023). The Committee was launched in 2001, three years after the adoption of the Protocol.

average, successful finalisation of an application via the African Commission could take up to a decade, if one considers the backlog of cases and prolonged litigation at the domestic courts.

4.7 *Slow Ratification of the Protocol on the African Court of Justice and Human Rights (ACJHR)*

As mentioned earlier, it is hoped that providing leverage for the African Children's Committee to access the African Court could bridge the fragmentation among the different institutions, and reinforce the complementary role among the three monitoring bodies. Interestingly, this position seems to have resonated with the AU Assembly of Heads of State and Government, and subsequently inspired the drafting of the 2008 Protocol on the African Court of Justice and Human Rights (ACJHR), which merges the African Court with the African Court of Justice and Human Rights (African Court of Justice). Under article 30(c) of the 2008 Protocol, the African Children's Committee is listed as one of the 'entities eligible to submit cases to the Court'.[45] The insertion is undoubtedly a groundbreaking achievement for minor RAS and related NGOs to have (in)direct access to the Court. Still, in a pattern similar to its forerunner (the Court Protocol), ratification of the instrument has been slow and saddled with inertia. By March 2021, only eight AU member states had ratified the instrument, thus falling short of the 15 required accessions.[46] The lack of political commitment begs two discursive questions: whether dominant refugee host states will eventually become parties to the instrument; and whether the 2008 Protocol will enter into force any time soon. A positive response to these questions will be useful in advancing the rights of underage RAS under the auspices of the 2008 Protocol.

[45] Art 30(c) of the Statute of the African Court of Justice and Human Rights.

[46] AU 'List of countries which have signed, ratified/acceded to the Protocol on the Statute of the African Court of Justice and Human Rights' (2020) https://au.int/sites/default/files/treaties/36396-sl-PROTOCOL%20ON%20THE%20STATUTE%20OF%20THE%20AFRICAN%20COURT%20OF%20JUSTICE%20AND%20HUMAN%20RIGHTS.pdf (accessed 25 February 2023). State parties to the Protocol are Angola, Benin, Burkina Faso, Congo, Gambia, Libya, Liberia and Mali.

4.8 *The Paucity of Socio-Economic Rights Cases Before the African Court*

Although its seminal case relates to a refugee, the African Court took a step back from fleshing out the socio-economic entitlements of the applicant and similarly situated persons.[47] The lack of deliberation on this theme may be linked to the fact that the application did not merit such a discussion, as the applicant was merely seeking an order to forestall the prosecution of the refugee by the host state. More disturbingly, subsequent cases have followed a similar suit of alleging violations unrelated to socio-economic rights, thereby denying the African Court an opportunity to give life to this set of entitlements. The lack of socio-economic rights cases before the African Court has arguably undermined its competence in terms of forging a jurisprudence that bridges the gap between the textual guarantee of entitlement to social security and its actual realisation. In sum, the lack of opportunity of the African Court to grapple with a specific or related socio-economic rights case has deprived it of its prospect to clearly articulate its position on RAS' entitlement to social security, and more broadly socio-economic rights. It is therefore imperative that the African Court fosters cooperation with the African Commission to facilitate the transfer of relevant cases to the Court as a means of expanding its jurisprudence within this thematic area. Ultimately, given its competence as the authoritative adjudicative regional body, the African Court's decision on socio-economic rights may serve as a useful precedence for advancing people's access to social security, including RAS.

4.9 *Lack of Autonomy of the African Court*

While the African Court is textually and theoretically an autonomous institution, it is, in practice, subservient to the political architecture of the AU. Articles 14 to 20 of the Court Protocol place the operations of the African Court under the direct supervision of the AU Assembly. In addition, the AU Assembly is responsible for deciding on the appointment, suspension, removal and replacement of judges. This role by the Assembly ultimately compromises the independence and neutrality of judges, as some might seek to satisfy the whims of the Assembly to extend their tenure.

[47] *Michelot Yogogombaye v The Republic of Senegal* Application 001/2008.

4.10 Non-Compliance by States

The success of any international legal regime largely depends, amongst other things, on the willingness of states parties to respect and comply with its decisions.[48] Unfortunately, the AU, as an organisation, is composed of members who are unamenable to the (rational) decisions of its organs.[49] To be exact, a considerable number of these states have flagrantly disregarded the decisions of the African Commission and proceeded to perpetrate abuses against victims. Notable victims include Nigeria's Ken Saro-Wiwa, Botswana's Mariette Bosch and Libya's Saif al-Islam Gaddafi.[50] Arguably, the large-scale non-compliance in the region may be tied to the notions of sovereignty and territorial integrity which proscribe excessive intrusion in a state's domestic affairs; and the ineffective role of the AU Assembly to monitor the conduct of their members.[51] Thus, without effective supranational entities to regulate the internal affairs of AU states, many individuals have been subjected to grave human rights abuses with little or no external intervention.

In the arena of socio-economic rights, despite the groundbreaking decision in the *SERAC* case, Ogoniland continues to face massive oil exploitation in a manner that is inconsistent with the decision of the African Commission.[52] Suffice it to note that this hostility might not be limited to the African Commission, but might extend to the African Court as states are often disobliging to decisions of international (quasi)judicial bodies.[53] To avert this impediment, article 29 of the Court Protocol charges the AU Council of Ministers (CoE) to monitor the operationalisa-

[48] B Nkrumah 'Opening Pandora's box: A legal analysis of the right to food in South Africa' (2019) 52 *De Jure Law Journal* 47 at 48.

[49] F Viljoen and L Louw 'State compliance with the recommendations of the African Commission on Human and Peoples' Rights, 1994–2004' (2007) 101 *American Journal of International Law* 1.

[50] V Brittain 'Ken Saro-Wiwa: A hero for our times' 2015 56 *Race & Class* 5 at 10; GK Antigegn 'The role of the African Court on Human and Peoples' Rights for human rights protection: The case of Libyan crises' (2020) 7 *Advanced Journal of Social Science* 38 at 39.

[51] A Chayes et al. 'Managing compliance: A comparative perspective' in EB Weiss and H Jacobson (eds.) *Engaging countries: Strengthening compliance with international environmental accords* (1998) 39.

[52] *Social and Economic Rights Action Centre (SERAC) & Another v Nigeria* (2001) AHRLR 60 (ACHPR 2001) para 2.

[53] F Viljoen 'The African human rights system and domestic enforcement' in M Langford, C Rodríguez-Garavito and J Rossi (eds.) *Social rights judgments and the politics of compliance: Making it stick* (2017) 351.

tion of the African Court's decisions by states parties. Still, any findings of non-compliance by the CoE ought to be submitted to the AU Assembly. As the final decision-making body, the AU Assembly may approve or disapprove any interventions or sanctions which might be instituted against an uncooperative state.

Thus, considering the AU Assembly's chequered track record of holding member states accountable for refusing to comply with the decisions of its organs, it is likely that the operationalisation of the African Court's decisions could be achieved based on the good faith of the target state, rather than coercion.[54] Ultimately, while the Court's Protocol obliges the judicial body to report non-execution of judgements to the CoE, it remains to be seen whether the AU Assembly might take a bold step and impose a collective sanction on uncooperative states. In light of these challenges, the next section of the chapter delves into practical recommendations on how individuals, NGOs and the African Court could overcome these dominant barriers to promote the socio-economic rights of RAS.

5 Recommendations

Legal entitlements are often weighed by the extent to which they satisfy the needs of the target group, instead of the restitution they might trigger when denied. This niche has been well carved by the African Court, which has been a prolific actor in terms of providing legal interpretations of the rights contained in the African Charter. Nevertheless, since compliance with the decisions of supranational entities is still rare across the continent, it seems that the panacea for improving the socio-economic rights of RAS rests on strengthening collaboration between the African Court and national courts. This collaboration may have two merits, which are discussed next.

5.1 *Expanding on Existing Socio-Economic Jurisprudence*

Like the African Commission, the African Court has been accorded overarching protective powers to issue advisory opinions on key economic and

[54] AO Enabulele 'Incompatibility of national law with the African Charter on Human and Peoples' Rights: Does the African Court on Human and Peoples' Rights have the final say?' (2016) 16 *African Human Rights Law Journal* 1 at 14.

social rights issues.[55] The African Court must use this mandate carefully, by building on the existing jurisprudence of the African Commission, in terms of creatively interpreting the right to life to give effect to rights that are not explicitly set out in the African Charter. However, since the African Court on its own cannot proffer an opinion without a request to do so, it is important that RAS and related NGOs table such requests. Article 4(1) of the Court Protocol and Rule 82 of the Rules of Court indicate that aside from AU institutions, other African organisations which have been recognised by the structures of the AU may file a request for an advisory opinion. The import of these provisions may be construed as applying to NGOs which are geologically located in the African region, composed of Africans, and advancing the cause of Africans. Flowing from this interpretation, RAS-related organisations with observer status before, for instance, the African Commission may be deemed eligible for seeking an advisory opinion on the measures host states ought to take to improve the living conditions of RAS within their jurisdiction.[56]

5.2 *Awareness Creation*

The African Court ought to channel some resources towards increasing its visibility at the local level. One may rightly claim that not many RAS crammed in Cape Town's Central Methodist Church or camps in *Bidi bidi* or *Kakuma* are aware of the existence of a human rights court in Arusha, Tanzania. With limited knowledge of its existence, the group might not consider it as an option in cases where national courts are unsympathetic to their plea for improved living conditions. This limited awareness may not only be displayed by RAS alone, but may also be widespread among RAS-related NGOs, lawyers and public interest litigators (PILs) who might be interested in advocating for the socio-economic rights of this vulnerable population. Overcoming this limitation might entail embarking on large-scale information dissemination and visibility campaigns on the existence of the African Court. The campaign ought to be launched around the continent, from the (sub)regional to the (sub)national level.

[55] Rule 29(b) of the Rules of Court of the African Court on Human and Peoples' Rights (1 September 2020) http://www.african-court.org/wpafc/wp-content/uploads/2020/10/4-RULES-OF-THE-COURT-25-September-2020.pdf (accessed 25 February 2023).

[56] Assembly of the African Union Eleventh Ordinary Session, AU Doc Assembly/AU/Dec.1(I) xi.

5.3 *Education Around the African Court's Procedural Requirements*

As illustrated in the *Falana v AU* case, a disproportionate percentage of applications before the African Court have been declared inadmissible as they fail to adhere to the procedural requirements in submitting complaints before the regional body. As the African Court commits to enhancing its presence in the region, it ought to channel some resources to provide legal training to RAS, relevant NGOs and PILs on the requirements for seizing the African Court. These may include exhaustion of local remedies unless they are unduly prolonged; that the matter is not before the African Commission, the African Children's Committee or another international (quasi)judicial body; the application is submitted within a reasonable time after the alleged violation; the alleged violation is not based exclusively on media reports; the right violated is protected by the African Charter; the language used in the application is not disparaging or insulting; the application contains the name of the plaintiffs, even if anonymity is required; and the application must reference jurisprudence and not be merely formulaic.

5.4 *Tapping into the Role of the Special Rapporteur on Refugees, Asylum Seekers, Internally Displaced Persons and Migrants in Africa*

Appointed in 2004, the Rapporteur is mandated to conduct fact-finding missions and entreat states to comply with their human rights obligations towards RAS. Since its launch, the Office of the Rapporteur has been influential in using print and electronic media to provide wide visibility on issues confronting RAS. Thus, in the instance where there is evidence of grave deprivation of essential resources to RAS, the Rapporteur could encourage the African Commission to file an application with the African Court for interim measures. Under such circumstances, the African Commission may impose interim measures on the concerned state or request the African Court to impose such a directive order to forestall irreparable harm. While an interim order does not constitute a final finding of the African Court, it imposes a legal obligation on the relevant state to act, refrain or undertake certain actions. The conventional practice is that the order is often imposed before considering the admissibility or procedural requirement of the application. This leverage, to a greater extent, may give the African Commission considerable time to prepare their submissions before the African Court, while the state undertakes steps to address the needs of RAS before the case goes to trial. Suffice it to note that the large-scale deprivation faced by RAS in contemporary times presents an opportunity for the African Commission to present such an application to the African Court to urge receiving states to provide adequate resources for RAS. The submission of such an application ought to be guided by three cardinal principles: the likelihood of the respondent state disregarding the African Commission's provisional orders; the degree of deprivation faced by RAS; and urgency for intervention. Having said that, it remains to be seen whether this approach would be effective, as the operations of the Rapporteur have been hindered by inadequate human and financial resources.

5.5 *Ordering Provisional Measures Before Considering the Admissibility of the Application*[57]

This argument tilts in favour of exigency over decorum or strictures. This sense of urgency and immediate reaction by the African Court could forestall possible grave danger to the lives of vulnerable African RAS. Since the establishment of the African Court, the African Commission has submitted two applications on the question of interim orders. In the first case, the African Court issued a provisional measure ordering Kenya to halt the eviction of the *Ogiek* (an indigenous population) from the Mau forest.[58] In terms of the second, the African Court responded by instructing Libya to refrain from further acts of violence inflicted on the victim.[59] It further obliged the state to provide feedback within two weeks on the steps taken to safeguard the victim. Yet, to avert mismanagement of the African Court's resources and time, the African Commission ought to scrutinise the admissibility criteria of such communication before approaching the African Court. Overcoming deficiencies in procedural requirements or exhausting local remedies has two merits. First, this will enable the African Court to fast-track its decision on interim orders, particularly if it is

[57] Rule 118(4) of the 2010 Rules of Procedure.

[58] The other provisional measure relates to *African Commission v Kenya (Ogiek)*, App 6/2012, Order for Provisional Measures (15 March 2013).

[59] *African Commission (Saif Al-Islam Kadhafi) v Libya*, App 002/2013, Order of Provisional Measures (15 March 2013).

evident that the applicants utilised local legal mechanisms before ascending to the regional arena. Also, they have the prospects of enhancing compliance by states parties. Indeed, these two observations reinforce the African Court's role in scrutinising applications submitted by the African Commission, particularly if it perceives such applications as manifestly inadmissible in the first instance. To this end, the African Commission ought to build an impeccable reputation in its assessment of admissibility criteria submitted by applicants, thereby removing any doubts of partiality which might incite the state or the African Court to undertake a full assessment of procedural and substantive findings of the African Commission.

5.6 *Handing Down Modest (Socio-Economic) Decisions*

The African Court's orders must be informed by the economic position of the host state to avoid court decisions that outweigh the economic strength of the state. In circumstances where the Court's order places an overly onerous burden on the state's resources, the state may have a justifiable reason to side-step the African Court decision. This can thereby create tension between the state and the African Court on the one hand, as well as between citizens and migrants on the other. A reasonable order requiring a meagre allocation of food, water, housing and healthcare for fellow Africans is more likely to appeal to the conscience and ethical values of many host states and citizens. To avoid any ambiguity in the operationalisation of an order, the African Court could provide practical or step-by-step guidance on how the states ought to assist the target group, with specific timeframes within which each court-ordered obligation must be fulfilled.

5.7 *Increasing Ratification of the Court's Protocol and Article 34(6) Declarations*

With virtually all major RAS host states not making the declaration, this limits the prospect of this vulnerable group and relevant NGOs approaching the African Court. Perhaps it is high time that the drafters of the Court Protocol amend article 34(6) to pave the way for individuals and NGOs to submit applications. This will also concretise the rights of vulnerable populations. Direct access to the African Court for victims and NGOs ought to be prioritised as it is these actors who are meant to benefit from the protective mandate of the Court, and not states parties or the African Commission, which presently have automatic access. Ultimately, such an amendment will be determined by the willingness of the legislative organ of the AU, the Assembly of Heads of State. Mobilising governments to amend the article 34(6) claw-back clause could be achieved through infrapolitics or lobbying of African leaders to consent to such an amendment. This effort could be intensified through local activism by civil societies and human rights commissions in urging their governments to amend the Court Protocol or ratify the Protocol, and submit the article 34(6) declaration concurrently.

6 Conclusion

Whilst RAS originally enjoyed a generous reception in the immediate post-colonial Africa, contemporary developments across the region indicate that this hospitality has waned. Although the regional organisation, the AU, has established several institutions to safeguard the welfare of Africans, regardless of their citizenship status, the effective operationalisation of the mandates of these institutions seems to be curtailed by a normative and political hurdle. One of these institutions is the African Court. The Court has been allocated overarching protective powers to provide advisory opinions on and remedies for violations of the rights entrenched in the African Charter. While the institution is well placed to execute this mandate, it suffers from several weaknesses.

At the normative level, the insufficient number of states parties to the Court Protocol limits its jurisdiction and ability to monitor the human rights situation across the continent, particularly in the case of access to basic socio-economic necessities among RAS. Also, the insertion of 34(6) in the Court Protocol limits the prospect of RAS and related NGOs directly accessing the protection of the African Court. Other limitations identified by the chapter include the historical problem of exhaustion of domestic remedies, lack of visibility of the African Court at the local level, and lack of compliance with decisions of international bodies. To this end, the chapter makes five key recommendations, namely: there should be a rigorous awareness campaign on the socio-economic rights of RAS; an increase in the visibility of the African Court may be achieved through information dissemination at the local level; enhanced collaboration between the African Court and domestic courts will improve socio-economic litigation at the local level; legal education should be provided to local judges to better understand the socio-economic rights of RAS; and states should be lobbied to ratify the Court Protocol and submit the declaration to provide direct access for RAS and related NGOs.

Bibliography

Books

Nkrumah, B *Seeking the right to food: Food activism in South Africa* (Cambridge University Press 2021)

Chapters in Books

Chayes, A, Chayes, AH & Mitchell, RB 'Managing compliance: A comparative perspective' in Weiss, EB & Jacobson, H (eds) *Engaging countries: Strengthening compliance with international environmental accords* (1998 Cambridge University Press)

Nkrumah, B 'The potential of the African human rights system in addressing poverty' in Durojaye, E & Mirugi-Mukundi, G (eds) *Exploring the link between poverty and human rights in Africa* (Pretoria: Pretoria University Law Press 2020)

Viljoen, F 'The African human rights system and domestic enforcement' in Langford, M; Rodriguez-Garavito, C & Rossi, J (eds) *Social rights judgments and the politics of compliance: Making it stick* (Cambridge University Press 2017)

Journal Articles

Antigegn, GK 'The role of African Court on Human and Peoples' Rights protection: The case of Libyan crises' (2020) 7 *Advanced Journal of Social Science* 213

Bhorat, H; Oosthuizen, M & Stanwix, B 'Social assistance amidst the COVID-19 epidemic in South Africa: A policy assessment' (2021) 89 *South African Journal of Economics* 63

Brittain, V 'Ken Saro-Wiwa: A hero for our times' (2015) 56 *Race & Class* 5

Daly, TG & Wiebusch, M 'The African Court on Human and Peoples' Rights: Mapping resistance against a young court' (2018) *International Journal of Law in Context* 294

De Beco, G 'The interplay between human rights and development the other way round: The emerging use of quantitative tools for measuring the progressive realisation of economic, social and cultural rights' (2010) 4 *Human Rights & International Legal Discourse* 265

Devereux, S 'Social protection responses to COVID-19 in Africa' 2021 (21) *Global Social Policy* 421

Enabulele, AO 'Incompatibility of national law with the African Charter on Human and Peoples' Rights: Does the African Court on Human and Peoples' Rights have the final say?' (2016) 16 *African Human Rights Law Journal* 1

Fassin, D; Wilhelm-Solomon, M & Segatti, A 'Asylum as a form of life: The politics and experience of indeterminacy in South Africa' 58 *Current Anthropology* 160

Foster, M *International refugee law and socio-economic rights: Refuge from deprivation* (Cambridge: Cambridge University Press 2007)

Gordon, SL 'Welcoming refugees in the rainbow nation: Contemporary attitudes towards refugees in South Africa' (2016) 35 *African Geographical Review* 1

Kapindu, RE 'No return to persecution or danger: Judicial application of the principle of *non-refoulement* in refugee law in South Africa and Malawi' (2020) 10 *Constitutional Court Review* 107

Khan, F & Lee, M 'Policy shifts in the asylum process in South Africa resulting in hidden refugees and asylum seekers' (2018) 4 *African Human Mobility Review* 1205

Maphosa, F & Ntau, C 'Undocumented migrants as *homo sacer*: Cases from Botswana and South Africa' (2021) 56 *Journal of Asian and African Studies* 872

McGary, H 'Reconciliation and reparations' (2010) 41 *Metaphilosophy* 546

Moagi, M; Wyatt, G; Mokgobi, M; Loeb, T; Zhang, Davhana-Maselesele, M 'Mozambican immigrants to South Africa: Their xenophobia and discrimination experiences' (2018) 28 *Journal of Psychology in Africa* 196

Momodu, S 'Africa most affected by refugee crisis' (2017) 30 *Africa Renewal* 28

Moyo, I 'On borders and the liminality of undocumented Zimbabwean migrants in South Africa' (2020) 18 *Journal of Immigrant & Refugee Studies* 60

Mukumbang FC, Ambe AN, Adebiyi BO 'Unspoken inequality: How COVID-19 has exacerbated existing vulnerabilities of asylum-seekers, refugees, and undocumented migrants in South Africa' (2020) 19 *International Journal for Equity in Health* 1

Nkrumah, B 'Food protest in South Africa: "Them belly full, but we hungry"' (2018) 19 *ESR Review* 4

Nkrumah, B 'Opening Pandora's box: A legal analysis of the right to food in South Africa' 52 *DeJure Law Journal* 47

Okoloise, C 'Circumventing obstacles to the implementation of recommendations by the African Commission on Human and Peoples' Rights' (2018) 18 *African Human Rights Law Journal* 27

Viljoen, F 'Understanding and overcoming challenges in accessing the African Court on Human and Peoples' Rights' (2018) 67 *International & Comparative Law Quarterly* 63

Viljoen, F & Louw, L 'State compliance with the recommendations of the African Commission on Human and Peoples' Rights, 1994-2004' (2007) 101 *American Journal of International Law* 1

Zurayk, R 'Pandemic and food security: A view from the Global South' (2020) 9 *Journal of Agriculture, Food Systems, and Community Development* 17

Case Law

African Commission (Saif Al-Islam Kadhafi) v Libya, App 2/2013, Order of Provisional Measures (15 March 2013)

African Commission v Kenya (Ogiek), App 6/2012, Order for Provisional Measures (15 March 2013)

Falana v African Union, App 1/2011, Judgment (26 June 2012)

Inbabire Victoire Umuhoza v Rwanda, App 3/2014, ruling on 3 June 2016

Michelot Yogogombaye v The Republic of Senegal Application 001/2008

Rencontre Africaine pour la Défense des Droits de l'Homme v Zambia (2000) AHRLR 321 (ACHPR 1996)

Social and Economic Rights Action Centre (SERAC) & Another v Nigeria (2001) AHRLR 60 (ACHPR 2001)

AU Documents

African Union, African Union Convention for the Protection and Assistance of Internally Displaced Persons in Africa (Kampala Convention), 23 October 2009

African Union, Protocol to the African Charter on Human and People's Rights on the Rights of Women in Africa, 11 July 2003

Assembly of the African Union Eleventh Ordinary Session, AU Doc Assembly/AU/Dec.1(I) xi

OAU, African Charter on Human and Peoples' Rights (Banjul Charter), 27 June 1981, CAB/LEG/67/3 rev. 5, 21 ILM 58 (1982)

OAU, African Charter on the Rights and Welfare of the Child, 11 July 1990, CAB/LEG/24.9/49 (1990)

OAU, Convention Governing the Specific Aspects of Refugee Problems in Africa ('OAU Convention'), 10 September 1969, 1001 UNTS 45

UN Documents

UN General Assembly, Convention on the Rights of the Child, 20 November 1989, United Nations, Treaty Series, vol 1577, p 3

Internet Sources

ACHPR 'Network: Non-governmental organizations' (2021) https://www.achpr.org/ngos (accessed 25 February 2023)

AU 'ACERWC 2015-2019 Strategic Plan' https://au.int/sites/default/files/pages/32903-file-acerwc_strategic_plan_2015-2019.pdf (accessed 25 February 2023)

AU (African Union) 'List of countries which have signed, ratified/acceded to the Protocol on the Statute of the African Court of Justice and Human Rights (2020) https://au.int/sites/default/files/treaties/36396-slPROTOCOL%20ON%20THE%20STATUTE%20OF%20THE%20AFRICAN%20COURT%20OF%20JUS TICE%20AND%20HUMAN%20RIGHTS.pdf (accessed 25 February 2023)

Easton-Calabria, E 'Uganda has a remarkable history of hosting refugees, but its efforts are underfunded' *The Conversation* 26 August 2021 https://theconversation.com/uganda-has-a-remarkable-history-of-hosting-refugees-but-its-efforts-are-underfunded-166706 (accessed 25 February 2023)

Humanitarian Aid 'Refugees at risk of hunger and malnutrition, as relief hit in Eastern Africa' (2020) https://news.un.org/en/story/2020/08/1071062 (accessed 25 February 2023)

Rules of Court of the African Court on Human and Peoples' Rights. O1 September 2020. < https://www.african-court.org/en/images/Basic%20Documents/Rules_of_Court_-_25_September_2020.pdf >. (accessed 25 February 2023)

UN 'Migration dynamics, refugees and internally displaced persons in Africa' https://www.un.org/en/academic-impact/migration-dynamics-refugees-and-internally-displaced-persons-africa (accessed 15 March 2022)

UNHCR (United Nations High Commissioner for Refugees) 'Ethiopia refugee crisis explained' (2019) https://www.unrefugees.org/news/ethiopia-refugee-crisis-explained/ (accessed 25 February 2023)

UNHCR (United Nations High Commissioner for Refugees) 'Africa' (2021) Africa https://www.unhcr.org/africa.html (accessed 15 March 2022)

CHAPTER 6

Contextualising the Socio-Economic Rights of the Refugee Child: An Evaluation of the Position of the African Charter on the Rights and Welfare of the Child

Robert Doya Nanima

1 Introduction

Statistics show that the number of refugees across the world is high.[1] Reports from the United Nations High Commissioner for Refugees (UNHCR) indicate that up to 82.4 million people across the globe have been displaced, 26.6 million are refugees and asylum seekers, and 30 million originate from Africa.[2] While 42 per cent of the 82.4 million (35

[1] UNHCR 'Africa: Figures at a glance' (2021) https://www.unhcr.org/figures-at-a-glance.html (accessed 9 January 2022).

[2] As above.

R. D. Nanima (✉)
Department of Criminal Justice and Procedure, Faculty of Law, University of the Western Cape, Cape Town, South Africa
e-mail: rnanima@uwc.ac.za

E. Durojaye et al. (eds.), *Realising Socio-Economic Rights of Refugees and Asylum Seekers in Africa*, Politics of Citizenship and Migration, https://doi.org/10.1007/978-3-031-16548-1_6

million) are children, 44.4 per cent of the 26.6 million (11.8 million) are refugee children.[3] This number has been on an upward trajectory since 1951 (from 2 million people) since the adoption of the UN Refugee Convention.[4] The discussion below shows the growth in the number of refugees over the last 70 years.[5] The UNHCR states that 44 million people in sub-Saharan Africa are displaced and 60 per cent are internally displaced persons.[6] A 2019 report shows that the number of refugee children has soared exponentially. The number increased beyond 80 per cent between 2010 and 2019 and at least 13.5 million children live as refugees, migrants and internally displaced persons in Africa.[7] Children and their families face the destructive effects of violence, poverty or climate change and make the painful decision to leave their homes in search of safety and a more hopeful future.[8] There are indications that one in every four migrants in Africa is a child and 59 per cent of the 6.8 million refugees in African countries are children. Africa's population of displaced children includes four million refugees and seven million internally displaced children.[9] The challenge related to these figures is not only the upward trend, but that these vast numbers lead to escalating humanitarian crises such as shortages of food and inadequate essential services like education and health for vulnerable children.[10]

A study by the African Committee of Experts on the Rights and Welfare of the Child (African Children's Committee) indicates that the key drivers

[3] UNICEF 'Child displacement' (2021) https://data.unicef.org/topic/child-migration-and-displacement/displacement/ (accessed 9 January 2022).

[4] UN General Assembly, Convention Relating to the Status of Refugees, 28 July 1951, United Nations, Treaty Series, vol. 189, p 137. See M Hussein and M Haddad 'Visualising 70 years of refugee journeys' *Al Jazeera* 20 June 2021 https://www.aljazeera.com/news/2021/6/20/infographic-world-refugee-day-journey (accessed 9 January 2021).

[5] Hussein and Haddad (n 4).

[6] UNHCR Planning figures 2023 https://reporting.unhcr.org/globalappeal2023/pdf?page=10 (accessed 5 May 2023).

[7] '13.5 million children now uprooted in Africa - including those displaced by conflict, poverty and climate change' *UNICEF press release* 9 February 2019 https://www.unicef.org/press-releases/135-million-children-now-uprooted-africa-including-those-displaced-conflict-poverty (accessed 3 June 2022).

[8] As above.

[9] As above.

[10] See footnotes 1–5.

of children on the move from one country to another include armed conflict, tension and strife, socio-economic challenges, and accompanying their parents who are in search of greener pastures.[11] There is no universal consensus in Africa on how to deal with the refugee (child). It is on this basis that various countries adopt different approaches to engaging refugees generally. Approaches range from integration to encampment.[12]

In Kenya, for example, the encampment policy requires refugees to be placed in refugee camps.[13] This is further amplified by the fact that while the refugees use Kenya's curriculum, education is managed by private organisations like the UNHCR and UNICEF.[14] Other countries like South Africa apply the integration policy to refugees. This does not act as a panacea to the challenges that refugees face. South Africa's Department of Home Affairs still requires that children have residence permits to take the final examinations in both primary and secondary school.[15]

In the light of the above, this chapter proceeds with an evaluation of the normative guidance under the African Charter on the Rights and Welfare of the Child. It seeks to show the relevance of the current framework as a competent instrument to enforce the socio-economic rights of the child. Subsequently, the chapter reflects upon the emerging jurisprudence and highlights various attempts by the African Committee to continually realign its engagements with the normative guidance under the African Charter on the Rights and Welfare of the Child. While the

[11] ACERWC 'Mapping children on the move within Africa' (2018) https://reporting.acerwc.africa/en/resources/publications/mapping-children-move-within-africa (accessed 2 May 2023) generally.

[12] R Jaji 'Social technology and refugee encampment in Kenya' (2012) 25 *Journal of Refugee Studies* 221.

[13] NA Kerubo 'Refugees' rights vs responsibilities: An analysis of Kenya's refugee encampment policy' (2013) https://bit.ly/2J6yOjs (accessed 23 May 2022). See also A Maina Securitization of Kenya's asylum space: Origin and legal analysis of the encampment policy' in JD Schmidt, L Kimathi and MO Owiso (eds.) *Refugees and forced migration in the Horn and Eastern Africa: Trends, challenges and opportunities (advances in African economic, social and political development)* (2019) 81.

[14] UNHCR 'Briefing note on education in Dadaab refugee camps: Version 13 September' (2020) https://data2.unhcr.org/ar/documents/download/31025 (accessed 25 May 2022). For instance, according to the UNHCR, there are 22 primary schools in Dadaab Camp with a classroom ratio of one teacher per 100 learners and a desk ratio of one desk for seven learners.

[15] See *Minister of Home Affairs v Watchenuka* [2004] 1 All SA 21 (SCA).

Committee has to a great extent lived up to the task of promoting the rights of the refugee child in Africa, much can still be done.

The international law on refugees is discussed extensively in Chap. 1 and thus does not warrant repetition here.[16] The author makes a cautious but deliberate decision to question the extent to which the African Charter and its African Committee align with the normative and jurisprudential developments on the internally displaced child and child refugee.

2 Normative Guidance of the African Children's Charter

The African Charter on the Rights and Welfare of the Child provides for a child-centred approach that engages the four principles. These include; non-discrimination,[17] the best interests of the child,[18] participation,[19] and the right to life, survival and development.[20] This is informed by the deliberate engagement of the realities of the Child in Africa that include various problems such as armed conflict,[21] child marriages[22] and harmful child practices[23].[24] The use of a child rights-based approach and the added value to the protection of the Child in Africa is instructive to understanding the normative and jurisprudential guidance emerging from the African Charter

[16] See Chap 1. For further reading, see the UN Convention Relating to the Status of Refugees (n 4); OAU, Convention Governing the Specific Aspects of Refugee Problems in Africa (OAU Convention), 10 September 1969, 1001 UNTS 45. See also UN General Assembly, International Covenant on Civil and Political Rights, 16 December 1966, United Nations, Treaty Series, vol. 999, p 171; UN General Assembly, International Covenant on Economic, Social and Cultural Rights, 16 December 1966, United Nations, Treaty Series, vol. 993, p 3; OAU, African Charter on Human and Peoples' Rights (Banjul Charter), 27 June 1981, CAB/LEG/67/3 rev 5, 21 ILM 58 (1982). See also OAU, African Charter on the Rights and Welfare of the Child, 11 July 1990, CAB/LEG/24.9/49 (1990). This is discussed at length in Sect. 3.

[17] Article 3 of the ACRWC.

[18] Article 4 of the ACRWC.

[19] Article 7 of the ACRWC.

[20] Article 5 of the ACRWC.

[21] Article 22 of the ACRWC.

[22] Article 21(2) of the ACRWC.

[23] Article 21(1) of the ACRWC.

[24] For a detailed discussion on the added value of the African Children's Charter, see BD Mezmur 'Happy 18th birthday to the African Children's Rights Charter: Not counting its days but making its days count' (2017) 1 *Africa Human Rights Yearbook* 125.

on the Rights and Welfare of the Child. The chapter now turns to the normative provisions on refugees.

The relevant provision states that

> States Parties to the present Charter shall take all appropriate measures to ensure that a child who is seeking refugee status or who is considered a refugee in accordance with applicable international or domestic law shall, whether unaccompanied or accompanied by parents, legal guardians or close relatives, receive appropriate protection and humanitarian assistance in the enjoyment of the rights set out in this Charter and other international human right and humanitarian instruments to which the States are parties.[25]

This provision, in itself, provides an instructive position that embraces vulnerabilities on two fronts: firstly, it embraces the vulnerable position of the child, and secondly, the added vulnerable position of the child as a refugee. This is a cardinal point of distinction from other international instruments such as the United Nations Convention on the Rights of the Child that is silent on the position of refugee children.[26]

Firstly, the existence of a provision pertaining to the refugee child is not sufficient unless it is conceptualised and contextualised. To this end, the foregoing provision mandates the provision of normative guidance on matters concerning the refugee child.[27] This is evident from the use of the word 'shall' in response to the obligations. Further, the extent to which a state is obligated to meet the requirement depends on the applicable international and regional law. This position is affirmed by the ability of the Committee to rely on persuasive human rights jurisprudence of the United Nations and other regional laws as long as it supports the protection of the rights of the child.[28]

Secondly, a refugee child is not necessarily automatically entitled to the enjoyment of socio-economic rights in the host country.[29] This is evident from the lack of appreciation of the importance of whether the child is unaccompanied or accompanied by parents, legal guardians or close relatives. This highlights the fact that the immigration status of the refugee child in the host state is of no consequence. It also indicates lack of

[25] Article 23 of the ACRWC.
[26] Mezmur (n 47).
[27] Article 23 of the ACRWC.
[28] Article 46 of the ACRWC.
[29] Article 23 of the ACRWC.

commitment to the promotion and protection of the right to life, survival and development of the refugee child through approaches that lead to the holistic development of the child in all aspects.

Thirdly, the Charter provides for the protection of specific children. This is evident in the wording that protection extends to children when they are unaccompanied or accompanied by parents, legal guardians or close relatives.[30] Two insights can be garnered from this provision. Firstly, it speaks to the vulnerabilities that a child faces such as being an accompanied or unaccompanied minor. Secondly, this deliberate inclusion of specific protection for children echoes the added value of the Charter towards the protection of the rights of the child. This concept embraces the child rights-based approach, especially the principle of non-discrimination. As widely observed, the principle of non-discrimination is provided for across most international instruments. The African Children's Charter calls on states to promote and protect the rights of children without discrimination, and that such protection and promotion should not be affected by the status of the child.

Fourthly, the child is entitled to appropriate protection for the enjoyment of his or her rights.[31] To this end, it is argued that the protection accorded to the child has to be commensurate to the realities that he or she experiences. Often, when states indicate the form of protection for children generally, they tend to allude to the adoption policies, enactment of laws, and use of government programmes that speak to the promotion and protection of the rights of the child. While this is appreciated, these initiatives have to be supported by deliberate plans that show actual quantifiable changes in the life of the child. This calls for states to use due diligence in the measures that they take to improve the position of the child. A discussion on the use of due diligence follows next in the discussion on emerging jurisprudence.

The fifth critical point lies in the mandatory directive to states, to use humanitarian assistance in addition to the measures used by the state to offer appropriate protection. This is instructive as it recognises the fact that at times, refugees and internally displaced children are in areas where there is a limited supply of essential services.[32] For instance, the right to education may be very limited or lacking in quality. The same may apply

[30] As above.

[31] As above.

[32] As above.

to the continued lack of adequate health services and facilities for the refugee child. This is exacerbated by the fact that children are not a homogenous group—requiring that different modes of engagement are used for different children. As such, it is advised that humanitarian assistance be tailored to the challenges faced by the refugee child in each environment. The use of humanitarian assistance is associated with the initiatives by the state in providing protection; the question of the appropriateness of such protection is tailored to fit the position of the affected refugee child.

In addition, the article stipulates that the source of appropriate protection and humanitarian assistance finds its place in both human rights and humanitarian law.[33] This is interesting as it allows the Charter, which is premised on human rights, to draw insights from both human rights law and humanitarian law. The critical question that one has to ask is how to balance this provision. It is argued that this guiding principle should be informed by the best interests of the child. As widely observed, this principle is not defined but rather contextualised to address the position of the children that require its application. It is thus a moving target aimed at ensuring that the best interests of the child principle is informed by the living realities of the child. It also ensures non-discrimination, participation and the right to life, survival and development. The best interests of the child principle therefore requires that humanitarian law be applied if it offers appropriate protection. The same applies to human rights law.

Furthermore, the Charter requires that states parties shall undertake to

> cooperate with existing international organizations which protect and assist refugees in their efforts to protect and assist such a child and to trace the parents or other close relatives of an unaccompanied refugee child in order to obtain information necessary for reunification with the family.[34]

There is no drafting history of the African Children's Charter that can inform our understanding of the article. It is thus prudent that the intent of the drafter is deduced from the text. Arguably, they intended that states should not act in isolation but must engage organisations that have worked with refugees. This would allow for nuanced approaches to be applied. Such approaches would arise out of collegiality and the concerted identification of methods of working that holistically improve the well-being of

[33] As above.

[34] Article 23(2) of the ACRWC.

the child. The purpose of the cooperation between states and international organisations is to ensure the protection of the rights of the child refugee and at the same time to support children to reunite with their families.

3 Emerging Jurisprudence

The emerging jurisprudence of the African Committee of Experts is informed by its various methods that are provided for in the African Charter on the Rights and Welfare of the Child.[35] For instance, the consideration of state reports from states parties leads to the handing down of concluding observations, while the consideration of communications from states parties leads to the granting of recommendations on the communications received. In addition, the Committee may also research modes of improvement of the promotion and protection of the rights of the refugee child. A look at the emerging jurisprudence as informed by the mandate of the Committee is explored next.

3.1 Concluding Observations on States Party Reports

In its concluding observations, the Committee has reiterated the need to improve the enjoyment of socio-economic rights, and the plight of refugees across Africa. For example, in its Concluding Observations on the report of South Africa, the Committee noted

> with concern that access to basic services by asylum seeking, migrant, and refugee children and their parents/caregivers is mostly dependent on being in possession of valid refugee/asylum-seeker documentation issued by the Department of Home Affairs (DHA). Reported community xenophobia, and at times attack, is also a serious concern that needs a concerted and effective legislative, administrative and other appropriate response.[36]

[35] Article 42 on the mandate of the African Committee of Experts on the Rights and Welfare of the Child.

[36] Concluding Recommendations by the African Committee of Experts on the Rights and Welfare of the Child (ACERWC) on the Republic of South Africa Initial Report on the Status of Implementation of the African Charter on the Rights and Welfare of the Child, para 22. See also paras 55 and 56.

A similar recommendation was evident in the African Children's Committee Concluding Observations on the Report of the Republic of Mozambique. It called on the states party to ensure

> that no child is left uneducated by lifting barriers such as the requirement of identity cards for refugee and stateless children and guaranteeing access to education for pregnant girls.[37]

This recommendation is consistent with the contemporary states party narrative that insists upon valid documentation from refugees as a condition for receiving basic services such as primary education and health services. It speaks volumes to the interpretation of article 1 on the obligations of the state under the African Charter on the Rights and Welfare of the Child. The Committee urges states parties to employ legislative, administrative and other appropriate responses. It is argued that the language used by the Committee to express states' obligations implies that states parties should be prepared to respond to needs in innovative ways and not be limited to an exhaustive or standard list of responses. The states party is expected to take on a non-exhaustive list of responses. It may be argued that this might mean that states should inculcate the use of progressive realisation of socio-economic rights. This argument, however, is not viable as the interpretation of the Concluding Observations has to be informed by the overall interpretation of the Charter. In respect of the impugned Concluding Observation, it may be argued that though it does not call for the progressive realisation of the rights, it does urge the states party to use a variety of responses to give effect to the rights. This denotes that a non-exhaustive list of responses should be employed by the states party.[38]

The protective mandate also lies in the Committee's use of its principles to be applied as a framework for the enjoyment of rights under the African Charter on the Rights and Welfare of the Child. At its core, the Committee

[37] See also Concluding Recommendations by the African Committee of Experts on the Rights and Welfare of the Child (ACERWC) on the Republic of Mozambique's Report on the Status of Implementation of the African Charter on the Rights and Welfare of the Child, para 24.

[38] This is reiterated in para 23, where the Committee calls on South Africa to 'take all the necessary measures to ensure that these groups of children are not discriminated against, and in particular undertake measures to avoid unnecessary barriers to accessing basic education, healthcare, child protection services, and birth registration services, and guarantee among others the rights of asylum seeking, migrant, and refugee children'.

uses principles that inform the protection of civil and political rights as a framework for the subsequent protection and promotion of socio-economic rights. To this end, the Committee uses critical principles such as the use of birth registration and the granting of birth certificates as a precursor to the protection of the rights of the refugee child. In considering the obligations of the state towards the enjoyment of the rights of the child, it should be borne in mind that the Charter does not differentiate between civil and political rights and socio-economic rights.[39]

In its Concluding Observations to South Africa's Report, the Committee noted that many foreign children born to undocumented migrant women and unaccompanied foreign children without asylum claims do not have birth certificates.[40] The Committee aptly links this to the denial of the enjoyment of socio-economic rights such as healthcare services, education, grants, protection services or alternative care. Furthermore, it

> recommends that the [South Africa] should avoid any barriers as well as address the complex checks and burdens of proof on caregivers who do not necessarily fit the married nuclear family unit required to register births and, where in the best interests of a child requires, also to where in the best interests of a child requires also to consider giving nationality to refugee and migrant children.[41]

This recommendation is vital as it aligns with the use of the best interests of the child as one of the four child rights-based approaches that aid the child's enjoyment of his or her rights. Further, the Committee also reiterated the need for the states party to regularly monitor and ensure the implementation of national law that relates to birth and death regulations to enable the enjoyment of the rights of child immigrants.[42]

A similar recommendation is given in Kenya's Second Periodic Report that calls on the states party to

[39] See the discussion in Sect. 3 on the normative guidance of the African Charter on socio-economic rights.

[40] Paragraph 30 of the Concluding Observations on South Africa Report.

[41] As above.

[42] See Concluding Observations on South Africa. Paragraph 31 shows that the state party has to ensure that the 'Birth and Death Registration Act and Regulations of 1st March 2014 does not serve to be a hindrance for the registration of the births of children in South Africa including non-citizens'.

> increase the accessibility of civil registry services through decentralization, remove the administrative hindrances that discourage birth registration, and create awareness about the importance of birth registration. Besides, the Committee recommends that birth registration services be extended to Refugee and IDP camps.[43]

This recommendation shows that access to civic services should not be an onerous burden on the refugee. The states party retains the obligation to ensure the accessibility of birth registration and other civic services.[44] This is crucial as the states party cannot rely on refugee policies such as encampment or integration to escape its obligations. This is evident in the specific initiatives that the Committee recommends to states parties when they apply encampment policies, which often impede access to civic and basic services due to significant geographical distances between camps and the locations where services are rendered.[45] A case in point is the recommendation to Kenya to ensure the provision of services for children to give effect to the enjoyment of the socio-economic rights of refugees. This was evident in the recommendation to the states party to

> continuously undertake children's rights education in refugee camps, inform the refugee community about the Gender Desks and ensure that the personnel is well trained to utilize child-friendly services to assist children who need care and protection.[46]

This further supports the Committee's desire that states parties take all necessary measures at their disposal to ensure the promotion and protection of the socio-economic rights of the refugee child.[47]

[43] Concluding Recommendations by the African Committee of Experts on the Rights and Welfare of the Child (ACERWC) on the Republic of Kenya's Second Periodic Report on the Status of Implementation of the African Charter on the Rights and Welfare of the Child, para 31. See also ACERWC, General Comment 2 on article 6 of the African Charter on the Rights and Welfare of the Child: The right to a name, registration at birth, and to acquire a nationality, 16 April 2014, ACERWC/GC/02 (2014) para 60.

[44] See para 31 of the Concluding Observations on South Africa Report.

[45] Nanima (22 above) generally.

[46] Paragraph 60 on education of Kenya's Second Periodic Report. See also para 61 on health and safe drinking water.

[47] As above.

3.2 General Comments

General comments offer insights into the interpretation of the specific articles. In the context of this study, the position of the promotion and protection of the socio-economic rights of the refugee child is interrogated.

3.2.1 Use of a Child Rights-Based Approach

Firstly, the link between refugee children and socio-economic rights is not aptly developed. Rather, there is a nexus between the well-being of the child refugee and the child rights-based approach. This is informed by the general thematic approach that connects the child rights-based approach to the content of the general comment. This is not what is desired, however. It is expected that the link of the child rights-based approach reflects the realities that affect the Child in Africa, such as their refugee status. The principle of the right to life, survival and development and the registration of deaths are instructive in ensuring future sustenance of life, especially where there are enormous numbers of child deaths in refugee settlements or internally displaced persons camps.[48] In addition, the Joint General Comment of the ACHPR and the African Children's Committee on Ending Child Marriage use this principle to protect the child refugee. The requisite paragraph states that

> Child marriage poses a considerable threat to the survival and development of women and children, especially girls, children with disabilities, migrant children, children who are refugees and children in child-headed households. Child marriage is correlated with early and frequent pregnancy, which in turn is associated with significantly higher rates of maternal morbidity, maternal mortality and infant mortality. Child marriage also curtails the right to development, as those who marry young are often forced to drop out of school or are precluded from participating in economic, political, social and other activities.[49]

A refugee child's protection emerges from the Committee's reiteration of states parties' obligation to protect them. The Committee has stated that states must protect children who are asylum seekers, refugees,

[48] Paragraph 20 of General Comment 2 on article 6.

[49] In the Joint General Comment by the ACHPR and the ACERWC on ending child marriage (2017) para 12 https://www.right-to-education.org/sites/right-to-education.org/files/resource-attachments/ACERWC_ACHPR_joint_GC_ending_child_marriage_2017_En.pdf (accessed 7 January 2022).

migrants, returnees or internally displaced persons against all forms of violence. States must also take measures to ensure their physical, psychological, social and legal protection.[50] A more radical and instructive method is to call for a holistic and robust approach by states parties to the Charter. States should be urged to use other initiatives to ensure the right to life, survival and development. The relevant general comment specifically calls on

> States … to adopt a holistic approach, which is facilitated by adopting a system's strengthening approach … The Committee has noted that complimenting the African Children's Charter, the SDGs serve as a tool to address implementation of children's rights to survival, development and protection in Africa, particularly the realisation of socio-economic rights, through good governance, targeted policies and adequate provision of the required services.[51]

While this does not categorically refer to the refugee child, it speaks volumes to the promotion and protection of the socio-economic rights of children generally.

3.2.2 Use of a Wider Mandate of the Committee

Secondly, general comments continue to reiterate the wide mandate of the Committee in drawing on inspiration from other international instruments to ensure the enjoyment of thematic aspects of the general comment.[52]

3.2.3 Deliberate Thematic Approach to the Content of General Comments

Thirdly, a closer reading of general comments shows different contextual understandings of the protection of the socio-economic rights of the refugee child. First, there is an emphasis on the theme covered by the general

[50] As above.

[51] ACERWC, General Comment 5 on state party obligations under the African Charter on the Rights and Welfare of the Child (Article 1) and systems strengthening for child protection (2018) para 4.3. acerwc.africa/general-comments (accessed 23 May 2022).

[52] It should be recalled that the Committee may engage article 46 of the African Charter on the Rights and Welfare of the Child to draw on inspiration from other international and regional laws. Concerning the General Comment on article 6, para 59 calls on states parties to use the African Union Convention for the Protection and Assistance of IDPs to protect refugees.

comment with a lesser connection to the enjoyment of the socio-economic rights of the refugee child.[53] A similar thematic approach that reiterates refugees as a vulnerable group that suffers from social challenges and mal-practices such as child marriages is also evident.[54] The General Comment on Article 6 only mentions 'socio-economic rights' twice. Other General Comments do not mention the terms 'refugee' and 'socio-economic rights' at all.[55]

The only thematic articulation of the socio-economic rights of refugee children appears in General Comment 5 on States Party Obligations under the African Charter on the Rights and Welfare of the Child (article 1) and systems strengthening for child protection, which unpacks the implementation of article 1 on states party obligations.[56] The General Comment recognises the Charter's non-distinction between different rights (civil, political, social, economic or cultural rights) concerning states parties' obligation to implement[57] interdependence, indivisibility and mutual reinforcement of all rights.[58] This articulation extends to the recommendation that states parties should undertake 'all possible positive measures' to realise the 'rights of the child contained in the African Children's Charter' concerning disadvantaged and marginalised groups.[59] There is a deliberate emphasis by the Committee on states parties adopting legislative measures to protect vulnerable groups such as refugees,[60] and using system strengthening methods and budget and resource mobilisation for efficient utilisation of all children's rights including refugees.[61]

[53] See paras 23, 35, 50, 51 and 57. See para 58 that reiterates the benefit of birth registration to refugees themselves as far as it facilitates their return to their country of origin, and aids the proof of identity and lineage.

[54] Paragraph 3 of the Joint General Comment by the ACHPR and the ACERWC on ending child marriage (n 52).

[55] In ACERWC, General Comment on article 30 of the African Charter on the Rights and Welfare of the Child, ACERWC/GC/01 (2013), adopted by the Committee at its twenty-second Ordinary Session (04–08 November, 2013), the closest link to a socio-economic right is the recognition of the application of the International Covenant on Economic, Social and Cultural Rights; see para 18. There is no mention of the term refugee.

[56] General Comment 5.

[57] Part III, 5 of General Comment 5.

[58] See also part III, 5 of General Comment 5. See para 25 of General Comment 2 on article 6. The Committee reiterates that the enjoyment of economic, social and cultural rights is inextricably intertwined with the enjoyment of civil and political rights.

[59] See also part III of General Comment.

[60] Paragraph 4.3.1 of General Comment 5.

[61] See also para 6.1 of General Comment 5.

It is notable that the purposive interpretation of the jurisprudence of the African Children's Committee needs to be engaged in reading into the socio-economic rights of the refugee child. For instance, the General Comment on Article 6 of the African Charter on the Rights and Welfare of the Child[62] reiterates the importance of the right to birth registration as an ineptly implemented right by states parties.[63] This has been greatly informed by the low rate of birth registration.[64] To deal with this problem, the Committee calls on the use of capacity building programmes for legislators and policymakers to use a human rights approach to birth registration and its significance for the political, social and economic development of the country.[65] The critical question to ask would be how this leads to the enjoyment of the socio-economic rights of the refugee child. This question is addressed in the General Comment's emphasis on the interconnectivity of rights.[66] An effective and fully functioning, universal, free and accessible birth registration system (as a civil and political right) needs to be integrated with other services.[67] The General Comment creates a nexus between the provision of civic services and socio-economic services. This is evident from the following:

> From a socio-economic point of view, a functioning birth registration system integrated with other civil registration services informs government social services agencies on the details of the current beneficiaries of services as well as on those who no longer qualify for them because they have died or exited the requisite age to benefit from those services.

A fully functioning birth registration system contributes to the good economic governance of the country as it provides accurate statistical data for planning purposes. It is important to note that the General Comment recognises various socio-economic factors in the community such as

[62] General Comment 2.

[63] Paragraph 3 of General Comment 2.

[64] Paragraph 3 of General Comment 2.

[65] Paragraph109 of General Comment 2.

[66] At para 111, the General Comment calls on states parties that respect the principle of international law that statelessness shall be avoided, and in particular that, as required by art 6(4), a child who, at the time of birth, is not granted nationality by any other state in accordance with its laws acquires the nationality of the state in the territory of which he or she has been born.

[67] This is evident in para 109; these services include the provision of education and health, and the right to safe drinking water.

'poverty, lack of education, discrimination against women some vulnerable groups such as refugees or migrants'.[68] The General Comment on Article 22 of the African Charter on the Rights and Welfare of the Child guides the interpretation of Article 22 on the protection and promotion of the rights of the child in conflict situations.[69] It is instructive to note that this General Comment is informed by one of the various aspects of the added value of the African Children's Charter.

3.3 *Research by the African Committee of Experts*

The Committee continues to research as part of its mandate under Article 42 of the Children's Charter. Various recommendations that generally speak to the need to improve the welfare of the refugee child have not gone unnoticed.[70] For instance, in the Continental Study on the impact of conflict and crisis on children, the Committee makes various recommendations to include the provision of a legal identity to every person as the first step to protection. The guiding framework for the granting of identity requires accessible birth registration without discrimination (including one's immigration status).[71] It should be recalled that birth registration is a recognised human right under Article 6 of the African Children's Charter. As such, the registration of children secures their recognition before the law and safeguards their rights against possible violations in all situations.[72]

The Committee reiterates the use of the birth registration of more vulnerable children like refugees as a platform to secure the enjoyment of all their rights, especially where the children are affected by situations of conflict. The same study also recommends the engagement of counter-intuitive measures to protect the child and ensure the enjoyment of specific rights. For instance, in situations where there is radicalism and extremism, especially where children affected by armed conflict and accompanying refugees are targeted by terrorist groups, the Committee recommends the use of practical measures such as

[68] Paragraph 3 of General Comment 2.

[69] As above.

[70] There are various studies by the Committee. The study only makes reference to the ACERW studies of 2016 and 2018.

[71] Paragraph g of the Recommendations in the ACERWC 'Continental Study on the impact of conflict and crises on children in Africa' (2016).

[72] Paragraph g of Recommendations in the ACERWC Continental Study.

> [Adopting] a more hands-on approach involving relevant ministries in dealing with radicalization. For example, the Ministry of Education should be involved in removing teachers who are contributing to radicalization; the matter cannot be left to the schools alone.[73]

This approach ensures that socio-economic rights such as the right to education for refugee children are enjoyed. It is further reiterated by the need to use a top-to-bottom approach where the African Union

> Consider(s) setting standards for the protection and alternative care of unaccompanied, separated and refugee children. This would ensure the timely placement of these children in a protective environment to prevent them from being subject to protection abuses and to work on tracing and reunification with their families. This should involve both Governments and NGOs.[74]

The Committee in its research appreciated this move. However, it speaks to support for the refugee child from the context of children in situations of conflict.

Other important research such as the study on the mapping of children on the move in Africa has reiterated the use of the expansive mandate of the African Charter that draws inspiration from other international or regional instruments. This specific study reiterates the protection of the rights of the child under the Refugee Convention and the OAU Convention Governing Specific Aspects of Refugee Problems in Africa. It is interesting to note that the Refugee Convention (under Article 3) and the OAU Convention (under Article 4) require states to protect the rights of refugees without discrimination. A similar position is reiterated in the Revised Migration Policy Framework for Africa and Plan of Action (2018–2027), which underscores that refugee protection is a central aspect of international, regional and national efforts to protect persons fleeing persecution'.[75]

[73] Paragraph h of the Recommendations in the ACERWC Continental Study.

[74] Paragraph d of the Recommendations in the ACERWC Continental Study.

[75] AU, Revised Migration Policy Framework for Africa and Plan of Action (2018–2027) Para 6.1. This is a confirmation of other pieces of jurisprudence such as article 23(4) of the ACRWC. *Institute for Human Rights and Development in Africa (IHRDA) and Open Society Justice Initiative (on behalf of Children of Nubian Descent in Kenya) v the Government of Kenya* ACERWC Decision 002/Com/002/2009 (22 March 2011), paras 167 and 168.

While this is appreciated, there is a lack of deliberate engagement in the socio-economic rights of refugees. The reference to the need to enjoy socio-economic rights is applicable to all children and not necessarily only the refugee child.[76] A great deal more could be done to continually realign the deliberate engagement of the socio-economic rights of refugee children.

3.4 *Communications*

Few decisions from the African Children's Committee speak to the socio-economic rights of refugee children. This is partly because the communications procedure has not been used optimally concerning the Committee.[77] It suffices to note that about 16 cases have been concluded since this procedure was introduced to the Africa Children's Charter at its adoption in 1999.[78] This is a stark contrast to the African Commission's use of the same procedure, which shows that over 300 communications have been dealt with.[79] This notwithstanding, a look at a few of these decisions points to the fact that there is a growing engagement of the socio-economic rights of all children using different approaches. Two such communications, the *Nubian Children's case* and the case against *Mauritania*, are looked at. Both decisions deal with the socio-economic rights of vulnerable children.

In the *Kenyan Nubian Children's case*, the facts are as follows. Before independence, the British colonial authorities allocated land to their ancestors, in Kibera, but did not grant them British citizenship.[80] At the granting of Kenya's independence (1963), the citizenship status of the Nubians was not directly addressed, and they were consistently treated by the

[76] The report highlights this position, thus 'states have an obligation to ensure that children on the move are integrated into receiving communities in order to ensure effective realisation of their fundamental freedoms and human rights and access to socio-economic services in an equal manner to the citizens'. See also CRC, General Comment 14 (2013) on the right of the child to have his or her best interests taken as a primary consideration (art 3, para 1), 29 May 2013, UN Doc CRC/C/GC/14 (2013) para 41.

[77] See the list of communications at ACERWC 'Table of communications' acerwc.africa/table_of_communications (accessed 23 May 2022).

[78] The African Children's Charter was adopted in 1991 but came into force about 1999.

[79] See ACHPR 'Communications' https://www.achpr.org/communications (accessed 9 January 2021).

[80] Paragraphs 2–5 of *The Nubian Children's Case.*

government of Kenya as 'aliens'.[81] They argued that the refusal by the Kenyan Government to recognise the Nubians' claim to the land was closely linked with the government's denial of Nubians to Kenyan citizenship.[82] The complainants alleged a violation of articles 6(2), (3) and (4) by the state concerning the right to birth registration, and to acquire a nationality at birth, prohibition on unlawful/unfair discrimination and consequential violations to article 11(3) on equal education and article 14 on equal access to healthcare.[83]

The Committee held that the decision by the government not to grant this group citizenship led to statelessness that affected the children's realisation of their socio-economic rights such as access to healthcare and access to education.[84] In addition, the position of statelessness was an antithesis to the best interests of children.[85] The Committee reiterated the importance of recognising or granting nationality to a child to inform the enjoyment of socio-economic rights. It stated that it is important to ensure that the future of children is secured through dealing with issues of statelessness. The Committee stated that

> Statelessness is particularly devastating to children in the realisation of their socio-economic rights such as access to health care, and access to education. In sum, being stateless as a child is generally an antithesis to the best interests of children.[86]

Another critical aspect that the Committee engaged with was the use of the best interests principle as critical to providing a platform (nationality through grant or recognition) to ensure the enjoyment of socio-economic rights. While the Committee does not deal with the question of the socio-economic rights of refugees, it has indicated that all children should be able to enjoy socio-economic rights.

In the case of *Minority Rights Group International and SOS-Enclaves on behalf of Said Ould Salem and Yarg Ould Salem v Mauritania*, the minors were born to a slave class (called the Haratine) and were slaves to

[81] As above.
[82] As above.
[83] Paragraph 7 of *The Nubian Children's Case.*
[84] Paragraph 46 of *The Nubian Children's Case.*
[85] As above.
[86] Paragraph 46 of the *Nubian Children's Case.*

the El Hassine family.[87] As slaves, these minors were subjected to long hours of work, corporal punishment and poor nutrition.[88] An attempt to seek justice through the courts by the complainants was unsatisfactory.[89] While the complainants alleged the state's violation of its obligations under the African Children's Charter (article 1), the right against non-discrimination (article 3), the best interests of the child (article 4), and the right to survival and development (article 5), the African Children's Committee used these provisions to find a violation of social economic rights.[90]

Firstly, the African Children's Committee reiterated the critical place of article 1 concerning the obligation of states parties to take legislative, administrative, judicial and other measures to realise the rights of the child and protect him or her from acts of slavery and inevitable consequences.[91] This without a doubt includes steps taken to realise socio-economic rights without the use of progressive realisation.[92]

Secondly, regarding the right to education, the Committee found that children worked throughout the week without going to school, unlike their counterparts in the same household.[93] The use of deferential treatment of these children amounted to discrimination through the non-implementation of the Anti-Slavery Law.[94] Furthermore, the violation of the right to education was evident in the failure of the state to take special measures to ensure that disadvantaged children have access to education.[95]

Thirdly, concerning the violation of the right to health, the African Children's Committee found that the state violated the principle of the right to life, survival and development because it did not aid the realisation

[87] *Minority Rights Group International and SOS-Enclaves on behalf of Said Ould Salem and Yarg Ould Salem v The Government of the Republic of Mauritania* ACERWC Decision 003/2017 (15 December 2015) para 6.

[88] Paragraph 7 of the *Mauritania* case.

[89] Paragraphs 9–11 of the *Mauritania* case.

[90] Paragraph 12 of the *Mauritania* case.

[91] Paragraph 36 of the *Mauritania* case.

[92] J Sloth-Nielsen 'The protection of children's economic, social and cultural rights under the African Children's Charter' in D Chirwa and L Chenwi (eds.) *The protection of economic, social and cultural rights in Africa: International, regional and national perspectives* (2016) 155–179. See also BD Mezmur 'The African Children's Charter versus the UN Convention on the Rights of the Child: A zero-sum game?' (2008) 23 *SA Publiekreg, SA Public Law* 1.

[93] Paragraph 59 of the *Mauritania* case.

[94] Paragraphs 60–61 of the *Mauritania* case.

[95] Paragraphs 74–75 of the *Mauritania* case.

of the right to health, let alone protect the children from abuse, torture and child labour.[96] With the aid of inspiration from the UN Committee on the Rights of the Child General Comment,[97] the African Children's Committee found that the physical and physiological well-being of the child was violated because of the insensitive or abusive treatment of the child.[98] The African Children's Committee also found a violation of the right to leisure, recreation and cultural activities because it affected the holistic development of the child—an intrinsic link to the violation of the right to health.[99] In addition, the finding of the violation of the prohibition on harmful social and cultural practices under article 21 not only violated the principle of the right to life, survival and development, but also violated the right to health.

4 Where to from Here?

Despite the lack of in-depth and deliberate focus on the rights of the refugee child across the Committee's jurisprudence, the African Union continues to create awareness across states parties to take appropriate legal, social and economic measures to address harmful practices like child marriage.[100]

The normative mandate of the African Charter points to the use of the child rights-based approach that inculcates the best interests' principle, the right to life, survival and development, non-discrimination and participation of the child. A look at the emerging jurisprudence shows limited and slow-paced use of these principles and the added value in the context of the socio-economic rights of the refugee child. For instance, concerning the child rights-based principles and the socio-economic rights of refugees, there is some indulgence in the right to life, survival and development. In relation to the added value, the jurisprudence reiterates the thematic underpinnings that generally affect all children such as the definition of a child as a person below the age of 18 years, protection of the refugee child, and protection against harmful practices in the context of the jurisprudence. In some isolated instances, there is an implicit reference to

[96] Paragraph 71 of the *Mauritania* case.

[97] This was in line with art 44 of the Charter. See paras 71–73 of the *Mauritania* case.

[98] As above.

[99] Paragraphs 76–78 of the *Mauritania* case.

[100] See Joint General Comment by the ACHPR and the ACERWC on ending child marriage (n 52) note 2.

the use of the mandate of the African Children's Committee under Article 46. While it is appreciated that jurisprudence is often informed by its context and thematic approach (e.g. communications and general comments), any deliberate actions that seek to have the socio-economic protection of the rights of refugee children should start from a deconstruction of this limited engagement.

The emerging jurisprudence from the concluding observations, the general comments, research and communications points to the continued use of the child rights-based approach and the added value that the African Children's Charter brings to the table. However, there is a lack of deliberate effort to speak specifically to the socio-economic rights of refugee children. As such, the issue of refugee children and their socio-economic rights must be highlighted on all fronts: in both the normative and the emerging jurisprudence. This will give it the necessary support for the enjoyment of the socio-economic rights of the child. This should not be a preserve of only the Committee, but also other stakeholders such as civil society and states parties.

5 Conclusion and Recommendations

As widely acknowledged, the refugee child in Africa is a victim of circumstances that are not of his or her making. This chapter has evaluated the normative guidance under the auspices of the African Charter on the Rights and Welfare of the Child. It has shown that the current framework is sufficient for enforcing the socio-economic rights of the child. An engagement of the emerging jurisprudence shows various aspects that reflect on the attempts by the African Committee to continually realign its engagements with the normative guidance under the auspices of the African Charter on the Rights and Welfare of the Child. While the Committee has to a great extent lived up to the task of promoting the rights of the refugee child in Africa, a great deal can still be done to harness its strengths in streamlining its mandate. It is proposed that specific and deliberate measures by the African Committee should be geared towards encouraging states parties to take the necessary measures to ensure the immediate and urgent realisation of the rights of the refugee child. The governments have a key role to play in the use of due diligence as a tool to ensure result-oriented obligations. To this end, states should take deliberate measures to protect and promote the rights of children. This includes measures to support the education, health and sanitary living conditions of refugee children in their territories.

Bibliography

Books

P Weis (1990) *The Refugee Convention, 1951: The Travaux préparatoires analysed with a commentary* (UNHCR 1990)

Chapters in Books

Sloth-Nielsen, J 'The protection of children's economic, social and cultural rights under the African Children's Charter' (2016) in Chirwa, D & Chenwi, L (eds) *The protection of economic, social and cultural rights in Africa: International, regional and national perspectives* (Cambridge University Press 2016)

Maina, A 'Securitization of Kenya's asylum space: Origin and legal analysis of the encampment policy' in Schmidt, JD; Kimathi, L & Owiso, MO (eds) *Refugees and forced migration in the Horn and Eastern Africa: Trends, challenges and opportunities (advances in African economic, social and political development)* (Springer 2019)

Journal Articles

Jaji, R 'Social technology and refugee encampment in Kenya' (2012) 25 *Journal of Refugee Studies* 221

Mezmur, BD (2017) 'Happy 18th birthday to the African Children's Rights Charter: Not counting its days but making its days count' (2017) 1 *Africa Human Rights Yearbook* 125

Mezmur, BD 'The African Children's Charter versus the UN Convention on the Rights of the Child: A zero-sum game?' (2008) 23 *SA Publiekreg, SA Public Law* 1

Nanima, RD 'The right to education of the refugee girl affected by armed conflict in Kenya: Insights from the jurisprudence of the African Committee of Experts on the Rights and Welfare of the Child (2021) 25 *Law, Democracy and Development* 119

Case Law

Institute for Human Rights and Development in Africa (IHRDA) and Open Society Justice Initiative (on behalf of Children of Nubian Descent in Kenya) v the Government of Kenya ACERWC Decision 002/Com/002/2009 (22 March 2011)

Minister of Home Affairs v Watchenuka [2004] 1 All SA 21 (SCA)

Minority Rights Group International and SOS-Enclaves on behalf of Said Ould Salem and Yarg Ould Salem v The Government of the Republic of Mauritania ACERWC Decision 003/2017 (15 December 2015)

Statutes

Constitution of the Republic of Kenya, 2010
Constitution of the Republic of Uganda, 1995

ACERWC Documents

ACERWC 'Continental study on the impact of conflict and crises on children in Africa' (2016)
ACERWC, General Comment 2 on article 6 of the African Charter on the Rights and Welfare of the Child: The right to a name, registration at birth, and to acquire a nationality, 16 April 2014, ACERWC/GC/02 (2014)
ACERWC, General Comment 5 on state party obligations under the African Charter on the Rights and Welfare of the Child (article 1) and systems strengthening for child protection (2018a)
ACERWC, General Comment on article 30 of the African Charter on the Rights and Welfare of the Child, ACERWC/GC/01 (2013)
ACERWC Report on 'Mapping of Children on the Move within Africa' (2018b)

AU Documents

AU, Revised Migration Policy Framework for Africa and Plan of Action (2018-2027)
OAU, African Charter on Human and Peoples' Rights (Banjul Charter), 27 June 1981, CAB/LEG/67/3 rev 5, 21 ILM 58 (1982)
OAU, African Charter on the Rights and Welfare of the Child, 11 July 1990, CAB/LEG/24.9/49 (1990)
OAU, Convention Governing the Specific Aspects of Refugee Problems in Africa (OAU Convention), 10 September 1969, 1001 UNTS 45

UN Documents

UN Children's Committee, General Comment 14 (2013) on the right of the child to have his or her best interests taken as a primary consideration (art 3, para 1), 29 May 2013, UN Doc CRC/C/GC/14 (2013)
UN General Assembly, Convention Against Torture and Other Cruel, Inhuman or Degrading Treatment or Punishment, 10 December 1984, United Nations, Treaty Series, vol 1465, p 85

UN General Assembly, Convention Relating to the Status of Refugees, 28 July 1951, United Nations, Treaty Series, vol 189, p 137

UN General Assembly, International Covenant on Civil and Political Rights, 16 December 1966, United Nations, Treaty Series, vol 999, p 171

UN General Assembly, International Covenant on Economic, Social and Cultural Rights, 16 December 1966, United Nations, Treaty Series, vol 993, p 3

UNHCR 'The principle of non-refoulement as a norm of customary international law. Response to the questions posed to UNHCR by the Federal Constitutional Court of the Federal Republic of Germany in Cases 2 BvR 1938/93, 2 BvR 1953/93, 2 BvR 1954/93' (31 January 1994)

UNHCR 'Briefing note on education in Dadaab refugee camps: Version: 13 September' (2020) https://data2.unhcr.org/ar/documents/download/31025 (accessed 25 May 2022)

Concluding Recommendations

Concluding Recommendations by the African Committee of Experts on the Rights and Welfare of the Child (ACERWC) on the Republic of Kenya's Second Periodic Report on the Status of Implementation of the African Charter on the Rights and Welfare of the Child

Concluding Recommendations by the African Committee of Experts on the Rights and Welfare of the Child (ACERWC) on the Republic of Mozambique's Report on the Status of Implementation of the African Charter on the Rights and Welfare of the Child

Concluding Recommendations by the African Committee of Experts on the Rights and Welfare of the Child (ACERWC) on the Republic of South Africa Initial Report on the Status of Implementation of the African Charter on the Rights and Welfare of the Child

Internet Sources

'13.5 million children now uprooted in Africa - including those displaced by conflict, poverty and climate change *UNICEF press release* 9 February 2019 https://www.unicef.org/press-releases/135-million-children-now-uprooted-africa-including-those-displaced-conflict-poverty (accessed 3 June 2022)

ACERWC 'Table of communications' acerwc.africa/table_of_communications (accessed 23 May 2022)

ACHPR 'Communications' https://www.achpr.org/communications (accessed 9 January 2021)

Hussein, M & Haddad, M 'Visualising 70 years of refugee journeys' *Al Jazeera* 20 June 2021 https://www.aljazeera.com/news/2021/6/20/infographic-world-refugee-day-journey (accessed 9 January 2021)

Joint General Comment by the ACHPR and the ACERWC on ending child marriage (2017) https://www.right-to-education.org/sites/right-to-education.org/files/resource-attachments/ACERWC_ACHPR_joint_GC_ending_child_marriage_2017_En.pdf (accessed 7 January 2022)
Kerubo, NA 'Refugees' rights vs responsibilities: An analysis of Kenya's refugee encampment policy' (2013) https://bit.ly/2J6yOjs (accessed 23 May 2022)
UNHCR 'AfricaGlobal Trends 2020 (2021): Figures at a glance' (2021) https://www.unhcr.org/figures-at-a-glance.html (accessed 9 January 2022)
UNHCR 'States parties to the 1951 Convention relating to the Status of Refugees and the 1967 Protocol' https://www.unhcr.org/en-ie/3b73b0d63.pdf (accessed 23 May 2022)
UNHCR 'UNHCR note on the principle of non-refoulement' (November 1997) https://www.refworld.org/docid/438c6d972.html (accessed 9 January 2022)
UNICEF (2021) 'Child displacement' (2021) https://data.unicef.org/topic/child-migration-and-displacement/displacement/ (accessed 9 January 2022).

CHAPTER 7

Transnational African Child Rights Civil Society Architecture: A *Cul De Sac* Initiative Addressing the Socio-Economic Rights of Child Refugees?

Musavengana Winston Theodore Chibwana

1 Introduction

The African Union Agenda 2063 aims to build an integrated, prosperous, and peaceful Africa, driven and managed by its citizens, representing a dynamic force in the international arena. The goal of having a cohesive, collaborative continent for mutual progress and development is at the core of this agenda. Aspiration 2 of Agenda 2063 expresses clearly this desire to have a closely knit continent where there will be free movement of people. The deliberate efforts towards integration which started with regional economic communities and other regional mechanisms, beckons a

M. W. T. Chibwana (✉)
Institute of Gender and Africa Studies, University of the Free State, Bloemfontein, South Africa

E. Durojaye et al. (eds.), *Realising Socio-Economic Rights of Refugees and Asylum Seekers in Africa*, Politics of Citizenship and Migration, https://doi.org/10.1007/978-3-031-16548-1_7

growing need for a different kind of civil society. A civil society unfettered by national borders has become necessary to ensure the accountability of duty bearers.

Transnational child rights civil society networks (TCRNs) have gradually developed with a broad mandate in child rights governance and advocacy. The networks comprise national child rights networks across regions which form a conglomerate of regional child rights networks.[1] As demonstrated in the third section of this chapter, they form strategic partnerships to improve the realisation of children's rights in collaboration with other regional child rights duty bearers such as the African Committee of Experts on the Rights and Welfare of the Child (ACERWC). This chapter gives an overview of the socio-economic rights of the African refugee child. It uses the constructivist approach to enunciate the challenges that child refugees face.

2 Constructivism, Refugees, and Transnational Child Rights Civil Society

'Constructivism' envisages reality as dynamic and subjective, based on historical and cultural context.[2] Rouke further notes that constructivism focuses on the peculiarity of social values, norms, and assumptions in rationalising social and political happenings. This indicated the need for stakeholders to support refugees and asylum seekers, based on the availability of resources. While this points to the progressive realisation of socio-economic rights in the general dispensation, it does not cater to the immediate realisation of socio-economic rights under the ACRWC.[3] However, it suffices to note that 'individuals or states cannot be separated from a context of normative meaning which shapes who they are and the possibilities available to them'.[4] In addition to shaping possibilities in their midst, all stakeholders are (by implication) obligated to improve the lives of the people around them. To this end, stakeholders are obligated under

[1] In the context of this essay, 'regional' refers to the five regions of Africa namely West Africa, Southern Africa, Central Africa, Eastern Africa, and Northern Africa.

[2] L Rourke et al. 'Assessing social presence in asynchronous text-based computer conferencing' (2001) 14 *Journal of Distance Education* 17.

[3] See discussion above in Sect. 2.

[4] KM Fierke 'Constructivism' in T Dunne, M Kurki & S Smith *International relations theories: Discipline and diversity* (2007) 4, 173.

international law to improve the status of the child refugee in our communities.

The scope of constructivism includes defined structures such as states, multinational institutions, international civil societies, alliances, or international institutions that bring together people from different backgrounds to construct their values and norms, based on the content of the human nature of the historical, cultural, and political forms of the societies that they originate from. This alludes to a global village that embraces persons from various backgrounds regardless of their status. Constructivism provides for the expression of peculiarities in history, culture, and political settings to find expression in the institutions that go beyond their borders as they interact with the rest of the world. The underlying notion is that actors have distinct identities shaped by the cultural, social, political, and material circumstances in which they are embedded.

One of the criticisms of constructivism is that it has been primarily state-centric, neglecting other forms of agency, such as civil society. Price echoed this sentiment when he noted the following

> But focusing solely on the state as an actor diverts attention from other sources of agency and socialization, sources that have been particularly important in generating norms in a variety of issue areas on the global agenda.[5]

The use of constructivism to understand the agency of the transnational civil society provides the flexibility that is needed to appreciate how the global and regional social, cultural, and political processes have shaped this kind of civil society on the continent. In this chapter, constructivism assists in the comprehension of global and regional vicissitudes that directly or implicitly shape the civil society landscape on the continent. Constructivism also helps to critically analyse processes with which the author of this chapter was profoundly involved in during the formation and establishment of some of the TCRNs in Africa. As a result, the author reflects upon some of the challenges encountered regarding the sustainability of an initiative started with counterparts in the child rights sector of the continent. The following section deconstructs the conceptual nuances of TCRNs in Africa.

[5] R Price 'Reversing the gun sights: transnational civil society targets land mines' (1998) 52 *International Organization* 613.

2.1 Conceptualising Transnational Civil Society Networks

The concept of 'civil society' is a normative issue and is ideal within any society. Its conceptualisation can be traced to the evolution of the state.[6] Its direct equivalent in Latin is *societas civilis* and a close equivalent in ancient Greek *politike koinona*.[7] The latter referred to a 'political society', with active citizens shaping institutions and policies. It was a law-governed society in which the law was seen as the expression of public virtue, the Aristotelian 'good life'.[8] Gramsci popularised the term 'civil society', and he considered it an 'ensemble of private interests' located somewhere between the 'economic structure' and the 'super-structure'. By this he meant public life and the state.[9] In other words, civil society is the process through which individuals negotiate, argue, struggle against, or agree with each other and the centres of political and economic authority. Individuals can act publicly through voluntary associations, movements, parties, and unions.[10] Hitherto, the term has been broadly used to refer to an independent, mission-driven, non-profit, voluntary citizens' group. Further, civil society has been defined as a sphere of ideas, shared values, and the building of institutions, organisations, networks, and individuals between the family, the state, and the market.[11] Seckinelgin submits that the term has been used recently to reflect an attempt to bring people into the development process in Africa, Asia, and elsewhere.[12] In Africa, civil society denotes an aspirational formation enabling people to act for themselves for desired policy outcomes.[13]

The abovementioned conceptualisation of civil society applies mainly to national jurisdictions. Over the years, civil society has evolved into transnational groups. The term 'transnational' is used in consonance with

[6] J Hearn 'The "uses and abuses" of civil society in Africa' (2001) 28 *Review of African Political Economy* 43.

[7] M Church et al. 'Participation, relationships and dynamic change: New thinking on evaluating the work of international networks' (2002), generally.

[8] IG Shivji *Silences in NGO discourse: The role and future of NGOs in Africa* (2008).

[9] A Mafeje 'Democracy, civil society and governance in Africa' in *Proceedings of the Second DPMF Annual Conference on Democracy, Civil Society and Governance in Africa II* (1998) 7–10.

[10] M Kaldor 'The idea of global civil society' *International affairs* (2003) 79583.

[11] As above.

[12] H Seckinelgin 'Civil society as a metaphor for western liberalism' (2002) 16 *Global society* 357.

[13] As above.

Risse-Kappen's reference to interactions across national boundaries for non-state agents in pursuit of the desired policy outcome that is not bound by a state's territorial and institutional spaces.[14]

There are several reasons warranting the need for transnational civil society. They have the soft power to pressurise governments into meeting their obligations to all persons in their geographical territories. Through appeals to international authorities, civil societies can indirectly create political platforms and exert pressure on national governments. The efforts of civil society can also have what is termed the 'boomerang effect'. This means that civil society can appeal to the international community instead of directly addressing their plight or complaint to governments. By doing so, pressure may be put on a state party to respect their obligations in terms of the international instruments which they ratified or acceded to.[15] For child rights civil society, the point of convergence is the UNCRC, its Optional Protocols, and General Comments at the international level. The ACRWC is the coalescing point for transnational child rights civil society at the continental level.

Civil society engages beyond its borders through networks and coalitions, in the same way that child rights issues traverse borders within regions. This is due to many commonalities amongst countries within the same region, which therefore warrant transnational responses in dealing with the issues. These issues include inter alia response to scourges like Ebola, child marriages, recruitment and use of children in conflict situations, addressing terrorism, responding to statelessness, and attending to bad governance that jeopardises the fulfilment of children's rights. The symbiotic relationship between transnational civil societies and refugees is the interface between peoples across borders. Unfortunately, this interface across various borders carries a negative prospect of cross-border child rights violations like child trafficking and unregulated migration, which may result in the exploitation of children. At the heart of such violations, is the perennial lack of data since most of the violations happen tacitly. The violations inhibit any enjoyment of critical socio-economic rights such as the right to education, health, and privacy.

[14] T Risse-Kappen *Bringing transnational relations back in non-state actors, domestic structures and international institutions* (2009). See interesting insights in RD Lipschutz & J Mayer *Global civil society and global environmental governance: The politics of nature from place to planet* (1996).

[15] Interesting observations in M Keck & K Sikkink *Activists beyond borders* (1998).

3 Setting the Scene: The Refugee Child in Africa

Statistics indicate that Africa is home to over 50 percent of the world's refugees. This is evident from the reported numbers of refugees received by some African countries. Uganda has 1,421,133 refugees which makes it the leading refugee host, followed by Sudan with 1,040,308, Ethiopia with 800,464, the Democratic Republic of Congo with 490,243, and Chad with 478,664.[16] A closer look at these figures reveals that nearly 50 percent of these numbers are children.[17] As of February 2019, another report by UNICEF indicated that approximately 13,500,000 children (including those displaced by conflict, poverty, and climate change) have moved from one territory to another.[18] This is a very high number punctuated by the fact that it does not include refugees on the other continents of the world.

Children can be economic refugees, who move to a different jurisdiction in search of economic activities.[19] Therefore, in implementing the Agenda 2063 flagship programme of the Continental Free Trade Area, place of refugees in the development agenda should deliberately be dealt with.[20]

3.1 Socio-Economic Rights Challenges of the Refugee Child

Refugee children face various rights violations, such as unlawful military recruitment into armed forces and groups, sexual exploitation and abuse,

[16] Statista 'African countries with the most refugees as of 2020' https://bit.ly/3Mv4YAo (accessed 19 April 2022).

[17] UNICEF 'Child displacement' (September 2021) https://bit.ly/3yQ0kcP (accessed 23 May 2022).

[18] '13.5 million children now uprooted in Africa – Including those displaced by conflict, poverty and climate change' *UNICEF press release* 9 February 2019 https://www.unicef.org/press-releases/135-million-children-now-uprooted-africa-including-those-displaced-conflict-poverty (accessed 25 March 2022).

[19] OHCHR *The economic, social and cultural rights of migrants in an irregular situation* (2014) https://www.ohchr.org/Documents/Publications/HR-PUB-14-1_en.pdf (accessed 23 May 2022).

[20] IOM & AUC *Africa Migration Report: Challenging the narrative* (2019) 47.

and other grave violations.[21] Due to their vulnerability, refugee children should be afforded protection and assistance to find durable solutions.[22] More than half of the refugee population in Africa are children.[23] Conflicts create emergency conditions that disrupt family and community ecosystems and cause acute shortages of resources. This significantly affects the physical and psychological well-being of refugee children. The nature of conflicts is such that children are often the first and most frequent victims of violence, disease, and malnutrition. These conditions lead to population displacement and the refugee status.[24] The entire experience affects children's psychosocial and spiritual well-being, leaving indelible damage on the life of these children. In some cases, the emergency responses to the refugee challenges homogenise children with the rest of the population due to a lack of awareness of the fact that child refugees might have their own peculiar needs.

3.2 Normative Guidance on the Protection of the Refugee Child

Refugees are protected under both international and regional/continental law. Under international law, the 1951 Convention Relating to the Status of Refugees (Refugee Convention) is the main instrument.[25] The instrument defines 'persecution' based on five grounds: religion, race, nationality, membership in a particular social group, and political opinion.[26] The Refugee Convention has maintained this list for over seventy years.

[21] UN General Assembly, Protection and assistance to unaccompanied and separated refugee children: Report of the Secretary-General, 7 September 2001, UN Doc A/56/333 (2001) para 6. See also V LeBlanc 'Implementation of the 1989 Convention on the Right of the Child and the work of the United Nations High Commissioner for Refugees' in E Verhellen (ed) *Understanding children's rights: Collected papers presented at the First International Interdisciplinary Course on Children's Rights* (1996) 404, who notes that '[t]hey are a group of children most likely to lack survival amenities and to have their basic rights violated. When resources are scarce, they are the first to die too'.

[22] T Kaime 'The protection of refugee children under the African human rights system: Finding durable solutions in international law' in J Sloth-Nielsen (ed) *Children's rights in Africa: A legal perspective* (2008) 183–197.

[23] UNHCR 'Refugee children: Guidelines on protection and care' https://www.unhcr.org/3b84c6c67.pdf (accessed 3 June 2022).

[24] As above.

[25] The UN General Assembly, Convention Relating to the Status of Refugees, 28 July 1951, United Nations, Treaty Series, vol 189, p 137 (Refugee Convention).

[26] Article 1(A)(2) of the Refugee Convention.

Protection under the Refugee Convention confirms that these grounds or criteria are consistent with other instruments. It should be noted that the existence of the Refugee Convention has created some form of uniformity in promoting or protecting the rights of refugees. These include the right to religion and religious education,[27] public education,[28] health,[29] and housing among others.[30] Similar instruments on the regional level include the OAU Convention Governing the Specific Aspects of Refugee Problems in Africa.[31]

Other international instruments also provide protection to refugees. Such protection includes guidance on the protection of the rights of all persons without discrimination on account of their status. The enjoyment of civil and political rights under the International Covenant on Civil and Political Rights[32]; the International Covenant on Economic, Social, and Cultural Rights[33]; the African Charter on Human and Peoples' Rights,[34] and regarding children, the African Charter on the Rights and Welfare of the Child (ACRWC) afford protection.[35]

The ACRWC does not distinguish between civil and political rights on the one hand and socio-economic rights on the other.[36] This is a departure from the international law position on socio-economic rights that calls on states to progressively realise socio-economic rights.[37] The International Covenant on Economic, Social and Cultural Rights requires states

[27] Article 4 of the Refugee Convention.

[28] Article 22 of the Refugee Convention.

[29] Article 23 of the Refugee Convention.

[30] Article 21 of the Refugee Convention.

[31] OAU, Convention Governing the Specific Aspects of Refugee Problems in Africa (OAU Convention), 10 September 1969, 1001 UNTS 45 https://bit.ly/3dCwX1P (accessed 9 December 2021).

[32] Articles 4(1) and 26 of the UN General Assembly, International Covenant on Civil and Political Rights, 16 December 1966, United Nations, Treaty Series, vol 999, p 171 (ICCPR).

[33] Articles 2(2) and 10(3) of the ICCPR.

[34] Article 28 of the OAU, African Charter on Human and Peoples' Rights (Banjul Charter), 27 June 1981, CAB/LEG/67/3 rev 5, 21 ILM 58 (1982).

[35] Article 3 of the OAU, African Charter on the Rights and Welfare of the Child, 11 July 1990, CAB/LEG/24.9/49 (1990).

[36] MW Chibwana 'Towards a transformative child rights discourse in Africa: A reflexive study' (2021) African *Human Rights Law Journal, 21(1), 126–148.*

[37] JG Akech 'Exacerbated inequalities: Implications of COVID-19 for the socio-economic rights of women and children in South Sudan' (2020) 20 *African Human Rights Law Journal* 584.

> [I]ndividually and through international assistance and co-operation, especially economic and technical, to the maximum of its available resources, to achieve progressively the full realization of the rights recognized in the present Covenant by all appropriate means, including particularly the adoption of legislative measures.[38]

This has been encapsulated in the General Comment of the Committee on Economic, Social and Cultural Rights, which recommends that states use legislative, administrative, financial, educational, and social measures to realise socio-economic rights.[39]

In the case of the ACRWC, the Committee obliges states to:

> Recognize the rights, freedoms and duties enshrined in this Charter and [to] undertake the necessary steps, following their constitutional processes and with the provisions of the Charter, to adopt such legislative and other measures as may be necessary to give effect to the provisions of this Charter.[40]

This indicates that all rights under the ACRWC must be accorded the same degree of emphasis and weight, regardless of their nature.[41] Secondly, on this basis, the necessary steps taken by the state should flow from the grund norm, usually the national constitutions, and trickle down to the various principles and subsidiary legislation, policies, and administrative practices. Thirdly, the measures which the state takes must be positively qualified through the extent to which they successfully ensure the enjoyment of the rights under the ACRWC.

Article 23 of the ACRWC provides critical normative guidance on promoting and protecting the rights of the refugee child. While various principles are evident, six stand out. First, the states parties' measures must be tailored to the refugee child's challenges. This is the spirit of the law in 'appropriate measures' mentioned in the article.[42] Secondly, these

[38] Article 2(1) of the UN General Assembly, International Covenant on Economic, Social and Cultural Rights, 16 December 1966, United Nations, Treaty Series, vol 993, p 3.

[39] Paragraphs 5 and 7 of the UN Committee on Economic, Social and Cultural Rights (CESCR), General Comment 3: The nature of states parties' obligations (Art 2, Para 1, of the Covenant), 14 December 1990, UN Doc E/1991/23 (1990).

[40] Art 1(1) and (2) of the ACRWC.

[41] ACERWC, General Comment 5 on state party obligations under the African Charter on the Rights and Welfare of the Child (article 1) and systems strengthening for child protection (2018).

[42] Article 23(1).

measures must be applied regardless of the status of the impugned child. Thus, the measures should extend to all situations regardless of whether the child is unaccompanied or accompanied by parents, legal guardians, or close relatives.[43] Thirdly, this protection is measured by the extent to which the successful attempt embraces human rights or humanitarian law. This wording is also elucidated in article 22 of the ACRWC, which requires that the protection of a child affected by armed conflict should either emerge from human rights law or humanitarian law, depending on the option that offers the best protection for the rights of the child.[44] Fourthly, added value for the protection of the refugee child is in the call for cooperation between the states and international organisations that offer protection and assistance to the child so that he or she can trace and be reunited with the family.[45] It is this call that brings into contention the role of TCRNs in response to addressing the plight of child refugees.

3.3 Locating the Place of TCRNs in Addressing Child Refugees' Rights

Whilst regional civil society has existed for a long time on the continent, the 'regionality' of this civil society was primarily based on the existence of programmes in the region's different countries.[46] In most instances, the interventions from one country to another were not interconnected. Little cross-border programming existed. What is different now is that with increased regional and continental cohesion through migration, there is a need for transnational interventions to address cross-border violations that may take place as the borders are opening up with high volumes of goods and services and people moving.

A classic example of a response to migration that demonstrates the need for transnational interventions for unaccompanied minors is offered in what follows hereafter. A 2015 report by the United Nations High Commission for Refugees noted an estimated 65,000 refugees in South Africa. These refugees came from countries such as the Democratic

[43] As above.

[44] As such, the protection of a refugee child who is affected by armed conflict should embrace the best interests of the child on the basis of both human rights and humanitarian law.

[45] Article 23(2)–(3).

[46] F Söderbaum 'Regionalisation and civil society: The case of Southern Africa' (2007) 12 *New Political Economy* 319.

Republic of Congo, Somalia, Burundi, Ethiopia, and Zimbabwe.[47] The report further noted that an estimated 50 percent of these refugees were children, some of whom had entered the country unaccompanied. Appreciating the role of non-governmental organisations and/or civil society organisations in supporting vulnerable populations is important. In some countries, these organisations remind states about their obligations in international law. In South Africa, for example, Scalabrini Centre of Cape Town does charity work and litigation to support refugees, asylum seekers, and vulnerable communities.[48] Islamic Relief South Africa is part of a large NGO that empowers communities to strengthen their resilience against calamities and disasters.[49] Through their work, these organisations illustrate the transnational nature of their services that impact the status of a foreigner (as a refugee or asylum seeker). Closely related is the fact that their activities are informed by thematic engagement. For instance, while Scalabrini Centre deals with vulnerable communities, Islamic Relief South Africa leans towards humanitarian support to communities generally.[50] The lack of sustainability remains a challenge, especially when the operations for a given project end. The project-orientated nature of the work of these organisations results in a lack of sustainability insofar as the promotion and protection of child refugees and asylum seekers are concerned. When a project ends it is highly likely that the protection of rights it extended, will end too.

One of the challenges in dealing with cross-border issues is the reliability of the data since countries may not have similar disaggregation criteria. As a result, Vearey and Nunez raised caution on the migration of

[47] UNHCR Briefing Notes 'Seven factors behind movement of Syrian refugees to Europe' (25 September 2015) http://www.unhcr.org/560523f26.html (accessed 19 September 2021).

[48] Scalabrini Centre https://www.scalabrini.org.za (accessed 25 May 2022). Some of the notable cases involving refugees where Scalabrini has been involved include: *Scalabrini Centre, Cape Town v Minister of Home Affairs* 2013 (3) SA 531 (WCC); *Scalabrini Centre, Cape Town v Minister of Home Affairs* 2018 (4) SA 125 (SCA); *Scalabrini Centre of Cape Town and Another v Minister of Social Development* 2021 (1) SA 553 (GP).

[49] Islamic Relief South Africa https://www.islamic-relief.org.za/about-us/ (accessed 25 April 2022).

[50] See Scalabrini Centre (n 36) and Islamic Relief South Africa (n 37).

unaccompanied children.[51] This is one example of a transnational issue that one country will not solve. Meanwhile, classical civil societies may not be able to adequately respond to such an issue as it has many nuances which may be beyond their scope. Such a realisation has prompted the emergence of transnational networks designed to respond to the emerging issues of cross-border child rights violations.

TCRNs are one such avenue to respond to pan-African and regional developmental vicissitudes of the continent.[52] Whilst these networks are important in addressing cross-border child rights violations and issues of commonality in their respective regions, their sustainability is not guaranteed.[53] This is primarily because most of the funding for the child rights governance work comes from Western countries. Meanwhile, these countries have been undergoing political changes, and may therefore rather prioritise projects and interventions that address immediate national interests. With the dwindling financial support from the West, civil society on the African continent has to think innovatively and explore new ways of ensuring sustainability. To respond to the exogenous challenges, this chapter provides some ideas that civil societies, especially TCRNs, can use to mitigate their sustainability challenges as they continue their accountability work on child rights. The chapter uses three sections to address the foregoing challenges. The first section provides a snapshot historiography of civil society whilst linking it to the emergence of TCRNs on the African continent. This section also explores the value addition that transnational networks bring in addressing the rights of child refugees. The second section delves into the situation of child refugees on the continent and the crucial role that TCRNs play in the fulfilment of their rights. The last section presents possible opportunities which civil society may embrace and exploit to ensure sustainability.

At this juncture is necessary to provide a few caveats: first, it is a deliberate approach to focus on TCRNs working precisely on child rights governance broadly and child refugees in particular. The reason for focusing on

[51] J Vearey & L Nunez 'Towards improving forced migrant access to health and psychosocial rights in urban South Africa - A focus on Johannesburg' (2011). Consortium For Refugees and Migrants in South Africa 'Protecting refugees, asylum seekers and immigrants in South Africa' (2010).

[52] D Spini 'Civil society and the democratisation of global public space' in D Armstrong et al. (eds) *Civil society and international governance: The role of non-state actors in global and regional regulatory frameworks* (2010) 18.

[53] Spini (n 40) 16.

this typology of networks is that they have not enjoyed substantial academic interest, as is evidenced by the limited scholarly literature on such networks on the African continent. Indeed, most of the issues which the chapter raises can apply to other forms of civil societies on the African continent. The second caveat is that the author of this chapter has been profoundly involved in forming and establishing these networks, which coordinate child rights advocacy on the African continent. The author thus shares some ontological reflections on the issues which he grappled with as a leader because such issues are also raised in this chapter and they affect the sustainability of TCRNs. The last caveat is that some of the sustainability strategies proposed might have been tested by using forms of civil societies which do not exist on the African continent. As such, the suggested sustainability mechanisms are prognostic since these emerging networks are yet to embrace and exploit them.

4 Attention to Child Refugees? The Value Proposition of Transnational Networks

The creation of effective child rights transnational networks succour in pushing the regional child rights agenda effectively with regional duty bearers such as the ACERWC, regional economic communities, and other regional mechanisms.[54] Their effectiveness in the context of this conversation requires finding the extent to which these networks deal with the plight of refugee children. This is because belonging to a transnational network brings a feeling of empowerment through its strength of network ties and its belief system.[55] Empowerment involves the extent to which rights are enjoyed or remedied in case of human rights violations.[56] For a transnational network to empower individuals (such as children for this matter), it is expected that they have a fair understanding of the contextual

[54] There are eight regional economic communities and other regional mechanisms namely Southern Africa Development Community (SADC), East African Community (EAC), Arab Maghreb Union (UMA), Common Market for Eastern and Southern Africa (COMESA), Community of Sahel-Saharan States (CEN-SAD), Economic Community of Central African States (ECCAS), Economic Community of West African States (ECOWAS), and Intergovernmental Authority on Development (IGAD).

[55] NS Glick & A Çağlar 'Towards a comparative theory of locality in migration studies: Migrant incorporation and city scale' (2009) 35 *Journal of Ethnic and Migration Studies* 177.

[56] This may be covered in the institutional plans of the transnational networks, which may form part of the implementation.

picture of the children in the host country from the national to the regional or provincial level like towns and cities where most of the movement and settlement occurs.[57] For instance, a recent study by the ACERWC on Children on the Move reveals various reasons such as armed conflict and economic reasons.[58] While the study is scant on the role of transnational networks, it offers an instructive source for transnational networks to use to learn more about the contextual issues of refugee children for purposes of deliberate and intended advocacy and support programmes.

While it is appreciated that TCRNs also initiate, consolidate, and sustain democratic social change through citizen participation, it is important to evaluate the participation of other vulnerable groups such as refugee children.[59] This creates pathways that speak to the improvement in the enjoyment of the rights and welfare of children. There are three pertinent advantages of engaging with regional duty bearers through TCRNs on child rights advocacy. First, TCRNs enable the members to amplify their voices to achieve greater influence with both national and regional child rights duty bearers. As such, network members collectively realise what ordinarily, the individual members would not be able to achieve if they work alone. To this end, vulnerable groups such as refugee children are given a platform and empowered to be heard. Secondly, by encapsulating a plethora of players and an expansive range of social identities, TCRNs tend to lend legitimacy and credibility to child rights organisations with governments, critical constituencies, and the general public. This creates a stronger advocacy base that inculcates various players in the context of refugee children. Since transnational networks typically involve their members in some form of joint communication, decision-making, and governance, they can also serve as positive models of democratic forms of organisation.[60] Thirdly, in the context of shrinking civic space where individual child rights organisations come under tough scrutiny or even harassment by government security forces, increased strength comes in numbers.[61] Being a member of a larger network can serve to protect

[57] Glick & Çağlar (n 57). See also R Snyder 'Scaling down: The subnational comparative method' (2001) 36 *Studies in Comparative International Development* 93.

[58] ACERWC 'Mapping children on the move' (2019) https://www.acerwc.africa/mapping-children-on-the-move/ (accessed 13 May 2022).

[59] See AA Muñoz 'Transnational and domestic processes in the definition of human rights policies in Mexico' (2009) 31 *Human Right Quarterly* 35.

[60] AK Singh & R Stevens *Networking: Towards a better tomorrow* (2007).

[61] As above.

national civil society in harsh contexts by making them less isolated and vulnerable. This is mainly important when dealing with polemical advocacy issues which may be considered to be antagonistic to the state.

5 Making the Nexus: Transnational Child Rights Networks, Sustainability, and Socio-Economic Rights

Based on the foregoing platform on value proposition, an appreciation of the link between the transnational networks and their value proposition cannot be complete if the trinity (addition of the place of socio-economic rights) is not done. There is evidence across Africa that points to the role of these networks in fighting for children's rights—and more importantly in the field of socio-economic rights. A look at some of the transnational networks across Africa follows, and their role in advocating for the enjoyment of the socio-economic rights of the refugee child, is questioned. This is based on the position that the realisation of socio-economic rights in the context of the African Children's Charter requires immediacy rather than progressiveness, which forms the entry point for the relevance of transnational networks.

5.1 *Transnational Child Rights Civil Society Architecture*

Since 2009, there have been new TCRNs on the continent of Africa that did not exist before. The broad mandate of these networks has been mainly child rights governance advocacy. The TCRNs are composed of national child rights networks and coalitions that coalesce at the regional level to form a regional child rights network.[62] At the Pan-African level, there is the Civil Society Forum on the African Charter on the Rights and Welfare of the Child (hereinafter the CSO Forum) which was formed in 2009.[63] The CSO Forum has been designed as a framework for a strategic partnership aimed at improving children's rights in Africa, engaging with the African Committee of Experts on the Rights and Welfare of the Child (ACERWC) in its mandate to promote and protect the rights of children.[64]

[62] In the context of this essay, 'regional' refers to the general five regions of Africa namely West Africa, Southern Africa, Central Africa, Eastern Africa, and Northern Africa.

[63] Children Forum https://childrencsoforum.africa/ (accessed 15 May 2022).

[64] As above.

The network also provides a platform for partnership, networking, and advocacy on the rights and welfare of children in Africa.[65] The CSO Forum brings together regional child rights networks and like-minded institutions.[66] The founding leadership developed a philosophy that made the Forum rely on the strength of the regional child rights networks.[67] These regional networks also rely on the strength of national child rights networks and coalitions.[68] The challenge to this is the question of to what extent the CSO Forum deliberately deals with issues concerning children's socio-economic rights. A consideration of their remarks over the past five years at the various sessions of the ACERWC reveals much in terms of advocacy for children's rights ranging from children affected by armed conflict, and child marriages among others.[69]

For Southern Africa, the Child Rights Network for Southern Africa (CRNSA) was established in 2012, to galvanise child rights advocacy starting with Southern Africa up to the continental level.[70] CRNSA also pitched its work differently than other networks, by primarily focusing on child rights governance. This clarity of purpose and niche made CRNSA a model which was replicated in other regions. Following the CRNSA template, East African child rights civil society formed the East Africa Child Rights Network (EACRN) in 2014 and Central Africa introduced the Network for the Rights of the Child in Central Africa (REDEAC) in 2018.[71] North Africa has not been able to establish such a network due to geopolitical dynamics in the region and simple logistical challenges for the CSO Forum leadership to provide necessary support. West Africa has had a vibrant network, but it became riddled with governance challenges. This approach imbibes the use of child participation in matters that affect them regardless of their environments.

[65] A above.

[66] As above.

[67] As above.

[68] As above.

[69] See ACERWC 'State reports' https://reporting.acerwc.africa/ (accessed 15 May 2022).

[70] The network was established in 2012 to improve child rights governance in Southern Africa. With a mandate to strengthen country child rights networks that protect and promote the rights of children to ensure appropriate child development and child participation in decisions that affect them. See Child Rights Network for Southern Africa (CRNSA) https://bit.ly/3lcXTsB (15 May 2022).

[71] J Kaberi & E Foley 'Leave no child behind: A 12th CSO Forum Conversation, Bamako, Mali 21–23, April, 2018' (2018) https://childrencsoforum.africa/wp-content/uploads/2020/11/Copy-of-CSO-Forum-Report-Final-1.pdf (accessed 15 May 2022).

The CSO Forum at the Pan-African level derives its legitimacy and credibility from the strength of the regional networks. Meanwhile, the regional networks also rely on national networks.[72] As such, the whole ecosystem of TCRNs relies on one another for content, credibility, and legitimacy.[73] However, the national networks are at the base of this structure, as the foundational building blocks of the regional networks. It is of mutual interest that the national child rights networks observe good corporate governance and operate above board.[74] If they are found in contravention of good corporate governance standards, they will be discredited by their respective governments, which will compromise the legitimacy and credibility of the whole ecosystem. As such, the leadership of the CSO Forum and regional networks place a premium on ensuring that national civil societies are not found wanting due to flouting good corporate governance and misappropriation of funds, issues which the same civil societies will be lobbying governments to correct.[75] Of course in some contexts, civic space is shrinking, hence there is a need for civil societies to operate beyond reproach themselves. A 2019 report of the CSO Forum indicated a critical sense of direction towards dealing with issues of statelessness, refugees, and durable solutions. The socio-economic rights of the child refugee were tackled, but not deliberately to a great degree.[76]

5.2 *The Question of Sustainability*

It is acknowledged that alluding to the sustainability of transnational networks in a discussion that is supposed to consider how they may aid the improvement of the welfare of the refugee child is to a great extent 'misplaced'. However, without prejudice to the foregoing, it is noted that the

[72] N Gabriel 'The millennium development goals: Towards a civil society perspective on reframing poverty reduction strategies in Southern Africa' Paper presented at the Southern Africa MDGs Forum, Johannesburg (July 2003) 2–4.

[73] M Chibwana 'Status of national child rights networks in southern Africa' Commissioned by the Child Rights Network for Southern Africa (2018) 17 https://bit.ly/3lwzvT1 (accessed 23 May 2022).

[74] Chibwana (n 72) 11.

[75] This remains a challenge that often affects the sustainability of the TRCNs.

[76] See 'Report of the Civil Society Forum on year of refugees, returnees and internally displaced people: Towards durable solutions to forced displacement in Africa, following proceedings on 12 October 2019'. https://www.chr.up.ac.za/images/researchunits/dce/resources/CIVIL_SOCIETY_FORUM_ON_YEAR_OF_REFUGEES_REPORT.pdf (accessed 25 March 2022).

non-existence of these TCRNs affects the possible traction towards a transnational approach by conglomerates of CSOs whose agenda is to advocate for the rights and welfare of the impugned child. This discussion engages the position of sustainability from the position of placing the refugee child at the centre of the interventions by the African refugee child. Against this background, this chapter now turns to the question of sustainability.

The sustainability of TCRNs remains an existential challenge for many reasons.[77] At its core, the sustainability of child rights civil society in Africa is affected mainly by the unavailability of predictable and long-term funding.[78] Currently, the funding of transnational child rights civil society is characterised by short-term small grants, making it difficult to create formidable momentum in addressing both cross-border child rights violations and issues of commonality demanding a regional response.[79] This is majorly due to the lack of specific niche areas of confluence that transnational organisations fail to engage in.[80] It is argued that grappling with a specific African problem such as child refugees always remains a platform on which other intricate concerns such as education, health, human trafficking, and human smuggling can still be engaged in from the central position of a refugee child. This would create opportunities for engagement with various organisations and stakeholders who are like-minded in dealing with a secondary thematic approach informed by the child refugee platform as the dominant or primary theme.[81]

Another factor that militates against the durability of TCRNs is that its leadership is preoccupied with finding resources instead of investing its time in coming up with conceptually grounded, value-driven strategies

[77] G Francia & J Gillett-Swan 'Special Issue: Children's rights from a sustainability perspective: The UNCRC in Dialogue with Agenda 2030' (2021) 10 *Social Sciences* https://www.mdpi.com/journal/socsci/special_issues/children_rights_sustainability (accessed 23 May 2022).

[78] N Banks, D Hulme & M Edwards 'NGOs, states, and donors revisited: Still too close for comfort?' (2015) 66 *World Development* 707.

[79] As above.

[80] A look at the reports of the African Committee on the Rights and Welfare of the child indicates that the CSO Forum largely contributes to unfolding thematic issues, without a latch on a specific aspect. While this is a noteworthy approach, there is a lack of consistency in what the CSO Forum engages in other than generally contributing to the agenda of the Committee as and when the thematic need arises.

[81] The dominant thematic position would be child refugees and any other thematic aspect that arises is secondary.

that would make civil society more effective in playing its role.[82] Oftentimes, in various circles, the stakeholders forget that the child is the 'final user' of all engagements by organisations that are aligned to the spirit and purpose of the African Charter on the Rights and Welfare of the Child. Any other perspective that distracts an organisation from the goal to have an Africa fit for children and children fit for Africa, will inevitably make it lose sight of the bigger picture. Disputes about resources and funding will result in the unsustainability of TCRNs.

Transnational child rights civil societies face peculiar challenges compared to national civil society organisations. Generally, international donors prefer local initiatives where there may be quick wins because project cycles are an average of three to five years. Meanwhile, transnational civil society networks are not able to demonstrate the impact of ratification, the promulgation of law, or ensure adherence by a state party to its obligations because there are many variables. Funding partners are 'results' orientated and often choose to support initiatives that yield concrete outcomes (such as passing of law or a state's ratification of an instrument) overtime as already mentioned. Funders are reluctant to fund initiatives which only contribute to solutions. Transnational governance initiatives do not have a 'direct reach' per se, which most funding partners would want to broadcast on their website to demonstrate their impact. High networth individuals who are interested in development often prefer programmes that establish tangible goals such as the building of schools, the number of children on the scholarship programmes, and so forth. Transnational child rights governance initiatives are not able to achieve any of the aforesaid.

5.3 *Engaging SERs*

As indicated earlier, the ACRWC does not distinguish between civil and political rights on the one hand and socio-economic rights on the other hand.[83] The foregoing identification of the critical roles of the TCRNs in light of their value addition creates an opportunity to identify synergies across the spectrum that aids the enjoyment of the socio-economic rights of the refugee child.

[82] This unfortunate approach has led to the breakup of various transnational initiatives.

[83] M Chibwana 'Transformative child rights advocacy: An ergonomic conceptual framework' (2021) 29 *The International Journal of Children's Rights* 541.

The ACRWC's normative recognition of the need for immediacy in realising socio-economic rights offers the TCRNs an opportunity to deliberately guide the conversation. There is an opportunity for the use of the available soft power to pressurize states parties to urgently meet their socio-economic rights obligations. Appeals to international authorities may increase pressure on national governments through the 'boomerang effect' that leads states parties to uphold their obligations. In the context of the socio-economic rights of refugees, the discussions must start with identifying the plight of the refugee child as part of the national community in any country.[84] This approach will add traction to the protection of the refugee child.[85]

The plans of regional civil society must move beyond the existence of programmes in the region's different countries,[86] to cross-border programming that inculcates the enjoyment of socio-economic rights. Various initiatives such as Agenda 2063 and 2040, the SDG Agenda 2030 call for increased continental interventions to address cross-border human rights issues. For instance, the call for Africa to be an economic powerhouse by 2063 requires nuanced approaches that protect all youths and children regardless of their immigration status. In the same vein, the SDG Agenda has recognised the refugee gap and embraced SDG 10.7.4. At its core, SDG 10 calls for a reduction in inequality within and among countries, with Goal 7 requiring the facilitation of orderly, safe, regular, and responsible migration and mobility of people, through the implementation of planned and well-managed migration policies.[87] Target 10.7.4 addresses the issue of refugees by inquiring into the proportion of the population who are refugees, by country of origin.[88] This initiative offers the transnational rights networks an entry point to pose questions about the enjoyment of the rights of refugees in the grand scheme of things, followed by

[84] States use various approaches to refugee populations such as encampment and integration. A discussion on first, the need to uphold the rights of the refugee child in all environments is critical to setting the scene for more robust discussions between transnational child rights networks and states parties.

[85] Article 23(2)–(3).

[86] European Union Agency for Fundamental Rights 'Challenges facing civil society organisations working on human rights in the EU' https://bit.ly/3GaLxLd (accessed 23 May 2022).

[87] UN SDG Goal 10.7: Facilitate orderly, safe, regular, and responsible migration and mobility of people, including through the implementation of planned and well-managed migration policies.

[88] SDG Goal 10: Reduce inequality within and among countries https://unstats.un.org/sdgs/metadata/?Text=&Goal=10&Target=10.7 (accessed 15 May 2022).

the enjoyment of the rights of the refugee child. This offers an opportunity to add to an enhanced mode of engagement that is not driven by working in silos, but rather by working with existing initiatives to create traction around the rights and welfare of the refugee child.

6 Conclusion

Transnational child rights civil society networks are a strategic institution for ensuring the accountability of duty bearers to meeting their obligations regarding children. Their primary purpose is to address governance issues that fall into two categories. Firstly, they have an important role in addressing cross-border child rights violations, which may be increasing in light of the increased free movement of people, goods, and services across the continent. Secondly, the networks address common child rights issues within their regions using harmonised approaches while anchoring their work on global and regional child rights instruments that states parties have ratified. With the aid of constructivism, this study calls for defined structures that are evident in alliances such as TCRNs to construct their values and norms based on various formations in society. The use of the child refugee as a platform of engagement, particularly in socio-economic rights, is a place of subsequent engagement on making child refugees a critical agenda of the ACERWC. The TCRNs offer a vehicle of transnational engagement where advocacy and appropriate pressure can be placed on governments, to use policies that are inclusive of both citizens and refugees. In dealing with sustainability, it is strategic that TCRNs place the refugee child as an entry point to engage with other like-minded stakeholders, like organisations working with refugees, persons, or organisations dealing with other intricate aspects like the SDG Agenda, human trafficking, and human smuggling. This will go a long way in enhancing synergies from various stakeholders in dealing with the issue of the socio-economic rights of refugees in Africa.

Bibliography

Books

Keck, M & Sikkink, K *Activists beyond borders* (Cornell University Press 1998)
Lipschutz, RD & Mayer, J *Global civil society and global environmental governance: The politics of nature from place to planet* (Sunny Press 1996)

Risse-Kappen, T *Bringing transnational relations back in non-state actors, domestic structures and international institutions* (Cambridge University Press 2009)

Shivji, IG *Silences in NGO discourse: The role and future of NGOs in Africa* (Fahamu/Pambazuka 2007)

Singh, AK & Stevens, R *Networking: Towards a better tomorrow* (South Asian Network for Social & Agricultural Development 2007)

Chapters in Books

Kaime, T 'The protection of refugee children under the African human rights system: Finding durable solutions in international law' in Sloth-Nielsen, J (ed) *Children's rights in Africa: A legal perspective* (Routledge 2008)

LeBlanc, V 'Implementation of the 1989 Convention on the Right of the Child and the work of the United Nations High Commissioner for Refugees' in Verhellen, E (ed) *Understanding children's rights: Collected papers presented at the First International Interdisciplinary Course on Children's Rights* (Ghent, Children's Rights Centre, University of Ghent 1996)

Spini, D 'Civil society and the democratisation of global public space' in Armstrong, D; Bello, V; Gilson, J & Spini, D (eds) *Civil society and international governance: The role of non-state actors in global and regional regulatory frameworks* (Routledge 2010)

Journal Articles

Akech, JG 'Exacerbated inequalities: Implications of COVID-19 for the socio-economic rights of women and children in South Sudan' (2020) 20 *African Human Rights Law Journal* 584

Banks, N; Hulme, D & Edwards, M 'NGOs, states, and donors revisited: Still too close for comfort?' (2015) 66 *World Development* 707

Chibwana, M 'Transformative child rights advocacy: An ergonomic conceptual framework' (2021a) 29 *The International Journal of Children's Rights* 541

Chibwana, M 'Towards a transformative child rights discourse in Africa: A reflexive study' (2021b) *African Human Rights Law Journal, 21(1), 126-148.*

Fierke, KM 'Constructivism' in Dunne, T; Kurki, M & Smith, S *International relations theories: Discipline and diversity* (2007)

Francia, G & Gillett-Swan, J 'Special issue: Children's rights from a sustainability perspective: The UNCRC in Dialogue with Agenda 2030' (2021) 10 *Social Sciences* https://www.mdpi.com/journal/socsci/special_issues/children_rights_sustainability (accessed 23 May 2022)

Glick, NS & Çağlar, A 'Towards a comparative theory of locality in migration studies: Migrant incorporation and city scale' (2009) 35 *Journal of Ethnic and Migration Studies* 177

Hearn, J 'The "uses and abuses" of civil society in Africa' (2001) 28 *Review of African Political Economy* 43
Kaldor, M 'The idea of global civil society' *International affairs* (2003) 79
Muñoz, AA 'Transnational and domestic processes in the definition of human rights policies in Mexico' (2009) 31 *Human Right Quarterly* 35
Price, R 'Reversing the gun sights: Transnational civil society targets land mines' (1998) 52 *International Organization* 613
Rourke, L; Anderson, T; Garrison, DR & Archer, W 'Assessing social presence in asynchronous text-based computer conferencing' (2001) 14 *Journal of Distance Education* 17
Seckinelgin, H 'Civil society as a metaphor for western liberalism' (2002) 16 *Global society* 357
Snyder, R 'Scaling down: The subnational comparative method' (2001) 36 *Studies in Comparative International Development* 93
Söderbaum, F 'Regionalisation and civil society: The case of Southern Africa' (2007) 12 *New Political Economy* 319

Case Law

Scalabrini Centre, Cape Town v Minister of Home Affairs 2013 (3) SA 531 (WCC)
Scalabrini Centre, Cape Town v Minister of Home Affairs 2018 (4) SA 125 (SCA)
Scalabrini Centre of Cape Town v Minister of Social Development 2021 (1) SA 553 (GP)

Papers and Reports

Consortium for Refugees and Migrants in South Africa 'Protecting refugees, asylum seekers and immigrants in South Africa' (2010)
Church, M; Bitel, M; Armstrong, K; Fernando, P; Gould, H; Joss, S & Vouhé, C 'Participation, relationships and dynamic change: new thinking on evaluating the work of international networks' (2002)
Gabriel, N 'The millennium development goals: Towards a civil society perspective on reframing poverty reduction strategies in Southern Africa' Paper presented at the Southern Africa MDGs Forum, Johannesburg (July 2003)
IOM & AUC *Africa Migration Report: Challenging the narrative* (2019) 4
Vearey, J & Nunez, L. 'Towards improving forced migrant access to health and psychosocial rights in urban South Africa - A focus on Johannesburg' (2011)

ACERWC Documents

ACERWC, General Comment 5 on state party obligations under the African Charter on the Rights and Welfare of the Child (article 1) and systems strengthening for child protection (2018)

AU Documents

OAU, African Charter on Human and Peoples' Rights (Banjul Charter), 27 June 1981, CAB/LEG/67/3 rev 5, 21 ILM 58 (1982)
OAU, African Charter on the Rights and Welfare of the Child, 11 July 1990, CAB/LEG/24.9/49 (1990)
OAU, Convention Governing the Specific Aspects of Refugee Problems in Africa (OAU Convention), 10 September 1969, 1001 UNTS 45

UN Documents

UN Committee on Economic, Social and Cultural Rights (CESCR), General Comment 3: The nature of states parties' obligations (Art 2, Para 1, of the Covenant), 14 December 1990, UN Doc E/1991/23 (1990)
UNHCR 'Global consultations on international protection/third track: Refugee children' 25 April 2002, UN Doc EC/GC/02/9 (2002)
UN General Assembly, Assistance to unaccompanied refugee minors: Resolution adopted by the General Assembly, 24 February 2004, UN Doc A/RES/58/150 (2004)
UN General Assembly, Convention Relating to the Status of Refugees, 28 July 1951, United Nations, Treaty Series, vol 189, p 137
UN General Assembly, International Covenant on Civil and Political Rights, 16 December 1966, United Nations, Treaty Series, vol 999, p 171
UN General Assembly, International Covenant on Economic, Social and Cultural Rights, 16 December 1966, United Nations, Treaty Series, vol 993, p 3
UN General Assembly, Protection and assistance to unaccompanied and separated refugee children: Report of the Secretary-General, 7 September 2001, UN Doc A/56/333 (2001)
UN General Assembly 'Report of the United Nations High Commissioner for Refugees, questions relating to refugees, returnees and displaced persons and humanitarian questions: Report of the 3rd Committee: General Assembly, 54th session' 1 December 1999, UN Doc A/54/600 (1999)
UN SDG Goal 10.7: Facilitate orderly, safe, regular and responsible migration and mobility of people, including through the implementation of planned and well-managed migration policies

Internet Sources

'13.5 million children now uprooted in Africa - including those displaced by conflict, poverty and climate change' UNICEF 9 February 2019 (2022) https://www.unicef.org/press-releases/135-million-children-now-uprooted-africa-including-those-displaced-conflict-poverty (accessed 25 March 2022)

ACERWC 'Mapping children on the move' (2019) https://www.acerwc.africa/mapping-children-on-the-move/ (accessed 13 May 2022)

ACERWC 'State reports' https://reporting.acerwc.africa/ (accessed 15 May 2022)

AU 'Agenda 2063: The Africa we want' https://au.int/en/agenda2063/overviewau.int (accessed 23 May 2022)

Chibwana, M 'Status of national child rights networks in southern Africa' Commissioned by the Child Rights Network for Southern Africa (2018) https://bit.ly/3lwzvT1 (accessed 23 May 2022)

Children Forum https://childrencsoforum.africa/ (accessed 15 May 2022)

Child Rights Network for Southern Africa (CRNSA) https://bit.ly/3lcXTsB (15 May 2022)

European Union Agency for Fundamental Rights 'Challenges facing civil society organisations working on human rights in the EU' https://bit.ly/3GaLxLd (accessed 23 May 2022)

Islamic Relief South Africa, https://www.islamic-relief.org.za/about-us/ (accessed 25 April 2022)

Kaberi, J & Foley, E 'Leave no child behind: A 12th CSO Forum Conversation, Bamako, Mali 21-23, April, 2018' (2018) https://childrencsoforum.africa/wp-content/uploads/2020/11/Copy-of-CSO-Forum-Report-Final-1.pdf (accessed 15 May 2022)

OHCHR The economic, social and cultural rights of migrants in an irregular situation (2014) Migrants in an irregular situation, https://www.ohchr.org/Documents/Publications/HR-PUB-14-1_en.pdf (accessed 23 May 2022)

'Report of the Civil Society Forum on year of refugees, returnees and internally displaced people: towards durable solutions to forced displacement in Africa, following proceedings on 12 October 2019' https://www.chr.up.ac.za/images/researchunits/dce/resources/CIVIL_SOCIETY_FORUM_ON_YEAR_OF_REFUGEES_REPORT.pdf (accessed 25 March 2022)

Scalabrini Centre https://www.scalabrini.org.za (accessed 25 May 2022)

SDG Goal 10: Reduce inequality within and among countries, https://unstats.un.org/sdgs/metadata/?Text=&Goal=10&Target=10.7 (accessed 15 May 2022)

UNHCR Briefing Notes 'Seven Factors behind Movement of Syrian Refugees to Europe' (25 September 2015) http://www.unhcr.org/560523f26.html (accessed 19 September 2021)

UNHCR 'Refugee children: Guidelines on protection and care' https://www.unhcr.org/3b84c6c67.pdf (accessed 3 June 2022)

UNICEF 'Child displacement' (September 2021) and refugees, https://bit.ly/3yQ0kcP (accessed 23 May 2022)

CHAPTER 8

The Rule of Law and the Principle of Non-Refoulement: An Appraisal of the Human Rights Protection of Refugees in South Africa

Gerard Emmanuel Kamdem Kamga and Rashri Baboolal-Frank

1 Introduction

The purpose of this chapter is to review the extent to which South Africa complies with its commitments to refugee protection in general and the principle of non-refoulement. The recent refugee situation in the country,

G. E. K. Kamga (✉)
Research and Postgraduate Division, Free State Centre for Human Rights, University of the Free State, Bloemfontein, South Africa
e-mail: kamdemkamgage@ufs.ac.za

R. Baboolal-Frank
Department of Procedural Law, Faculty of Law, University of Pretoria, Pretoria, South Africa
e-mail: rashri.baboolal@up.ac.za

E. Durojaye et al. (eds.), *Realising Socio-Economic Rights of Refugees and Asylum Seekers in Africa*, Politics of Citizenship and Migration, https://doi.org/10.1007/978-3-031-16548-1_8

characterised by state abandonment, bureaucratic slowness,[1] mistreatment in detention camps such as the private Lindela facility, corruption and the convulsive impact of repeated attacks (termed xenophobia/Afrophobia according to critics or mere criminality according to the government) since 2008, have become a serious concern that results in refugees being abused and forced to leave the country. A report by Human Rights Watch observed that xenophobic violence in the country is often interpreted as a popular and spontaneous reaction to the government's perceived failures in relation to service delivery, a lack of jobs and mounting income inequality as well as the influx of foreign nationals over the past few years. Within this context, the link between government's failures and the realisation of socio-economic rights becomes evident irrespective of whether those involved are individual citizens or foreign nationals. Xenophobic/Afrophobic violence is more deeply rooted in the South African state and society, because it is much more organised than it appears as it does not necessarily take place in the very poorest neighbourhoods only, but is often provoked by powerful actors who have an economic or political interest in large-scale looting, displacement of people and the administration of mob justice.[2] As a largely politically and economically stable country, South Africa has indeed been experiencing a massive influx of people from other parts of the continent and even the rest of the world. The mechanisms of protection of persons fleeing their country because of dictatorship, conflict, corruption, extreme poverty, underdevelopment, neo-colonialism and lack of opportunities in a bid to seek a better life in South Africa or simply passing through South Africa as a transit point towards more distant destinations such as for instance Europe, America or Oceania, will be our focus in this chapter. The country is host to a considerable population not only from the Southern African region such as Zimbabwe,[3]

[1] There appears to be a lack of coordination within the administration on cross-cutting issues such as migration. More generally, each level of government in the country (national, provincial and local) has a tendency to function in an autonomous rather than a coordinated manner. For further details, see J Crisp & E Kiragu 'Refugee protection and international migration: A review of UNHCR's role in Malawi, Mozambique and South Africa' PDES/2010/10; United Nations High Commissioner for Refugees Policy Development and Evaluation Service (PDES), PDES/2010/10 (2010) https://www.unhcr.org/4c629c4d9.html (accessed 18 June 2022).

[2] As above.

[3] A Bloch 'The right to rights? Undocumented migrants from Zimbabwe living in South Africa' (2010) 44 *Sociology* 233.

Malawi, Angola, Mozambique, and the Democratic Republic of Congo,[4] but from other parts of the continent, namely Kenya, Nigeria, and Ethiopia and from further afield notably Bangladesh, China, India and Pakistan. There are reasons for this mass exodus of populations. One of our key concerns in this chapter is to focus on the situation of refugees and/or asylum seekers who are not to be mixed with other kinds of immigrants. Indeed, owing to their vulnerability, refugees almost always rely on others to survive in the host country.[5] Can one become a refugee or asylum seeker by choice? Though the mass exodus of people from their country of origin to South Africa is a phenomenon that can be anticipated and prevented, the true culprits may not necessarily be the people in distress. In most cases, compliance with the rule of law is an issue in these countries; the rule of law is considered the preeminent factor to legitimate political ideals in the world today, even though there are still disagreements about its proper meaning.[6] Yet, as a general juristic phenomenon, the concept of the 'rule of law' gives rise to, first, the fundamental conditions that have to be satisfied for the existence of any legal system and secondly, to a morally cherishable expression of commitments to the dignity and equality of individuals.[7] The correlation between human rights' violations and the influx of refugees is not an accidental one where humanitarian intervention is justified merely by the presence of refugees.[8] If one agrees on these premises, then the issue of refugees' protection in terms of compliance with the rule of law and their socio-economic rights, which is the main focus of this chapter, becomes tangible.

The principle of non-refoulement means that a state may not expel or deport a refugee to another state where he or she can be subjected to ill treatment, torture and even death. One of the issues with this principle is that states may not directly expel or deport refugees, but the possibility exists that such refugees may be treated in such a way that they find

[4] See S Masuku & S Rama 'Challenges to refugees' socioeconomic inclusion: A lens through experiences of Congolese refugees in South Africa' (2020) 20 *The Oriental Anthropologist* 82.

[5] See CA Labys, C Dreyer & JK Burns 'At zero and turning in circles: Refugee experiences and coping in Durban, South Africa' (2017) 54 *Transcultural Psychiatry* 696.

[6] B Tamanaha *On the rule of law: History, politics, theory* (2004) 4.

[7] M Kramer *Objectivity and the rule of law* (2007) 102.

[8] G Loescher 'Refugees as grounds for international action' in E Newman E & J van Selm (eds) *Refugees and forced displacement: International security, human vulnerability, and the state* (2003) 42.

themselves in a situation having no choice but to leave the country on their own. For instance, it will be easy for a state not to fulfil the socio-economic rights of the refugees to deepen their vulnerability which will in turn hasten their 'voluntary' departure. It is rightly observed that preventing *refoulement* is an effective, and sometimes the only, means of preventing further human rights violations.[9] We will provide detailed developments regarding this principle and explore the extent to which this has an impact on the socio-economic rights of refugees in the country. South Africa is party to a number of international agreements on human rights protection. Chief among these instruments are the Convention Relating to the Status of Refugees adopted in 1951 in Geneva (UN Refugee Convention) and the International Covenant on Economic Social and Cultural Rights of 1966 (ICESCR).[10] As a result, South Africa is not permitted to close its borders to persons in distress who are seeking refuge in the country. More importantly, South Africa must meet their basic needs by providing them with food, water, housing and healthcare, amongst other things. Despite South Africa's clear obligations to refugees, it must be borne in mind that not all foreign nationals should be allowed to enter the country as not everyone is classified as a refugee automatically. To this end, it is important to first clarify who falls into the category of 'refugee'. The second paragraph of article 1 of the UN Refugee Convention provides the following lengthy definition of refugees. A refugee is a person whom,

> [a]s a result of events occurring before 1 January 1951 and owing to well-founded fear of being persecuted for reasons of race, religion, nationality, membership of a particular social group or political opinion, is outside the country of his nationality and is unable or, owing to such fear, is unwilling to avail himself of the protection of that country; or who, not having a nationality and being outside the country of his former habitual residence as a result of such events, is unable or, owing to such fear, is unwilling to return to it. In the case of a person who has more than one nationality, the term 'the country of his nationality' shall mean each of the countries of which he is a national, and a person shall not be deemed to be lacking the protection

[9] SC Joshi *Protecting human rights of refugees: Issues and international intervention* (2011) 34.

[10] UN General Assembly, Convention Relating to the Status of Refugees, 28 July 1951, United Nations, Treaty Series, vol 189, p 137; and UN General Assembly, International Covenant on Economic, Social and Cultural Rights, 16 December 1966, United Nations, Treaty Series, vol 993, p 3.

of the country of his nationality if, without any valid reason based on well-founded fear, he has not availed himself of the protection of one of the countries of which he is a national.

The foregoing provision is rooted in article 14 of the Universal Declaration of Human Rights[11] that enshrines the right for every person who seeks asylum from persecution in other states. We have observed that not everyone qualifies as an asylum seeker or refugee under the UN Refugee Convention. To determine the status of refugees, several factors must be taken into consideration. For example, where asylum seekers testify that they have left their country to avoid serious harm being inflicted upon them, both the general human rights record of the country of origin and similar situations of other people, should be considered as alternative means of establishing the objective risk associated with the person's return.[12] Despite this determination one must also keep in mind that there is a specific category of persons who may not be automatically entitled to the protection mechanisms available under the UN Refugee Convention. Such persons include persons who may be guilty of war crimes, genocide and other serious non-political crimes as well as refugees currently under the protection or assistance of the United Nations Agency. The refugees from Palestine who fall under the auspices of the United Nations Relief and Works Agency for Palestine are examples of persons who do not enjoy automatic protection.[13] It is against this backdrop that we will be assessing the extent to which South Africa complies with the standards of refugees' protection including their socio-economic rights. In other words, the question of how much protection in terms of socio-economic rights and the rule of law does South Africa provide to persons in distress crossing its borders will be considered. Another question which arises is what are the existing legal frameworks and mechanisms in place to implement such protection and are they efficient? Further, it will be determined to what extent does South Africa comply with the principle of non-refoulement, one of the key mechanisms of refugees' protection in international law.

The abovementioned questions are key to guiding our analysis. In the upcoming sections we will review the international, regional and domestic

[11] UN General Assembly, Universal Declaration of Human Rights, 10 December 1948, 217 A (III).

[12] JC Hathaway *The law of refugee status* (1991) 89.

[13] See UNHCR (The UN Refugee Agency) 'The 1951 Refugee Convention' https://www.unhcr.org/1951-refugee-convention.html (accessed 14 March 2021).

framework of refugee protection in South Africa and assess the extent to which they are implemented on the ground. The penultimate section of the chapter will be dedicated to the principle of non-refoulement and its level of implementation in South Africa.

2 The Legal Standard Relating to the Status of Refugees

It is important to distinguish between the international, regional and domestic standard of refugee protection. This section may appear to be descriptive, but it is imperative to review the legal framework if one intends to properly account for the principle of non-refoulement. The international standards on refugee protection are provided for in Chap. 1 and need not be repeated here. We analyse only the last two documents given their relevance compared to Article 14 of the Universal Declaration of Human Rights frames the protection of refugees in the following terms

(a) Everyone has the right to seek and enjoy in other countries asylum from persecution.
(b) This may not be invoked in the case of prosecutions genuinely arising from non-political crimes or from acts contrary to the purposes and principles of the United Nations.

The contents of article 14 are characterised by their universality given that there is no restriction as to who can seek and enjoy asylum from persecution in another state. Despite this assertion, there are nonetheless some criteria that need to be met to qualify for refugee status. The enjoyment of the right does not preclude anyone on the bases of sex, race, nationality, religion or gender. It applies to all human beings who, for one reason or another can be subject to persecution in their country of origin. This conforms to the spirit of the Declaration itself, that is, to extend protection from persecution and human rights abuses to all human beings. Even though legally and technically speaking a Declaration is a document that by its very nature is not binding on states, it is crucial to highlight that the Universal Declaration of Human Rights has acquired the status of international customary law and is part of the norm of *jus cogens*. As observed by the Supreme Court of Appeal of South Africa, the Universal Declaration of Human Rights is a 'fundamental text, whose mandatory character as "*jus cogens*" is undeniable'. The Court further held that the

'Universal Declaration of Human Rights is, at the very least, a customary rule of international law within the meaning of article 38, paragraph 1 b), of the Statute of the International Court of Justice'.[14] Therefore, it is unthinkable that states who signed this document will ignore its provisions in terms of the rule of law and the protection of refugees. As it was rightly observed, the Universal Declaration of Human Rights has become not only a constitution for human rights, but also the most cited human rights instrument in the world.[15] This instrument, published in 1948, sets the basis for another key instrument, that is, the UN Refugee Convention which came into force in 1954 and has since become the central piece of international refugee protection.

Historically, the Refugee Convention, as a post-Second World War instrument, was originally limited in scope to persons fleeing events occurring before 1 January 1951 and within Europe. The Protocol to the Refugee Convention removed these limitations and thus gave the Convention universal coverage.[16] This universal aspect regarding the rights granted to refugees is emphasised in article 5, which provides that '[N]othing in this Convention shall be deemed to impair any rights and benefits granted by a Contracting State to refugees apart from this Convention'. In the introductory section of this chapter, we have determined who can qualify as a refugee. It is therefore important to review their main protection mechanisms in terms of human rights provided for by the UN Refugee Convention. The Convention must apply to refugees without discrimination as to race, religion or country of origin (article 3). In addition, the Convention further requests states to accord to refugees within their territories, treatment at least as favourable as that accorded to their nationals with respect to freedom to practise their religion and freedom regarding the religious education of their children (article 4). It can then be said that the aim of the UN Refugee Convention is to design a framework where people fleeing their countries due to any kind of persecution are placed in a position where their rights are equal to those of other foreign nationals in the host country. The UN Refugee Convention further seeks to grant refugees the same rights and protection mechanisms

[14] *State v Rudman; State v Johnson; State v Xaso; Xaso v Van Wyk NO* 1989 (3) SA 368 (E) at 376.

[15] HJ Steiner, P Alston & R Goodman *International human rights in context* 3rd ed. (2008) 136.

[16] UNHCR (n 13).

as those granted to citizens of the state in which they find themselves. Overall, it provides three standards. Refugees should enjoy protection of their rights on a favourable basis and have equal enjoyment of their rights as other foreign nationals. The point is that in international law in general the relationships between states and refugees remain subject to clarification. The purpose of the UN Refugee Convention is therefore to place the obligations of the governments into a contractual agreement, attributing a high degree of importance to the refugees.[17] Not only does the UN Refugee Convention bring together a set of human rights and humanitarian law aspirations, but more importantly, it brings to the fore the issue of an exceptional immigration regime for refugees and asylum seekers in a host country. In other words, one has to understand that the international refugee protection system has been construed as offering human rights protection to a clear and distinct group of people who cannot or can no longer rely on their country of origin or habitual residence for protection.[18] Article 31(1) of the UN Refugee Convention, which falls under the section entitled 'refugees unlawfully in the country of refuge', requires states not to impose penalties on refugees who enter illegally or is present in the country without authority, if they come directly from a territory where their life or freedom was threatened. This is provided that they present themselves without delay to the authorities and show good cause for their illegal entry or presence. One of the key protection mechanisms in the UN Refugee Convention is the prohibition on the expulsion or deportation of refugees who may face danger in their country of origin. The protection is inherent in the principle of non-refoulement contained in article 33 of the UN Refugee Convention. This principle is reviewed in detail within the South African context in the next section of this chapter.

The African continent has been subject to imperialistic policies and practices and colonised for decades. Even after so-called independence, it has remained subject to various types of turmoil including conflict, rebellion, neo-colonialism, poverty, general disorder and instability. These phenomena by themselves constitute the key drivers of forced migration and mass displacement of people internally and externally. There was a crucial need to conceptualise the AU Convention in a way that it benefits millions of people across the continent. This explains why its scope is broader than

[17] LW Holborn *Refugees: A problem of our time – The work of the United Nations High Commissioner for Refugees, 1951–1972* vol 1 (1975) 158–159.

[18] J Van der Klaauw 'Refugee rights in times of mixed migration: Evolving status and protection issues' (2009) 28 *Refugee Survey Quarterly* 59 at 61.

that of the UN Refugee Convention. Whenever there is an influx of persons seeking refuge within the borders of another state, the AU Convention does not deny the status of refugees to such persons. As a result, some people may be covered by the provisions of the AU Convention on the ground of being nationals from a particular country. This differs from the current practices in various states where the determination of the status of refugees follows a particular procedure.[19]

Despite expanding the category of people who may qualify as refugees on the continent, the AU Convention, similarly to the UN Refugee Convention, provides for a group of persons who do not fall under its protection. Persons excluded from the category of refugees who enjoy protection include: those who voluntarily regained the protection of their home country; those who lost their nationality, but voluntarily re-acquired it and those who were involved in serious non-political crimes outside their country of refuge after their admission to that country. Further, the AU Convention is not applicable to those who have seriously infringed its purposes and objectives.[20] It may be evident that despite its broad scope, the AU Convention remains grounded in the principles of the rule of law. Individuals who have been found guilty of serious human rights violations and breaching the rule of law in their country of origin and elsewhere cannot hide under the blanket provisions of the AU Convention and escape from their liabilities. The AU Convention brings about a legal architecture where provisions of humanitarian law, human rights and the rule of law have successfully been merged into a single document aimed at mitigating the suffering of populations.

The African Charter on Human and Peoples' Rights adopted in 1981 and entered into force in 1986 is the second key document dealing with refugee issues on the continent. It is a document that considers freedom, equality, justice and dignity as essential objectives for the achievement of the legitimate aspirations of the African people.[21] The African Charter re-emphasises its attachment to the universal principles of human rights available in other key documents such as the Universal Declaration of Human Rights. In its first article, the African Charter marks its opposition to any sort of discrimination as its provides that every individual shall be entitled to the enjoyment of the rights and freedoms without distinction of any

[19] N Nathwani *Refugees and human rights: Rethinking refugee law* (2002) 2.

[20] Article 1(4) of the OAU Convention.

[21] See Preamble.

kind such as race, ethnic group, colour, sex, language, religion, political or any other opinion, national and social origin, fortune, birth or other status. This provision can be analysed to include the refugee's context, but there is no point to such an analysis, because the African Charter contains specific provisions dedicated to the problem of refugees on the continent. On this account, the third paragraph of its article 12 provides as follows: 'Every individual shall have the right, when persecuted, to seek and obtain asylum in other countries in accordance with laws of those countries and international conventions'.

A similar provision which frames the refugee issue, appears in article 23(2)(a) and (b) of the African Charter. These provisions require persons enjoying the right of asylum under article 12, not to engage in subversive activities against their country of origin or any other states party and to use their asylum territories as bases for subversive or terrorist activities against the people of any other states party to the African Charter. Similarly, to the AU Refugee Convention, one can notice the consistency of the African Charter in terms of the principles of human rights, humanitarian law and the rule of law.

The Refugees Act 130 of 1998 is the main instrument which frames refugee matters in South Africa. The end of the apartheid regime in the country came along with a sharp increase in migratory influx. A report by the United Nations High Commissioner for Refugees found that South Africa has a substantial population of people from nearby parts of Africa (for example, Angola, Malawi and Mozambique) and from further afield (for example, Nigeria, and increasingly, from Bangladesh, China, India and Pakistan). A study depicts the extent to which the immigration policies of the country are especially geared towards economic migrants from other African states. As a result, most of them decide to opt for the asylum seekers' permit.[22] The current Refugees Act provides for a legal framework on such matters across the country.

It is crucial to observe that potential refugees finding themselves in South Africa also fall under the protection of the Constitution of the Republic of South Africa, 1996, which is considered, first, as the supreme law of the Republic and, secondly, as one of the most advanced in the world in terms of human rights protection, especially in the Bill of Rights in Chap. 2.

[22] R Amit 'No refuge: Flawed status determination and the failure of South Africa's refugee system to provide protection' (2011) 23 *International Journal of Refugee Law* 458 at 459.

3 South Africa and the Principle of Non-Refoulement

It is important to provide a brief overview of this principle before assessing the extent to which South Africa complies with it.

3.1 A Brief Overview of the Principle of Non-Refoulement

The principle of non-refoulement equates to the prohibition of rejection at the frontier, expulsion and deportation. It means that persons who qualify as refugees cannot be forcefully returned to a country where they can be subject to torture, persecution, death and other human rights violations. The prohibition of rejection at the frontier, expulsion and deportation apply whenever persons seeking refuge in a particular country find themselves either in that country or at its borders. It is a fundamental mechanism of protection of refugees and asylum seekers. This principle is relevant to the extent that it has acquired the status of customary international law. It is worth noting that the principle of non-refoulement does not mean an obligation to grant asylum exists. States remain completely sovereign in their choice to admit people on their territory or not. The principle of non-refoulement is provided for by article 33(1) of the UN Refugee Convention as follows

> No Contracting State shall expel or return ('refouler') a refugee in any manner whatsoever to the frontiers of territories where his life or freedom would be threatened on account of his race, religion, nationality, membership of a particular social group or political opinion.

The principle of non-refoulement is echoed in article 12(5) of the African Charter that prohibits the mass expulsion of non-nationals. It further mentions that mass expulsion shall be that which is aimed at national, racial, ethnic or religious groups. In the same vein, article 3 of the African Convention also provides for the principle of non-refoulement as follows

> No person shall be subjected by a Member State to measures such as rejection at the frontier, return or expulsion, which would compel him to return to or remain in a territory where his life, physical integrity or liberty would be threatened for the reasons set out in Article I, paragraphs 1 and 2.

Refoulement or expulsion can occur directly such as for instance following deportation, and indirectly[23] when receiving states behave in such a way that refugees find themselves in devastating conditions and are left with no choice but to leave the country.[24] A further analysis of this will follow later. Next, however, it is crucial to firstly review South Africa's compliance with the principle of non-refoulement.

3.2 *South Africa Compliance with the Principle of Non-Refoulement*

There is a general sentiment that most migrants feel that South Africa has a moral obligation to African countries that opposed apartheid and should therefore embrace and welcome foreign migrants.[25] In *Union of Refugee Women v Director: Private Security Industry Regulatory Authority*, the Constitutional Court held that 'during the liberation struggle many of those who now find themselves among our country's leaders were refugees themselves, forced to seek protection from neighbouring states and abroad'.[26] South Africa's stand on the principle of non-refoulement is distinctly pronounced.[27] The Refugee Act, the standard domestic legal framework dealing with refugee matters, complies with international and regional agreements. The country's stand on the principle of non-refoulement is articulated early in the Refugees Act. Under the section entitled 'general prohibition of refusal of entry, expulsion, extradition or return to other country in certain circumstances', the second article provides as follows:

> 2. Notwithstanding any provision of this Act or any other law to the contrary, no person may be refused entry into the Republic, expelled, extradited or returned to any other country or be subject to any similar measure, if as

[23] It has to be noted that the principle of non-refoulement is further reflected in the Torture Convention.

[24] G Clayton *Immigration and asylum law* 3rd ed. (2008) 409.

[25] R Modi *Migration to South Africa: A human rights perspective* (2001) 11.

[26] *Union of Refugee Women v Director: Private Security Industry Regulatory Authority* 2007 (4) SA 395 (CC) para 30.

[27] See JD Mujuzi 'The principle of non-refoulement in South African and the exclusion from refugee status of asylum seekers who have committed offences abroad: A Comment on *Gavric v Refugee Status Determination Officer, Cape Town and Others*' (2018) 43 *South African Yearbook of International Law* 20.

a result of such refusal, expulsion, extradition, return or other measure, such person is compelled to return to or remain in a country where-

(a) he or she may be subjected to persecution on account of his or her race, religion, nationality, political opinion or membership of a particular social group; or
(b) his or her life, physical safety or freedom would be threatened on account of external aggression, occupation, foreign domination or other events seriously disturbing or disrupting public order in either part or the whole of that country.

Rejection at the frontier, extradition, expulsion or deportation remain processes at the disposal of the South African government when coping with irregular migrants. It can become a tricky procedure when it comes to determining who qualifies as an asylum seeker. We have previously mentioned that non-compliance with the principle of non-refoulement can occur directly or indirectly. We now turn to the review of these two methods considering the recent developments on the ground to account for the extent to which South Africa complies with this principle. In terms of direct refoulement, it is demonstrated that since the end of apartheid and the advent of democracy, the country has consistently expelled 'undocumented migrants'. In 1998, the very same year that the Refugee Act was enacted, a report released by Human Rights Watch, indicated that the number of return or expulsion of undocumented migrants out of the country, reached close to 200,000 people in 1997.[28] The report further explained how suspected undocumented migrants are identified by the authorities through unreliable means such as the skin complexion of the person, his accent or whether or not they have inoculation marks. Human Rights Watch documented cases of persons who claimed they were arrested for being 'too black', having a foreign name, or in one case, walking 'like a Mozambican'.[29] This section of the report refers to 'undocumented migrants' and not specifically to 'refugees' or 'asylum seekers'. But the latter category of persons is not very different from the former. Our assumption derives from reports by Human Rights Watch, that many of those arrested, that is, up to 20 per cent of the total in some areas, were actually

[28] Human Rights Watch 'PROHIBITED PERSONS': Abuse of undocumented migrants, asylum-seekers, and refugees in South Africa' (1998) https://www.hrw.org/legacy/reports98/sareport/ (accessed 21 May 2021).

[29] As above.

South African citizens or lawful residents, who often have to spend several days in detention while attempting to convince officials of their legitimate status.[30] These practices of refoulement are still happening today and it is in this sense that despite having a robust legal architecture to protect refugees and asylum seekers, South Africa sometimes fails to comply with its commitments.[31]

In terms of indirect refoulement, we live in an era where information moves fast. As a result, individual actors and state entities do not want to be exposed, named and shamed publicly by the civil society and the media whenever they fail to comply with their commitment in terms of good governance, human rights or the fight against poverty. Therefore, a state that does not intend to directly and officially expel, deport or deny entry of persons seeking refuge on its territory will generally rely on indirect refoulement. We have depicted it as a way of treating refugees or asylum seekers in a manner that they will be left with no choice but to 'voluntarily' leave the country. South Africa formally committed itself to the international refugee law after signing a Basic Agreement with the United Nations High Commissioner for Refugees (UNHCR) in 1993 and becoming a party to the Organisation of African Unity (OAU) and United Nations Refugee Conventions in 1995 and 1996, respectively. Despite signing up for this responsibility, there are numerous instances where the state has not done much to protect refugees' socio-economic rights and thereby inciting in them the desire to leave the country. It has been alleged that the police was not responsible for the shootings which killed 34 miners at Marikana. A Commission of Inquiry was set up to investigate deaths of only the South African nationals who were killed during this unfortunate tragedy. As a result, the families of the victims would be paid R1.2 million, plus other benefits. On the other hand, no commission of inquiry was instituted to investigate the killing of foreign nationals who were part of the group of people gunned down by the same police that day.[32] Therefore no foreign victim would ever see retributive justice. On the other hand, it

[30] As above.

[31] See F Khan 'Does the right to dignity extend equally to refugees in South Africa?' (2020) 20 *African Human Rights Journal* 261.

[32] Parliamentary Monitoring Group 'Issues that affect migrants and citizens: Engagement with NGOs & stakeholders' (29 October 2019) https://pmg.org.za/committee-meeting/29180/ (accessed 18 June 2022).

is well known that the mining industry, a key sector of South Africa's economy, employs several undocumented migrants including those still waiting to be granted a formal asylum or refugee status for their cheap labour. The fact that the state and other entities, including among others the civil society and the media, did not do much to account for the killing of non-nationals, can lead to a sentiment of unfairness and incite such non-nationals to leave a country where they feel abandoned by law and its institutions.

A further example of an instance where the right of undocumented migrants or those awaiting a refugee or asylum status have not been protected is the abuse which occurs in some detention camps such as the private Lindela facility near Johannesburg, which is operated on behalf of the Department of Home Affairs. Human Rights Watch found numerous serious human rights abuses. The non-governmental organisation photographed more than ten people who claimed to have been beaten by security personnel in three separate incidents within a week. These incidents were confirmed by medical reports documenting the injuries. The situation of a young man from Lesotho was reported and it appeared that he had been brutally beaten over a period of several hours after complaining to security guards about the theft of his music tapes by security personnel. Although the Lindela management was aware of some of these incidents, no internal investigation appeared to have been instituted.[33] From the above examples, it can be said that indirect refoulement proceeds from the actions or inactions of the state that do not participate much in protecting the rights of persons seeking refuge within South African borders. It is within this context that it was observed that when asylum seekers, coming by sea, land or air, are denied entry to a country and are obliged to continue their journey to another destination, there is a strong argument that they have in effect been rejected at the border.[34] No one would want to live in an environment where he or she can be assaulted without the authorities doing anything to sanction the culprits. Humans by nature desire to live in a safe and secured environment and this is the first prerequisite to seek refuge.

The last instances that can lead to indirect refoulement and departure of refugees and asylum seekers from South Africa amount to what has

[33] Human Rights Watch (n 36).
[34] Joshi (n 9) 60.

been termed xenophobic attacks,[35] Negrophobia or Afrophobia[36] which amounts to attacks on foreign nationals mostly from African countries by mostly black South African nationals. This is not an apparent issue as the matter has been subject to controversies given that state officials perceive these attacks as nothing but criminality. According to Human Rights Watch:

> Anti-foreigner feelings have also increased alarmingly. Politicians, the press, and the South African public commonly blame foreigners for exacerbating social problems such as rising crime, unemployment, or even the spread of diseases, and undocumented migrants have been subject to abuse by officials from the Department of Home Affairs, the police, and the army, as well as by the general public.[37]

Whether it is about criminality or anti-foreign nationals' attacks, either instance can well constitute a genuine ground for refugees and asylum seekers to leave the country. As a matter of fact, the treatment of undocumented or illegal or irregular migrants is basically the same as persons holding an asylum seeker permit issued by the authorities. An example is the situation of an undocumented migrant who is not allowed to open a bank account just like anyone holding an asylum seeker permit. In the same vein, even when guarantees are provided to cover their monthly payments, some medical aid schemes in South Africa systematically reject applications of asylum seekers on the ground that they do not deal with this category of documents yet issued by the government of the Republic. The same also applies when it comes to refugees, who, lacking a proper shelter live in harsh conditions. It is reported that despite the generous provisions of the Constitution, practical access to public services is limited, while only occasional support is available from NGOs, churches and other members of civil society, including refugee community associations. Many

[35] As reported by Human Rights Watch, Xenophobia has taken two recent forms in South Africa. First, and despite the generous provisions of the Constitution, practical access to public services such as education and health is often very difficult for foreign nationals. Foreign nationals are also subject to abuse, exploitation and discrimination by employers (sometimes migrants find that they are dismissed or arrested just before pay-day). Second, refugees, asylum seekers and migrants in South Africa live in constant fear that large-scale violence of the type witnessed in May 2008 will erupt once again. For further details, see Human Rights Watch (n 36).

[36] L Thela et al. 'Counting the cost of Afrophobia: Post-migration adaptation and mental health challenges of African refugees in South Africa' (2017) 54 *Transcultural Psychiatry* 715.

[37] Human Rights Watch (n 36).

are obliged to live in what Doctors without Borders [or Medicine sans frontiers] (MSF) describes as 'bad buildings', where they have to pay rent, but where they do not have access to reliable water, electricity and sanitation systems.[38] As we have previously observed, immigration issues are a matter of sovereignty and a state is not compelled to admit everyone into its territory. Nonetheless it remains the primary bearer in terms of guaranteeing the human rights and safety of those living on its territory, whether citizens or foreign nationals. If the state is not up to this task, then this can be a constitutive failure to comply with international commitments in terms of refugee protection. When it comes to the principle of non-refoulement, it is evident that despite its international commitments in terms of human rights protection and despite its robust domestic legal framework, there are nonetheless documented cases and several instances attesting to the fact that South Africa has sometimes failed to comply with such a principle.

4 Relationship Between the Principle of Non-Refoulement and the Socio-Economic Rights of Refugees

The relationships between the principle of non-refoulement and refugees' socio-economic rights are intertwined. When a country of refuge becomes a ground of hostility, the use of protection of liberties falls away. The two concepts are strongly linked and dependent upon each other. Whether it is about direct or indirect refoulement, it is our contention that the state that succumbs to the former or the latter somehow retreats from its obligations in terms of the provision of socio-economic rights to refugees. The mistreatment of refugees and asylum seekers whether deliberately or indirectly is flagrant of international treaties and norms. We have seen the extent to which some refugees and asylum seekers in South Africa are abused, violated, degraded, detained, prohibited from opening a bank account or joining a medical aid and denied the possibility of renting a proper place to stay despite providing additional guarantees. This has to do with the dignity of refugees. It is not conceivable that basic socio-economic rights such as the right to health, shelter or to work be denied to people already in distress. When asylum seekers are not allowed to open

[38] Crisp & Kiragu (n 1).

a bank account, this means that there is no possibility for them to be hired by potential employees. It is crucial to understand that with the spectrum of rights that refugees and asylum seekers are entitled to, there are rights that require the intervention of the state to be functional. If instead of implementing such rights, the state as the main duty bearer is the first to infringe upon their rights, this would amount to a death sentence for those in distress. The interconnection between the principle of non-refoulement and the socio-economic rights of refugees is a fact that cannot be denied. There is a correlation between the former and the latter and if something goes wrong this can lead to a tragedy. Direct refoulement can be interpreted as a way for the state to openly oppose the provision of socio-economic rights to refugees. Indirect refoulement on the other hand, can still occur whenever asylum seekers, despite being allowed within the country, find themselves in a position of not having access to housing, healthcare services, food, employment etc. It is a misinterpretation of the exceptional character of this immigration regime that was designed for the purpose of restoring the humanity and dignity of people in distress fleeing their country or ordinary residence for whatever reason. As a result, the principle of non-refoulement will only make sense if it is accompanied by the willingness of the hosting country to provide those in distress with the basic service delivery necessary for their survival. So far, this has not been the case and South Africa needs to be held accountable for its non-fulfilment of its obligations. Only when accountability and transparency is maintained within state and government departments, will imminent change occur. This has a particular connotation especially within the South African context where socio-economic rights are justiciable. In other words, the failures of the state to realise the right to housing, food, healthcare, employment and water to a section of the population can lead to legal actions in courts. Unfortunately, if proactive change is not undertaken by government to protect refugees and asylum seekers, then litigation compelling government to give effect to those rights, becomes the only option, which is costly if not sponsored fully by a non-governmental agency.

5 Conclusion

The aim of this analysis was to assess South Africa's compliance with its commitments in terms of refugees' protection including the provision of refugees' socio-economic rights and the principle of non-refoulement.

The country is party to key international instruments pertaining to refugee matters notably, the UN Refugee Convention, the AU Convention and the International Covenant on Civil and Political Rights. In addition to this, the country has a robust domestic law, that is, the Refugee Act protecting these categories of persons. The legal architecture for refugees and asylum seekers in the country is consistent with other international human rights instruments such as for instance the Universal Declaration of Human Rights.

Nonetheless, despite the comprehensive mechanisms at its disposal, South Africa is still struggling to fully implement them to realise the socio-economic rights of refugees. The recurrent abuses of undocumented and even documented migrants either by the police, officials of Home Affairs, the rise of anti-foreign national sentiments and the recurrent attacks they have been subjected to for years remain the principal hurdles that the government still needs to overcome. Despite these challenges, refugee and other immigration issues are yet to occupy a more relevant place on the national agenda comprised of crucial issues including, among others, violence against women, poverty, growing inequalities, high unemployment rate, service delivery and more recently, the Covid-19 pandemic.[39] As it stands, the country is a young democracy facing stringent governance issues marred by corruption scandals and various other issues. Nonetheless the country is endowed with great potential that is a guarantee of improvement in terms of human rights and the rule of law for the benefit of all.

Bibliography

AU Documents

The 1951 United Nations Convention Relating to the Status of Refugees (1951) 189 UNTS 150.

The African Charter on Human and Peoples' Rights 1981, OAU Doc. CAB/LEG/67/3 rev. 5.

The African Charter on the Rights and Welfare of the Child 1990, CAB/LEG/153/Rev.2.

The Organisation of African Unity Convention Governing Specific Aspects of Refugee Problems in Africa 1969 1001 UNTS 45.

[39] FL Zanker & K Moyo 'The Corona virus and migration governance in South Africa: Business as usual?' (2020) 55 *Africa Spectrum* 100.

Books

G Clayton. *Immigration and Asylum Law* 3rd ed (2008).

HJ Steiner, P Alston and R Goodman *International Human Rights in Context* 3rd edition (2008).

JC Hathaway. *The Law of Refugee Status* (1991).

MH Kramer, *Objectivity and the rule of law* (Cambridge University Press 2007).

SC Joshi. *Protecting Human Rights of Refugees: Issues and International Intervention* (2011).

Tamanaha, B *On the rule of law: History, politics, theory* (Cambridge University Press 2004).

Cases

State v. Rudman, State v. Johnson, State v. Xaso, Xaso v. Van Wyk No [1989] 3 SA (SCA) 368.

Union of Refugee Women v Director: Private Security Industry Regulatory Authority and Others 2007 (4) SA (CC) Para 30.

Journal Articles

Bloch, A 'The right to rights? Undocumented migrants from Zimbabwe living in South Africa' (2010) 44 *Sociology* 233

FL Zanker and K Moyo. 'The Corona Virus and Migration Governance in South Africa: Business As Usual?' 55(1) *Africa Spectrum* (2020).

G Loescher. 'Refugees as Grounds for International Action' in E Newman E and J van Selm (eds) *Refugees and Forced Displacement: International Security, Human Vulnerability, and the State* (2003).

Van der Klaauw J. 'Refugee rights in times of mixed migration: Evolving status and protection issues' (2009) 28 *Refugee Survey Quarterly.*

JD Mujuzi. 'The Principle of Non-Refoulement in South African and the Exclusion from Refugee Status of Asylum Seekers who have Committed Offences Abroad: A Comment on *Gavric v Refugee Status Determination Officer, Cape Town and Others*' (2018) *SAYIL.*

L Thela, A Tomita, V Maharaj, M Mhlongo & JK Burns. 'Counting the cost of Afrophobia: Post-migration adaptation and mental health challenges of African refugees in South Africa' Transcultural Psychiatry 54(5-6) (2017).

Labys, CA; Dreyer, C & Burns, JK 'At zero and turning in circles: Refugee experiences and coping in Durban, South Africa' (2017) 54 *Transcultural Psychiatry* 54

LW Holborn. *Refugees: A Problem of Our Time – The Work of the United Nations High Commissioner for Refugees, 1951-1972* vol. 1 (1975).

Masuku, S & Rama, S 'Challenges to refugees' socioeconomic inclusion: A lens through experiences of Congolese refugees in South Africa' (2020a) 20 *The Oriental Anthropologist* 82.

N Nathwani. *Refugees and Human Rights: Rethinking Refugee Law* (2002).

R Amit. 'No refuge: flawed status determination and the failure of South Africa's refugee System to provide protection' 2011 (23) *International Journal of Refugee Law*.

R Modi. *Migration to South Africa: A Human Rights Perspective* (2001).

S Masuku & S Rama. 'Challenges to Refugees' Socioeconomic Inclusion: A Lens Through Experiences of Congolese Refugees in South Africa' 20(1) (2020b).

See F Khan. 'Does the right to dignity extend equally to refugees in South Africa?' (2020) 20 *African Human Rights Journal*.

UN Documents

Declaration on Territorial Asylum, G.A. res. 2312 (XXII), 22 U.N. GAOR Supp. (No. 16) at 81, U.N. Doc. A/6716 (1967).

The Universal Declaration of Human Rights of 1948.

Internet Sources

Crisp, J & Kiragu, E 'Refugee protection and international migration: A review of UNHCR's role in Malawi, Mozambique and South Africa PDES/2010/10; dar-background' United Nations High Commissioner for Refugees Policy Development and Evaluation Service (PDES) PDES/2010/10 (2010) https://www.unhcr.org/4c629c4d9.html

Human Rights Watch "PROHIBITED PERSONS" Abuse of Undocumented Migrants, Asylum-Seekers, and Refugees in South Africa available at https://www.hrw.org/legacy/reports98/sareport/

Parliamentary monitoring group. Issues that affect migrants and citizens: engagement with NGOs & stakeholders available at https://pmg.org.za/committee-meeting/29180/.

Refworld Fact Sheet No.20, Human Rights and Refugees available at https://www.refworld.org/pdfid/4794773f0.pdf

United Nations Human High Commissioner for Refugees (The UN Refugee Agency) 'Convention and protocol relating to the status of refugees' available at https://www.unhcr.org/1951-refugee-convention.html

CHAPTER 9

Maternal Health Rights of Refugee Women in Uganda: Confronting the Multiple Layers of Vulnerability

Emma Charlene Lubaale

1 Introduction

The late Anguko Jennifer went into labour at 11:00 am at Arua Regional Referral Hospital and started bleeding at around 2:00 pm. The nurses left Ms. Anguko unattended and told her sister and husband to try and stop her bleeding with old pieces of cloth. A doctor was not called until 7:30 pm. He was delayed in arriving and Anguko and her child died at the hospital.[1]

[1] *Center for Health, Human Rights and Development (CEHURD) v Attorney General* (Constitutional Petition 16 of 2011) [2020] UGCC 12 (19 August 2020) 1–88 (*CEHURD* case).

E. C. Lubaale (✉)
Faculty of Law, Rhodes University, Grahamstown, South Africa
e-mail: e.lubaale@ru.ac.za

E. Durojaye et al. (eds.), *Realising Socio-Economic Rights of Refugees and Asylum Seekers in Africa*, Politics of Citizenship and Migration, https://doi.org/10.1007/978-3-031-16548-1_9

Maternal health rights generally encompass the health rights of women 'during pregnancy, childbirth and the postnatal period'.[2] A total of 16 Ugandan women die daily due to childbirth-related causes, with most of these deaths being largely preventable.[3] From the above quote, the late Anguko, a Ugandan woman, was another statistic adding to these overall statistics. The situation is already dire among Ugandan women. However, it is much worse for refugee women. While they experience similar barriers to maternal rights as other Ugandan women, many of these barriers are exacerbated by the refugee context. Reports reveal that in refugee settlements, the maternal mortality ratio stands at 123 for every 1000 live births,[4] with most of the deaths resulting from primary postpartum hemorrhage.[5]

Uganda is ranked as the largest refugee hosting country in Africa after Kenya and Ethiopia and globally, it takes third position.[6] Currently, Uganda hosts about 1.4 million refugees, the majority of whom come from neighbouring countries with long histories of conflict including the Democratic Republic of Congo and South Sudan.[7] Uganda's framework on refugee protection allows refugees to move and interact freely within the country, to get involved in gainful employment and to set up/engage in business/income-generating activities just like other Ugandan nationals. All things considered, Uganda is deemed to have one of the most progressive frameworks on refugee protection globally despite its high refugee burden. Its approach to refugee integration has even been lauded as a model implementation of the United Nations Framework on refugee

[2] WHO 'Maternal health' (2022) https://www.who.int/health-topics/maternal-health (accessed 5 April 2022); see also BK Twinomugisha 'Maternal health rights, politics and the law: Professorial Inaugural Lecture' (2016) 13 https://law.mak.ac.ug/news/maternal-health-rights-politics-and-law-professorial-inaugural-lecture (accessed 20 May 2021).

[3] *CEHURD* case, 16.

[4] UNHCR 'Refugee Health Report Uganda' (May 2019) 1–8.

[5] UNHCR (n 4). Primary postpartum haemorrhage PPH is defined as 'blood loss from the genital tract of 500 ml or more following a normal vaginal delivery (NVD) or 1000 mL or more following a cesarean section within 24 hours of birth'. For the foregoing definition, see S Ngwenya 'Postpartum hemorrhage: Incidence, risk factors, and outcomes in a low-resource setting' (2016) 8 *International Journal of Women's Health* 647.

[6] UNHCR 'Uganda' (2021) https://www.unhcr.org/uganda.html (accessed 20 May 2021).

[7] As above.

integration.[8] Free movement in Uganda has allowed refugees to have access to the socio-economic rights that other Ugandan nationals are entitled to including the right to health, the right to work and the right to education.

But amidst such resounding praise, an issue that remains far from clear is whether such progressiveness extends to the rights of refugee women. Concern for the rights of refugee women is particularly critical for various reasons. Notably, women continue to suffer the brunt of discrimination that goes back in history. Furthermore, refugee women experience other layers of prejudice because of the humanitarian contexts, such as armed conflict and poverty, which they often find themselves in. Moreover, refugee women are generally considered a 'vulnerable group'.[9] Emphasis on the rights of refugee women is critical because they make up a significant percentage of the refugee population. In Uganda, 82 per cent of the 1.4 million refugees are women and children.[10]

Generally, women and girls continue to suffer from violence and discrimination. The statistics on violence against women is extremely frightening.[11] This brings into focus the rights of women and the extent to which host countries are accorded due regard to their rights. One of the rights unique to women is the right to maternal health. This right falls under the umbrella of the right to health which is guaranteed under several international treaties. This chapter engages with this right in the context of Uganda, demonstrating that despite the resounding praise regarding Uganda's refugee framework, Uganda continues to lag behind in its enforcement of key socio-economic rights of women, one such right being maternal health.

Much has been written on the right to maternal healthcare. Some scholars have approached the subject from a social and humanities

[8] United Nations Development Programme *Uganda's contribution to refugee protection and management* (2017) 1–15; Africa Renewal 'Uganda stands out in refugee's hospitality' (2019) https://www.un.org (accessed 20 May 2021).

[9] The Forced Migration Research Network, University of New South Wales (Australia) 'The world's biggest minority? Refugee women and girls in the global compact on refugees' (2017) 1–2 https://www.unhcr.org/events/conferences/59e5f4447/worlds-largest-minority-women-girls-global-compact-refugees-extended.html (accessed 20 May 2021).

[10] UNHCR 'Uganda: Refugee statistics April 2020' (2020) 1.

[11] HRW 'Human Rights Watch submission to the UN Special Rapporteur on Violence Against Women' (22 May 2020) https://www.hrw.org/news/2020/05/22/human-rights-watch-submission-un-special-rapporteur-violence-against-women (accessed 20 May 2021); WHO *Changing cultural and social norms that support violence* (2009) 1–18.

perspective.[12] There is also literature that has engaged in comparative studies on this subject.[13] Literature also abounds on the right to maternal healthcare in other countries including South Africa.[14] There is also a plethora of research on barriers to the enjoyment of maternal health rights.[15] Being a health issue, literature also abounds on the maternal health rights of women through the lens of science.[16] However, hardly any research studies have engaged with the overlapping layers of discrimination and disadvantage that refugee women in Uganda experience regarding this right. In addition, no work has thus far engaged critically with the subject of maternal health rights in light of the recent judicial developments in Uganda. Against this backdrop, after demonstrating the multiple layers of disadvantage that refugee women in Uganda experience in accessing maternal health services, the chapter unpacks the August 2020 Constitutional Court of Uganda landmark case of *Center for Health, Human Rights and Development (CEHURD) v Attorney General* (*CEHURD* case)[17] and highlights how some key rulings in the decision could constitute tools for addressing some of the vulnerabilities of refugee women in Uganda.

[12] See, for example, H Mwenyango & G Palattiyil 'Health needs and challenges of women and children in Uganda's refugee settlements: Conceptualising a role for social work' (2019) 62 *International Social Work* 1535 https://doi.org/10.1177/0020872819865010 (accessed 21 June 2022).

[13] See, for example, JN Hakim, A Lansink & EC Lubaale 'The right to maternal healthcare of migrant and refugee women in South Africa and Uganda: Criminal accountability as a tool to addressing violation' in A Budoo-Scholtz & EC Lubaale (eds) *Violence against women and criminal justice: Sexual violence and vulnerability* (2021).

[14] See, for example, TS Mashanguri *Realising the right of access to maternal health care services for refugee women in South Africa*, LLM thesis, University of Kwazulu-Natal, 2015.

[15] See, for example, Twinomugisha (n 2) 15; BK Twinomugisha 'Exploring judicial strategies to protect the right of access to emergency obstetric care in Uganda' (2007) 7 *African Human Rights Law Journal* 283.

[16] See, for example, Ngwenya (n 5) 15.

[17] *CEHURD* case at 16.

2 The Legal Status of Socio-Economic Rights in Uganda and Their Progressive Realisation

Uganda's Constitution,[18] through its Bill of Rights and the Directive Principles of State Policy (DPSP), recognises a number of socio-economic rights. The socio-economic rights expressly guaranteed under Uganda's Bill of Rights include the right to education under article 30, rights of persons with disabilities under article 35, the right to a clean and healthy environment under article 39, protection from deprivation of property under article 26 and economic rights under article 40. The DPSP also recognises a number of rights including the right to development, water, food and health, however, these are not justiciable.[19] It may, however, be argued that the rights under the DPSP are justiciable in light of the fact that the Constitution makes it explicit that DPSP shall guide courts when applying or interpreting the Constitution or any other law.[20] Moreover, in terms of article 45 of the Constitution, the rights not specifically mentioned in the Bill of Rights are not considered as excluded. By implication, rights such as the right to health not explicitly mentioned under the Bill of Rights are included and therefore justiciable.

The socio-economic rights under Uganda's Constitution are not just black ink on paper. They are judicially enforceable. In terms of article 50 of the Constitution, any person who claims that a right guaranteed by the Constitution has been infringed upon or threatened can apply to a competent court for redress. The courts in Uganda have on numerous occasions enforced some of the socio-economic rights under the Constitution. In addition to the *CEHURD* case that will be discussed later in this chapter, another notable case is *British American Tobacco (BAT) v The Environment Action Network*, that dealt with the right to a clean environment.[21]

Uganda's Constitution does not make use of the notion of 'progressive realisation' in the Constitution. However, this term has been used by the ICESCR, a treaty to which Uganda is party. The Committee on Economic Social and Cultural Rights (Committee) explains that progressive realisation recognises that 'full realization of all economic, social and cultural

[18] Constitution of the Republic of Uganda, 1995.

[19] Constitution of the Republic of Uganda, 1995, para IX and XIV DPSP.

[20] Constitution of the Republic of Uganda, 1995, Para I DPSP.

[21] *British American Tobacco (BAT) v The Environment Action Network (TEAN)* Civil Application 27/2003

rights will generally not be able to be achieved in a short period of time'.[22] The Committee, however, emphasises that such recognition shouldn't deprive socio-economic rights of their meaningful content.[23] Chenwi comments that 'the progressive realisation qualification requires a state to strive towards fulfilment and improvement in the enjoyment of socio-economic rights to the maximum extent possible, even in the face of resource constraints'.[24] The courts in Uganda have sometimes made mention of the term 'progressive realisation' and have been guided by it to arrive at their decisions in as far as the realisation of socio-economic rights are concerned. In the *CEHURD* case, for example, the Constitutional Court, in finding that the state was in violation of the maternal health rights of women in Uganda, ruled that while providing healthcare depends largely on the availability of resources,

> the constitutional obligation of the state to provide these services to uphold the rights of women and fulfil their reproductive rights and needs cannot be ignored. What the government failed to do was to annually at the time of budgeting prioritise funding to the maternal health sector and disburse all the budgeted amount to the specific centers.[25]

It is clear from the Court's ruling that while Uganda is financially constrained and as such incapable of achieving the realisation of maternal healthcare within a short period of time, it is expected to make tangible and targeted steps within its available resources, at least annually, towards the realisation of this constitutionally guaranteed right.

3 Maternal Health: The International Human Rights Framework

A discussion of the international human rights framework on maternal health is a vital starting point because it constitutes a standard against which Uganda's approach to maternal health for refugee women is

[22] UN Committee of Economic Social and Cultural Rights, General Comment No 3 The Nature of States Parties Obligations UN doc E/1991/23 (1990) para 9.

[23] As above.

[24] L Chenwi, 'Unpacking "progressive realisation", its relation to resources, minimum core and reasonableness, and some methodological considerations for assessing compliance' (2013) *De Jure* 743.

[25] *CEHURD* case at 55.

measured. The right to health, which includes maternal health, is entrenched in very strong and clear terms under several international instruments to which Uganda is party. By virtue of ratification of these treaties, Uganda is under an obligation to enforce the right to health as contained in these treaties in good faith. The International Covenant on Economic, Social and Cultural Rights (ICESCR) is notable.[26] Article 12 of the ICESCR guarantees the right to health in general terms, underscoring that everyone is entitled 'to the enjoyment of the highest attainable standard of physical and mental health'. In its General Comment 14, the Committee on Economic Social and Cultural Rights (CESCR or the Committee) has observed that this right includes sexual and reproductive health.[27] The Committee has observed further that this right extends to underlying determinants of the enjoyment of the right to health including accessibility, availability, acceptability and quality healthcare.[28] With regard to maternal health and reproductive healthcare, the Committee underscores that states are to ensure that measures are in place to improve maternal health through access to pre-natal and postnatal care, emergency obstetric services and access to information.[29] A key principle highlighted by the Committee in the enforcement of the right to health, is the elimination of all forms of discrimination on multiple grounds including gender.[30] One could extend the grounds further to include nationality. Moreover, often, nationality is a basis for discrimination against refugees, whether directly or indirectly. However, General Comment 20 of the Committee underscores that nationality should not bar anyone from accessing rights guaranteed under the ICESCR.[31] The Committee made it explicit that the rights under the ICESCR are enjoyable by all including refugees and asylum seekers.[32]

[26] UN General Assembly, International Covenant on Economic, Social and Cultural Rights, 16 December 1966, United Nations, Treaty Series, vol 993, p 3.

[27] UN Committee on Economic, Social and Cultural Rights (CESCR), General Comment 14: The Right to the Highest Attainable Standard of Health (art 12 of the Covenant), 11 August 2000, E/C.12/2000/4.

[28] As above.

[29] As above.

[30] As above.

[31] UN Committee on Economic, Social and Cultural Rights (CESCR), General Comment 20: Non-discrimination in economic, social and cultural rights (art 2, para 2, of the International Covenant on Economic, Social and Cultural Rights), 2 July 2009, E/C.12/GC/20 para 30.

[32] As above.

Article 12 of the Convention on the Elimination of All Forms of Discrimination Against Women (CEDAW)[33] and article 24 of the United Nations Convention on the Rights of the Child (CRC),[34] both contain similar provisions on the right to maternal health. In its General Recommendation 24 pertaining to the right to health under article 12, the Committee on the Elimination of Discrimination Against Women (the Committee) has buttressed the obligation of states regarding this right by noting that states' duty to ensure women's right to emergency obstetric care and safe motherhood is a fundamental right that ought to be given the priority it deserves.[35] The Committee on the Rights of Child has also added its voice to the interpretation of the right to maternal health. In its General Comment 15, the Committee on the Rights of Child has provided a similar breakdown of the right to maternal health, highlighting the obligation of states to ensure that mothers have access to healthcare before, during and after pregnancy.[36] In addition to the aforementioned instruments at the United Nations level, both the International Convention on the Elimination of All Forms of Racial Discrimination[37] and the International Convention on the Protection of the Rights of All Migrant Workers and Members of Their Families[38] guarantee the right to health in very strong terms. The Universal Declaration of Human Rights (UDHR), though not binding, also declares that '[mothers and children] are entitled to special care and assistance'.[39]

[33] UN General Assembly, Convention on the Elimination of All Forms of Discrimination Against Women, 18 December 1979, United Nations, Treaty Series, vol 1249, p 13.

[34] UN General Assembly, Convention on the Rights of the Child, 20 November 1989, United Nations, Treaty Series, vol 1577, p 3.

[35] UN Committee on the Elimination of Discrimination Against Women (CEDAW), CEDAW General Recommendation 24: Article 12 of the Convention (Women and Health), 1999, A/54/38/Rev.1, chap I.

[36] UN Committee on the Rights of the Child (CRC), General Comment 15 (2013) on the right of the child to the enjoyment of the highest attainable standard of health (art 24), 17 April 2013, CRC/C/GC/15.

[37] Article 5(e)(iv) of the UN General Assembly, International Convention on the Elimination of All Forms of Racial Discrimination, 21 December 1965, United Nations, Treaty Series, vol 660, p 195.

[38] Articles 25(1)(a), 28, 43(1)(e) and 70 of the UN General Assembly, International Convention on the Protection of the Rights of All Migrant Workers and Members of their Families, 18 December 1990, A/RES/45/158.

[39] Article 25(2) of the UN General Assembly, Universal Declaration of Human Rights, 10 December 1948, 217 A (III).

At the African regional level, the African Charter on Human and Peoples' Rights guarantees the right to health among the broad catalogue of socio-economic rights.[40] A similar guarantee is evident in article 14 of the Protocol to the African Charter on Human and Peoples' Rights on the Rights of Women in Africa (Maputo Protocol) which protects women's right to health, including sexual and reproductive health.[41] The African Commission on Human and Peoples' Rights has given interpretive guidance on article 14 of the Maputo Protocol, thus, making states' obligations regarding this right clear and free from ambiguity. It is worth noting that, studies have shown that states including Uganda have generally not been keen on committing sufficient funds towards the realisation of the right to health.[42] In instances where resources have been allocated, the finances have not been targeted to those who are most in need of assistance. Consequently, the poor and most vulnerable are still left in limbo, because of the multiple barriers that prevent them from benefiting from the allocated funds.[43] In giving interpretive guidance to this right, the African Commission has emphasised that states are under an obligation to 'allocate adequate financial resources for strengthening of public health'. This, in the African Commission's view, includes 'making specific budget allocation under the health budget at the national and local levels'.[44] Emphasis on targeted budget allocations has also been buttressed by the United Nations Technical guidance on the application of a human rights-based approach to the implementation of policies and programmes to

[40] Article 16 of the OAU, African Charter on Human and Peoples' Rights (Banjul Charter), 27 June 1981, CAB/LEG/67/3 rev. 5, 21 ILM 58 (1982).

[41] African Union, Protocol to the African Charter on Human and People's Rights on the Rights of Women in Africa, 11 July 2003.

[42] 'Uganda government takes Shs1.7 trillion for jet fighters' *Monitor* 26 March 2011 https://www.monitor.co.ug/uganda/news/national/uganda-government-takes-shs1-7-trillion-for-jet-fighters-1488866 (accessed 20 May 2021); Twinomugisha (n 2) 31.

[43] WHO 'Public financing for health in Africa: From Abuja to the SDGs' (2016) 8; F Castrol-Leal et al. 'Public spending on health care in Africa: Do the poor benefit?' (2000) 78 *Bulletin of the World Health Organisation* 66.

[44] Paragraph 62. See also African Union's 2001 Abuja Declaration on funding national health budgets. In this Declaration, heads of state in Africa pledged to allocate at least 15 per cent of annual expenditure to health.

reduce preventable maternal morbidity and mortality.[45] These guidelines offer direction to states on how to plan, budget, implement, account and monitor the financial resources directed towards prevention of maternal morbidity and mortality. Of relevance to refugee women and poor women generally is the United Nations' emphasis on budget allocations being accompanied by accountability measures that ensure access to maternal health services to the poor.[46] For refugee women in Uganda and elsewhere, this is particularly important because this category of women is generally financially constrained.[47] Therefore, targeted allocation and accountability, taking into account the plight of poor women, becomes indispensable in the realisation of maternal health rights.

Although not legally binding, the African region also has several principles, guidelines, resolutions, campaigns and agendas lending impetus to the effective realisation and enforcement of the right to maternal health for refugee women. Notable instruments include the African Commission on Human and Peoples' Rights Principles and Guidelines on the Implementation of ESCR in the African Charter,[48] the African Union Campaign on Accelerated Reduction of Maternal Mortality in Africa,[49] the Pretoria Declaration on ESCR in Africa,[50] Resolution on the Programme of Essential Medicines for Children and their Mothers[51] and the Resolution on Maternal Mortality Rate in Africa by the African Commission.[52]

[45] HRC 'Technical guidance on the application of a human rights-based approach to the implementation of policies and programmes to reduce preventable maternal morbidity and mortality: Report of the United Nations High Commissioner for Human Rights' UN Doc A/HRC/21/22 (2 July 2012).

[46] HRC (n 44) para 52.

[47] CH Logie et al. 'Exploring resource scarcity and contextual influences on wellbeing among young refugees in Bidi Bidi refugee settlement, Uganda: Findings from a qualitative study' (2021) 15 *Conflict and Health* 3 https://conflictandhealth.biomedcentral.com/articles/10.1186/s13031-020-00336-3 (accessed 21 June 2022).

[48] African Commission on Human and Peoples' Rights (The Commission) Principles and Guidelines on the Implementation of Economic, Social and Cultural Rights in the African Charter on Human and Peoples' Rights (2010).

[49] African Union, Campaign on Accelerated Reduction of Maternal Mortality in Africa (2009).

[50] African Commission on Human and Peoples' Rights, Pretoria Declaration on Economic, Social and Cultural Rights in Africa (2004).

[51] OAU, Resolution on the programme of essential medicines for children and their mothers, CM/Res. 1164 (XLVIII) (1988).

[52] African Commission on Human and Peoples' Rights, Resolution on Maternal Mortality Rate in Africa, ACHPR/Res.135(XXXXIV)08 (2008).

While the above international instruments do not make explicit provision for the right to maternal healthcare for refugee women, a progressive interpretation of the provisions contained therein makes room for their application to the unique circumstances of refugee women in Uganda, whose maternal health rights continue to be threatened. These instruments' reference words such as 'everyone', is testament to the fact that they encompass all categories of individuals including refugee women. It is unfortunate that both the United Nations Convention relating to the Status of Refugees[53] and the Organisation of African Unity (now African Union) Convention Governing the Specific Aspects of Refugee Problems in Africa,[54] make no explicit provision for the right to health. Commendably, however, both make explicit provision for some key socio-economic rights including the right to work and some welfare rights. These Conventions require states to guarantee the rights of refugees, including the right to work, without discrimination.[55] The realisation of the right to work and other social welfare rights may be a gateway to the realisation of the right to maternal health. If the right to work is realised among refugee women, the income generated from work-related ventures can help refugees to access financial services that would otherwise be inaccessible to them.

Moreover, while the United Nations Convention relating to the Status of Refugees is silent on some socio-economic rights, in article 5, the Convention makes it clear that 'nothing in [the UN Convention on Refugees] shall be deemed to impair any rights and benefits granted by a Contracting State to refugees apart from [the] Convention'.[56] There are rights guaranteed under various Conventions which, though not making specific mention of maternal health rights, are interrelated to the right to maternal health.[57] At the World Conference on Human Rights in Vienna on 25 June 1993, during which the Vienna Declaration and Programme of Action was adopted, states resolved that

[53] UN General Assembly, Convention Relating to the Status of Refugees, 28 July 1951, United Nations, Treaty Series, vol 189, p 137.

[54] OAU, Convention Governing the Specific Aspects of Refugee Problems in Africa (OAU Convention), 10 September 1969, 1001 UNTS 45.

[55] Article 3 of the UN Refugee Convention (n 54); art 4 of the OAU Convention (n 55).

[56] Article 5 of the UN Refugee Convention (n 54).

[57] See for example the wide catalogue of rights guaranteed under the ACHPR, ICESCR and the ICCPR.

> all human rights are universal, indivisible and interdependent and interrelated. The international community must treat human rights globally in a fair and equal manner, on the same footing, and with the same emphasis.[58]

Several rights are related to the right to maternal health; therefore, the violation of maternal health rights directly undermines these rights and vice-versa. The right to life, dignity, equality and freedom from torture/cruel/inhuman/degrading punishment are notable. Many women, including refugee women, have succumbed to death due to failure by states to respect, protect and fulfil the right to maternal health. The *Anguko* case in the introduction section above serves as a vivid example. It is therefore easy to see how the right to maternal health is directly related to the right to life. These two rights are thus indivisible, interdependent and interrelated. Effectively, provisions such as article 5, as well as other rights such as the right to life guaranteed under both national constitutions and human rights treaties, create an entry point for the realisation of the right to maternal healthcare. Also, respect, protection and fulfilment of maternal health rights directly result in the realisation of other rights including the right to dignity and life.

From the brief discussion in this section, it is clear that there is an obligation on Uganda to ensure that the maternal health rights of refugee women are guaranteed. In terms of the 2012 decision of the Constitutional Court in *Uganda v Thomas Kwoyelo*,[59] it was settled that the Constitution of Uganda not only recognises, but also legitimises the direct application of international human rights instruments to court proceedings in Uganda. Therefore, Ugandan courts can draw directly on these instruments in the adjudication of human rights complaints.

4 Maternal Health Rights in Uganda

This section demonstrates that while Uganda has a legal framework at the national level which provides a foundation for the enforcement of maternal health rights, there is a complex web of barriers that make the realisation of this right a myth. The section also demonstrates that the barriers

[58] Paragraph 5 of the UN General Assembly, Vienna Declaration and Programme of Action, 12 July 1993, A/CONF.157/23.

[59] *Uganda v Thomas Kwoyelo*, Constitutional Appeal 1 of 2012.

to access are exacerbated among refugee women, and this increases the rate of violation of the maternal health rights of refugee women in Uganda.

At the national level, the Constitution of Uganda does not make explicit provision for maternal health rights.[60] This is a gap in the law that has impacted negatively on the judicial enforcement of these rights for both Ugandan women and refugee women. However, the Constitution has a wide range of rights which have a bearing on maternal health rights. In line with the notion of interdependence of rights under human rights law,[61] the realisation of these rights contributes to the realisation of maternal health rights and the violation of these rights leads to the violation of maternal health rights. Likewise, the violation of maternal health rights undermines the enjoyment of other rights and the realisation of maternal health rights impacts positively on other rights such as the right to life, dignity, equality, freedom from torture, cruel and inhuman treatment and the right to security of person.

Other key explicitly entrenched provisions critical to the realisation of maternal health rights are: the obligations of the state 'to ensure provision of medical services to the population' and 'to encourage and promote proper nutrition'.[62] The Constitution also makes explicit provision for women's rights, amongst which, is the mandate to 'protect women and their rights, taking into account their unique status and natural maternal functions in society'.[63] The Refugees Act of Uganda mentions refugee women and makes it clear that they are

> entitled to equal enjoyment and protection of all human rights and fundamental freedoms in economic, social, cultural, civil or any other fields as provided for in the Constitution and other relevant laws in force in Uganda and international and regional instruments to which Uganda is a party.[64]

[60] Under Uganda's Constitution, mention of health is in a section referred to as National Objectives and Directive Principles on State Policy (NDSP) rather than the section on guaranteed rights. In terms of NDSP XX, 'The State shall take all practical measures to ensure the provision of basic medical services to the population'.

[61] In *Serac v Nigeria* AHRLR 20 (ACHPR 2001), The African Commission on Human and Peoples' Rights observed that the right to health and other rights are inseparably linked.

[62] Objective XX and XXII of the NODPSP.

[63] Article 33(3) of the Constitution of the Republic of Uganda, 1995.

[64] Section 33 of the Refugees Act 2006.

In terms of lived experiences, generally, there are gaps in access to healthcare among refugees in Uganda. Discrimination remains rife, with refugee women always feeling like they do not belong.[71] Sexual and reproductive health services remain inaccessible to a significant number of refugee women.[72] Refugee women in camps report that they have experienced stigma and discrimination.[73] They are often discriminated against based on nationality when accessing healthcare, as services are not equitably distributed.[74] Refugee women face financial constraints resulting from the challenges of accessing the employment market.[75] This makes their access to healthcare services a challenge particularly where they have to pay to access certain services. Challenges of access to healthcare are exacerbated by language barriers which make it difficult for refugee women to communicate effectively with health practitioners, locals, Ugandan nationals and fellow refugees.[76] In a bid to cope and blend into the Ugandan community, some women have resorted to marrying Ugandan men.[77] It is assumed that marriage will provide them some form of protection from the harsh realities of life in refugee camps.[78] Unfortunately, some refugee girls have ended up being married off at a young age and this has led to early pregnancy and exposed them to maternal health challenges.

Literature abounds on the barriers to the realisation of maternal health rights in Uganda. The work of scholars like Twinomugisha[79] and researchers from organisations such as the UNCHR[80] have gone to great lengths to demonstrate the true state of maternal health in Uganda. This literature

[71] H Mwenyango et al. 'Health needs and challenges of women and children in Uganda's refugee settlements: Conceptualising a role for social work' (2021) *International Social Work*, https://doi.org/10.1177/002087281986501

[72] R Nara et al. 'A Multi-Methods Qualitative Study of the Delivery Care Experiences of Congolese Refugees in Uganda' (2020)4 *Maternal Child Health Journal* 1073–1082. doi: https://doi.org/10.1007/s10995-020-02951-1.

[73] Refugee Law Project, 'Psychosocial Challenges among Refugee Women and Girls in Nakivale Refugee Settlement' (2015) *Research Report* 38 & 43.

[74] As above.

[75] Refugee Law Project (n 74) 40.

[76] Refugee Law Project (n 74) 41.

[77] Refugee Law Project (n 74) 42.

[78] As above.

[79] Twinomugisha (n 2) 1–55.

[80] See, for example, A Whelani et al. 'Evaluation of quality, access to and use of reproductive health services for refugees and internally displaced persons' (2004) United Nations High Commissioner for Refugees and United Nations Population Fund.

demonstrates the mismatch between the excellent national and international laws on the one hand, and the enforcement of maternal health rights on the other. However, not much of the engagement has linked these barriers to refugee women as a vulnerable group. The literature has divided these barriers into two categories, namely, immediate causes/barriers and structural causes.[81] Amongst the immediate causes of death among mothers are hypertensive disorders, postpartum hemorrhage, complications resulting from unsafe abortion, obstructed labour, prolonged labour and lack of access to skilled healthcare services.[82]

There are also multiple structural barriers to the realisation of this right. The financial cost involved in accessing maternal healthcare and other related health services is a barrier. At the heart of structural barriers is the neo-liberal culture in Uganda which is characterised by the market model to public services.[83] As a result of this model, there is now limited government involvement in the delivery of essential services such as healthcare.[84]Public hospitals which ideally ought to be platforms for states' actual fulfilment of the right to maternal health have been crippled by privitisation. Most public hospitals in Uganda now have private service and public service options.[85] The private service option, of course, on account of coming at a hefty price, generally offers better services than the public service option. Unfortunately, many women in Uganda, especially the most vulnerable, cannot afford the hefty price that comes with such services, and it is these very women that have often succumbed to death and formed part of the maternal mortality rate statistics.

The issue of financial accessibility and poverty brings sharply into focus the vulnerable women in Uganda, amongst which are refugee women. For refugee women, who often have no reliable source of income, with some still finding their feet financially,[86] poverty is tantamount to death because

[81] Twinomugisha (n 2) at 20–21.

[82] As above.

[83] Twinomugisha (n 2) at 20.

[84] As above.

[85] Twinomugisha (n 2) at 25.

[86] United Nations High Commissioner for Refugees Uganda 'Women and girls Fact Sheet - Southwest Uganda' (2014) 1–4; World Bank 'Uganda refugee and host communities' (2018) http://documents1.worldbank.org/curated/en/571081569598919068/pdf/Informing-the-Refugee-Policy-Response-in-Uganda-Results-from-the-Uganda--Refugee-and-Host-Communities-2018-Household-Survey.pdf (accessed 20 May 2021); Logie et al. (n 46).

they cannot afford private services to save their lives. Effectively, the risk of them succumbing to death is exacerbated by the vulnerable circumstances under which they find themselves. There are Non-Government Organisations that have intervened to address the plight of refugee women.[87] These, however, can only go so far and the question remains, what is the quality of service in public health facilities? It is notable that most of the well-equipped hospitals are located in Kampala, the capital city of Uganda. Most refugee women, however, are based in the rural areas of Uganda.[88] Most of the hospitals in the rural areas of Uganda have a shortage of specialised professionals, equipment and skilled workers.[89] The majority of these rural-based hospitals cannot attend to the complex maternal health needs of refugee women.[90]

It is on record that in most of the hospitals in rural Uganda, there is a shortage of skilled health professionals to attend to complications that require surgery.[91] The government has also conceded to this challenge, yet no clear and targeted solutions have been explored to address this gap.[92] In some public health facilities, medical practitioners are known to absent themselves from work. They commit more time to their private health practices.[93] This causes more challenges to the already strained public health system. Aside from the foregoing, corruption in hospitals remains

[87] OCHA 'CERF: Providing maternal health care in a refugee camp in Uganda' (2012) https://www.unocha.org/story/cerf-providing-maternal-health-care-refugee-camp-uganda (accessed 20 May 2021).

[88] J Kasozi et al. 'Access to health care by urban refugees and surrounding host population in Uganda' (2018) 3 *World Journal of Public Health* 32. According to the study by Kasozi et al., only a minority of refugees reside in rural areas (about 34,000 of the 1.4 million refugees in Uganda). While they have access to equipped health facilities compared to their counterparts in rural areas, they are constrained by the financial cost that comes with accessing these facilities. The situation is much worse in rural areas because there is a lack of access to the good quality facilities. This challenge is coupled with the price that sometimes comes with the price attached to the service in these rural facilities.

[89] G Babughirana et al. 'Maternal and newborn healthcare practices: Assessment of the uptake of lifesaving services in Hoima District, Uganda' (2020) 20 *BMC Pregnancy and Childbirth* 686 https://doi.org/10.1186/s12884-020-03385-x

[90] *CEHURD* case, at 15–21.

[91] As above.

[92] As above.

[93] R Tweheyo et al. 'I have no love for such people, because they leave us to suffer': a qualitative study of health workers' responses and institutional adaptations to absenteeism in rural Uganda' (2019) *BMJ Global Health*, https://gh.bmj.com/content/4/3/e001376

rife,[94] with the poor being on the extreme end of the vulnerability continuum. Thus, refugee women are not only barred from accessing these equipped hospitals in Kampala physically, but they also cannot access them financially. Effectively, healthcare has become a commodity in Uganda that only the wealthy can afford. It has been highly privatised and monetised, leaving vulnerable women, including refugee women with little to no access. In this regard, the disadvantage experienced by refugee women is aggravated.

Generally, the national framework on health in Uganda is structured in a manner that oppresses the poor and vulnerable. Incidentally, the law which ought to be a tool for the realisation of maternal health rights has also brought with it a layer of oppression against vulnerable women. Some laws on health practice, though seemingly neutral, have had the effect of oppressing the vulnerable in society. For example, these laws allow health practitioners to levy reasonable charges for the services offered.[95] Twinomugisha rightly submits that the lack of definitive content to the term 'reasonable' has left this term vague and open to abuse by health practitioners who levy extremely high fees that the poor and vulnerable in Uganda's society cannot afford.[96] These abnormal prices have not been checked by the government despite the obligation of states to protect women from abuse meted out on them by third parties.[97] In this regard, the obligation to protect remains illusory in as far as pricing of maternal health services in Uganda is concerned. Twinomugisha aptly states that 'in Uganda, those unable to pay for maternal health services in the market have to accept their fate and die or suffer debilitating injuries'.[98] Of course, amongst those struggling to pay and eventually accept the fate of death are refugee women.

[94] Twinomugisha (n 2) at 27.

[95] See, for example, sec 42 of the Medical and Dental Practitioners' Act Cap 272 Laws of Uganda; and sec 49 of the Nurses and Midwives Act Cap 274 Laws of Uganda.

[96] Twinomugisha (n 2) at 20.

[97] In *Asero v Attorney General* HCCC Petition 409 of 2009 (20 April 2012). the High Court at Nairobi ruled that the obligation of the state regarding rights does not merely entail refraining from violating a right in issue, but also, protecting individuals from violations by non-state actors.

[98] Ministry of Health Uganda 'The Annual Health Sector Performance Report 2018/2019' (2019) http://library.health.go.ug/publications/performance-management/annual-health-sector-performance-report-20182019 (accessed 20 May 2021).

Laws that criminalise abortion also reportedly undermine the realisation of maternal health rights.[99] Unsafe abortions account for 5 per cent of maternal deaths in Uganda.[100] The laws criminalising abortion have effectively exposed already vulnerable women to unsafe methods of terminating pregnancies. In an interview with one medical doctor, Dr. Kiggundu of Kawempe Hospital in Uganda it was commented that,

> what is documented for Kawempe alone shows that more than 800 women seek post-abortion services from the hospital when the situation is already out of hand and many of them show with advanced complications and can't be saved... lives are lost when doctors are still weighing between helping victims because of the likely repercussions to them.[101]

Lives are not only lost when doctors are weighing the option of whether or not to offer a service, but also when refugee women, who risk deportation for breaking the law, have to choose between seeking medical help or dealing with the consequences of unsafe abortions. For refugee women therefore, the risk of deportation on account of the criminal act of abortion adds another layer of vulnerability and ultimately impacts on their enjoyment of maternal health rights.

Local integration is praiseworthy as it ensures that refugees have an opportunity to enjoy a broader catalogue of socio-economic rights in the host country. However, if not properly managed, it could increase the risk of abuse and discrimination against refugee women. Uganda, as already alluded to, has been lauded for performing exceptionally well in as far as local integration of refugees is concerned. While this is positive, it could also be negative particularly where there are no measures in place to ensure access. Because refugee women are expected to be integrated into the

[99] K Singh & SS Ratnam 'The influence of abortion legislation on maternal mortality' (1998) 5 *International Journal of Gynecology & Obstetrics* S123 https://doi.org/10.1016/s0020-7292(98)00194-5; E Koch et al. 'Abortion legislation, maternal healthcare, fertility, female literacy, sanitation, violence against women and maternal deaths: a natural experiment in 32 Mexican states' (2015) 5 *BMJ Open* e006013; FE Okonofua 'Contribution of anti-abortion laws to maternal mortality in developing countries' (2008) 3 *Expert Review of Expert Review of Obstetrics & Gynecology* 147.

[100] J Nteziyaremye 'Abortion, maternal mortality and the law in Uganda: Mini-review' (2020) 10 *Primary Health Care* 343.

[101] International Federation of Gynaecology and Obstetrics 'End preventable deaths and disability from unsafe abortion' (2020) https://www.figo.org/news/end-preventable-deaths-and-disability-unsafe-abortion (accessed 20 May 2021). Interview with Dr. Kiggundu.

maternal healthcare system in Uganda, often no effort is made to ensure that where such access is a challenge, additional measures are put in place to support them. Based on the discussion thus far, it goes without saying that access to the highest attainable standard of maternal health rights comes with a price that not many refugees are able to pay. Local integration effectively creates an illusion of access. However, the reality on ground is that most refugee women only have access to rural or poor health facilities which are often incapable of addressing complex and unique maternal health needs.[102]

Access remains a major barrier, with reports revealing the dire state that refugee women often find themselves in. For example, even though refugee women are generally considered locally integrated, financial constraints have meant that some of them walk for tens of kilometres to access a health facility that may be too poorly equipped to meet their maternal health needs.[103] Access has also been undermined by discrimination. Reports reveal that many refugee women are discriminated against based on their marital status.[104] Some health practitioners have demanded details of the men responsible for their pregnancies, where such information is not satisfactory, refugee women are deemed as lacking in morals and not worthy of receiving a service.[105] Such demands are not just unrealistic, but also problematic given the circumstances under which some refugee women conceive. For some, conception has resulted from sexual violence against them during armed conflict, forced and early marriage, etc.[106] Some leave their countries of origin abruptly, leaving their spouses behind. Access has also been undermined due to the requirement of identification. In some instances, health practitioners have demanded women to prove their identity before offering a health service.[107] Again, these expectations are out of step with reality because some refugee women, in fleeing their countries of origin, did not have the time to carry identity documents along. For some identification documents were destroyed during the con-

[102] UNHCR Uganda 'Women and girls Fact Sheet - Southwest Uganda' (2014) 1–4.

[103] Whelani et al. (n 76).

[104] M Tanabe et al. 'Intersecting sexual and reproductive health and disability in humanitarian settings: Risks, needs, and capacities of refugees with disabilities in Kenya, Nepal, and Uganda' (2015) 33 *Sexuality & Disability* 411.

[105] As above.

[106] UNHCR Uganda, Fact Sheet (n 102).

[107] M Addaney 'A step forward in the protection of urban refugees: The legal protection of the rights of urban refugees in Uganda' (2017) 17 *African Human Rights Law Journal* 218.

flict. Furthermore, some refugee women are unable to communicate in the languages spoken in Uganda such as English and Luganda.[108] For these women, local integration remains a myth and continues to undermine their maternal health rights as they cannot effectively communicate with health practitioners.[109]

Crenshaw has advanced a concept referred to as 'intersectionality' that helps us to make sense of the multiple layers of vulnerability that individuals encounter as a result of their multiple identities. Crenshaw first coined the term 'intersectionality' in 1989 to underscore that individuals can have cross-cutting identities and these identities overlap to heighten discrimination.[110] Because of differences in identity by individuals, a general approach to addressing the disadvantage that various individuals experience may fall short due to failure to address the unique realities and experiences of these individuals. Refugee women in Uganda carry a number of identities. They are mostly black, of the female gender, non-nationals of Uganda and often from a poor social class. Therefore, they experience discrimination based on race, gender, nationality and class. These multiple identities place them in disadvantaged positions. Such disadvantage overlaps or compounds, thus, heightening the nature of discrimination that they experience in accessing basic rights including maternal healthcare. It follows that a 'one-size fits all' response that fails to take cognisance of these various layers of disadvantage perpetuates disadvantage against refugee women. For example, if maternal healthcare is made available without Uganda taking targeted steps to address the fact that women refugees are non-nationals, who cannot communicate in the local languages of Uganda, policy interventions will still not deliver on their intended outcomes.

In sum, the realisation of maternal health rights in Uganda remains a challenge for women generally. While refugee women experience similar

[108] See, for example, the discussion by L Hanmer & M Elefante 'Refugee women face complex barriers to proving identity' (2020) https://blogs.worldbank.org/dev4peace/refugee-women-face-complex-barriers-proving-identity (accessed 20 May 2020).

[109] 'Language barrier hindering refugee access to health services' *Monitor* 11 July 2018 https://www.monitor.co.ug/uganda/special-reports/language-barrier-hindering-refugee-access-to-health-services-1767568 (accessed 20 May 2021); A Walnycki et al. *Towards more inclusive urban health systems for refugee wellbeing* (2019) 1–21; J Jesuthasan et al. 'Health-related needs and barriers for forcibly displaced women: A systematic review' (2019) 3 *Gender and the Genome* 1.

[110] Kimberle Crenshaw, 'Demarginalizing the Intersection of Race and Sex: A Black Feminist Critique of Antidiscrimination Doctrine, Feminist Theory and Antiracist Politics' (1989) *The University Of Chicago Legal Forum* 139–167.

barriers to maternal health rights as other Ugandan women, many of these barriers are exacerbated by the refugee context in which these women find themselves. Uganda boasts of a solid international human rights framework, national legal framework and national policies on health,[111] yet, most of these remain unimplemented.[112] Could the recent *CEHURD* decision on maternal health rights be instructive on how to confront some of these barriers? How would an intersectional lens ensure the best outcomes for its implementation regarding refugee women?

5 The *CEHURD* Case and Its Instructiveness in Addressing Refugee Women's Vulnerability

This section engages with the *CEHURD* case. The discussion in the section is with a view of identifying key rulings that are instructive in addressing the multiple layers of disadvantage that refugee women experience in accessing maternal health services. The facts and decision of the case are discussed first. After this, the implication of the decision for refugee women's maternal health rights, when viewed through an intersectionality lens, is dealt with.

5.1 The CEHURD *Case*

The *CEHURD* case dealt with maternal health rights in the context of Uganda. CEHURD and others lodged a petition against the government of Uganda before the Constitutional Court alleging failure on the part of the government to deliver on its mandate to guarantee maternal health rights in Uganda. The case of Jennifer Anguko who bled to death due to delays in having a skilled medical practitioner attend to her was notable.[113] Both mother and child died as a result of negligence and the absence of skilled medical practitioners at the hospital at the time.

The petition in the *CEHURD* case was first heard in 2012 in the Constitutional Court of Uganda.[114] CEHURD and others contended that

[111] On Policies, see for example, Ministry of Health 'Roadmap for accelerating maternal and neonatal morbidity and mortality rate in Uganda' (2007); Ministry of Health 'Reproductive maternal new born and child health sharpened plan for Uganda' (2013).

[112] *CEHURD* case, at 7–11.

[113] As above.

[114] As above.

the inadequate allocation of financial resources to the health sector, coupled with poor healthcare services in public health facilities contributed significantly to the high maternal mortality rate in Uganda. Effectively, CEHURD and others argued that Uganda was in violation of its obligation to guarantee maternal health rights in these facilities. The state argued in response that the petition raised political and policy issues that were not within the mandate of the judiciary to pronounce itself on. It was the state's submission that political and policy matters were the preserve of other arms of the government, in this regard, the executive. The state further argued that to therefore allow the judiciary to pronounce itself on these issues would be to undermine the principle of the separation of powers which bars, inter alia, the interference by one arm of government into the functions of another arm of government. The Constitutional Court ruled that it would not hear the matter on its merits based on the principle of the separation of powers.

CEHURD and others appealed against the decision of the Constitutional Court in the Supreme Court, Uganda's highest appellate court.[115] The Supreme Court ordered that the matter be sent back to the Constitutional Court for it to be heard on its merits. The Supreme Court reasoned that the Constitutional Court was under no circumstance being called upon to interfere in the functioning of other arms of government. On the contrary, the petitioners required the Court to rule on the issue of whether the government of Uganda had taken necessary steps to ensure the realisation of maternal health rights of women in Uganda.

The Constitutional Court proceeded to hear the matter on its merits, keenly taking note of the submissions of both CEHURD and the state. It took nine years for the Constitutional Court to arrive at its decision on this very critical subject of maternal health rights in Uganda. In arriving at its decision, very persuasive reasons were given, some of which are noteworthy. First, although the Constitution of Uganda does not explicitly entrench the right to health generally and maternal health rights specifically, the court elevated this right to a constitutionally guaranteed right.[116] This decision is therefore critical in that it settles this debate in Uganda in as far as the justiciability of the right to health/maternal health is concerned.

[115] *Center for Health, Human Rights and Development v Attorney General* (2015), Constitutional Appeal 01 of 2013 Uganda, Supreme Court.

[116] As above.

Secondly, the Court mapped out the contours of minimum core obligations in the enforcement of socio-economic rights in Uganda.[117] The state had argued that Uganda is a low-income country with meagre resources and as such, not in a position to deliver on the demands made by the petitioners.[118] But drawing on the international human rights framework on socio-economic rights as well as comparative case law from South Africa,[119] the Court ruled that the states' argument cannot justify non-compliance with core obligations.[120] The Court added that the state was in fact under an obligation to demonstrate concrete and targeted steps taken to address the maternal health needs of women. It is therefore not enough for Uganda to raise the defence of limited resources as a blanket barrier to the realisation of maternal health rights. Ultimately, the Court found the government in violation of the Constitution and made several orders including the provision of emergency obstetric care in public health facilities, training of staff in hospitals within two years, the prioritisation of funding for maternal healthcare within one year and an order requiring the Minister of Health to report back to Parliament on the progress of implementation of the orders made.

5.2 *The* CEHURD *Case and Its Implications for Refugee Women's Maternal Health Rights*

The *CEHURD* decision appears to be a general one in the sense that it addresses the plight of women generally. However, some of the orders made by the Court, if implemented, will go a long way in addressing some maternal health needs specific to refugee women. A discussion of all the orders is beyond the ambit of this chapter. For this reason, only two of the orders will be discussed in this section. The Court ruled that

> in order to meet the constitutional obligation of the state to uphold the right of women and fulfil their reproductive rights, the government should in the next financial year prioritise and provide sufficient funds in the national budget for maternal health care.

[117] *CEHURD* case, at 24–28.
[118] As above.
[119] As above.
[120] As above.

This ruling is particularly critical for refugee women who, as consistently demonstrated, are often constrained financially to pay the high price that comes with quality health services mostly available in Kampala. In the past years, Uganda has failed to accord the health sector the funding it deserves. The government of Uganda can therefore be criticised for failing to prioritise health. For example, a significant portion of Uganda's budget is devoted to sectors that are not worth the expenditure they are allotted to. The military and police take up the biggest chunk of Uganda's income. At some point, income in the amount of 740 million dollars (1.7 trillion Uganda shillings) was devoted to the purchase of military jets.[121] Approximately 600 million shillings (over 200,000 US dollars) is spent on the President daily.[122] Disturbingly, in 2016, 773 billion Ugandan shillings was spent on presidential campaigns for a president who has been in leadership since 1986 (37 years as of 2023).[123] Amidst such extravagant expenditure, the state has on several occasions argued that there are no resources to increase funding for the health sector.[124] Of course, financially stable women hardly experience the violations that result from such thoughtless and extravagant expenditure because they are wealthy enough to access quality health services. For refugee women, however, there is a triple injustice resulting from such abuse—first as not-citizens of Uganda who continue to suffer discrimination on account of nationality, secondly as women and thirdly as a vulnerable group in society. It is submitted that Uganda's position regarding funding for maternal health rights is not just an afront to the Maputo Protocol,[125] but also the Abuja Declaration which requires states to apportion 15 per cent of its national funds to the health sector.[126]

The ruling which required the state to be deliberate in budgeting effectively for maternal health demands the government of Uganda to revisit its

[121] *Monitor* (n 42).

[122] Twinomugisha (n 2) 31.

[123] 'Museveni spent Shs773b on 2016 campaign – Report' *Monitor* 9 July 2016 https://www.monitor.co.ug/uganda/news/national/museveni-spent-shs773b-on-2016-campaign-report%2D%2D1657050 (accessed 20 May 2021).

[124] See, for example, the state submission in *CEHURD* case.

[125] For example, in terms of article 26 of the Maputo Protocol: 'States Parties undertake to adopt all necessary measures and in particular shall provide budgetary and other resources for the full and effective implementation of the rights herein recognised'.

[126] See African Union's 2001 Abuja Declaration on funding national health budgets. In this Declaration, heads of state in Africa pledged to allocate at least 15 per cent of annual expenditure to health.

From the foregoing provision, it can be deduced that, 'reference to instruments that Uganda is party' to does suggest that protection of refugee women requires Uganda to have recourse to various international frameworks that provide guidance to maternal, health rights of women. These very strong guarantees, coupled with the multiple international treaties to which Uganda is party seemingly create a water-tight framework for the enforcement of the maternal health rights of all women in Uganda, including refugee women.

It is, however, notable that the maternal mortality rate in Uganda remains alarmingly high despite the exemplary legal framework. In Uganda, as of 2020, it was estimated that the maternal mortality ratio was 336 deaths for every 100,000 live births.[65] There are some health facilities in Uganda with maternal mortality ratios as high as 2578 per 100,000 live births.[66] Although there are no specific figures on the maternal mortality rate among refugee women in Uganda, studies reveal that the situation is much worse among them. In an empirical study conducted by Rustad et al. among refugee women in Northern Uganda, it was established that while public health services were available to both Ugandan women and refugee women, the latter category was 6 per cent less likely to receive antenatal care services than the former. Refugee women in this study were 4 per cent more likely to feel discriminated against than Ugandan women.[67] In terms of actual access to health facilities, the study established that there was a gap between refugee women and Ugandan women, with 10.5 per cent and 5.5 per cent of refugee women and Ugandan women, respectively, not being able to give birth at a medical facility.[68] Furthermore, refugee mothers felt less respected and welcomed than Ugandan women and this impacted directly on the quality of maternal health services they received.[69] Overall, the study found that refugee women felt generally dissatisfied with the antenatal care services offered in healthcare facilities compared to their Ugandan counterparts.[70]

[65] *CEHURD* case, at 16.

[66] *CEHURD* case at 16.

[67] Rustad et al. 'Maternal health care among refugees and host communities in Northern Uganda: Access, quality, and discrimination' (2021) *Frontiers in Global Women's Health* https://doi.org/10.3389/fgwh.2021.626002 (accessed 21 June 2022).

[68] As above.

[69] As above.

[70] As above.

budget and its priorities. This step may even require that some adjustments be made to sectors such as the military that have for decades taken up the biggest chunk of Uganda's budget. Furthermore, it has been noted in the preceding sections that most refugee women can only access hospitals in rural areas, where most of these facilities are poorly equipped. This ruling requires health facilities to be made a priority in funding. This is with a view of ensuring that they are not merely accessible to refugee women, but also capable of providing refugee women quality health services. Moreover, both the UN Convention on Refugees and the AU Convention on Refugees underscore that refugees must be given 'the most favourable treatment accorded to nationals'.[127] Drawing on the *CEHURD* case, this international obligation places a demand on the government of Uganda to go a notch higher in as far as funding for the maternal health rights of refugee women is concerned. Moreover, in line with the notion of intersectionality as discussed above, in allocating resources, it is important that the various identities of refugee women that cause discrimination are considered so that their unique realities are responded to appropriately.

The other ruling is that

> the government of Uganda through the Minister responsible for health is directed to ensure that all the staff who provide maternal health care services in Uganda are fully trained and all health centers are equipped within the next 2 financial years (2020/2021 and 2021/2022).

This ruling is critical for refugee women. As noted, many of them visit health facilities that are poorly resourced. This increases their risk of maternal death because of their vulnerable situations. This ruling is a positive one for these women as it addresses the injustice that results from their lack of access to the services of qualified health practitioners. However, a generalised implementation of this ruling may still fail to address the plight of refugee women. An intersectionality-based approach to the implementation of this ruling requires that staff are sensitised about the unique realities of refugee women, their various identities, how these identities compound to cause disadvantage and how staff should attend to refugee women's maternal health needs in light of these layers of vulnerability. For example, where the norm might be to speak to patients in local languages,

[127] See the UN Refugee Convention generally.

for refugee women who may not understand local languages, an intersectionality-based approach may require that health practitioners take language barriers into account and explore means of addressing these barriers. An intersectionality lens may also call for a rethinking of the market model to access to maternal healthcare in light of the financial constraints refugee women face which compound with other factors such as gender, race and non-national status to heighten discrimination against them. An intersectionality-based approach should generally require that available funds be allocated in a manner that pays particular attention to vulnerable groups such as refugee women—who are black, female, poor and not nationals of Uganda.

6 Conclusion

Maternal health rights continue to be under threat in Uganda. While most women in Uganda are victims of a failure by Uganda to meet its obligations in as far as this right is concerned, the risk of death is higher for refugee women. Before the *CEHURD* decision of 2020, there was no instructive judicial decision on the exact steps to be taken by the government of Uganda to protect women. With this decision, the task has been cut out for the Ugandan government. There is now a need for adequate monitoring of the implementation of the orders made. For refugee women, specific monitoring needs to be directed at addressing the intersectionality of the complex and overlapping disadvantages, prejudices and discriminations that they experience—as women, as black, as non-citizens and as a vulnerable group.

Acknowledgment The author would like to acknowledge funding from the National Research Foundation (Funding to EC Lubaale, Grant No: 127504) towards the funding of a writing retreat that informed the conceptual development and writing of this chapter.

Bibliography

Books

Walnycki, A et al. *Towards more inclusive urban health systems for refugee wellbeing* (IIED: Kampala 2019)

Chapters in Books

Hakim, JN et al. 'The right to maternal healthcare of migrant and refugee women in South Africa and Uganda: Criminal accountability as a tool to addressing violation' in Budoo-Scholtz, A & Lubaale, EC (eds) *Violence against women and criminal justice: Sexual violence and vulnerability* 303-337 (Switzerland: Springer 2021)

Theses and Papers

Mashanguri, TS 'Realising the right of access to maternal health care services for refugee women in South Africa' LLB thesis, University of Kwazulu-Natal, 2015

World Health Organisation 'Public financing for health in Africa: From Abuja to the SDGs' (2016).

Refugee Law Project, 'Psychosocial Challenges among Refugee Women and Girls in Nakivale Refugee Settlement' (2015) Research Report.

Journal Articles

Abebe, TT 'Breaking Africa's cycle of forced displacement' *Institute of Security Services* (2019) https://issafrica.org/iss-today/breaking-africas-cycle-of-forced-displacement (accessed 20 May 2021)

Addaney, M 'A step forward in the protection of urban refugees: The legal protection of the rights of urban refugees in Uganda' (2017) 17 *African Human Rights Law Journal* 218

Awolowo, A 'Fundamental objectives and directive principles of state policy as a panacea for national transformation and sustainable development in Nigeria' (2017) 65 *Journal of Law, Policy and Globalisation* 23

Castrol-Leal, F *et al.* 'Public spending on health care in Africa: Do the poor benefit?' (2000) *Bulletin of the World Health Organisation* 66

Chenwi, L 'Unpacking "progressive realisation", its relation to resources, minimum core and reasonableness, and some methodological considerations for assessing compliance' (2013) *De Jure* 742

Crenshaw, K 'Demarginalising the Intersection of Race and Sex: A Black Feminist Critique of Antidiscrimination Doctrine, Feminist Theory and Antiracist Politics' (1989) *The University Of Chicago Legal Forum* 139

Jesuthasan, J *et al.* 'Health-related needs and barriers for forcibly displaced women: A systematic review' (2019) 3 *Gender and the Genome* 1

Kasozi, J *et al.* 'Access to health care by urban refugees and surrounding host population in Uganda' (2018) 3 *World Journal of Public Health* 32

Koch, E *et al.* 'Abortion legislation, maternal healthcare, fertility, female literacy, sanitation, violence against women and maternal deaths: a natural experiment in 32 Mexican states' (2015) 5 *BMJ Open* e006013

Logie, CH *et al.* 'Exploring resource scarcity and contextual influences on wellbeing among young refugees in Bidi Bidi refugee settlement, Uganda: findings from a qualitative study' (2021) 15 *Conflict and Health* 3 https://conflictandhealth.biomedcentral.com/articles/10.1186/s13031-020-00336-3 (accessed 21 June 2022)

Mwenyango, H & Palattiyil, G 'Health needs and challenges of women and children in Uganda's refugee settlements: Conceptualising a role for social work' (2019) 62 *International Social Work* 1535 https://doi.org/10.1177/0020872819865010 (accessed 21 June 2022)

Mwenyango, H *et al.* 'Health needs and challenges of women and children in Uganda's refugee settlements: Conceptualising a role for social work' (2021) *International Social Work*, https://doi.org/10.1177/002087281986501

Nara, R *et al.* 'A Multi-Methods Qualitative Study of the Delivery Care Experiences of Congolese Refugees in Uganda' (2020) 4 *Maternal Child Health Journal* 1073-1082. doi: https://doi.org/10.1007/s10995-020-02951-1

Ngwenya, S 'Postpartum hemorrhage: Incidence, risk factors, and outcomes in a low-resource setting' (2016) 8 *International Journal of Women's Health* 647

Nteziyaremye, J 'Abortion, maternal mortality and the law in Uganda: Mini-review' (2020) 10 *Primary Health Care* 343

Okonofua, FE 'Contribution of anti-abortion laws to maternal mortality in developing countries' (2008) 3 *Expert Review of Obstetrics & Gynecology* 147

Olaiya, T 'Interrogating the non-justiciability of constitutional directive principles and public policy failure in Nigeria' (2015) 8 *Journal of Policy and Law* 23

Onyemelukwe, C 'Access to anti-retroviral drugs as a component of the right to health in international law: Examining the application of the right in Nigerian jurisprudence' (2007) 2 *African Human Rights Law Journal* 446

Singh, K & Ratnam, SS 'The influence of abortion legislation on maternal mortality' (1998) 5 *International Journal of Gynecology & Obstetrics* S123

Tanabe, M et al. 'Intersecting sexual and reproductive health and disability in humanitarian settings: Risks, needs, and capacities of refugees with disabilities in Kenya, Nepal, and Uganda' (2015) 33 *Sexuality & Disability* 411

Twinomugisha, BK 'Exploring judicial strategies to protect the right of access to emergency obstetric care in Uganda' (2007) 7 *African Human Rights Law Journal* 283

Case Law

Asero v Attorney General HCCC Petition 409 of 2009

British American Tobacco (BAT) v The Environment Action Network (TEAN) Civil Application 27/2003
Center for Health, Human Rights and Development (CEHURD) v Attorney General (CEHURD case) (Constitutional Petition 16 of 2011) [2020] UGCC 12 (19 August 2020)
Center for Health, Human Rights and Development v Attorney General (2015) Constitutional Appeal 01 of 2013 Uganda, Supreme Court
Serac v Nigeria AHRLR 20 (ACHPR 2001)
Uganda v Thomas Kwoyelo Constitutional Appeal 1 of 2012

AU Documents

African Charter on Human and Peoples' Rights, 1986
African Commission on Human and Peoples' Rights (The Commission) Principles and Guidelines on the Implementation of Economic, Social and Cultural Rights in the African Charter, 2010
African Commission on Human and Peoples' Rights, Pretoria Declaration on Economic, Social and Cultural Rights in Africa (2004)
African Commission on Human and Peoples' Rights, Resolution on Maternal Mortality Rate in Africa, ACHPR/Res.135(XXXXIV)08, 2008
African Union 2001 Abuja Declaration on funding national health budgets
African Union, Campaign on Accelerated Reduction of Maternal Mortality in Africa, 2009
Organization of African Unity (OAU), Convention Governing the Specific Aspects of Refugee Problems in Africa, 1969
Protocol to the African Charter on the Right of Women in Africa, 2003
Resolution on the programme of essential medicines for children and their mothers, CM/Res. 1164 (XLVIII) (1988)

UN Documents

UN Committee of Economic Social and Cultural Rights, General Comment No 3: The Nature of States Parties Obligations UN doc E/1991/23
UN Committee on Economic, Social and Cultural Rights (CESCR), General Comment 14: The Right to the Highest Attainable Standard of Health (art 12 of the Covenant), 11 August 2000, E/C.12/2000/4
UN Committee on Economic, Social and Cultural Rights (CESCR), General Comment 20: Non-discrimination in economic, social and cultural rights (art 2, para 2, of the International Covenant on Economic, Social and Cultural Rights), 2 July 2009, E/C.12/GC/20

UN Committee on the Elimination of Discrimination Against Women (CEDAW), CEDAW General Recommendation 24: Article 12 of the Convention (Women and Health), 1999, A/54/38/Rev.1, chap I

UN Committee on the Rights of the Child (CRC), General Comment 15 (2013) on the right of the child to the enjoyment of the highest attainable standard of health (art 24), 17 April 2013, CRC/C/GC/15

UN Development Programme 'Uganda's contribution to refugee protection and management' (2017)

UN General Assembly, Convention on the Elimination of All Forms of Discrimination Against Women, 18 December 1979, United Nations, Treaty Series, vol 1249, p 13

UN General Assembly, Convention on the Rights of the Child, 20 November 1989, United Nations, Treaty Series, vol 1577, p 3

UN General Assembly, International Convention on the Elimination of All Forms of Racial Discrimination, 21 December 1965, United Nations, Treaty Series, vol 660, p 195

UN General Assembly, International Convention on the Protection of the Rights of All Migrant Workers and Members of their Families, 18 December 1990, A/RES/45/158

UN General Assembly, International Covenant on Economic, Social and Cultural Rights, 16 December 1966, United Nations, Treaty Series, vol 993, p 3UN General Assembly, Convention Relating to the Status of Refugees, 28 July 1951, United Nations, Treaty Series, vol 189, p 137

UN General Assembly, Universal Declaration of Human Rights, 10 December 1948, 217 A (III)

United Nations High Commissioner for Refugees Uganda 'Women and girls Fact Sheet - Southwest Uganda' (2014a)

UN Human Rights Committee (HRC), CCPR General Comment 15: The Position of Aliens Under the Covenant, 11 April 1986, UN Doc HRI/GEN/1/Rev.6, (1986)

UN Human Rights Council 'Technical guidance on the application of a human rights-based approach to the implementation of policies and programmes to reduce preventable maternal morbidity and mortality: Annual report of the United Nations High Commissioner for Human Rights' UN Doc A/HRC/21/22 (2 July 2012)

United Nations, Sustainable Development Goals (2015) Goal 3: 'Ensure healthy lives and promote wellbeing for all at all ages'

Vienna Declaration and Programme of Action, Adopted by the World Conference on Human Rights in Vienna on 25 June 1993

Whelani, A et al. 'Evaluation of quality, access to and use of reproductive health services for refugees and internally displaced persons' (2004) United Nations High Commissioner for Refugees and United Nations Population Fund

National Laws and Policies

Constitution of the Republic of Uganda, 1995
Medical and Dental Practitioners' Act Cap 272 Laws of Uganda
Ministry of Health, 'Reproductive maternal newborn and child health sharpened plan for Uganda' (2013)
Ministry of Health 'Roadmap for accelerating maternal and neonatal morbidity and mortality rate in Uganda' (2007)
Nurses and Midwives Act Cap 274 Laws of Uganda
Refugees Act of Uganda, 2006

Internet Sources

Africa Renewal 'Uganda stands out in refugee's hospitality' (2019) https://www.un.org (accessed 20 May 2021)
Babughirana, G et al. 'Maternal and newborn healthcare practices: assessment of the uptake of lifesaving services in Hoima District, Uganda' (2020) 20 *BMC Pregnancy and Childbirth*, 686 https://doi.org/10.1186/s12884-020-03385-x (accessed 21 June 2022)
Central Emergency Response Fund 'CERF: Providing maternal health care in a refugee camp in Uganda' (2012) https://www.unocha.org/story/cerf-providing-maternal-health-care-refugee-camp-uganda (accessed 20 May 2021)
International Federation of Gynaecology and Obstetrics 'End preventable deaths and disability from unsafe abortion' (2020), https://www.figo.org/news/end-preventable-deaths-and-disability-unsafe-abortion (accessed 20 May 2021)
Hanmer, L & Elefante, M 'Refugee women face complex barriers to proving identity' (2020) https://blogs.worldbank.org/dev4peace/refugee-women-face-complex-barriers-proving-identity (accessed 20 May 2020)
Human Rights Watch 'Submission to the UN Special Rapporteur on Violence Against Women' (22 May 2020) https://www.hrw.org/news/2020/05/22/human-rights-watch-submission-un-special-rapporteur-violence-against-women (accessed 20 May 2021)
Ministry of Health Uganda, The Annual Health Sector Performance Report 2018/2019 (2019) http://library.health.go.ug/publications/performance-management/annual-health-sector-performance-report-20182019 (accessed 20 May 2021)
Monitor 'Language barrier hindering refugee access to health services' (2018) https://www.monitor.co.ug/uganda/special-reports/language-barrier-hindering-refugee-access-to-health-services-1767568 (accessed 20 May 2021)
Monitor 'Museveni spent Shs773b on 2016 campaign – Report' (2016) https://www.monitor.co.ug/uganda/news/national/museveni-spent-shs773b-on-2016-campaign-report%2D%2D1657050 (accessed 20 May 2021)

Monitor 'Uganda government takes Shs1.7 trillion for jet fighters' (2011), https://www.monitor.co.ug/uganda/news/national/uganda-government-takes-shs1-7-trillion-for-jet-fighters-1488866 (accessed 20 May 2021)

Rustad et al. 'Maternal health care among refugees and host communities in Northern Uganda: Access, quality, and discrimination' (2021) *Frontiers in Global Women's Health* https://doi.org/10.3389/fgwh.2021.626002 (accessed 21 June 2022)

Twinomugisha, BK 'Maternal health rights, politics and the law: Professorial Inaugural Lecture' (2016) 13 https://law.mak.ac.ug/news/maternal-health-rights-politics-and-law-professorial-inaugural-lecture (accessed 20 May 2021)

The Forced Migration Research Network, University of New South Wales (Australia) *The world's biggest minority? Refugee Women and Girls in the Global Compact on Refugees* (2017) 1–2 https://www.unhcr.org/events/conferences/59e5f4447/worlds-largest-minority-women-girls-global-compact-refugees-extended.html (accessed 20 May 2021)

Office of the High Commissioner for Human Rights 'Violence against women' https://www.ohchr.org/EN/Issues/Women/WRGS/Pages/VAW.aspx (accessed 20 May 2021)

United Nations High Commissioner of Human Rights 'Refugee data finder' (2021) https://www.unhcr.org/refugeestatistics/#:~:text=An%20estimated%2030%20%E2%80%93%2034%20million,age%20(end%2D2019).&text=Developing%20countries%20host%2086%20per,per%20cent%20of%20the%20total (accessed 20 May 2021)

United High Commissioner for Refugees, 'Africa' (2021) https://www.unhcr.org/africa.html (accessed 20 May 2021)

United Nations High Commissioner for Refugees Uganda 'Women and girls Fact Sheet - Southwest Uganda' (2014b)

United Nations Human Rights Office of the High Commissioner 'What are human rights?' (2021) https://www.ohchr.org/EN/issues/pages/whatarehumanrights.aspx (accessed 20 May 2021)

United Nations High Commissioner for Refugees 'Uganda' (2021) https://www.unhcr.org/uganda.html (accessed 20 May 2021)

World Bank 'Uganda refugee and host communities' (2018) http://documents1.worldbank.org/curated/en/571081569598919068/pdf/Informing-the-Refugee-Policy-Response-in-Uganda-Results-from-the-Uganda-Refugee-and-Host-Communities-2018-Household-Survey.pdf (accessed 20 May 2021)

United High Commissioner for Refugees 'Women' (2021) https://www.unhcr.org/women.html (accessed 20 May 2021)

World Bank 'Forced displacement: Refugees, internally displaced and host communities' (2020) https://www.worldbank.org/en/topic/forced-displacement (accessed 20 May 2021)

World Health Organisation *Changing cultural and social norms that support violence* (2009) https://apps.who.int/iris/handle/10665/44147 (accessed 21 June 2022)
World Health Organisation 'Maternal health' (2022) https://www.who.int (accessed 5 April 2022)
World Health Organisation 'Maternal mortality' (2019) https://www.who.int/news-room/fact-sheets/detail/maternal-mortality#:~:text=Key%20facts,dropped%20by%20about%2038%25%20worldwide (accessed 20 May 2021)

CHAPTER 10

The Tensions Between National Security and Refugee Protection Within the Context of the Boko Haram Insurgency in the Lake Chad Basin

Gerard Emmanuel Kamdem Kamga

1 Introduction

The aim in this chapter is to review the tensions between national security and refugee protection within the context of the Boko Haram insurgency in the Lake Chad basin. Relying on a bird's-eye view approach, insights are shared on the recent developments unfolding in a hostile environment characterised by the Boko Haram insurgency, the forced repatriation of refugees, and violation of the refugees' socio-economic rights and the rule of law. The violent rise and tenacity of the extremist organisation, Boko Haram, since 2009 brought about insecurity, a dire humanitarian situation, human rights abuses, a refugee crisis and serious governance and

G. E. Kamdem Kamga (✉)
Research and Postgraduate Division, Free State Centre for Human Rights, University of the Free State, Bloemfontein, South Africa

E. Durojaye et al. (eds.), *Realising Socio-Economic Rights of Refugees and Asylum Seekers in Africa*, Politics of Citizenship and Migration, https://doi.org/10.1007/978-3-031-16548-1_10

security issues. The bloody attacks perpetrated by Boko Haram, recently renamed 'Islamic State West Africa Province' after swearing allegiance to Islamic State or Daech, begun inside Nigeria and started to spill over Nigeria's northeastern border, Cameroon, Chad and Niger. The three countries share common borders that represent what is generally referred to as the Lake Chad basin. This chapter will focus specifically on Cameroon because for the past few years, the country has been at the forefront of news and the media for having orchestrated the forced returns of refugees from Nigeria who had been trying to escape from the Boko Haram insurgency. To further clarify, while the title of the chapter refers to the Lake Chad basin instead of Cameroon as the focus point of the study, it is because the events unfolding in this area are strongly linked to the dynamics in place across the entire region. In 2016, for example, the majority of attacks perpetrated by Boko Haram, that is, 52 per cent, occurred outside Nigeria, including 45 per cent in the northern region of Cameroon, up from 21 per cent in 2015. The following observation provides a brief context to the refugee debacle in the Lake Chad basin following the Boko Haram insurgency in the region:

> Nigeria has been dominated by violent civil conflict between opposition groups since 2009, which in addition to the 1.8 million people that have become internally displaced within Nigeria, has led an estimated 200,000 to flee to neighbouring Chad, Cameroon and Niger.[1]

While analysing the situation in Cameroon and reviewing the forced repatriation of Nigerian refugees and the national security paradigm, this chapter will also be touching on the developments across the Lake Chad basin that remain strongly connected. In so doing, a brief overview will be provided of the Boko Haram insurgency that originated not in Cameroon, but in Nigeria before spreading into neighbouring countries, namely, Cameroon, Chad and Niger. The declaration of a state of emergency by Nigerian authorities in Borno State coupled with the escalation of attacks by Boko Haram led to thousands of Nigerians fleeing to Cameroon to seek refuge. In November 2016, a note issued by the Peace and Security Council of the African Union underlined the serious impacts of Boko

[1] European Council of Refugees and Exile 'Cameroon forces Nigerian refugees back to violence' (25 January 2019) https://www.ecre.org/cameroon-forces-nigerian-refugees-back-to-violence/ (accessed 31 March 2021).

Haram's activities in Nigeria; activities that paved the way to a considerable refugee crisis and humanitarian disaster. In terms of the provisions of article 1(2) of the United Nations Convention Relating to the Status of Refugees of 1951, the term refugee means the following:

> As a result of events occurring before 1 January 1951 and owing to well-founded fear of being persecuted for reasons of race, religion, nationality, membership of a particular social group or political opinion, is outside the country of his nationality and is unable or, owing to such fear, is unwilling to avail himself of the protection of that country; or who, not having a nationality and being outside the country of his former habitual residence as a result of such events, is unable or, owing to such fear, is unwilling to return to it. In the case of a person who has more than one nationality, the term 'the country of his nationality' shall mean each of the countries of which he is a national, and a person shall not be deemed to be lacking the protection of the country of his nationality if, without any valid reason based on well-founded fear, he has not availed himself of the protection of one of the countries of which he is a national.

With regard to the legal framework of refugee protection, Cameroon has ratified a number of international standards on refugee matters, notably the 1951 Refugee Convention and the OAU Convention on the Specific Aspects of Refugee Problems in Africa. More importantly, in 2005 the country took another important step towards the protection of persons seeking refuge within its borders. A key law framing refugee matters, namely Law N° 2005/006 of 27 July 2005 establishing the Status of Refugees was enacted by the country's parliament. It is worth noting also that Cameroon is a party to the International Covenant on Economic, Social and Cultural Rights and other similar instruments. But the unfolding of the refugee crisis in the country depicts the gap between ratifying international instruments and implementing such instruments as will soon be portrayed in this chapter.

The first incursion of Boko Haram in Cameroon left the country marred by kidnappings, suicide bombings, theft and other crimes for the first time in 2013. The invasion occurred concurrently with a massive influx of refugees who were desperately knocking on Cameroon's door at its northern borders. This was not the first time that the country was experiencing a significant influx of people in distress. Given its position and status as a peaceful country in a region afflicted by recurrent conflicts and political instability, Cameroon has been host to a substantial population in distress from various parts of the continent for the past decades. To provide a proper picture of refugees' influx into the country one may consider, as of October 2019, the country recorded about 1,575,403 people of concern, including 271,960 Central African and 106,761 Nigerian refugees.[2] Despite these clarifications, in 2017 reports published by various organisations portrayed the extent to which Cameroon forcefully returned thousands of refugees from Nigeria, despite the obvious threats and deadly activities of Boko Haram across the region. In a bid to justify this move, Cameroon authorities claimed that people disguised as refugees orchestrated some of the suicide attacks that led to the loss of innocent lives. In other words, the authorities deemed thousands of Nigerian refugees a threat to national security to justify their forceful repatriation and thereby violated its international commitments to refugee protection and the rule of law. As a result, in April and May 2017, 13,000 returned from the camp to Nigeria, some of whom were killed in early September after Boko Haram attacked the Banki displacement camp where many had ended up.[3] As illustrated, the move by Cameroon attests to the violation of the key socio-economic rights of the refugees including, the right to housing, to education, to health, to food, to work and other rights. In the upcoming discussion the violation of such rights will be reviewed in detail.

The concept of national security is a complex one and over the past few years, it has become extremely popular. Increasingly, such a concept appears as a magic wand to resolve various issues especially when one does not intend to abide by laws and pre-established procedures. Wolfers rightly opines that when political formulas such as 'national interest' or 'national security' gain popularity, they need to be scrutinised with particular care. Indeed, they may not mean the same thing to different people, but more importantly they may not have any precise meaning at all.[4] The intersection between national security and refugee protection in an area subject to terrorist attacks requires further attention. How do we find the right

[2] Reliefweb 'UNHCR Cameroon Factsheet – October 2019' (31 October 2019) https://reliefweb.int/report/cameroon/unhcr-cameroon-factsheet-october-2019 (accessed 24 April 2021).

[3] Human Rights Watch '"They forced us onto trucks like animals": Cameroon's mass forced return and abuse of Nigerian Refugees' (27 September 2017) https://www.hrw.org/report/2017/09/27/they-forced-us-trucks-animals/cameroons-mass-forced-return-and--abuse-nigerian (accessed 24 April 2021).

[4] As quoted by JA Tapia-Valdes 'A typology of national security policies' (1982) 9:10 *The Yale Journal of World Public Order* 10.

balance between the protection of individual refugees and that of the entire society in the midst of terrorist threats? What are the criteria of national security and can a threat to such security justify the violation of the socio-economic rights of refugees along with key international instruments? If this is the case, what will the implications be? These are the key questions that will guide the upcoming discussions in this chapter. To understand the issue at stake, it is crucial to begin this analysis by outlining the legal status of socio-economic rights and their progressive realisation within the context of Cameroon, then proceed by reviewing the rise of Boko Haram that led to the refugee crisis in the Lake Chad basin. The third section of this chapter reviews the forced returns of Nigerian refugees and the issue of national security. The penultimate section is dedicated to the implications of such forced returns while reviewing failures to comply with the socio-economic rights of the refugees.

2 The Legal Status of Socio-Economic Rights and Their Progressive Realisation Within the Context of Cameroon

In this section, we firstly review the legal status of socio-economic rights in Cameroon before looking at the concept of progressive realisation.

2.1 *The Legal Status of Socio-Economic Rights*

In Cameroon, socio-economic rights are recognised by the state. At the international level, the country has been a party to the International Covenant of Economic Social and Cultural Rights since 1984. Nonetheless, it is worth mentioning that Cameroon is yet to sign and ratify the optional protocol to the International Covenant of Economic Social and Cultural Rights adopted in December 2008 and which entered into force on 5 May 2008. Similarly, at the regional level, Cameroon is party to a number of treaties which protect socio-economic rights including, the African Charter on Human and Peoples' Rights which it ratified on 21 October 1986, the African Cultural Charter of 1981, ratified on 29 June of the same year, and the African Charter on the Rights and welfare of the child of 1989, ratified in 1997. These international treaties may have pre-eminence over national laws. Section 45 of law No 96-06 of 18 January 1996 to amend the constitution of 2 June 1972, provides that 'duly approved or ratified treaties and international agreements shall, following their publication, override national laws, provided the other party implements the said treaty or agreement'.

At the domestic level, socio-economic rights are mentioned by the preamble to the above-mentioned law of 18 January 1996. It is important to emphasise that there is no specific section of the constitution dedicated to such rights as they are scattered across the preamble and sometimes intermingled with other rights and obligations in generic terms such as 'The State shall guarantee all citizens of either sex the rights and freedoms set forth in the Preamble of the Constitution' or 'Affirm our attachment to the fundamental freedoms enshrined in the Universal Declaration of Human Rights, the Charter of United Nations and the African Charter on Human and Peoples' Rights, and all duly ratified international conventions'. The fact that such rights reside in the preamble and not in the body of the constitution gave rise to a debate for many years. Before a new constitution was released in 1996, the question was whether the provisions available in the preamble were mere philosophical aspirations or genuine provisions vested with the same legal force as those embedded in the body of the supreme law. Since the enactment of the law of 18 January 1996, that is, the new constitution of Cameroon, the debate over the legal force of the preamble has been closed. In fact, section 65 provides that the preamble shall be part and parcel of the Constitution.

2.2 *The Progressive Realisation of Socio-Economic Rights*

In February 2019, the Committee on Economic, Social and Cultural Rights concluded its review of the fourth periodic report of Cameroon on its efforts to implement the provisions of the International Covenant on Economic, Social and Cultural Rights. During this review, the representative of Cameroon reaffirmed the equal status afforded to civil and political rights, and economic, social and cultural rights, as well as the right to development. He went on to emphasise the acceleration of growth, the creation of jobs and poverty reduction across the country. According to him, the state initiated legislative, institutional and judicial measures to strengthen the protection of economic, social and cultural rights, notably the right to education and health. With regard to the right to education for example, the report refers to the government that constructed facilities, adopted special measures for students in the north-west and south-west regions of the country, recruited teachers and improved education.

In the same vein, the report mentioned the emphasis placed on the provision of adequate food, water, energy and decent housing as well as concerns relating to decent work and the strengthening of social security.[5] Following this report, a Committee Member and Country Rapporteur raised concerns that somehow confirm that the realisation of socio-economic rights in the country is not as efficient as that of civil and political rights. In so doing, observations were made regarding the lack of strategy to ensure the economic, social and cultural rights of people subjected to attacks in the far north of the country, and in the Anglophone regions of north-west and south-west that produced more than 400,000 internally displaced persons and more than 4 million people being affected. Overall, it can be said that with regard to the progressive realisation of socio-economic rights within Cameroon context, the system of implementation is different from that of the first generation of rights, that is civil and political rights. These rights are subject to immediate realisation and justiciable, which is not the case with socio-economic rights. This probably explains why there is a chronic lack of infrastructures and basic service delivery while the right to health, education, food, shelter and work are poorly implemented. The report also mentions that since 2013, Cameroon had been threatened by the Boko Haram terrorist group whose repeated attacks had already led to the loss of thousands of lives, kidnapping, destruction of property, and the use of children as human bombs, combatants or sexual objects. This is the object of the next section.

3 A Brief Overview on the Rise of Boko Haram and the Refugee Crisis

This section will firstly review the rise of Boko Haram before turning to the refugee crisis.

3.1 *The Rise of Boko Haram*

In 2016, the Global Terrorism Index labelled the extremist organisation, Boko Haram, the world's second-deadliest terrorist group. This is a step down from its position as the deadliest in 2015. From a historical

[5] Committee on Economic, Social and Cultural Rights reviews Cameroon's report. https://www.ohchr.org/en/news/2019/02/committee-economic-social-and-cultural-rights-reviews-cameroons-report.

perspective, the Boko Haram group came into being in 2002 under the aegis of Mohammed Yusuf, known as one of several Nigerian clerics who embraced Saudi Arabia's Wahhabi/Salafi strain of Islam in the mid-1990s and who had settled in the northern region of Nigeria, an area inhabited mostly by Muslims. Boko Haram translates loosely as 'Western education is forbidden' and is the nickname in Hausa language of this extremist organisation officially known in Arabic as '*Jama'atu Ahlis Sunna Lidda'awati wal-Jihad*', which means 'People committed to the propagation of the prophet's teachings and Jihad'. The group leader, Yusuf, who claimed that Western education (translated as 'boko' in Hausa language) and the holding of government jobs are religiously prohibited, or haram, under Islam, established the tenets of this sect.[6] It is noticeable from the onset that the nickname of the organisation along with its teachings amount to an explosive mixture and a challenge to the Nigerian state and established legal order. Indeed, in an aggressive rhetoric and preaching to a growing number of followers, Yusuf called upon Muslims to remove, including by force, Nigeria's secular government and replace it with an Islamic State. The statement of Abubakar Shekau, Yusuf's deputy and current leader of a faction of the extremist group following the capture of Gwoza, Borno State in August 2014 is unequivocal:

> We are grateful to Allah for the big victory he granted our members in Gwoza and made the town part of our Islamic Caliphate. Oh you people, here I am Abubakar Shekau, still standing on my feet. I am still the leader of Jama'atu Ahlissunnah Lid Da'awati wal Jihad, that county called Nigeria; a name we don't believe; but forced to address as such because it has not better name. For us there is nothing like Nigeria but Islamic Caliphate.[7]

Tensions between the Nigerian authorities and Boko Haram escalated in July 2009 when following an altercation between members of the sect and the officers in charge of fighting violence and crime in Borno State, the former refused to comply with the instruction of the latter to wear helmets as required of motorcycle passengers. This resulted in several people being shot and wounded by the police. In retaliation, Yusuf along with

[6] UM Sani 'The popular discourses of Salafi radicalism and Salafi counter-radicalism in Nigeria: A case study of Boko Haram' (2012) 42 *Journal of Religion in Africa* 118.

[7] 'Boko Haram leader, Shekau, claims captured Gwosa now "Islamic Caliphate"' *Premium Times* 24 August 2014 https://www.premiumtimesng.com/news/167248-boko-haram-leader-shekau-claims-captured-gwosa-now-islamic-caliphate.html (accessed 14 March 2021).

his group initiated an armed uprising, breaking into a prison, attacking state symbols such as buildings as well as police stations; an uprising that quickly spread across five northern states and lasted for several days. In response, the federal government sent soldiers to restore peace and order. This resulted in more than 1000 dead, including among others Yusuf who was executed while in police's custody. Boko Haram was subsequently banned and its mosques demolished while its surviving members scattered and went underground.[8]

That day in July 2009 was followed by a year of inactivity, which later appeared to be the calm before the storm. In mid-2011, a new surge of violent attacks was directed towards churches and people of the Christian faith. Around the same time, Boko Haram came to the forefront of news and media around the world when a suicide bomber ploughed an explosive-laden car through two security barriers and into the lobby of the United Nations' offices in Abuja, killing nearly two dozen people and wounding another eighty.[9] During Christmas day church services in 2011, in a region heavily populated by migrants, many churches were bombed. In addition to this, attacks against state symbols resumed notably with the bombing of the heavily secured national police headquarters and party offices and the killing of candidates for the April 2011 national elections.

Since 2016, Boko Haram has split into two opposing factions that regularly fight each other. Its better-known faction, headed by Yusuf's deputy, Abubakar Shekau, has mainly based itself in the sprawling Sambisa forest, and is characterised by its use of women and children as suicide bombers targeting mosques and markets. The rival faction that is based in the Lake Chad region is led by the son of the founder, Abu Musab al-Barnawi who swore allegiance to Islamic State well known as IS, ISIS, ISIL or Daech, a fearsome extremist organisation that emerged in Syria, Iraq and Libya.[10] Since 2009, Boko Haram has successfully attacked schools, churches, mosques, abducted thousands of people including the 276 Chibok schoolgirls in 2014. The group members are wreaking havoc and claiming peoples' lives on a full-time basis. They have expanded their cynical activities across several borders, spilling blood and sowing

[8] J Bavier & B Kurzen 'Nigeria: Boko Haram 101' *Pulitzer Center* 17 January 2012 https://pulitzercenter.org/stories/nigeria-boko-haram-101 (accessed 14 March 2021).

[9] As above.

[10] J Zenn 'Leadership analysis of Boko Haram and Ansaru in Nigeria' (2014) 7 *CTC Sentinel: Special Issue* 23 https://www.ctc.usma.edu/leadership-analysis-of-boko-haram--and-ansaru-in-nigeria/ (accessed 14 March 2021).

desolation all over. Boko Haram's definition of 'legitimate' targets has considerably expanded and as a result, Muslims not aligned with Boko Haram's ideology and understanding of Sharia law find themselves outlawed and targeted following the process of takfir, whereby people are literally expelled from the universe of Muslim believers to become unfaithful. Reports on Boko Haram's modus operandi account for extreme brutality, including abduction and execution of anyone trying to escape, attacks on civilians, both Christian and Muslim, targeting of public spaces, such as markets and schools, and stoning of people suspected of adultery.[11] Over the years, the business of killing seems to have crossed the threshold of absolute insanity as their target is no longer confined to Christians, but Muslims and rival factions. At the time of writing, there are repeated reports referring to the (possible) death of Abubakar Shekau who may have detonated his suicide vest when rival fighters of the faction headed by al-Barnawi, tried to capture him in his hideout in Sambisa forest in northeastern Nigeria on 19 May 2021. These reports were met with mixed reactions and are yet to be confirmed by the Nigerian officials who said they are still investigating. Nonetheless, about two weeks later, on 6 June 2021, a recorded voice believed to be that of al-Barnawi in Kanuri language seems to confirm the death by suicide of Abubakar Shekau who, after being hunted in the Sambisa forest for five days 'preferred humiliation in the afterlife rather than humiliation on earth after triggering an explosive'. Whether this information is a fact or not, one needs to acknowledge that it is an unusual occurrence for a wanted terrorist to willingly announce the death of his peer. Interestingly, a few months later, in October of the same year, the Chief of Defence Staff of Nigeria's military, announced the death of al-Barnawi without providing any details of the circumstances of this death, which was first reported in September. To date, the Boko Haram insurgency has led to millions of people deserting the area to find refuge in states surrounding the Lake Chad basin, notably Cameroon, Chad and Niger.

3.2 *The Refugee Crisis*

The refugee crisis that is taking place across the Lake Chad basin was caused by the Boko Haram insurgency. There is a clear relationship of

[11] S Ladbury et al. 'Jihadi groups and state-building: The case of Boko Haram in Nigeria' (2016) 5 *Stability: International Journal of Security & Development* 1.

cause and effect between the two phenomena. Since its inception, the insurgency has led to more than 40,000 deaths and forced displacements of over 3.5 million people across the region. In 2013, the terrorist organisation started its incursion in the northern part of the country. The conflict has killed nearly 2000 people alone in that part of the state and has led to a humanitarian crisis. The Minawo camp in the northern region of Cameroon symbolises a humanitarian crisis and the refugee debacle as a whole. The camp opened its doors in July 2013 in the Far North's Mayo Tsanga department for the purpose of hosting Nigerian nationals who fled from the Boko Haram insurgency. Initially it hosted 18,000 refugees, but as of 2017, this number rose to 60,000 people, that is, three times its official capacity. At the time, 150 more people arrived on a weekly basis, while 60 babies were born during the same timeframe. In terms of size, the Minawo camp covers 623 hectares, as the authorities decided to expand the camp rather than setting up a second site in the Mayo Danay department, as proposed by the United Nations High Commissioner for Refugees (UNHCR), the United Nations agency in charge of providing assistance and protection to refugees.[12] Despite its 623 hectares, the continued influx of refugees and asylum seekers along with the intensification of Boko Haram's deadly enterprise across the region, it can be said that the refugee crisis is not nearing its end. Already, at the early stage of the crisis in 2014, it was reported that over 1500 Nigerian families crossed into Cameroon where they were mainly sheltering with host families or in local mosques, churches and schools, but following renewed Boko Haram attacks, some of these schools have been destroyed and refugees have had to flee further into Cameroon's interior. An estimate of 43,000 Nigerians had fled to Cameroon, including 26,753 refugees registered by UNHCR.

The overcrowding in Minawo camp is a genuine crisis which violates the socio-economic rights, particularly the right to housing, of refugees and asylum seekers. Moreover, it constitutes a violation of article 21 of the UN Refugee Convention which provides as follows:

[12] International Crisis Group 'The humanitarian fallout from Cameroon's struggle against Boko Haram' (21 February 2017) https://www.crisisgroup.org/africa/central-africa/cameroon/humanitarian-fallout-cameroons-struggle-against-boko-haram (accessed 2 May 2021).

> As regards housing, the Contracting States, insofar as the matter is regulated by laws or regulations or is subject to the control of public authorities, shall accord refugees lawfully staying in their territory treatment as favourable as possible and, in any event, not less favourable than that accorded to aliens generally in the same circumstances.

It is evident that the refugees in the Minawo camp in the northern region of Cameroon, have been living in degrading conditions which impact negatively on their well-being. Indeed, in a bid to ameliorate the overpopulation of the camp, the UNHCR suggested that a new area be set up for new refugees. This suggestion was ignored by Cameroon's authorities who instead preferred to expand the camp. The expansion is likely to contribute to the precarious conditions that characterise the lives of Nigerian refugees. There are numerous instruments that guarantee the right to housing especially for refugees. Yet contracting parties have almost systematically failed to comply with their obligations.

In September 2014, another report indicated that 13,900 Nigerian refugees crossed into Cameroon and Chad.[13] The report also mentioned that Nigerians were arriving hungry, exhausted, with wounded feet from the long journey, and with a high rate of respiratory infections among the children. The refugees explained that insurgents had attacked their villages in the areas of Gwoza, Bama, Pulka and Idagala in Borno State, and stole everything before burning down their houses. They escaped, walking for days until they reached Cameroon. The villages remain mostly deserted on the Nigerian side, with only the elderly and persons with disabilities remaining.[14] The following testimonies from some of these people in distress allude to the scale of the crisis and dire humanitarian situation that characterises the region. John Shetima, a refugee in Kolofata in the northern region of Cameroon, observes as follows:

> We thank the Cameroonian authorities for accepting us on their land. Despite the fear of Ebola, the government of Cameroon has let us cross the border. I come from the village of Kerawa. We were attacked in the village

[13] 'Cameroon border towns no safe haven for Nigerian refugees' *The New Humanitarian* 17 September 2014 https://www.thenewhumanitarian.org/fr/node/254862 (accessed 5 April 2021).

[14] As above.

by Boko Haram and I don't even know where my two sons could be found today.[15]

This account emphasises that the non-realisation of the right to housing is not the only issue faced by refugees. Concerns about other key socio-economic rights such as the right to food and the right to healthcare are also brought to light. These rights are core rights from which other rights are derived and without which a dignified life cannot be lived. Such rights must be realised without discrimination and irrespective of whether we are in a time of war or in a time of peace. The fact that there are hungry refugees with health issues across the Minawo camp is concerning and depicts yet another violation of their fundamental rights despite relevant international commitments. One of these recent commitments is Goal 2 of the Sustainable Development Goals (End hunger, achieve food security and improved nutrition and promote sustainable agriculture).[16] Since the invasions by Boko Haram, the socio-economic rights of refugees have been systematically violated by host countries.

An account from Lydia Ali, another refugee from Borno State, depicted the extent to which they have been negatively affected: 'Life is hopeless. My village is now in the hands of Boko Haram. People ran away and some people were killed, and some were captured by Boko Haram. We feel safer in Cameroon'.[17] During that period, the growing estimates about the massive movement of people across the Lake Chad basin were concerning. In 2014, an estimate of 75,000 people fleeing Nigeria to Cameroon, Chad and Niger led the UNHCR and its partners to call for more funding to boost the response to the growing refugee crisis.[18]

It is not an unusual occurrence for people in distress to seek refuge within Cameroon's borders. The country has a history of hosting refugees

[15] As above.

[16] Other commitments include the Rome Declaration on World Food Security and the World Food Summit Plan of Action (adopted at the Food and Agriculture Organization's (FAO) World Food Summit 1996), the adoption of General Comment 12: The Right to Adequate Food (Article 11) by the Committee on Economic, Social and Cultural Rights (CESCR 1999), the appointment of a Special Rapporteur on the Right to Food by the Human Rights Commission (2000), and the adoption of the Voluntary Guidelines on the Progressive Realisation of the Right to Adequate Food in the Context of National Food Security by the FAO Council (2004).

[17] As above.

[18] As above.

who fled neighbouring states in turmoil. Due to the political instability and ongoing armed rebellion in the Central African Republic (CAR), Cameroon previously experienced a similar influx of refugees from the eastern borders. As of 2017, a report by International Crisis Group provides relevant details about the number of refugees and the dire humanitarian situation in the country. The report mentions that the Far North hosts 87,000 of Cameroon's over 360,000 refugees, 191,000 internally displaced people (IDPs) and 36,000 Cameroonian returnees. The report further highlights that, including local Cameroonians, an estimated 1.6 million people in the Far North need urgent humanitarian assistance, and that more than half of 2.9 million people share the same plight throughout the country.[19] It is not an overstatement that the Boko Haram insurgency has so far led to a genuine refugee debacle in the Lake Chad basin in general and Cameroon in particular. Therefore, the forced return of Nigerian refugees by Cameroon security forces on the ground of national security was a disturbing occurrence that deserves detailed analysis, which is the focus of the next section.

4 Forced Return of Nigerian Refugees and the Issue of National Security

This section, first, contextualises the forced returns of Nigerian refugees before reviewing the issue of national security.

4.1 Forced Return of Nigerian Refugees

In 2018, following the forced return of Nigerian refugees and asylum seekers who fled from the Boko Haram violence, the UNHCR reiterated to Cameroonian authorities the need to protect the refugees. In a report, the United Nations agency observed that since the beginning of 2018, 385 Nigerian refugees and asylum seekers were forcibly returned from Cameroon. In May 2017, the UNHCR published two reports documenting the return of over 90,000 Nigerian refugees since 2015. As of mid-July 2015, despite the denial from authorities, additional evidence confirmed that Cameroon has indeed continued to unlawfully deport hundreds of asylum seekers at a time.[20] A report by Human Rights Watch

[19] See International Crisis Group (n 11).
[20] See Human Rights Watch (n 3).

captured the extent to which Cameroon forcefully deported Nigerian refugees. It provides the following:

> Since early 2015, the Cameroonian authorities have summarily deported at least 100,000 Nigerians living in remote border areas back to war, displacement, and destitution in Nigeria's Borno State. At least 4,402 are known to have been deported in the first seven and a half months of 2017. In carrying out these deportations, Cameroonian soldiers have frequently used extreme physical violence. Some, including children, weakened after living for months or years without adequate food and medical care in border areas, have died during or just after the deportations, and children have been separated from their parents.[21]

It is a surprising occurrence when a state traditionally considered as a host country for persons in distress to orchestrate the forced repatriation of refugees to an area subject to violence by a deadly terrorist organisation. Given the modus operandi of this extremist group, these unlawful deportations literally amount to a death sentence for those in distress. The publication of such reports by international organisations can be perceived as a call upon Cameroonian authorities and actors of the international arena to refrain from carrying out such practices that undermine human dignity. Unfortunately, the reports did not dissuade security forces from resuming entry denial and the forced repatriation of Nigerian refugees. Until recently, additional reports described how non-admissions at the border and forceful deportations were intensified by the authorities. In November 2018, more than 80,000 Nigerians were forcibly displaced in the north-east of the country, due to an upsurge of violent clashes between Nigerian security forces and members of Boko Haram. Civilian populations who fled the violence were denied refuge by Cameroon authorities who forcibly sent them back across the border.[22] In the same vein, a Boko Haram attack on the Nigerian town of Rann on 14 January 2019, during which buildings were destroyed, looted and burned to the ground compelled more than 9000 people to leave an area that looked like a graveyard and flee into Cameroon. At the time, the UNHCR continued to grow concerned about the forced return of thousands of Nigerian refugees from Cameroon following the return of 267 refugees two days later, on 16 January. Due to these occurrences, the UN refugee agency expressed its

[21] As above.

[22] See European Council of Refugees and Exile (n 1).

disagreement with such unexpected actions that put the lives of thousands of refugees at risk. It appealed to Cameroon to maintain its open door, hospitable policy and practices, to immediately halt repatriations, and to ensure full compliance with its refugee protection obligations. Similarly, the Norwegian Refugee Council called this development 'a breach of international and regional agreements' including the Tripartite Agreement signed in March 2017, which guarantees the protection and human rights of forcibly displaced persons.[23]

The forced repatriation of Nigerian refugees by Cameroon authorities violates section V of the 1969 Organisation of African Unity (OAU) Convention on voluntary repatriation. In addition to the OAU Convention that has a binding effect regarding voluntary repatriation, section 35 of the European Union (EU) Directive in 2011 should be noted. The concept of voluntary repatriation along with that of local integration are processes aiming to end the status of refugee.[24] From the above, it is evident that Cameroon failed to comply with the provisions of section V of the 1969 OAU Convention and section 35 of the 2011 EU Directive. These failures indirectly amount to non-compliance with the socio-economic rights of refugees, which constitute the backbone of refugees' protection. The forced repatriation implies that the right to housing, healthcare, education, food, water and other similar rights have been subject to serious violations by Cameroon, a contracting party to the international Covenant on Economic, Social and Cultural Rights.

Thus far, the analysis has focused only on the forced returns of Nigerian refugees from Cameroon followed by condemnation. Next, it must be inquired on which ground (should there be any) Cameroon, a states party to numerous international agreements which protect refugees, openly violates such agreements. Authorities argue that the forced return of Nigerian refugees was a matter of national security. This is the focus of the next section.

[23] As above.

[24] Sergio Carciotto & Cristiano d'Orsi 'Access to socio-economic rights for refugees: A comparison across six African countries' The Scalabrini Institute for Human Mobility in Africa (March 2017) http://sihma.org.za/reports/Final_report.pdf (accessed 2 April 2022).

4.2 Issue of National Security

After several forced deportations of Nigerian Refugees by Cameroonian authorities, an emergency meeting with representatives of the National Emergency Management Agency, Borno State Emergency Management Agency and civil society groups at the Government Reservation Area took place. During that meeting, the UNHCR regional representative in Nigeria stressed the following:

> The Cameroonian government has severally claimed that the refugees from Nigeria currently taking refuge in Kolofata, Minawawo, Marua and other communities in Cameroon constituted security and economic threats to its corporate existence.[25]

From the above quote, it transpires that Cameroonian authorities put forward the argument of national security to forcibly return refugees to a war zone where it is highly likely that they will not survive. The question of which arises is whether forced repatriation on the ground of national security can be a reasonable argument. The concept of 'national security' is relatively new and recently entered the strategic dictionary amidst the classic terms such as military affairs, external and military policy. National security is a term that is at present linked almost exclusively to a sovereign state's protection of its physical integrity.[26] Originally, the idea of national security was understood in the same context as the term 'national defence'. 'National defence' involved military activities aimed at the protection of the physical integrity, independence and sovereignty of nations against external threats from other states. In the contemporary society and since the end of the Second World War, this dynamic has changed. The external threat feature that until recently was the distinguished character of the national security paradigm has shifted. The threat can now also be found inside the borders of the state. In recent times, a strong emphasis has been put on the internal threat. The following observation attests to this new conception:

[25] N Musa & O Richards 'UN opposes forced return of Nigerian refugees from Cameroon' *The Guardian* 17 July 2017 https://guardian.ng/news/un-opposes-forced-return-of--nigerian-refugees-from-cameroon/ (accessed 9 April 2021).

[26] A Grizold 'The concept of national security in the contemporary world' (1994) 11 *International Journal on World Peace* 40.

> Today, the real focus of national security is the sphere of domestic politics and policies. Generally, a power elite posits a situation of 'belligerent peace' which blurs the distinctions between internal and external affairs. This elite proclaims the essential relation of security to the development of a sound economy, thus legitimizing the restrictions it may place on constitutionally mandated rights and freedoms.[27]

The above observation accounts for the recent developments within the context of Cameroon where the distinction between refugees/asylum seekers (considered here as an internal threat) and Boko Haram insurgents (the genuine external threat) has been blurred. The massive influx of refugees fleeing violence is considered by local authorities as 'security and economic threats to its corporate existence' following the above statement by the UNHCR regional representative in Nigeria. To mitigate such a 'threat' the authorities resort to drastic steps by expelling refugees and sending them back to Boko Haram-controlled areas, in violation of their human rights as well as national and international rule of law. The rationale behind Cameroon's forced repatriation of refugees amidst violence perpetrated by a deadly terrorist group is not evident and ought to be grappled with. Even though evidence is yet to be provided (which may be a matter of national security), there were allegations that Boko Haram fighters have been found among refugees returning to northeast Nigeria from Cameroon. The Borno State Emergency Management Agency alleged that during screening of the returnees at the Nigerian border town of Banki by security personnel at least nine Boko Haram insurgents and 100 accomplices were identified and arrested among 920 Nigerian refugees who returned from Marwa in Cameroon.[28] Despite these allegations, it is suggested that some of the detained may have been forced to work for Boko Haram when their village fell under the control of the latter. It could have been a significant mistake to forcibly return those Boko Haram defectors and escapees who were seeking refuge in Cameroon.

There were additional allegations that some Boko Haram insurgents had infiltrated the camps or the surrounding villages and perpetrated suicide bombings, causing death and sorrow. Reports of problems between established and newly arrived refugees in camps soon emerged. The

[27] Tapia-Valdes (n 4) 11–13.

[28] 'Boko Haram fighters found posing as refugees: Nigeria' *News24* 1 July 2017 https://www.news24.com/news24/Africa/News/boko-haram-fighters-found-posing-as-refugees-nigeria-20170701 (accessed 1 June 2021).

community often suspect refugees of being Boko Haram sympathisers. They question not only the timing of their arrival at a time when Boko Haram was weakened, but also how they managed to survive that long in Boko Haram-controlled areas. These suspicions explain why the earlier refugees remain reluctant to allow new ones to join their 184 strong camp security group, or the camp's nine committees dealing with issues like environment, water, youth and women's needs.[29] In addition to the fact that such suspicions take little account of the complex route many new arrivals have taken to get to the camp as observed by Human Rights Watch, it is of concern that Cameroonian authorities regard national security as a ground for deportation as the appropriate solution to dealing with the massive influx of refugees. Cameroon legal architecture does not deal with the concept of national security. Local legislation also does not provide for, repatriation, deportation or expulsion. The first chapter of the second book of the Cameroon Penal Code deals specifically with the notion of state security.[30] According to this Code, offences against state security encompass offences against the external security of the state on the one hand[31] and offences against the internal security of the state on the other.[32] The former is about hostility against the fatherland, sanctioned by capital punishment.[33] The latter refers to secession, civil war, spreading of false information, revolution, armed bands and insurrection, sanctioned by life imprisonment.[34] If it happens that there were indeed Boko Haram insurgents among the refugees and that local authorities intercepted them, the question of why they did not implement the provisions of the Penal Code on state security remains. In addition to the Penal Code, in 2014, to intensify the fight against Boko Haram, the Cameroonian Parliament enacted law N° 2014/028 of 23 December 2014 on the suppression of acts of terrorism. Insights into this legislation were recently made available elsewhere.[35]

[29] Human Rights Watch (n 3).

[30] Cameroon Penal Code, Book 2, Chapter 1, 'Felonies and misdemeanors against the state'.

[31] Cameroon Penal Code (n 30) sec 1.

[32] Cameroon Penal Code (n 30) sec 2.

[33] Cameroon Penal Code (n 30) sec 102.

[34] Cameroon Penal Code (n 30) secs 111, 112, 114, 115(1).

[35] For further details, see GE Kamdem Kamga 'Killing two birds with one stone: insights into the recent counterterrorism legislation in Cameroon' (2020) 53 *VRÜ Verfassung und Recht in Übersee* 190.

The insights on the legislation explain why Cameroon opted to expel the Boko Haram group as opposed to dealing with them in terms of the law. It is therefore understandable why Cameroon authorities when dealing with 'terrorists' from the Boko Haram group, expelled them from the country instead of dealing with them in accordance with the legal architecture of the state. Any terrorist or potential terrorist would appreciate being deported from the host country as a sanction. These considerations lead to the conclusion that thousands of Nigerian refugees were forcibly repatriated from Cameroon, not because they were a potential threat to national security, but for another reason that is not clear. Human Rights Watch believes that the failure to protect refugees is the result of the Cameroonian government's arbitrary decision to punish Nigerian refugees based solely on their nationality, for Boko Haram attacks carried out in Cameroon's Far North Region and to discourage Nigerians from seeking asylum in Cameroon.[36] These reasons are, however, debatable. The pretext of national security put forward by Cameroon to forcibly expel Nigerian refugees can be explained by the following observation

> As of late July 2017, international donors had funded less than ten percent of UNHCR's appeals for their Cameroonian operations on behalf of refugees from the Central African Republic and Nigeria. This significant shortfall risks sending Cameroon a message that donor governments do not care about what happens to Nigerian refugees and that Cameroon should deal with the significant challenges it faces in protecting and assisting refugees on its own. This is unlikely to encourage the authorities to be tolerant of Nigerian refugees and stop abusing them.[37]

From the above quote, it seems that insufficient funding is at the heart of the deportations. Imaginably, Cameroon (just like Niger and Chad) has been bearing most of the refugees' burden while expecting some assistance from the international community; assistance that is substantially withheld. If this scenario is plausible, it would be considered a strategy to increase pressure on the international community to provide more funding. This would not be the first time in the history of refugees that such a strategy is used by a host country. The case of President Erdoğan of Turkey threatening to open the door to Syrian refugees en route to Europe is an example. In December 2020, the European Commission and Turkey signed the final contracts under the operational budget for 6 billion euros

[36] Human Rights Watch (n 3).
[37] As above.

for the facility for refugees in Turkey. The conclusion of the remaining eight contracts for an amount of 780 million euros purport to cover the basic needs, healthcare, shelters, employment, food and infrastructure for refugees and asylum seekers in that country.

The fact that Cameroon has not received funding to comply with its humanitarian obligations towards the refugees is an unfortunate situation. This is especially true considering the case of Turkey where the remaining amount of 780 million euros were aimed at ensuring the basic needs, healthcare, housing, food, water and employment of refugees. It is enlightening to see that the purpose of this money was to realise the full array of refugees' socio-economic rights in that country. For Cameroon, as a host country to be expected to fulfil similar rights of thousands of Nigerian refugees, the international community should have done better. Unfortunately, this failure appears to be a collective one that contributed to worsening the critical situation that the Nigerian refugees find themselves in. To fulfil their legal obligations in respect of refugees, host states should be assured through a legally binding commitment, that the principle of international burden sharing will be upheld. Additionally, this principle should be infused with substantive content.[38]

Nonetheless this does not justify the forced return of refugees by Cameroonian authorities who could have dealt with the situation differently. The forced return of Nigerian refugees under the guise of national security could be a strategy by Cameroonian authorities to obtain similar concessions as in the case of Turkey. This contention is supported by the fact that even though it is a vague concept, the idea of national security must comply with certain key principles.

According to Vojin Dimitrijevic there are five characteristic features of national security. These include (1) ensuring the existence of the state as a political community, existence of the nation (which is not identical with the existence of a particular state) and the physical survival of its population; (2) protecting territorial integrity as the basic right of the state. The other facets include (3) maintaining political independence as an attribute of internationally recognised national status of the state; (4) ensuring quality of life; and (5) embedding of the vital interest of the state in the national security policy.[39]

[38] BS Chimni 'Perspectives on voluntary repatriation: A critical note' (1991) 3 *International Journal of Refugee Law* 544.

[39] As quoted by Grizold (n 25) 40.

The question of whether or not the mass influx of refugees fleeing Boko Haram was a threat to the national security of Cameroon remains. It is highly likely that in this context, some or at least the majority of the above-mentioned five features were not subject to threats from refugees and asylum seekers. It can be assumed that authorities rely on the ambiguous concept of national security, a concept that can easily justify their conduct, and that (always) legitimately obscures policies, ignorance of the rule of law and human rights violations. It is a concept that can absolve past, present and future sins irrespective of the scale of horror and damages suffered by victims. It is within this framework that the following observation must be interpreted

> If a crisis of human rights exists where the new notions of national security are applied, it is because national security has put democracy itself in jeopardy. The task, therefore, is to make national security compatible with democracy and its fundamental tenet, the rule of law.[40]

Some policies, when implemented on the ground of a threat to national security (real or alleged), can lead to serious implications. This is discussed in greater detail in the next section.

5 Implications of the Forced Return of Nigerian Refugees

There are numerous implications of the forced repatriation of Nigerian refugees from Cameroon. First, these amount to a gross violation of the socio-economic rights of refugees including the right to housing, food, work, education, healthcare and infrastructure. Even though this chapter is essentially dedicated to the socio-economic rights of refugees, it is worth emphasising the gravity of the situation that also results in the violation of core rights including non-derogable rights such as the right to life, freedom from torture and other cruel, inhuman or degrading treatment or punishment and the right to recognition everywhere as a person before the law. Reports also showed that most of the repatriated refugees have not been registered incamps. Communities suffer from severe overcrowding, water scarcity, scarcity of housing, insufficient healthcare, lack of education and poor infrastructures, which contradict the promotion and

[40] Tapia-Valdes (n 4) 35.

protection of socio-economic rights, yet guaranteed by the Constitution of Cameroon. It is true that socio-economic rights are not justiciable within the context of Cameroon. Still, it is unthinkable that refugees can experience this degree of humanitarian disaster not because of terrorists, but due to a state's refusal to protect them against a terrorist organisation. This refusal may worsen a security situation that has already entered a critical stage. Refugees and asylum seekers forcibly driven out of Cameroon and deprived of key fundamental rights are highly likely to fall prey to human trafficking and various other forms of exploitation or become the target of Boko Haram. An update from the United Nations Office for the Coordination of Humanitarian Affairs Lake Chad on 18 September 2017, confirmed the increased attacks targeted at sites for displaced people. Reference was made to Cameroon's Far North that witnessed an increase in incidents and attacks as well as a geographical shift in violent incidents from Logone-and-Chari to Mayo Sava department. Similarly, the update provides a report about the number of suicide bombers in northeast Nigeria that had become four times higher in 2017 than for the entire year of 2016.[41] In some cases, refugees had no choice, but to join Boko Haram as they had been left alone with no support, vulnerable, exposed to extreme poverty and the threat of death in an environment where the terrorist organisation is actively recruiting new members especially amongst displaced persons.

Secondly, another key implication of the forced repatriation of refugees is the violation of international, regional and domestic commitments of refugee protection and other key human rights texts such as for instance the two United Nations Covenants. Cameroon acceded to the 1951 Convention relating to the Status of Refugees in 1961 and to its 1967 Protocol in 1967. At the regional level, the country is party to the 1969 OAU (now African Union) Convention on the Specific Aspects of Refugee Problems in Africa and to the African Charter on Human and Peoples' Rights. In the same vein, in 2005, the country enacted Law N° 2005/006 of 27 July 2005 relating to the status of refugees and the Decree N° 2011/389 of 28 November 2011 on refugee management structures. The 2005 refugee law is enforced in parallel with Law N° 97/12 of 10 January 1997 relating to the conditions of entry, stay and exit of foreign

[41] Reliefweb 'Lake Chad Basin: Crisis Update No 19 (18 September 2017)' https://reliefweb.int/report/nigeria/lake-chad-basin-crisis-update-no-19-18-september-2017 (accessed 4 June 2021).

nationals that monitor the entry and residence of persons who fall outside the ambit of refugees and asylum seekers. It is evident that a robust legal architecture on refugee protection is available in Cameroon; an architecture that has been overlooked on the ground of national security. The forced repatriation of refugees amounts to the violation of international agreements on refugee protection and the rule of law. For instance, one can refer to the African Charter on Human and Peoples' Rights, which in article 12 provides as follows: 'Every individual shall have the right, when persecuted, to seek and obtain asylum in other countries in accordance with laws of those countries and international conventions'.

More importantly, non-compliance by Cameroon amounts to the violation of the core principle of international refugee law, namely the principle of non-refoulement. It is a principle provided for by article 33 of the 1951 UN Refugee Convention.[42] This principle also appears in article 3 of the AU Convention.[43] The principle of non-refoulement is further reiterated in Cameroon domestic law. Article 7 of the 2005 Refugee Law provides that

> no person shall be turned back at the border, nor subject to any measure, whatsoever, that may force him to return to or remain in a territory where his life, physical integrity or freedom is threatened by any reasons mentioned in Section 2 of this law.

The forced return of Nigerian refugees from Cameroon is an occurrence that has repeatedly been confirmed. In addition to the available legal framework preventing the expulsion of refugees, it is crucial to mention that the developments in Cameroon occurred in defiance of the 2016 UNHCR's plea to all governments not to return anyone to northeastern Nigeria until such a time that the security and human rights situation have

[42] Article 33(1) of the UN General Assembly, Convention Relating to the Status of Refugees, 28 July 1951, United Nations, Treaty Series, vol 189, p 137: 'No Contracting State shall expel or return ("refouler") a refugee in any manner whatsoever to the frontiers of territories where his life or freedom would be threatened on account of his race, religion, nationality, membership of a particular social group or political opinion'.

[43] Article 2(3) of the OAU, Convention Governing the Specific Aspects of Refugee Problems in Africa (OAU Convention), 10 September 1969, 1001 UNTS 45 provides for the principle of non-refoulement in the following terms: 'No person shall be subjected by a Member State to measures such as rejection at the frontier, return or expulsion, which would compel him to return to or remain in a territory where his life, physical integrity or liberty would be threatened for the reasons set out in Article I, paragraphs 1 and 2'.

improved considerably. A few months after the plea, a tripartite agreement of the voluntary return of refugees was signed between Cameroon, Nigeria and the UNHCR on 2 March 2017.[44] Therefore, as stressed by the UNHCR, the current forced repatriation is in gross violation of this tripartite agreement. When expressing concern about the situation, the representative of the UNHCR pointed out that there is a convention that no person or government will be allowed to flout the agreement concerning the plight of refugees.[45]

Thirdly, another key implication of the forced return of Nigerian refugees from Cameroon, is the possibility of worsening the refugee crisis across the whole region. It must be mentioned that Niger and Chad, the two other countries in the Lake Chad basin, host 250,000 and 125,000 displaced people respectively. It is unthinkable what may happen if these two countries were to emulate what has been unfolding in Cameroon. The degradation of diplomatic relations and escalation of tensions between Cameroon and Nigeria are not to be excluded. Recent developments between the two countries may be indicative of what may be viewed as a retaliatory tit-for-tat move. In June 2017, the Nigerian authorities responded to Cameroon's pressure by sending military vehicles over the border to help Cameroon deport almost 1000 asylum seekers.[46] A few months later, in January 2018, the UNHCR grew concerned about the forced return by Nigeria of some 47 Cameroonians, who were handed over to Cameroon authorities on 26 January 2018. It was further reported that most of the individuals in question had submitted asylum claims. Such returns were carried out despite the efforts of the UNHCR to engage with Nigerian authorities.[47] If such occurrences were to happen again, the victims in this case would be the vulnerable refugees and asylum seekers.

[44] The Tripartite Commission on the voluntary repatriation of Nigerian refugees from Cameroon held its first meeting from 10 to 12 August 2017 in Abuja, Nigeria. A similar tripartite agreement between the three parties was recently held on 21 February 2021 in Maroua, Cameroon.

[45] Musa & Richards (n 25).

[46] Human Rights Watch (n 3).

[47] UNHCR, 1 February 2018 'UNHCR condemns forced returns of Cameroon asylum-seekers from Nigeria' (1 February 2018) https://www.unhcr.org/afr/news/press/2018/2/5a731fcf4/unhcr-condemns-forced-returns-cameroon-asylum-seekers-nigeria.html (accessed 29 May 2021).

6 Conclusion

The purpose of this chapter was to review the tensions between national security and refugee protection within the context of the Boko Haram insurgency in the Lake Chad basin that resulted in the forced return of Nigerian refugees from Cameroon. It appears that the insurgency has led to a significant refugee crisis in the Lake Chad basin resulting in a dire humanitarian situation, human rights violations and failure to comply with national and international human rights law in terms of refugee protection. The forced repatriation of refugees is an affront to human dignity. It accounts for a situation where they have been treated not as Nigerians particularly but less than human beings. The lack of employment, housing, healthcare, education and food that characterises their conditions illuminates the extent to which socio-economic rights are still not considered as rights, but mere philosophical and ideological aspirations. The Boko Haram insurgency has a negative impact on the socio-economic, political and cultural life and the lived experiences of the refugees. The argument regarding national security put forward by Cameroonian authorities to justify their conduct and violation of local, regional and international agreements on refugee protection, remains subject to suspicion and scrutiny.

It becomes crucial to reach an understanding that the plight of the refugee is that of everyone. Relevant steps need to be initiated to address this issue in a sustainable manner. Otherwise, it can pave the way to a more complex situation with the potential of affecting everyone especially within the context of the Boko Haram insurgency. Since its inception, the extremist organisation has proven to be efficient especially in terms of recruiting displaced people, that is, refugees and asylum seekers. It is also vital to keep in mind that before becoming refugees, persons in distress fleeing violence and seeking refuge outside their country of origin, are first of all humans. Therefore, there is a duty to protect them and in so doing, states must abide by their international, regional and domestic commitments in terms of human rights in general and refugee protection in particular.

Bibliography

Journal Articles

Chimni, BS 'Perspectives on voluntary repatriation: A critical note' (1991) 3 *International Journal of Refugee Law* 544

Grizold, A 'The concept of national security in the contemporary world' (1994) 11 *International Journal on World Peace* 40

Kamdem Kamga, GE 'Killing two birds with one stone: insights into the recent counterterrorism legislation in Cameroon' (2020) 53 *VRÜ Verfassung und Recht in Übersee* 190

Ladbury, S et al. 'Jihadi groups and state-building: The case of Boko Haram in Nigeria' (2016) 5 *Stability: International Journal of Security & Development* 1

Sani, UM 'The popular discourses of Salafi radicalism and Salafi counter-radicalism in Nigeria: A case study of Boko Haram' (2012) 42 *Journal of Religion in Africa* 118

Tapia-Valdes, JA 'A typology of national security policies' (1982) 9:10 *The Yale Journal of World Public Order* 10

AU Documents

OAU, African Charter on Human and Peoples' Rights (Banjul Charter), 27 June 1981, CAB/LEG/67/3 rev 5, 21 ILM 58 (1982)

OAU, Convention Governing the Specific Aspects of Refugee Problems in Africa (OAU Convention), 10 September 1969, 1001 UNTS 45

UN Documents

UN General Assembly, Convention Relating to the Status of Refugees, 28 July 1951, United Nations, Treaty Series, vol 189, p 137

UN General Assembly, Universal Declaration of Human Rights, 10 December 1948, 217 A (III)

Internet Sources

'Boko Haram fighters found posing as refugees: Nigeria' *News24* 1 July 2017 https://www.news24.com/news24/Africa/News/boko-haram-fighters-found-posing-as-refugees-nigeria-20170701 (accessed 1 June 2021)

'Boko Haram leader, Shekau, claims captured Gwosa now "Islamic Caliphate"' *Premium Times* 24 August 2014 https://www.premiumtimesng.com/news/167248-boko-haram-leader-shekau-claims-captured-gwosa-now-islamic-caliphate.html (accessed 14 March 2021)

'Cameroon border towns no safe haven for Nigerian refugees' *The New Humanitarian* 17 September 2014 https://www.thenewhumanitarian.org/fr/node/254862 (accessed 5 April 2021)

Carciotto, S & D'Orsi, C 'Access to socio-economic rights for refugees: A comparison across six African Countries' The Scalabrini Institute for Human Mobility in Africa (March 2017) http://sihma.org.za/reports/Final_report.pdf (accessed 2 April 2022)

European Council of Refugees and Exile 'Cameroon forces Nigerian refugees back to violence' (25 January 2019) https://www.ecre.org/cameroon-forces-nigerian-refugees-back-to-violence/ (accessed 31 March 2021)

Human Rights Watch '"They forced us onto trucks like animals": Cameroon's mass forced return and abuse of Nigerian Refugees' (27 September 2017) https://www.hrw.org/report/2017/09/27/they-forced-us-trucks-animals/cameroons-mass-forced-return-and-abuse-nigerian (accessed 24 April 2021)

International Crisis Group 'The humanitarian fallout from Cameroon's struggle against Boko Haram' (21 February 2017) https://www.crisisgroup.org/africa/central-africa/cameroon/humanitarian-fallout-cameroons-struggle-against-boko-haram (accessed 2 May 2021)

Reliefweb 'Lake Chad Basin: Crisis Update No. 19 (18 September 2017)' https://reliefweb.int/report/nigeria/lake-chad-basin-crisis-update-no-19-18-september-2017 (accessed 4 June 2021)

Reliefweb 'UNHCR Cameroon Factsheet – 31 October 2019' (31 October 2019) https://reliefweb.int/report/cameroon/unhcr-cameroon-factsheet-october-2019 (accessed 24 April 2021)

'UN opposes forced return of Nigerian refugees from Cameroon' *The Guardian* 17 July 2017 https://guardian.ng/news/un-opposes-forced-return-of-nigerian-refugees-from-cameroon/ (accessed 9 April 2021)

United Nations Human High Commissioner for Refugees (The UN Refugee Agency) 'Convention and protocol relating to the status of refugees' https://www.unhcr.org/1951-refugee-convention.html (accessed on 14 March 2021)

Zenn, J 'Leadership analysis of Boko Haram and Ansaru in Nigeria' (2014) 7 *CTC Sentinel: Special Issue* 23 https://www.ctc.usma.edu/leadership-analysis-of-boko-haram-and-ansaru-in-nigeria/ (accessed 14 March 2021)

CHAPTER 11

Legal Protection of Socio-Economic Rights of IDPs, Refugees and Asylum Seekers in South Sudan: Prospects and Challenges

Joseph Geng Akech

1 Introduction

The world's youngest nation, the Republic of South Sudan, hosts more than 200,000 internally displaced persons (IDPs) residing in United Nations protection camps, 314,938 refugees and 3769 asylum seekers who are located across five states of Central Equatoria, Western Equatoria, Unity, Jonglei and Upper Nile.[1] The country is also one of the highest

[1] UNHCR 'Submission by the United Nations High Commissioner for Refugees (UNHCR) For the Office of the High Commissioner for Human Rights' Compilation Report – Universal Periodic Review: The Republic of Turkey' (June 2014) 2 https://www.refworld.org/docid/5541e6694.html (accessed 8 April 2021).

J. G. Akech (✉)
University of Juba, Juba, South Sudan

University of Pretoria, Pretoria, South Africa

E. Durojaye et al. (eds.), *Realising Socio-Economic Rights of Refugees and Asylum Seekers in Africa*, Politics of Citizenship and Migration, https://doi.org/10.1007/978-3-031-16548-1_11

contributors of refugees and asylum seekers who are mainly hosted in the region. To be precise, there are as more as 2,278,474 South Sudanese refugees living in Sudan, Ethiopia, Uganda, Kenya and the Democratic Republic of the Congo.[2] This makes 'South Sudan's refugee crisis the largest in Africa'[3] which is consistent with the finding that 'displacement has become one of Africa's most pressing human rights challenges'.[4] Furthermore, the country is used as a transit point for migrants aspiring to cross into Europe through Sudan and North Africa. Despite accession to key international and regional legal instruments for the protection of the rights of IDPs, refugees and asylum seekers, implementation remains a major challenge.

Limited implementation of legal protection mechanisms has undoubtedly, albeit partially, contributed to poor access to basic social services by the IDPs, refugees and asylum seekers. Seen from this perspective, one may argue that the aforementioned groups in fact face double vulnerabilities. The concept 'double vulnerabilities', means that socio-economic and political conditions worsen IDPs', refugees' and asylum seekers' access to socio-economic rights. It is an important way of describing the intersectionalities that put IDPs, refugees and asylum seekers into vulnerable situations. This is evident when one looks at women and children who are often among the most vulnerable groups when they are displaced and/or seeking asylum. To put this idea of double vulnerabilities into context, two examples may be cited. In the first example, there is inadequate legal protection arising from and coupled with poor implementation of legal and policy frameworks. In the second, there is limited access to social services such as education, water and sanitation, food, and basic health. This is worsened by a number of factors. The first factor is that South Sudan already faces an acute humanitarian crisis that is exacerbated by protracted armed conflict, intercommunal violence and corruption which have depleted public resources that could have been used to provide basic social

[2] See UNHCR database https://data2.unhcr.org/en/situations/southsudan (accessed 2 October 2021).

[3] UNHCR 'South Sudan regional refugee response plan: January 2019–December 2020' (2019) 5 https://reliefweb.int/sites/reliefweb.int/files/resources/67312.pdf (accessed 7 April 2021).

[4] See generally, R Adeola & BD Mezmur 'The protection of internally displaced children in Africa: A doctrinal analysis of article 23(4) of the African Children's Charter' (2021) 65 *Journal of African Law* 115.

services. The second factor is the Covid-19 pandemic which has significantly diminished economic activities of not only the IDPs and refugees but also of *zol meskin* (common person), generally.

Through an extensive literature review, the chapter examines three interrelated issues: first, there is an analysis of the lived context and situation of refugees, asylum seekers and IDPs in South Sudan; second, an assessment of the national legal regime on IDPs, refugees and asylum seekers in relation to applicable international and regional norms; and third, there is analyses of the socio-economic rights challenges faced by these groups.

This chapter is divided into six sections, the first of which provides the chapter's outline as a content map, whilst the second outlines the contextual background in terms of figures and socio-economic conditions of IDPs, refugees and asylum seekers in South Sudan. The third section discusses the legal frameworks that guarantee socio-economic rights of IDPs, refugees and asylum seekers. In the fourth section the legal frameworks are analysed to demonstrate how legal instruments guarantee access to socio-economic rights of IDPs, refugees and asylum seekers. This is complemented in Sect. 5 which discusses two examples of refugees and urban IDPs' access to basic social services such as the right to social protection and livelihoods. The last section concludes the chapter with policy recommendations for strategies to implement international norms and standards for refugees, IDPs and asylum seekers to access socio-economic rights in South Sudan.

2 Overview of the Situations of IDPs, Refugees and Asylum Seekers in South Sudan

South Sudan hosts a high number of IDPs, refugees and asylum seekers. Apart from IDPs who are displaced from their homes but residing in some other parts of the country, most of the refugees and asylum seekers living in South Sudan come from mainly the Republic of the Sudan, the Central African Republic, Ethiopia, the Democratic Republic of the Congo (DRC) and Eritrea. A refugee is any person who seeks the protection of a state after he or she fled from their legal domicile.[5] At a national level, the

[5] See Article 1 of the UN General Assembly, Convention Relating to the Status of Refugees, 28 July 1951, United Nations, Treaty Series, vol 189, p 137 for detailed characterisation.

Refugee Act provides a more progressive definition of a refugee. It describes a 'refugee' as any person, who for a well-founded fear of persecution or conflict (as recognised under applicable international and national law on refugees), is seeking recognition as a refugee or to be granted asylum in a country other than his or her own.[6] However, the same law limits this expansive right by stating that

> a person does not qualify for refugee status if there is reason to believe that such person committed [serious crimes including] non-political crimes outside South Sudan, *guilty of acts contrary to the objects and principles of the United Nations or the Organisation of African Unity* or [anyone who] enjoys protection of [another] country.[7]

The fact that refugee status may be denied or revoked on the ground that one was guilty of an alleged crime contrary to the United Nations and African Union is vague and could be arbitrarily applied to impede legal guarantees of refugees and asylum applications. As for IDPs, these are

> [individuals] or groups of persons forced to flee their homes or habitual residence as a result of or in order to avoid armed conflict, violence, human rights abuses, or disasters, and who have not crossed an internationally recognized State border.[8]

It is estimated that over 300 refugees from Ethiopia, the Democratic Republic of the Congo, the Central African Republic, and Sudan are settled in refugee camps largely located in the Upper Nile, Unity, Central Equatoria, Jonglei and Western Equatoria states.[9] Furthermore, over 200,000 South Sudanese who fled the 2013 and 2016 conflicts are living as IDPs. They reside in camps in five United Nations protected sites commonly referred to as protection of civilian camps (PoCs) located in Wau,

[6] Section 7(a)–(e) of the Refugee Act, 2012.
[7] Section 8(1)(a)–(d) of the Refugee Act (my emphasis).
[8] Article 1(k) of the Refugee Act.
[9] UNHCR 'South Sudan refugee population statistics' (2021) 1 https://reliefweb.int/sites/reliefweb.int/files/resources/SSD_REF_Statistics_31%20January%202020.pdf (accessed 12 April 2021).

Juba, Bor, Bentiu and Malakal.[10] Most of the IDPs reportedly 'fear retaliatory or ethnically targeted violence from armed groups who may be affiliated to either government or rebels'.[11] According to the United Nations High Commissioner for Refugees (UNHCR), '4.3 million people are displaced in South Sudan of which over two million are living as refugees in neighbouring countries – Sudan, Uganda, Kenya, Democratic Republic of Congo and Ethiopia'.[12] There is a caution that these 'numbers could rise as ethnic tension increases coupled with prospects for spontaneous and organised returns of refugees from neighbouring countries'.[13]

Prior to the independence of South Sudan in 2011, the region (southern Sudan) had been home to and a passage for migrants and refugees from neighbouring countries—some coming from as far as Somalia—who use the country as a transit to North Africa for their journeys to Europe. The transit journeys are reportedly a concern for possible trafficking as warned by the US State Department.[14] Migration into South Sudan also occurs along its permeable borders in the form of smuggling, trafficking, conflict and other socio-economic conditions affecting people in their countries of origin.[15] Other refugees came from Nuba Mountains and Blue Nile in Sudan who fled conflict that erupted as a result of legacy issues relating to the Comprehensive Peace Agreement (CPA). That conflict displaced thousands who sought refuge in South Sudan, a newly found state governed by former comrades in arms to the Sudan Peoples' Liberation Movement—North (SPLM-N). As already mentioned, condi-

[10] JG Akech 'Urban internally displaced persons (IDPs): The South Sudan's experience with a focus on Juba' (2020) 2 http://genida.org/wpcontent/uploads/2021/03/Policy-Brief-8-Akech.pdf (accessed 11 April 2021). The acronym PoCs is used here to refer to the Protection of Civilians as adopted by the United Nations Mission in South Sudan. It is not to be confused with the 'Person of Concern' as used by United Nations High Commissioner for Refugees.

[11] US State Department 'South Sudan 2019 human rights report' (2019) 20 https://www.state.gov/wp-content/uploads/2020/02/south-sudan-2019-human-rights-report.pdf (accessed 11 April 2021).

[12] UNHCR 'South Sudan refugee crisis' https://www.unrefugees.org/emergencies/south-sudan/ (accessed 8 March 2021). See also UNCHR dashboard https://data2.unhcr.org/en/documents/details/85396 (accessed 9 April 2021).

[13] Adeola & Mezmur (note 4 above) 2.

[14] See US State Department 'Trafficking in person's report' (2016) 342 https://2009-2017.state.gov/documents/organization/258876.pdf (accessed 17 April 2021).

[15] African Child Policy Forum (ACDF) 'Baseline assessment for the implementation of the East Africa Community (EAC) child policy in the republic of South Sudan' (2020) 29 (on file with author).

tions of these refugees are also affected by violence that erupted in 2013 and 2016, respectively.

The conflict and multiple displacement created undesirable conditions for IDPs, refugees and asylum seekers in the form of limited access to social services. Although primary basic needs of refugees and IDPs are catered for by the United Nations agencies through programmes implemented by several international and national non-governmental organisations, legal protection and social service gaps remain. While the drivers of migration and displacement are manifold, protracted violence, armed conflict and intercommunal violence are among the key causes.[16] Some have discussed 'climate induced displacement'[17] as other causes exacerbating the plight of refugees and IDPs resulting in floods and severe food shortages.

Having sketched the context of IDPs and refugees in South Sudan, we now turn to analyse the (in)adequacy of the legal regime on refugees and asylum seekers. This is undertaken to assess the consistency of such legal frameworks with applicable international and regional norms.

3 Legal Frameworks on IDPs, Refugees and Asylum Seekers

This section discusses the applicable legal frameworks for the protection of IDPs, refugees and asylum seekers in South Sudan. It analyses the (in) adequacy of the legal regime relevant to these groups including its conformity with applicable international and regional norms. The section commences with an analysis of international and legal standards adopted by South Sudan to promote and protect the rights of IDPs, refugees and asylum seekers.

3.1 International Legal Frameworks and Standards Applicable in South Sudan

The Republic of South Sudan has ratified several key regional and international instruments relating to IDPs, refugees and asylum seekers. At the regional level, it has ratified the OAU Convention Governing the Specific

[16] See generally Adeola & Mezmur (note 4 above).

[17] ET Achiume 'Race, refugees and international law' in C Costello et al. (eds) *The Oxford Handbook of International Refugee Law* (2021) 43.

Aspects of Refugees Problems in Africa, 1974, and the African Union Convention for Protection and Assistance of Internally Displaced Persons in Africa, 2012 (Kampala Convention).[18] The country is also a party to the International Conference on the Great Lakes Region Protocol on the Protection and Assistance to Internally Displaced Persons (Great Lakes Protocol).[19] In addition, it has ratified relevant United Nations conventions such as the Convention Relating to the Status of Refugees, 1951 and the Protocol Relating to the Status of Refugees, 1967, thereby becoming its 143rd states party.[20] These international instruments have been domesticated through national legislation as discussed below.

3.2 National Legal Frameworks—Constitution and Relevant Legislation

To ensure effective implementation of the above-mentioned regional and international legal standards, the government of the Republic of South Sudan adopted relevant national legal frameworks for the promotion and protection of the rights of IDPs, refugees and asylum seekers. This includes the Transitional Constitution, 2011 (as amended) which guarantees the rights of IDPs, refugees and asylum seekers. South Sudan has also enacted the Refugee Act which incorporates international norms and standards. In terms of citizenship by naturalisation, the country has enacted the Nationality Act, 2011 which deals with acquisition and loss of citizenship. The more specific legislation, however, is the Refugee Act which South Sudan adopted in 2012 to

> give effect to international treaties, conventions, principles, and standards relating to refugee protection; to provide for the reception into South Sudan of asylum seekers; to regulate applications for and recognition of refugee

[18] OAU, Convention Governing the Specific Aspects of Refugee Problems in Africa (OAU Convention), 10 September 1969, 1001 UNTS 45; and African Union, African Union Convention for the Protection and Assistance of Internally Displaced Persons in Africa (Kampala Convention), 23 October 2009. See also OAU/AU 'Treaties, Conventions, Protocols and Charters' https://au.int/en/treaties (accessed 2 October 2021).

[19] International Conference on the Great Lakes Region, Protocol on the Protection and Assistance to Internally Displaced Persons, 30 November 2006. See UNHCR UPR Report (note 1 above) 1.

[20] UNHCR 'South Sudan signs the 1951 Refugee Convention' (2018) https://www.unhcr.org/news/press/2018/10/5bb1c5fb4/south-sudan-signs-1951-refugee--convention.html (accessed 2 October 2021).

status; to provide for the rights and obligations flowing from such status; and to provide for related matters.[21]

It is instructive to note that the Refugee Act expressly enjoins the Refugee Commission Affairs and other bodies dealing with refugee affairs to interpret the Act in accordance with standards and norms laid out in the 'Convention Relating to Status of Refugees(1951) the Protocol Relating to Status of Refugees (1967) the OAU Convention Governing Specific Aspects of Refugee Problems in Africa (1974) and the Universal Declaration of Human Rights (1948)'.[22] The Refugee Commission Affairs was established in 2012 to 'be responsible for administrative matters concerning refugees, coordinate inter-ministerial and non-governmental activities and programmes relating to refugees [in South Sudan]'.[23]

The Refugee Act also established the Eligibility Committee which processes refugee applications,[24] and the office of the Commissioner for Refugees,[25] and the Refugee Appeals Board, whose function is to 'receive and hear appeals arising from decisions of Appeals Committee'.[26] It is to be noted that these institutions have weak institutional capacity owing to their limited budgetary and technical resources to effectively respond and manage IDPs, refugee and asylum seekers' issues. Together, these legal frameworks promote the rights of refugees and IDPs including asylum seekers and prohibit discrimination based on citizenship or refugee status.

3.2.1 Recognition of Refugee Status Under National Laws

A 'refugee', is any person, including his or her dependant who, by reason of a well-founded fear of persecution or conflict, is seeking legal protection as a refugee.[27] IDPs and refugees are persons who have been uprooted from their families, and in the case of South Sudan, these people have been displaced largely by conflict (internally and with neighbouring countries). These groups of people settle in places where they feel relatively safe, but access to services is normally challenging.

[21] Section 3 of the Refugee Act.
[22] Section 10(1) of the Refugee Act.
[23] Section 13(1) of the Refugee Act.
[24] Section 16(1) of the Refugee Act.
[25] Section 14 of the Refugee Act.
[26] Section 21(1) of the Refugee Act.
[27] Section 7 of the Refugee Act.

A host country is obliged to recognise a person, as described above, as a refugee and offer him or her the necessary protection under the applicable legal regime. Applications for refugee status are processed by the Eligibility Committee established under the Refugee Commission.[28] It is important for national legal frameworks to recognise the legal definition of 'refugee', because it is from this categorisation that legal protection ensues. In giving effect to this standard, the Refugee Act stipulates that 'every recognised refugee and his or family' has a right to

> enjoy rights contained in the international conventions to which South Sudan is party, full legal protection including bills of rights set out in the Transitional Constitution, remain in South Sudan, seek employment and the [enjoyment] of basic health services and primary education enjoyed by citizens.[29]

The effect of this provision is that refugees, IDPs and asylum seekers are entitled to all socio-economic rights enjoyed by South Sudanese nationals. Similarly, the reference to part two of the Transitional Constitution which set out the bill of rights contained in the Constitution and international law applicable to South Sudan, is instructive.[30] Consequently, the Refugee Act guarantees strong legal protection of the right to access work and employment and basic social service like health and education, to those with a well-founded fear of persecution albeit they fear persecution by tribes.[31] Providing access to work and employment can be a doorway to IDPs, refugees and asylum seekers to realise socio-economic rights,[32] local integration, resettlement or voluntary repatriation.[33]

[28] Section 24 of the Refugee Act.

[29] Section 33 of the Refugee Act.

[30] See arts 9–34 of the Transitional Constitution, 2011 (as amended).

[31] See UNHCR UPR Report (note 1 above) 1.

[32] S Carciotto & C D'Orsi 'Access to socio-economic rights for refugees: A comparison across six African countries' *The Scalabrini Institute for Human Mobility in Africa* (March 2017) https://sihma.org.za/reports/Final_report.pdf (accessed 11 April 2022).

[33] BS Chimni 'Perspectives on voluntary repatriation: A critical note' (1991) 3 *International Journal of Refugee Law* 541. See also, BS Chimni 'The meaning of words and the role of UNHCR in voluntary repatriation' (1993) 5 *International Journal of Refugee Law* 442; & BS Chimni 'The geopolitics of refugee studies: A view from the South' (1998) 11 *Journal of Refugee Studies* 350.

3.2.2 Guarantees of Non-refoulement

Asylum seekers often face the risk of being expelled, forcefully returned or extradited to their home countries. One of the ways to guard against this is to ensure that the national legal framework on refugees incorporates international best practices on non-refoulement. Non-refoulement is an international human rights legal principle that applies to 'all migrants at all times, irrespective of migration status'.[34] The principle of non-refoulement prohibits authorities in the state concerned from forcefully returning a person to a country where they risk human rights abuse and other irreparable harm. The principle of non-refoulement has been effectively incorporated into the Refugee Act. It is stated that

> no person may be expelled, extradited or returned to any other country or be subject to any similar measure, if as a result of such action, he or she may be subjected to persecution, subjected to physical and psychological harm.[35]

To ensure that refugees and asylum seekers are protected against refoulement, the Refugee Act adopts robust mechanisms for the application for asylum. It enjoins the Eligibility Committee and the Appeals Board to follow 'principles laid down in relevant international instruments'.[36] Despite the promulgation of both national and international legal regimes on IDPs, refugees and asylum seekers, implementation remains a serious challenge as discussed below.

4 Analysing Legal Frameworks on Access to Socio-Economic Rights

This section discusses the legal status and access challenges to the fulfilment of socio-economic rights by IDPs, refugees and asylum seekers in South Sudan. It discusses the concept of 'progressive realisation' of socio-economic rights with a focus on the right of access to social security and livelihoods and the right to survival and protection using the examples of Maban refugee camp and urban IDPs, respectively. The aim is to illustrate

[34] See OHCHR 'The principle of *non-refoulement* under international human rights law' https://www.ohchr.org/Documents/Issues/Migration/GlobalCompactMigration/ThePrincipleNon-RefoulementUnderInternationalHumanRightsLaw.pdf (accessed 17 April 2021).

[35] Section 6(a) & (b) of the Refugee Act.

[36] Section 38 of the Refugee Act.

the specific challenges of accessing basic social services by IDPs, refugees and asylum seekers in those two contexts.

4.1 *Legal Status of Socio-Economic Rights and the Concept of Progressive Realisation*

Socio-economic rights are legally provided for in the relevant legal regime applicable in South Sudan. This includes the International Covenant on Economic, Social and Cultural Rights, 1966 (ICESCR) which South Sudan recently ratified,[37] and the country's Constitution. The ICESCR obliges states parties to

> undertake steps, individually and through international assistance and co-operation, especially economic and technical, to the *maximum of its available resources*, with a view to achieving *progressively the full realization of the rights* by all appropriate means, including particularly the adoption of legislative measures (text italicised for emphasis only).[38]

The meaning and scope of progressive realisation of socio-economic rights has a three-part test:

- there must be immediate and tangible progress towards the realisation of rights;
- states cannot pursue deliberate retrogressive measures; and
- [states must adopt] and put in place special measures for vulnerable and disadvantaged groups.[39]

The Constitution of South Sudan recognises the progressive nature of socio-economic rights, and it lays out a robust economic objective aimed

[37] The Parliament adopted the International Covenant on Economic, Social and Cultural Rights, however, at the time of writing this essay, the President had just signed the instrument of ratification just awaiting deposition with respective mechanisms in the UN system to effect South Sudan's ratification status. See Eye Radio 'President Kiir signs four international conventions into law' (2023) https://www.eyeradio.org/kiir-signs-four-international-conventions-into-law/ (accessed 26 February 2023).

[38] Article 2(1).

[39] Lillian Chenwi 'Unpacking "progressive realisation", its relation to resources, minimum core and reasonableness, and some methodological considerations for assessing compliance' (2013) *De Jure* 744–746. See also; CESCR General Comment No 3 The Nature of States Parties Obligations UN doc E/1991/23 (1990) par 9.

at 'poverty eradication, attainment of [sustainable development goals], guaranteeing equitable distribution of wealth [to] redress imbalances of income and achieve a decent standard of life for the people of South Sudan'.[40]

This fiduciary obligation stipulated under the objective sections of the Constitution is further entrenched by the Constitution which commits all levels of government to take *necessary measures* to promote equitable access to economic opportunities, development and prosperity.[41] This includes 'taking reasonable legislative and policy measures within available resources to achieve the progressive realisation of rights'.[42]

4.2 Refugees, IDPs and Asylum Seekers' Access to Socio-Economic Rights: Two Case Studies

Access to socio-economic rights by refugees and IDPs is impeded by various challenges including poor implementation of existing laws and socio-political challenges experienced by the country. However, there are gaps in the implementation of the laws and efforts should therefore be directed at implementing existing legal frameworks to give effect to rights provided for under such instruments.[43] Thus, the existence of legal frameworks on the rights of IDPs, refugees and asylum seekers is one part of the solution to ensuring access to socio-economic rights.

There are diverse barriers to the effective implementation of legal frameworks on IDPs, refugees and asylum seekers in South Sudan. First, the government lacks adequate resources to fund social services such as education, healthcare, food and protection needs. Countries with weak social welfare systems and limited economic resources should promote the right of IDPs, refugees and asylum seekers to work or self-employment.[44] This would relieve pressure on refugee hosting states in meeting the socio-

[40] Article 37(1).

[41] Article (2)(a)–(f) & 3.

[42] Article 34(2).

[43] For a detailed analysis of gaps, see generally; R Adeola 'The impact of the African Union Convention on the Protection and Assistance of Internally Displaced Persons in Africa' (2019) 19 *African Human Rights Law Journal* 591.

[44] A Edwards 'Article 17' in A Zimmermann (eds) *The 1951 Convention relating to the Status of Refugees and its 1967 Protocol: A commentary* (2011) 951. See also; A Edwards 'Article 18' in A Zimmermann (eds) *The 1951 Convention relating to the Status of Refugees and its 1967 Protocol: A commentary* (2011) 973.

economic needs of the displaced. In addition, it must be noted that Covid-19 negatively impacted upon health, education and the livelihoods of people in South Sudan. The impact on the poor and other vulnerable groups (IDPs, refugees and asylum seekers) could only have been made worse especially in countries where social welfare services were already lacking or inadequate.

Whilst South Sudan is rich in natural resources, the cost of senseless war for ethnic dogmatism (toxic nationalism) is depleting public coffers. This has left the country with limited or no resources for public services. In fact, much of the public service delivery is done by international non-governmental organisations through the generous funding from the international community. Additionally, the absence of good governance and constitutional democracy has given rise or contributed to widespread corruption, lack of accountability and inter-ethnic conflicts. These conditions do not allow for economic growth and social integration of peoples, which are conditions necessary for IDPs, refugees and asylum seekers. Similarly, the demographics of refugees and asylum seekers (the majority coming from Sudan, the DRC and Eritrea) might be another barrier to their speedy integration into South Sudanese society.

Nonetheless, the legal frameworks in South Sudan could sufficiently protect the rights of IDPs, refugees and asylum seekers if implemented. The legal frameworks provide two strands of protection: First, they guarantee refugee rights within normative frameworks that are judiciable. This includes domestication of international best practices such as the recognition of refugee status and the principle of non-refoulement. Second, the legal frameworks establish and mandate relevant institutions such as the Refugee Commission Affairs, the Appeals Board and the Eligibility Committee.

Other than the above challenges to the implementation of normative frameworks, conflict and economic collapse has, in addition, severely diminished access to social services. In fact, one can argue that South Sudan has abandoned its duties in the fulfilment of socio-economic rights of citizens generally and refugees and IDPs, in particular. This is not to say that there is deliberate or inadvertent denial of basic social services to refugees or IDPs. The challenge lies in the government's inability to provide social welfare services to the public. At the time of writing this chapter, critical public services were provided by humanitarian organisations with funding from the international community and United Nations. Imaginably, with the reliance on handouts from humanitarian organisations and shared resources from host communities, access to health, housing and basics of livelihood is hardly available. Refugees and IDPs are among vulnerable populations whose socio-economic conditions were exacerbated by Covid-19.[45]

4.3 Are Refugees and IDPs Accessing Socio-Economic Rights? Cases Studies

4.3.1 A Case of Maban Refugee Camp

At this juncture we discuss the rights to basic needs, which include the right to water, food, education, shelter and basic income to live decently. Refugees in Maban are supported by UNHCR funded programmes that ensure every refugee has access to basic necessities. For instance, all refugees receive food assistance in the form of general food distribution from the World Food Programme.[46] Healthcare and sanitation programmes are also provided through 'government health facilities and those run by international or non-governmental organisations'.[47] These healthcare facilities provide critical healthcare services including HIV and Aids, immunisation and emergency care services.[48] Whilst refugees in Maban are among those with high levels of life skills, vocational and other competencies, their access to livelihoods is affected by a lack of work and employment opportunities.

Maban refugee camp is one of the largest refugee settlements in South Sudan. It hosts an estimated '136,462 refugees in four settlements of Doro, Gendrassa, Jamam, Kaya, and Yusif Batil'.[49] These refugees are exclusively Sudanese who fled the protracted conflict between the Sudan

[45] For detailed analysis of how Covid-19 affected socio-economic rights of vulnerable people in South Sudan, see JG Akech 'Exacerbated inequalities: Implications of Covid-19 for the socio-economic rights of women and children in South Sudan' (2020) 20 *African Human Rights Law Journal* 584.

[46] UNHCR, WFP and partners 'Joint assessment mission report' (2018) 8 https://reliefweb.int/sites/reliefweb.int/files/resources/68549.pdf (accessed 16 April 2021).

[47] UNHCR, WFP and partners (note 40 above) 35.

[48] UNHCR, WFP and partners (note 40 above) 9.

[49] REACH 'Conflict and tensions between communities around Gendrassa and Yusif Batil camps, Maban county: South Sudan refugee response' (2016) 3 https://reliefweb.int/sites/reliefweb.int/files/resources/reach_ssd_report_conflict_and_tensions_between_communities_around_gendrassa_and_yusif_batil_camps_maban_county_december_2016.pdf (accessed 15 March 2021).

People's Liberation Movement and Army–North (SPLM/A–N) and the Sudan Armed Forces (SAF). Due to competition over meagre resources as well as political division emanating from a split in the SPLM-N camp, refugees had to be separated in various settlements within Maban County. Over time, tension escalated among refugees on the one hand and with the host community on the other. These events arose due to a perception that the host community, the Mabanese, were not gaining any benefit from refugee programmes such as employment with humanitarian organisations operating in the County. Particular points of tension included the accusation from the host community that refugees were 'cutting trees for wood, depleting grazing lands, access to employment and access to land for farming'.[50] It is to be noted that refugees had better education and skills compared to the host community which resulted in more refugees being hired.

4.3.2 Right to Survival and Protection: A Case of Urban IDPs

The term 'urban' IDPs is used here to refer to displaced persons who have fled to camps in urban areas. Other than the PoCs, IDPs who fled inter-communal violence and floods in Jonglei State are settled in Mangala, Juba suburb. The means of survival of urban IDPs are particularly challenging even for those who receive handouts from mostly international non-governmental organisations. Safety risks include sexual violence, forced labour, eviction from land and persecution. However, access to basic healthcare and psychosocial well-being is guaranteed in South Sudan under the Constitution and the law. Effectively, refugees are entitled 'to the same basic health services enjoyed by all South Sudanese nationals'.[51]

According to a UNHCR report on urban IDPs,[52] sexual violence, domestic abuse, teenage pregnancy and child marriages are among common protection risks. Girls in particular are at greater risk of violence due to their vulnerability in a highly patriarchal society. While the law affords

[50] L Hutton 'Displacement, disharmony and disillusion understanding host-refugee tensions in Maban county' (2012) 18 https://danishdemininggroup.dk/media/1309840/Displacement-Disharmony-and-Disillusion-DDG-South-Sudan.pdf (accessed 9 April 2021). See also; P Mathew et al. 'The Michigan guidelines on the right to work' (2010) 31 *Michigan Journal of International Law* 293.

[51] Article 31 of the Transitional Constitution, 2011 (as amended); sec 33(g) of the Refugee Act.

[52] UNHCR 'South Sudan IDP protection assessment report' (2019) 13 [on file with author].

protection to all refugees and IDPs, these groups face various protection concerns including: physical, sexual and psychosocial violence; and denial of access to justice.[53] In terms of violence, IDPs and refugees fear reprisals from communities and armed groups. Access to justice in particular is a critical concern for IDPs whose lands and properties were illegally occupied during the conflict.

5 Conclusion: Strategies for Enhanced Legal Protection and Increased Access to Socio-Economic Rights

This chapter has examined the legal framework on refugees, asylum seekers and IDPs. It discussed challenges faced by these groups in accessing socio-economic rights. It has been shown that despite what appears to be a robust legal framework, implementation remains a challenge and that lack thereof is destructive to the enjoyment of socio-economic rights. Consequently, there is a need to take further action to ensure rights guaranteed under the legal frameworks are accessible by refugees and IDPs. The antecedent analysis reveals two critical policy implications to strengthen the protection of socio-economic rights of refugees, IDPS and asylum seekers in South Sudan. Firstly, it is essential for the government to initiate and implement integrated social service schemes that absorb refugees into the host community. As observed in the case of refugees in Maban County, most of the refugees in South Sudan who arrived from neighbouring countries come with technical skills which are good for the country's economic development. To benefit from such skill sets, the government should integrate refugees into the host community and allow them to access basic jobs which will in turn improve their livelihoods and at the same time serve as an effective means of refugee community integration.

The last aspect to guaranteeing socio-economic rights of refugees is to ratify and domesticate all normative frameworks on refugees and IDPs. Although the existing legal framework is commendable, South Sudan should move fast in ratifying the remaining key international refugee conventions such as the Convention concerning International Co-operation regarding Administrative Assistance to Refugees, 1985; the United

[53] UNHCR (note 46 above) 15.

Nations Declaration on Territorial Asylum, 1967; and the Convention relating to the Status of Stateless Persons, 1954.[54] Once ratified, the government should domesticate them by adopting necessary administrative and policy measures that ensure due and fair procedures for processing asylum applications and equal access to socio-economic rights.

Bibliography

Chapters in Books

Achiume, ET 'Race, refugees and international law' in C Costello et al. (eds) *The Oxford handbook of international refugee law* (OUP, 2021)

Edwards, A 'Article 17' in A Zimmermann (ed) *The 1951 Convention relating to the Status of Refugees and its 1967 Protocol: A commentary* (OUP, 2011a).

Edwards, A 'Article 18' in A Zimmermann (ed) *The 1951 Convention relating to the Status of Refugees and its 1967 Protocol: A commentary* (OUP, 2011b)

Journal Articles

Adeola, R 'The impact of the African Union Convention on the Protection and Assistance of Internally Displaced Persons in Africa' (2019) 19 *African Human Rights Law Journal* 591

Adeola, R & Mezmur, B 'The protection of internally displaced children in Africa: A doctrinal analysis of article 23(4) of the African Children's Charter' (2021) 65 *Journal of African Law* 115

Akech, JG 'Exacerbated inequalities: Implications of Covid-19 for the socio-economic rights of women and children in South Sudan' (2020a) 20 *African Human Rights Law Journal* 584

Chimni, BS 'Perspectives on voluntary repatriation: A critical note' (1991) 3 *International Journal of Refugee Law* 541

Chimni, BS 'The geopolitics of refugee studies: A view from the South' (1998) 11 Journal of Refugee Studies 350

[54] International Commission on Civil Status (ICCS), Convention on International Cooperation in the Matter of Administrative Assistance to Refugees, 3 September 1985; UN General Assembly, Declaration on Territorial Asylum, 14 December 1967, A/RES/2312(XXII); UN General Assembly, Convention Relating to the Status of Stateless Persons, 28 September 1954, United Nations, Treaty Series, vol 360, p 117. See also; UNHCR 'Collection of international instruments and legal texts concerning refugeesand others of concern to UNHCR' (2007) https://www.unhcr.org/455c71de2.html (accessed 2 October 2021).

Chimni, BS 'The meaning of words and the role of UNHCR in voluntary repatriation' (1993) 5 *International Journal of Refugee Law* 442
Mathew, P et al. 'The Michigan guidelines on the right to work' (2010) 31 *Michigan Journal of International Law* 293

AU Documents

African Union, African Union Convention for the Protection and Assistance of Internally Displaced Persons in Africa (Kampala Convention), 23 October 2009
OAU, Convention Governing the Specific Aspects of Refugee Problems in Africa (OAU Convention), 10 September 1969, 1001 UNTS 45

UN Documents

UN General Assembly, Convention Relating to the Status of Refugees, 28 July 1951, United Nations, Treaty Series, vol 189, p 137
UN General Assembly, Convention Relating to the Status of Stateless Persons, 28 September 1954, United Nations, Treaty Series, vol 360, p 117
UN General Assembly, Declaration on Territorial Asylum, 14 December 1967, A/RES/2312(XXII)
UN General Assembly, Protocol Relating to the Status of Refugees, 31 January 1967, United Nations, Treaty Series, vol 606, p 267
UN General Assembly, Universal Declaration of Human Rights, 10 December 1948, 217 A (III)

Other

International Commission on Civil Status (ICCS), Convention on International Cooperation in the Matter of Administrative Assistance to Refugees, 3 September 1985

Laws and Legislation

South Sudan Nationality Act, 2011
South Sudan Refugee Act, 2012
Transitional Constitution of the Republic of South Sudan, 2011 (as amended)

Internet Sources

Akech, JG 'Urban internally displaced persons (IDPs): The South Sudan's experience with a focus on Juba' (2020b) http://genida.org/wpcontent/uploads/2021/03/Policy-Brief-8-Akech.pdf (accessed 11 April 2021)

Hutton, L 'Displacement, disharmony and disillusion understanding host-refugee tensions in Maban county' (2012) https://danishdemininggroup.dk/media/1309840/Displacement-Disharmony-and-Disillusion-DDG-South-Sudan.pdf (accessed 9 April 2021)

REACH 'Conflict and tensions between communities around Gendrassa and Yusif Batil camps, Maban county' (2016) https://reliefweb.int/sites/reliefweb.int/files/resources/reach_ssd_report_conflict_and_tensions_between_communities_around_gendrassa_and_yusif_batil_camps_maban_county_december_2016.pdf (accessed 15 March 2021)

Carciotto, S & D'Orsi, C 'Access to socio-economic rights for refugees: A comparison across six African countries' The Scalabrini Institute for Human Mobility in Africa (March 2017) https://sihma.org.za/reports/Final_report.pdf (accessed 11 April 2022)

UNHCR 'South Sudan refugee crisis' https://www.unrefugees.org/emergencies/south-sudan/ (accessed 8 March 2021a)

UNHCR 'South Sudan refugee population statistics' (2021b) https://reliefweb.int/sites/reliefweb.int/files/resources/SSD_REF_Statistics_31%20January%202020.pdf (accessed 12 April 2021)

UNHCR 'South Sudan regional refugee response plan' (2019) https://reliefweb.int/sites/reliefweb.int/files/resources/67312.pdf (accessed 7 April 2021)

UNHCR 'UPR submission report on South Sudan' (2014) https://www.refworld.org/docid/5541e6694.html (accessed 8 April 2021)

UNHCR 'Collection of international instruments and legal texts concerning refugees and others of concern to UNHCR' (2007) https://www.unhcr.org/455c71de2.html (accessed 2 October 2021)

US State Department 'South Sudan 2019 human rights report' (2019) https://www.state.gov/wp-content/uploads/2020/02/south-sudan-2019-human-rights-report.pdf (accessed 11 April 2021)

CHAPTER 12

Unfulfilled Rights to Education and Development for Unaccompanied Child Refugees Under Zimbabwe's Encampment Policy

James Tinotenda Ndemera

1 Introduction

> It is no exaggeration to say that refugee children's well-being depends to a major degree on their school experiences, successes and failures ...[1]

After a chaotic presidential election in 2008, Zimbabwe embarked on a reform process that culminated in adopting a new Constitution in 2013. One of the key features of this Constitution was the mainstreaming of

[1] N Richman *In the Midst of the Whirlwind: A manual for helping refugee children* (1998) 142.

J. T. Ndemera (✉)
Rhodes University, Grahamstown, South Africa
e-mail: jamesndemera@priorygroup.com

E. Durojaye et al. (eds.), *Realising Socio-Economic Rights of Refugees and Asylum Seekers in Africa*, Politics of Citizenship and Migration, https://doi.org/10.1007/978-3-031-16548-1_12

human rights through the Declaration of Rights, which also brought about special protection for child rights. Importantly, the right to education was crystallised by section 81(f) of the Constitution, which declares that every child has the right to education.[2] Internationally it is accepted that children are vulnerable, and thus, constitutionalising their rights is an important step in the realisation of their rights in the country. While the right to education has long been advocated for, the realisation of this right has continued to be elusive for many children in Zimbabwe. Though it was once lauded, the education sector has fallen into disrepair over the last 20 years following an economic decline at the turn of the century.[3] The sector has been rapidly deteriorating. Inequalities have widened, and education has fast become a luxury which most people cannot afford. Underfunded schools, poorly remunerated teaching staff, dilapidated buildings and the proliferation of for-profit private schools are all part of a concoction of issues that has destroyed the public education sector.[4] Recently, teachers in public schools downed tools and embarked on nationwide strikes over salary increments.[5] Much worse, in 2008, the main teaching unions embarked on a strike that resulted in much of the academic year going to 'waste'.[6]

While the right to education has become elusive for Zimbabwean children, it is much worse for refugee children especially those who are unaccompanied while encamped at Tongogara Refugee Camp. Unaccompanied child refugees are an often-forgotten subgroup which requires special measures for protection. Often, their parents or guardians have died

[2] Zimbabwe's Constitution of 2013.

[3] T Moyo 'Zimbabwe: Millions now denied a right to education' *Daily Maverick* 6 December 2020 https://www.dailymaverick.co.za/article/2020-12-06-zimbabwe-millions-now-denied-a-right-to-education/ (accessed 15 January 2022).

[4] K Mazvarirwofa 'Private Schools in Zimbabwe Remain Elite and Expensive' *Global Press Journal* 23 April 2018 https://globalpressjournal.com/africa/zimbabwe/private-schools-zimbabwe-remain-elite-expensive/ (accessed 15 December 2021).

[5] N Chingono 'Zimbabwe's striking teachers told to return to work or lose their jobs' *The Guardian* 21 February 2022 https://www.theguardian.com/global-development/2022/feb/21/zimbabwes-striking-teachers-told-to-return-to-work-or-lose-their-jobs (accessed 1 March 2022).

[6] T Kondo 'Socio-economic rights in Zimbabwe: Trends and emerging jurisprudence' (2017) 17 *African Journal of Human Rights Law* 164 at 164–165.

during the violence or have been unable to continue the journey to safety. Though they may experience similar barriers of underfunded schools, many of the barriers are aggravated when the children do not have parents who can pay for private schooling or do not have birth documents which means they cannot access out of camp schools. There are more than 20,000 refugees and asylum-seekers in Zimbabwe, most of them come from the DRC and Mozambique. Tongogara camp hosts 18,800 refugees, of whom around 9500 are aged between 5 and 17.[7] Studies conducted by various Non-Governmental Organisations (NGOs) indicate that unaccompanied children are expected to fend for themselves, which means they do not go to school.[8] As a result, many unaccompanied refugee children who should be receiving a basic education are not enrolled in school and are instead restricted to domestic duties and part-time jobs rather than getting an education. Furthermore, the education centres in the camp (Tongogara Sabi Experimental Primary and St Michaels Secondary) are underfunded, and sometimes teachers do not show up save for when the UNHCR and other stakeholders intervene.[9] The world is facing a record number of displaced minors.[10] The UNHCR notes a fivefold increase in the emergence of unaccompanied and separated children seeking refuge since 2010.[11] When they search for protection, they are exposed to legal and administrative processes that are oriented towards adults. In countries that adopt encampment policies, children become an afterthought. The proliferation of armed conflicts and governments that are unable or unwilling to offer protection to their citizens is a common contributor to

[7] J Mhlanga & RM Zengeya 'Social work with refugees in Zimbabwe' (2016) 6 *African Journal of Social Work* 22.

[8] UNHCR & WFP 'UNHCR and WFP Joint Assessment Mission Report: Tongogara Refugee Camp, Zimbabwe' (2014) https://www.unhcr.org/5559a9ed9.pdf (accessed 24 June 2022).

[9] ML Badibanga 'Educational opportunities for refugee women and girls in Zimbabwe: A case study of women and girls of the Democratic Republic of Congo' MA dissertation, University of Zimbabwe, 2010, at 2.

[10] J Pobjoy 'Refugee children' in C Costello (ed) *The Oxford handbook of international refugee law* (2021) 745. See also UNICEF USA 'Child Refugees and migrants' https://www.unicefusa.org/mission/emergencies/child-refugees-and-migrants. (accessed 1 June 2020).

[11] SM King & NS Hall 'Unaccompanied minors, statutory interpretation and due process' (2020) 108 *Californian Law Review* 1 at 3–7.

refugees streaming into Zimbabwe.[12] For children, the consequences of perpetual violence coupled with their underdeveloped cognitive, physical and psychological understanding, often mean they are scarred for life.[13] There is also a heightened risk of sexual violence and exploitation of female children.[14] These realities suggest that countries need to ensure that they take up the responsibility of providing education for displaced children to break the cycle of poverty which will open up other opportunities for refugees instead of them relying on the state.

With the advent of the mainstreaming of children's rights and the entrenchment through the UN, much has been written on the right to education. Furthermore, progressive judicial decisions at the domestic, regional and international level coupled with global policy directives that seek to entrench this right abound.[15] There is also literature that has engaged in comparative studies on this right and its importance to the child's full development.[16] It is arguable that the right to education and subsequent development of the child form the bases of many issues that arise regarding the realisation of children's rights in the UNCRC or the ACRWC. Some have also explored the issue based on psychology, arguing for the cognitive benefits that education brings to a child and how this contributes to a peaceful world.[17]

[12] M Forster *International refugee law and socio-economic rights* (2007) 21–25. See also, O Awuku 'Refugee movements in Africa and the OAU Convention on Refugees' (1995) 39 *Journal of African Law* 79 at 79–86.

[13] A Kadir, S Shenoda & J Goldhagen 'The effects of armed conflict on children' (2018) 142 *Official Journal of the American Academy of Paediatrics* 2018 at 2031–2034.

[14] M Denov 'Children born of conflict-related sexual violence within armed groups - A case study of Northern Uganda' in MA Drumbl (ed) *Research handbook on child soldiers* (2019) 3–8.

[15] F Coomans 'Clarifying the core elements of the right to education' in F Coomans & GJH van Hoof (eds) The *right to complain about economic, social and cultural rights* (1995) 11–26. See also K Tomaševski 'Free and compulsory education for all children: The gap between promise and performance' (2001) *Right to Education Primers No 2*.

[16] D Phillips & A Lowenstein 'Early care, education and child development' (2011) 62 *Annual Review of Psychology* 483. See also AO Mace et al. 'Educational, developmental and psychological outcomes of resettled refugee children in Western Australia: A review of School of Special Educational Needs – Medical and mental health input' (2014) 50 *Journal of Paediatrics and Child Health* 985.

[17] I Derluyn & E Broekaert 'Unaccompanied refugee children and adolescents: The glaring contrast between a legal and a psychological perspective' (2008) 31 *International Journal of Law and Psychiatry* 319.

However, not much has been written on the provision of this right specifically to unaccompanied refugee children, especially those who find themselves in countries that apply the encampment policy as opposed to the integration methods followed by most Western states. No study has thus far engaged critically with the provision of this right to refugee children in Zimbabwe despite the progressive 2013 Constitution and general state policies that seek to enhance the right to education. Essentially these children are an afterthought, especially when they do not have parents to fight for their interests. It is important to note that without birth documents and parents' input, the chance of a refugee child to access education outside the camp is extremely limited. Thus, unaccompanied children become the most vulnerable under the circumstances. Zimbabwe has acceded to the 1951 UN Convention Relating to the Status of the Rights of Refugees[18] and the Organisation of African Unity (now African Union) Convention Governing the Specific Aspects of Refugee Problems in Africa[19] which were ratified and domesticated through the Refugees Act Chapter 4:03 and thus entrenched the rights of refugees.

Against this backdrop, the chapter considers how this policy presents an encumbrance on the right to education and subsequent child development. It argues that the policy undermines the right to education and tests the applicability of this policy within the confines of Zimbabwe's domestic and international obligations towards the education of all children despite their origin. The chapter commences by discussing the general international framework on the right to education and reveals that although it does not specifically cater for unaccompanied refugee children, they ought to be given special attention on account of their vulnerability. It further engages with the International Covenant on Economic, Social and Cultural Rights together with other child rights treaties. The chapter then examines the context in which Zimbabwe caters for refugees, exploring the economic downturn and its relationship to the realisation of the right to education and how positive policy measures are hindered by the encampment rules. This includes engagement with the 2013 Constitution and various relevant jurisprudence since then. After demonstrating the challenges, the chapter proposes a way forward, highlighting the

[18] UN General Assembly, Convention Relating to the Status of Refugees, 28 July 1951, United Nations, Treaty Series, vol 189, p 137.

[19] OAU, Convention Governing the Specific Aspects of Refugee Problems in Africa (OAU Convention), 10 September 1969, 1001 UNTS 45.

importance of integration in addressing some of the vulnerabilities of unaccompanied refugee children in Zimbabwe.

2 Justiciability and Constitutional Protection of Socio-Economic Rights in Zimbabwe

At the attainment of independence in 1980 Zimbabwe adopted the Lancaster House Constitution (LH Constitution) as a transitional document to address the injustices of the colonial past. This constitution did not have any provisions for socio-economic rights. The LH Constitution did, however, have provisions for the protection of everyone but with a focus on civil and political rights.[20] In 2013, Zimbabwe adopted a new constitution. Section 2(1) of the 2013 Constitution of Zimbabwe states that it is the supreme law of the land. Fundamental human rights and freedoms are entrenched while government action should be within the confines of the Constitution.[21] Chapter 4 of the 2013 Constitution of Zimbabwe entrenches the Declaration of Rights which expressly provides for socio-economic rights. There is a duty on the state to uphold, advance and implement them. This includes the right to freedom of profession, trade or occupation; labour rights; property rights; the rights to agricultural land; the right to education; the right to healthcare; and the right to food.[22] As a result, socio-economic rights have a significant level of constitutional protection. To ensure the realisation of these rights the Constitution has also made provision for domestic institutions such as the Zimbabwe Human Rights Commission and the courts.[23]

Zimbabwe adheres to international human rights agreements which impose an obligation on the courts to enforce socio-economic rights which the Constitution also entrenches. Therefore, according to section 85(1) of the Constitution, any citizen is entitled to approach the court and challenge any violation of socio-economic rights.[24] Judicial enforcement, therefore, ensures that the rights, freedoms and guarantees in the Constitution can be litigated on should they be violated.[25]

[20] I Magaya & R Fambisayi 'Giant leaps or baby steps? A preliminary review of the development of children's rights in Zimbabwe' (2021) 54 *De Jure Law Journal* 16 at 22.

[21] As Above.

[22] Zimbabwe's 2013 Constitution.

[23] Kondo (n 6) 174–178.

[24] Zimbabwe's 2013 Constitution.

[25] Kondo (n 6) 179.

2.1 *The International Framework on the Protection and Realisation of the Right to Education*

The right to education is recognised as a human right. This right is understood to establish an entitlement to an education that influences one's development. Article 26 of the Universal Declaration of Human Rights asserts the right to education for everyone, but article 26(1) emphasises that children are the main beneficiaries.[26] Thus, it is also linked to children's dignity as General Comment 1 of the UNCRC has observed that the aims of educating children are multifaceted.[27] The right includes, among others, a child's ability to contribute to a full and satisfying life within society, encourages respect for human rights, shapes a child's sense of identity and affiliation and importantly assists them to overcome persistent and entrenched challenges.[28] In turn, the state as the principal duty bearer will be held to account for failing to deliver on its obligations of respecting, protecting and fulfilling this right. The right, in essence, is meant to address, at least, primary basic education[29] and can be realised through various means such as free primary education and policy directives that make it compulsory for children to attend school. Global policy directives and aspirations also seek to further this right, for example, through the Sustainable Development Goals (SDG). The SDG's goal 4 sets out the need to ensure the provision of quality education that is inclusive and leads to relevant and effective learning outcomes for all children.[30] As of 2020, it was estimated that 270 million children worldwide were without access to education.[31] This is a conservative estimate if one is to consider the number of displaced children in the world and those who are unaccompanied.

[26] UN General Assembly, Universal Declaration of Human Rights, 10 December 1948, 217 A (III).

[27] UN Committee on the Rights of the Child (CRC), General Comment 1 (2001): Article 29(1): The aims of education, 17 April 2001, CRC/GC/2001/1 (2001).

[28] General Comment 1 at 2–4.

[29] As above.

[30] United Nations Department of Economic and Social Affairs 'Sustainable Development: Goal 4 – Ensure inclusive and equitable quality education and promote lifelong learning opportunities for all' https://sdgs.un.org/goals/goal4 (accessed 24 June 2022).

[31] UN 'Policy brief: Education during COVID-19 and beyond' (2020) https://www.un.org/development/desa/dspd/wp-content/uploads/sites/22/2020/08/sg_policy_brief_covid-19_and_education_august_2020.pdf (accessed 24 June 2022).

Zimbabwe has acceded to several international instruments that entrench the right to education in clear terms. An overarching and important treaty on education as a socio-economic right is the International Covenant on Economic, Social and Cultural Rights (ICESCR).[32] In relation to the right to basic education, it is said to be the most comprehensive description of the right to education for children in international law.[33] The treaty goes further in recognising compulsory education for all and envisions that it is provided for free at the primary level.[34] Importantly article 13(2)(e) states that signatories should endeavour to provide education even through fellowships. The Committee on Economic, Social and Cultural Rights (CESCR) in General Comment 13 on the right to education states that this fellowship system should enhance equality of educational access for individuals from disadvantaged groups.[35] Glancing at the position of unaccompanied refugee children, it is clear that states have an obligation to ensure that they access education. Article 13(2)(d) creates obligations for states to encourage and ensure access and the availability of education to those whose access may have been interrupted for various reasons. This can also include children who have been displaced; therefore, states are obliged to ensure that access to education is maintained during all phases of the displacement cycle. A key observation also made in General Comment 13 is that the availability of education relates to the state's duty to safeguard not only that educational institutions are available but also the availability of teachers and teaching materials in such institutions.[36] In Zimbabwe's context, this means that the government also has an obligation to ensure that teachers are remunerated, that building facilities are usable and that learning materials are readily available.[37] These are some of the major issues that have plagued the country's education sector.

[32] UN General Assembly, International Covenant on Economic, Social and Cultural Rights, 16 December 1966, United Nations, Treaty Series, vol 993, p 3.

[33] L Arendse 'The obligation to provide free basic education in South Africa: An international law perspective' (2011) 14 *PER/PELJ* 100.

[34] Article 13 of the International Covenant on Economic, Social and Cultural Rights.

[35] Paras 16(e), 26, 32 and 53 of the UN Committee on Economic, Social and Cultural Rights (CESCR), General Comment 13: The Right to Education (Art 13 of the Covenant), 8 December 1999, UN Doc E/C.12/1999/10 (1999).

[36] Para 6(a) of General Comment 13.

[37] S Dryden-Peterson 'Refugee education: A global review' (2011) UNHCR, *Ontario Institute for Studies in Education*, University of Toronto 55. See also TEM Mufakose 'The right to basic education for refugee children in South Africa and Zimbabwe: Challenges and Palliatives' LLM Dissertation, University of Venda, 2015.

The CESCR has reiterated that progressive realisation of this right implies a specific and continuing obligation on states to, as much as possible, be expeditious and effective in working towards the full realisation of the rights.[38]

Zimbabwe is also party to two child rights treaties, namely, the United Nations Convention on the Rights of the Child (UNCRC) and the African Charter on the Rights and Welfare of the Child (ACRWC),[39] which are the most authoritative international legal instruments for the protection of children's human rights, with nearly universal and regional acceptance respectively. The UNCRC, in its Preamble, states that 'children are entitled to special care and assistance' and acknowledges that 'the child by reason of his physical and mental immaturity, needs special safeguards and care, including appropriate legal protection, before as well as after birth'. Thus, in accordance with article 28 of the UNCRC, children have a compulsory right to education while secondary education should be made available. Article 29 further recognises that education must be directed at the full development of the children's talents, physical and mental abilities, their respect for human rights and freedoms and their respect for their own identity, language and values. This alludes to the importance of education as a development tool to ensure that an unaccompanied refugee child does not remain in a state of perpetual refuge. The Committee on the Rights of the Child's (CRC) General Comment 6 refers directly to unaccompanied and separated children. It states that every unaccompanied and separated child, irrespective of status, shall have full access to education in the country that they have entered.[40] Furthermore, the unaccompanied or separated child should be registered with appropriate school authorities as soon as possible and get assistance in maximising learning opportunities.[41]

Similarly, in the ACRWC refugee children are given a prominent position as individuals requiring special care.[42] One can assume that

[38] Para 44 of General Comment 13.

[39] UN General Assembly, Convention on the Rights of the Child, 20 November 1989, United Nations, Treaty Series, vol 1577, p 3; OAU, African Charter on the Rights and Welfare of the Child, 11 July 1990, CAB/LEG/24.9/49 (1990).

[40] UN Committee on the Rights of the Child (CRC), General Comment 6 (2005): Treatment of Unaccompanied and Separated Children Outside their Country of Origin, 1 September 2005, UN Doc CRC/GC/2005/6 (2005) 41–43.

[41] General Comment 6 at 42.

[42] Article 23 of the African Charter on the Rights and Welfare of the Child.

unaccompanied children can also be singled out. Article 11 of the ACRWC provides that every child has the right to education which shall be directed to the development of the child in all aspects, including personality, talent, mental and physical potential.[43] The ACRWC goes on to stipulate that the right to education shall be geared towards the strengthening and preserving of positive African morals, traditional values and culture.[44] Article 11(3)(a) makes the provision for compulsory and free basic education, while 11(3)(d) mandate states to ensure equal access to education through special measures for disadvantaged children. Complementary to the right to education, signatories concede that in implementing the provisions of the ACRWC, discrimination is strictly forbidden, including on grounds of 'national and social origin'.[45] It can be argued that the ACWRC has expanded the scope of this right which in turn positively influences the quality of education which states provide to children in Africa. To enhance one's understanding of the context in which the right to education for children operates, child rights treaties embody that the child's best interests must be taken as a primary consideration.[46]

Article 22 of the UN Refugee Convention requires states to accord refugees the same treatment as accorded to nationals. Importantly, favourable treatment should be given to refugees in respect of access to education coupled with the reduction of tuition costs while also promoting the provision of scholarships.[47] This suggests that Zimbabwe as a signatory, cannot blame the lack of finances or resources if encamped unaccompanied refugee children are failing to access education in the country. This makes this provision more inclusive and compulsory than the related right under article 13(2)(a) of the ICESCR. Hathaway notes that this provision means refugee children who have not completed their primary education are entitled to receive it even before full recognition as refugees are concluded.[48] The AU Refugee Convention, although silent on the right to education, does emphasise equal treatment between refugees and

[43] Article 11 of the African Charter on the Rights and Welfare of the Child.

[44] Article 11(2) of the African Charter on the Rights and Welfare of the Child.

[45] Article 3 of the African Charter on the Rights and Welfare of the Child.

[46] This Treaty focuses on the specific right of children in Africa. However, for the best interests' principle, it is verbatim with the UN Child Convention but with an extra caveat that obliges signatories to consider a child's interests as a primary concern.

[47] Article 22(2) of the UN Refugee Convention.

[48] JC Hathaway *Reconceiving international refugee law* 3 ed (1997) 214.

citizens.[49] Furthermore, the UNESCO Convention against Discrimination in Education in article 3(e) directs states parties to give foreign nationals, who reside within their territory, the same access to education as that given to their own nationals.[50] Article 4 obliges states to take measures against 'active' and 'static' discrimination, which in this case, may result in encampment with limited access to education. The African Charter on Human and Peoples' Rights in article 17 declares that every individual has the right to education. The Charter does not expand in its content on the right to education beyond this brief formulation; however, the term 'every individual' must be construed as meaning all children, including unaccompanied refugees. Regionally, the Southern African Development Community (SADC), which Zimbabwe is a member of, has various agreements on the rights of children, but relevant to this chapter, is the SADC Protocol on Education and Training.[51] Article 5 of the Protocol calls for states to improve primary education, which is set as a critical foundation for the tertiary level. Furthermore, each member must ensure that basic education is provided for a minimum of nine years with special support for disadvantaged groups in gaining admission.[52]

At a continental level, Africa hosts the largest number of children who are unable to access basic education.[53] However, with the progress of human rights and the migration towards recognising children as rights bearers, various initiatives have been launched to try and reduce this deficit. In 2016, the Continental Education Strategy for Africa was launched, with the intended target of implementation in 2025. In summary, the target is to improve access and quality of education on the continent.[54] Other campaigns such as 'AU Educates Her' focuses on increasing access to education for girls and 'African Youth Initiative' recognises the right of

[49] Article IV of the OAU Refugee Convention.

[50] UN Educational, Scientific and Cultural Organisation (UNESCO), Convention Against Discrimination in Education, 14 December 1960. There is no comparable provision in the International Covenant on Economic, Social and Cultural Rights.

[51] SADC Protocol on Education and Training (1997).

[52] As above.

[53] G Clacherty 'The world in a suitcase: Psychosocial support using artwork with refugee children in South Africa' in G Rambaldi et al. (eds) *Participatory learning and action* (2006) 54.

[54] AU 'Continental Education Strategy for Africa 2016-2025' https://au.int/sites/default/files/documents/29958-doc-cesa_-_english-v9.pdf (accessed 3 February 2022).

every young person to good quality education.[55] Therefore the various international and regional instruments including the non-binding initiatives discussed in this section make explicit provision for the right to education. Although there is often no clarity on the position of unaccompanied refugee children, a progressive interpretation makes room for their application on account of their vulnerability and non-discrimination. In particular, the recourse to wording such as 'everyone' or 'every child' in the various provisions is testament to the fact that they are intended to apply to all categories of individuals including unaccompanied refugee children. From the brief discussion in this section, it seems that the international legal framework on the right to education of children, even if they are refugees, is solid. The 2013 Constitution ushered in the applicability of international law in Zimbabwe. Section 326 establishes the role of international customary law, while section 327 recognises international conventions, treaties and agreements.[56] Through ratifying and acceding to the various treaties which entrench the right to education, the Zimbabwean government has committed itself to protecting and ensuring the rights of all children, including refugee children without discrimination.[57] Effectively, the provisions create an entry point for the right to education, as contained in the various international instruments, to be applied to unaccompanied refugee children in Zimbabwe.

3 The Right to Education in Zimbabwe

This section examines the right to education in Zimbabwe and demonstrates that the legal framework and policies at the national level have not resulted in the enforcement of this right for unaccompanied refugee children. The section also determines that despite the government's lauded education policies, various economic challenges have created a crisis in education which has denied many the right to education. This is not to

[55] AU 'AU/CIEFFA Launches Africa Educates Her Campaign a rallying call to get girls back to school' (11 September 2020) https://au.int/en/pressreleases/20200911/aucieffa-launches-africa-educates-her-campaign-rallying-call-get-girls-back#:~:text=%22Africa%20Educates%20Her%22%20is%20a,return%20back%20to%20school%20as (accessed 15 March 2023).

[56] Zimbabwe's 2013 Constitution signalled a time where the country was opening up to reform after a period of isolation following political unrest from 1998–2008.

[57] Action for the Rights of Children 'Critical issues in education' *ARC Resource Pack on Education* Revision Version 01 (2001) 4.

suggest that the challenges have only affected education but included is the attainment of various other socio-economic rights such as the right to health, water, housing and food. Although important for refugee children these are beyond the scope of this chapter.

The LH Constitution had no express provisions on socio-economic rights let alone any dedicated to children's rights.[58] Expectedly during the time this Constitution was drafted, socio-economic rights were not constitutionally protected in many jurisdictions and the underlying targets were mostly related to redressing the past injustices. This Constitution resulted in some decisions which ignored children's socio-economic rights. For example, in *Batsirai Children's Care v The Minister of Local Government, Public Works and Urban Development*[59] an orphanage had been destroyed during the government's urban clean-up campaign dubbed 'Clean the Filth'.[60] Despite the glaring impact on socio-economic rights such as housing, health and education, the legal remedy sought was that of spoilation.[61] This failed, and the children were left in limbo without protection. Towards the turn of the century as the UNCRC and the ACWRC gained prominence, the Zimbabwean judicial system seemed to gradually recognise the duty to protect the rights and interests of children within the broader context of human rights.[62] For example in *S v Juvenile*,[63] a 17-year-old male child was found guilty of assault and had been sentenced to receive corporal punishment of four cuts. The Supreme Court declared that judicial corporal punishment against juveniles violated the right not to be subjected to torture or inhuman or degrading punishment.[64] In *S v Zaranyika*,[65] the High Court declared that child offenders should not be sent to prison barring the commission of a serious offence that justified incarceration. Importantly, in *Dzvova v Minister of Education Sports and Culture*[66] a child enrolled at a public school had been suspended from

[58] M Ndulo 'Zimbabwe's unfulfilled struggle for a legitimate constitutional order' in LE Miller & L Aucoin (eds) *Framing the state in times of transition: Case studies in constitution making* (2010) 184–192.

[59] Unreported case number HC 2566/05.

[60] Magaya & Fambisayi (n 55)23.

[61] As above.

[62] Kondo (n 6) 165–171.

[63] 1989 2 ZLR 61 (SC).

[64] *S v Juvenile* (n 61) para 5.

[65] (B 660 of 2010) [2010] ZWHHC 131 (29 June 2010).

[66] (2007) AHRLR 189 (ZwSC 2007).

attending after his hair had grown and developed into dreadlocks. The father opposed this, stating that their religion as Rastafarians forbid him to cut his hair, hence the suspension was an infringement of his rights.[67] The Supreme Court ruled that every child has a constitutional right to freedom of conscience and religion. Furthermore, it stated that the school's actions of excluding the child were discriminatory and contravened constitutional provisions, as well as the Education Act which at the time confirmed the right to education.[68] Thus influenced by the prevailing contemporary international best practices and international law, the judiciary did from time to time reach progressive decisions.

In 2013, following a period of unprecedented levels of socio-political upheaval since 2008, Zimbabwe adopted a new constitution. In 2008, the presidential election was marred by violence while economically, the country attained the highest ever recorded inflation rate since the 1950s. The standard of life rapidly diminished and the state's capacity to fulfil basic rights including education was extremely limited. By the end of 2008 most schools had shut down as many teachers migrated out of the country with UNICEF stating that 90 per cent of rural schools had closed by early 2009.[69] These schools also served the majority of the children in the country, but the gains which had been achieved after the expansion of access to education in the years following independence had been jeopardised. Positively, following the intervention of various regional and international governments,[70] the year marked the start of Zimbabwe's transition and formation of a new constitution. After the worst violation and challenges to socio-economic rights since 1980, the transition resulted in the 2013 Constitution. The 2013 Constitution has been described as progressive in the recognition of various socio-economic rights and the explicit support for child rights.[71] A Declaration of Rights was added which serves the purpose of expanding on several rights to make them justiciable in the newly formed Constitutional Court and clarify the role of the state. This is in Chapter 4 of the Constitution, while in Chapter 2 some socio-economic rights were added as national objectives.[72] For a country recov-

[67] As above.

[68] Following the 2013 Constitution this right has now been elaborated in the amended Act and is now listed as a fundamental right.

[69] Kondo (n 6) 164–165.

[70] As above.

[71] Magaya & Fambisayi (n 55) 25.

[72] Zimbabwe's 2013 Constitution.

ering from a period of deep recession and having had many citizens suffer in deplorable living conditions, it was necessary to add socio-economic rights to the new Constitution. The applicability of international law was also clarified. The language and contents of the Declaration of Rights in the Constitution depicts the influence of ICESCR, UDR, UNCRC, ACRWC and the African Charter, which similarly give prominence to fundamental human rights.

One of the considerations which influenced the inclusion of socio-economic rights in the 2013 Constitution was that it would be an important step towards the adoption of a rights-based approach to social policy.[73] Mavedzenge and Coltart conclude that the new constitutional era is not only characterised by an expanded Declaration of Rights, but a constitutional dispensation founded on the rule of law, separation of powers, government accountability, good governance and respect for fundamental rights.[74] Examples of the change can be seen in cases such as *Bhila v Master of the High Court*[75] and *Mudzuru v Ministry of Justice, Legal & Parliamentary Affairs*.[76] In *Bhila*, the Court dealt with the common law position that excluded children born out of wedlock from inheritance after the father was deceased. The surviving spouse had only found out that the husband had three children out of wedlock after he passed away and tried to prevent the children from inheriting from the estate. The Court ruled that the common law position violated children's rights to equality, it was discriminatory and could not pass constitutional muster. *Mudzuru* involved an application for a declaratory order to the Constitutional Court asking that the minimum age of marriage be increased to 18 and that no person under this age should be allowed to enter a marriage. In terms of the then applicable law, the Marriage Act and the Customary Marriage Act, a girl above the age of 16 years was allowed to marry. The Court found that children fall into the category of weak and vulnerable persons in society and needed special protection. Furthermore, the Court read that section 78(1) only allowed persons over 18 rights to form a family, while section 81(1) of the Constitution considered everyone below 18 as a child. Thus, provisions in the Marriage Act and Customary Marriages

[73] T Masuka 'The new Constitution of Zimbabwe and its implications for social workers' (2014) 2 *Journal of Social Welfare and Human Rights* 29.

[74] A Mavedzenge & DJ Coltart *A constitutional law guide towards understanding Zimbabwe's fundamental socio-economic and cultural human rights* (2014) 75–81.

[75] (HC 4396 of 2013) [2015].

[76] ZWCC 12 (20 January 2016).

Act were declared unconstitutional, from the date of the judgment in 2016. The mainstreaming of socio-economic rights and consequently children's rights has therefore set the ground for a fledging jurisprudence in areas of child justice which unaccompanied refugee children should also be able to enjoy.

At the national level, the specific provisions of the 2013 Constitution relevant to this chapter and relating to children rights and the right to education are sections 19, 27, 75 and 81. Section 19 relates to children and 27 to education and are classified national objectives. Section 19 requires the state to adopt measures and policies that ensure the child's best interests. Additionally, the state should ensure that children receive appropriate care when removed from a family environment, be protected from maltreatment and have access to education.[77] Section 27 requires practical measures from the state towards ensuring education for children and affording girls and boys equal opportunities.[78] As constitutionally enshrined national objectives, these provisions lean towards supporting the right to education of unaccompanied refugee children as they are at risk of maltreatment and are already removed from a family environment. Section 75 falls under the Declaration of Rights and relates to fundamental human rights and freedoms under the 2013 Constitution. The provision states that every citizen and permanent resident has a right to state funded primary education which must be made progressively available by the state. The specificity of citizen and permanent resident must not be construed to mean that unaccompanied refugee children are excluded, because section 81 which provides an elaboration on the rights of children, entrenches equal treatment for every child under the law.[79] Moreover the provision states that every child has a right to education, to be protected from economic and sexual exploitation, from child labour, from maltreatment and neglect or any form of abuse.[80] This suggests that even children who have arrived as refugees in Zimbabwe should be accorded the right. The Convention Against Discrimination in Education also mentions, unequivocally, that the deprivation of access to any type of education

[77] Section 19 of the Zimbabwe's 2013 Constitution.

[78] In the context of unaccompanied refugee children practical steps may include integration and the provision of fellowships for them to attend schools.

[79] The proposition in the Constitution which limits education to citizens and permanent residents will likely not stand in court if challenged. This may have been an oversight by the drafters of the Constitution which also has clauses on non-discrimination.

[80] Section 81 of Zimbabwe's 2013 Constitution.

for a specific group of persons, the establishment of separate education systems for specific persons and groups or the imposition of lesser education conditions on one specific group of persons, is discriminatory.[81] Other key provisions in the Constitution to note are sections 44,[82] 51,[83] 56[84] and 85.[85] It is therefore clear that Zimbabwe boasts a solid international human rights framework, national legal framework and national policies on education.

The 2013 Constitution and international law have also resulted in the amendments to the Education Act with the intention that it becomes aligned with international best practices on the right to education. Section 5 provides for the entitlement of every child to compulsory basic state funded education. The provision therefore makes it clear that receiving state funded education is not optional, but compulsory and it is an offence for any parent or guardian to deprive a child of education. Removing a child from school for reasons such as non-payment of the fee, place of birth or importantly. social origin, is also prohibited.[86] In the case of *Ismael v ST Johns College*,[87] the applicant, who was the father of the minor made an application to halt the expulsion of his son. The minor son had been ordered to shave his beard as a pre-condition for the continuation of his studies. The respondent stated that the beard had grown beyond the parameters permitted in the school's rule book. The applicant contended that this was a religious requirement. The Court held that the pre-condition was of no force as it was an infringement on the right to equality, freedom of religion and would result in the child being denied a right to education as envisioned in section 81 of the Constitution. Despite the encampment policy, Zimbabwe has willingly participated in the formulation of the 'education for all goal', with the world and has contributed to the setting up of international and regional laws and frameworks relating to basic education and protection of refugees. Although the country has

[81] Article 1(a)–(d) of the Convention against Discrimination in Education.

[82] This provision creates an obligation for the state to respect fundamental human rights and freedoms.

[83] Relates to the right to human dignity for every person.

[84] Expands on the right to equality and non-discrimination. Importantly everyone should be treated fairly notwithstanding their nationally or social origin.

[85] This provision allows any person acting in their own interests or acting on behalf of another to entitlement to approach a court and enforce their rights.

[86] Section 3(b) of the Education Act [Chapter 25:04].

[87] (HH 24 of 2019, HC 167 of 2019).

been hailed for its literacy and numeracy rate, that alone is not an indication of the delivery of accessible quality education.

Economic challenges have gradually increased pressure on the public school system and those who can afford to, often opt for private schools.[88] This is also prevalent amongst politicians who either send their children abroad or enlist them in private schools.[89] Teachers are paid by the Government of Zimbabwe since they are civil servants. Reports have indicated that the quality of education, both primary and secondary, is affected by the strikes and financial problems experienced by the institution.[90] This is due to poor remuneration of teachers who are civil servants. Considering the position of unaccompanied refugee children, it would be impossible for them to pay such fees, nor do they have guardians who can source other opportunities for them outside of the camp. This means that the government also needs to increase its investment as without the inputs identified by the General Comment 13, learning will be impossible. Although the UNHCR and other NGOs do try to incentivise teachers, it is often unsustainable, and it results in the poor performance by the learners in their final examinations.[91] The permanent effect is that the children become adults, but they lack the ability to exit the camp for work opportunities or to qualify for relocation schemes that are sometimes linked to education opportunities. There are reports that indicate that at times children reach upper grades such as grade 7 and high school but can neither write a complete sentence in English nor communicate fluently in the taught languages.[92] This is an extreme disservice to children and the general principles of refugee protection and equality. Therefore, the state ought to shift from thinking that child refugees are a burden or afterthought, to acknowledging that they are individuals in need of continuity in their lives.

[88] S Mutsvara 'To what extent does Zimbabwe comply with its international obligations for the protection of unaccompanied and separated refugee children?' LLM Dissertation, University of Western Cape, 2015, at 67–72.

[89] As above.

[90] As above.

[91] Mufakose (n 33).

[92] As above.

As evidenced by the various international human rights instruments, every child possesses an inherent right to education.[93] As a result, despite that the government has put in place social and legislative mechanisms aimed at promoting the right to education to recognise the potential developmental gains, it has not been able to fully fulfil its obligations because its duty has been limited by the state's available resources. The implementation of international law and the 2013 Constitution is still a challenge. It is a challenge for the state to fulfil the economic needs of citizens. Therefore, the obligations in respect of unaccompanied refugee children can potentially remain unfulfilled. While the 2013 Constitution provides for the protection of socio-economic rights, this is not enough to ensure the realisation of these rights. The enforcement of the rights requires a sound institutional-based policy approach. Thus, most of the discussed human rights instruments and the 2013 Constitution also prescribe the establishment of domestic mechanisms and measures to protect and promote the right to education.

4 Protecting and Fulfilling the Right to Education for Unaccompanied Refugee Children in Zimbabwe

In Zimbabwe, the two central institutions for enforcing human rights are the Zimbabwe Human Rights Commission (ZHRC) and the courts which since 2013 include the Constitutional Court. The Declaration of Rights and Zimbabwe's commitment to the various human rights treaties that accord the right to education create an obligation for the state. Whenever the state fails, it is the role of the ZHRC and the courts to question such failures and give decisions that ensure the fulfilment of the right. Section 85(1) of the 2013 Constitution has opened up channels for a person to approach the court when acts that violate fundamental rights occur. A critical problem in addressing the challenges of unaccompanied refugee children is the definition states accord to them during the assessment process. When dealing with child refugees and their eventual encampment,

[93] See for example the following instruments: Article 26 of the Universal Declaration of Human Rights; article 13 of the International Covenant on Economic, Social and Cultural Rights; article 7 of the Convention on the Elimination of all forms of Racial Discrimination; the Convention on the Rights of the Child; and the African Charter on Human and Peoples' Rights.

the Zimbabwean government seems not to consider that children are often victims of some of the most devastating state-sanctioned and private human rights abuses.[94] When seeking protection, they are forced to navigate legal processes oriented towards adults as there are no unique processes in the Refugee Act. Nevertheless, their vulnerability is often the chief reason why they should be afforded special protection.

Education is considered a key factor in creating stability and security for children affected by forced displacement.[95] The Zimbabwean government is well aware of the duty to ensure that the right to education is accorded to every child as evidenced by the policies discussed earlier. However, it is always difficult or nearly impossible for vulnerable people such as unaccompanied child refugees to challenge violations of their rights,[96] because what makes their situation worse, is that they are oblivious to the procedures which exist to help them exercise their rights. Another significant impediment to their rights, is that in the absence of institutions that recognise their plight, the children lack the financial resources to pursue legal remedies. Further, the children often do not have any knowledge on how to assert their rights as their major concern is to secure a safe environment away from the wars they have escaped.[97] Refugees often need assistance to be made aware of their rights, but in a country that enforces the encampment policy, only a few are fully aware of the rights they are entitled to in Zimbabwe. These are scenarios where the ZHRC, as an institution created for the advancement of constitutionalism, can intervene and assist the unaccompanied child refugees. As an institution it also serves the purpose of amongst other things, the protection, promotion, development and attainment of fundamental rights and freedoms at all levels of society.[98] The term 'all levels of society' includes unaccompanied refugee children who find themselves encamped at Tongogara. Section 244(1) of the 2013 Constitution also allows the ZHRC authority to require state bodies to institute reports on the enforcement of the Declaration of Rights. Therefore, the Minister of Public Services, Labour and Social Welfare in charge of Tongogara Refugee camp, can be tasked with this. The ZHRC

[94] N Quenivet 'Does and should international law prohibit the prosecution of children for war crimes?' (2017) 28 *European Journal of International Law* 429 at 433–455. See also, *Hossein Shabazi and family v Telemark County* 2012/688 Norway Supreme Court para 19.

[95] Mutsvara (n 85) 67–72.

[96] As above.

[97] Mufakose (n 33).

[98] Section 243(1)(b) of the Constitution.

serves an important role and as the African Commission stated, such national human rights institutions are central to ensuring the indivisibility and interdependence of all human rights.[99] The Court in the ***Mudzuru*** case held that children have no capacity to approach a court on their own due to their incapacity arising from their status as minors, poverty and socially and economically disadvantaged positions.[100] The Court correctly placed a burden and duty on institutions such as the ZHRC to ensure that refugee children are accorded the same rights as citizens.

The primary responsibility for the provision of education to unaccompanied children rests with the state and only when capacity is limited should UNICEF, UNESCO, UNHCR and other UN agencies within their respective mandates be expected to enter the fray.[101] Taking General Comment 6 observations on the right to education into consideration, it is essential for the Zimbabwean authorities to allow the children an opportunity to integrate for the purposes of education. This will enable the unaccompanied child refugees at Tongogara the chance to attend other schools within the region. Additionally, the CESR suggests that private and government funded schools should award scholarships to the children in the camps.[102] To overcome the capacity constraints on the state and district schools, it is submitted that legislation for the adoption of unaccompanied children in refugee camps should be introduced. Already at an international and regional level there are discussions on the introduction of burden sharing of refugees during times of mass influx.[103] Considering that Tongogara Camp is over capacitated, suggestions for allowing adoption are therefore reasonable and in line with discourses already taking place at regional and international level.

Another essential recommendation is for the UNHCR and the Education Ministry to coordinate better on education for refugees. Currently, the UNHCR and other NGO partners deal with the Minister of Public Services, Labour and Social Welfare who appoints the Commissioner of Refugees in charge of Tongogara on behalf of the state.

[99] State Party Reporting Guidelines for Economic, Social and Cultural Rights in the African Charter on Human and Peoples' Rights: Tunis Reporting Guidelines.

[100] *Mudzuru* (n 73) para 24.

[101] SD Peterson 'Refugee education in countries of first asylum: Breaking open the black box of pre-resettlement experiences' (2015) 14 *Theory and Research in Education* 1.

[102] Paragraphs 16(e), 26, 32 and 53 of General Comment 13.

[103] M Sharpe 'Regional refugee regimes Africa' in C Costello (ed) *The Oxford handbook of international refugee law* (2021) 279–280.

This has led to a lack of coordination between the two bodies as the Public Services department does not have the capacity to deal with education issues. This chapter submits that NGO support, and international collaboration is vital for the realisation of the right to education for unaccompanied refugee children. International law has an 'all-inclusive approach' which extends the enjoyment of the right to basic education, beyond the nationality of the recipient. The design, implementation and legislation pertaining to the assistance programmes must intentionally look to enhance the position of unaccompanied child refugees. However, since Zimbabwe is a signatory to the refugee instruments and the child rights treaties, the state retains the primary responsibility for ensuring their protection. Consequently, assistance and partnership with the NGOs should not result in the state leaving their obligations to NGOs to fulfil.

4.1 Education as a Conduit for Socio-Economic Development

The CRC has observed that the state has an obligation to ensure the survival and development of the child.[104] 'Development' includes the child's social sphere which is entrenched by article 6 of the UNCRC.[105] This obligation together with the best interests of the child principle need to be applied even when assessing the right to education. There is a high dropout rate in the two schools that have been established in the Tongogara camp. Some of the challenges include early marriages and pregnancies, transactional sex coupled with child labour.[106] This reveals that child protection remains elusive in the camp setting which is worse for unaccompanied refugee children. The laws and policies that seek to protect, respect, and fulfil the right to basic education are derived from human rights instruments and the 2013 Constitution. Considering the encampment policy, refugees are rendered an afterthought. The inclusion of socioeconomic rights in Zimbabwe was designed to ensure domestic accountability for obligations that were already recognised through the ratified human rights treaties. Furthermore the 2013 Constitution is noteworthy in that it guarantees rights for children that are exclusive and apart from those granted to all Zimbabweans. This puts children in a particular category which requires distinct attention.

[104] Article 6 of the Convention on the Rights of the Child.
[105] As above.
[106] Mufakose (n 33).

It is essential to recognise that while article 13 of the ICESR emphasises the importance of education as a right, it also stipulates that this right is an indispensable means of realising other human rights. The adequate provision of education for children will therefore in future enable all persons to participate effectively in a free society. This means that education can also open up other socio-economic rights as beyond the theory learnt, the right also ensures that children are equipped with the skills and knowledge of how to satisfy other practical needs in life. Studies by Vervliet et al.[107] and Carlson et al.[108] have shown that unaccompanied refugees' mental health and long-term adjustment are influenced by the education and care they get during their early years following relocation, which creates their own desire to build a better future. This speaks to exceptional benefits of the right to education afforded to these children. They can rely less on the state, and they can also reconfigure their lives away from violence. The continuous growth of refugee movements, coupled with the blurring of lines between asylum seekers and economic migrants, has caused a shift in regional policies.[109] Beyond burden sharing, dialogue has also shifted to favouring nationalism, sovereignty and protection from influx migration, which provide excuses for the non-fulfilment of obligations towards protecting refugees. Often refugees, including child refugees. have been repeatedly thrust to the end of state concern.[110] However, considering the vulnerability of children, discourse needs to be repositioned to focus mainly on protection as opposed to migration-related issues. The collective intent of the international conventions discussed above is for the right to education to be all-inclusive and for it to apply to refugee learners even if unaccompanied.

The 2013 Constitution was introduced as a transformative constitution and for a correct understanding of the values it underpins. Realising that it was designed as a framework towards better service delivery and transformation of the state ethos in governance, makes accountability and

107 M Vervliet, J Lammertyn and E Broekaert "Longitudinal follow-up of the mental health of unaccompanied refugee minors" (2013) 23 *European Child and Adolescent Psychiatry* 337.

108 BE Carlson, J Cacciatore & B Klimek 'A risk and resilience perspective on unaccompanied refugee minors' (2012) 57 *Social Work* 259.

109 A Betts 'International relations and forced migration' in EF Qasmiyeh et al. (ed) *The Oxford handbook of refugee & forced migration studies* (2014) 60–74.

110 Z Vaghri, Z Tessier & C Whalen 'Refugee and asylum-seeking children: Interrupted child development and unfulfilled child rights' (2019) 11 *Children Basel* 1.

transparency essential. Such an understanding lays a platform for allowing measures that are beyond the ordinary in addressing the plight of unaccompanied refugee children. Refugee children, just like children in general, need special protection because they are among the most vulnerable members of society.[111] Most will be dependent on others such as their parents or guardians. Some may also be dependent on the community with which they travel during their escape to a country of safety, but unaccompanied children are alone. Hence in the spirit of transformation and in line with the UN Refugee Convention and the AU Refugee Convention which confer on all refugees in the host nations the entitlement to be afforded the same treatment on the basis of equality as is accorded to nationals, unaccompanied refugee children should be integrated. There is an urgent need to think beyond the short-term objective of just educating refugee children. A more extensive investment is needed in both the quality of teachers and the education afforded to refugee children.[112] If refugee children leave school with limited skills, their education will not translate into the future livelihoods they imagine for themselves or into social and economic dividends for their societies.[113] The ideals of the African Union on child education and the guarantees of the 2013 Constitution would also be lost. Considering that the UNCRC and the ACRWC enjoy near universal and continental support respectively, it should not be necessary to reposition the status of unaccompanied refugee children in the protection dialogue. It would be expected that like all other children, they also deserve protection and are not subjected to adult-oriented measures due to a lack of guardianship.

5 Conclusion

With the recognition of the importance of education to world peace and dignity, states have agreed that 'every child shall have the right to education'. Consequently, unaccompanied refugee children in Zimbabwe do not deserve any less. This chapter set out to examine the progressive realisation of the right to education with a specific focus on unaccompanied

[111] N Azmi & SM Basir 'The role of the Convention on the Rights of the Child (CRC) in protecting refugee children' (2019) 12 *International Journal of Asian Social Science* 681.

[112] SD Peterson 'Refugee education: Education for an unknowable future' (2017) 47 *Curriculum Inquiry* 14 at 15–17.

[113] As above.

refugee children under Zimbabwe's encampment policy. The right to education which in turn influences child development continues to be under threat for children in Zimbabwe. Moreover, the country's endemic economic hardships have resulted in the destruction of a once lauded education sector. This chapter has shown that while most children have become victims with limited access to this right, the impact is more significant on unaccompanied refugee children. The chapter has also demonstrated that international instruments Zimbabwe has acceded to and the 2013 Constitution instructively safeguard child rights allowing for progressive and promising policies. Notably the right to education has risen to prominence under the reform-based Constitution. Accordingly, in developing measures to entrench this right for unaccompanied refugee children, it is vital for the state to consider the long-term benefits and obligations towards these right-holders. Education leads to the development of the child including the opening of economic capacities that can also influence access to other socio-economic rights. Therefore, it is expected that when implementing the constitutional and international legal framework provisions, the government should ensure that unaccompanied refugee children are afforded the same opportunities to allow their full development. In terms of these human rights instruments, socio-economic rights are the indispensable and inalienable rights of all human beings. The promotion of integration by the state can lead to the enhancement of policy implementation measures that adequately address the unique challenges endured by refugee children. This means they do not remain an afterthought in camps, but a priority that requires equal treatment in the realisation of the right to education.

Bibliography

Books

Forster, M *International refugee law and socio-economic rights* (Cambridge University Press: Cambridge 2007)

Hathaway, JC *Reconceiving international refugee law* 3 ed (Martinus Nijhoff Publishers: London 1997)

Mavedzenge, A & Coltart, DJ *A constitutional law guide towards understanding Zimbabwe's Fundamental socio-economic and cultural human rights* (Harare 2014)

Richman, N *In the midst of the whirlwind: A manual for helping refugee children* (Trentham Books Ltd: Stoke on Trent 1998)

Chapters in Books

Betts, A 'International relations and forced migration' in EF Qasmiyeh et al. (eds) *The Oxford handbook of refugee & forced migration studies* (Oxford University Press: Oxford 2014)

Denov, M 'Children born of conflict-related sexual violence within armed groups – A case study of Northern Uganda' in Drumbl, MA (ed) *Research handbook on child soldiers* (Edward Elgar Publishing: Cheltenham, United Kingdom 2019)

Ndulo, M 'Zimbabwe's unfulfilled struggle for a legitimate constitutional order' in Miller, L & Aucoin, L (eds) *Framing the state in times of transition: Case studies in constitution making* (International IDEA: Stockholm 2010).

Pobjoy, J 'Refugee children' in Costello, C et al. (eds) *The Oxford handbook of international refugee law* (Oxford University Press: Oxford 2020)

Sharpe, M 'Regional refugee regimes Africa' in C Costello (ed) *The Oxford handbook of international refugee law* (Oxford University Press: Oxford 2020)

Journal Articles

Arendse, L 'The obligation to provide free basic education in South Africa: An international Law Perspective' (2011) 14 *PER/PELJ* 100

Awuku, O 'Refugee Movements in Africa and the OAU Convention on Refugees' (1995) 39 *Journal of African Law* 79

Azmi, N & Basir, SM 'The role of the Convention on the Rights of the Child (CRC) in Protecting Refugee Children' (2019) 12 *International Journal of Asian Social Science* 681

Carlson, BE; Cacciatore, J & Klimek, B 'A risk and resilience perspective on unaccompanied refugee minors' (2012) 57 *Social Work* 259

Derluyn, I & Broekaert, E 'Unaccompanied refugee children and adolescents: The glaring contrast between a legal and a psychological perspective' (2008) 31 *International Journal of Law and Psychiatry* 319

Kadir, A; Sehnoda, S & Goldhagen J 'The effects of armed conflict on children' (2018) 142 *Official Journal of the American Academy of Paediatrics* 2019

King, SM & Hall, NS 'Unaccompanied minors, statutory interpretation and due process' (2020) 108 *California Law Review* 1

Kondo, T 'Socio-economic rights in Zimbabwe: Trends and emerging jurisprudence' (2017) 17 *African Journal of Human Rights Law* 164

Magaya, I & Fambisayi, R 'Giant leaps or baby steps? A preliminary review of the development of children's rights in Zimbabwe' (2021) 54 *De Jure Law Journal* 16

Masuka, T 'The new Constitution of Zimbabwe and its implications for social workers' (2014) 2 *Journal of Social Welfare and Human Rights* 29

Mhlanga, J & Zengeya, RM 'Social work with refugees in Zimbabwe' (2016) 6 *African Journal of Social Work* 22

Peterson SD 'Refugee education in countries of first asylum: Breaking open the black box of pre-resettlement experiences' (2015) 14 *Theory and Research in Education* 1

Phillips, D & Lowestein, A 'Early care, education and child development' (2011) 62 *Annual Review of Psychology* 483

Quenivet, N 'Does and should international law prohibit the prosecution of children for war crimes?' (2017) 28 *European Journal of International Law* 429

Vaghiri, Z; Tessier, Z & Whalen, C 'Refugee and asylum-seeking children: interrupted child development and unfulfilled child rights' (2019) 11 *Children Basel* 1

Dissertations

Badibanga, ML 'Educational Opportunities for refugee women and girls in Zimbabwe: A case study of women and girls of the Democratic Republic of Congo' unpublished MA Dissertation, University of Zimbabwe, 2010

Mufakose, TEM 'The right to basic education for refugee children in South Africa and Zimbabwe: Challenges and Palliatives' unpublished LLM Dissertation, University of Venda, 2015

Mutsvara, S 'To what extent does Zimbabwe comply with its international obligations for the protection of unaccompanied and separated refugee children' unpublished LLM Dissertation, University of Western Cape, 2015

Internet Sources

Chingono, N 'Zimbabwe's striking teachers told to return to work or lose their jobs' *The Guardian* 21 February 2022 https://www.theguardian.com/global-development/2022/feb/21/zimbabwes-striking-teachers-told-to-return-to-work-or-lose-their-jobs (accessed March 2022)

Mazvarirwofa, K 'Private Schools in Zimbabwe Remain Elite and Expensive' *Global Press Journal* 23 April 2018 https://globalpressjournal.com/africa/zimbabwe/private-schools-zimbabwe-remain-elite-expensive/ (accessed 15 December 2021)

Moyo, T 'Zimbabwe: Millions now denied a right to education' *Daily Maverick* 6 December (2020) https://www.dailymaverick.co.za/article/2020-12-06-zimbabwe-millions-now-denied-a-right-to-education/ (accessed 15 January 2022)

UNHCR Africa 'Forced displacement passes 80 million by mid-2020 as COVID-19 tests refugee protection globally' (9 December 2020) UNHCR Forced Displacement 2020 https://www.unhcr.org/news/press/2020/12/

5fcf94a04/forced-displacement-passes-80-million-mid-2020-covid-19-tests-refugee-protection.html (accessed 15 February 2021)
UNHCR & WFP 'UNHCR and WFP Joint Assessment Mission Report: Tongogara Refugee Camp, Zimbabwe' (2014) https://www.unhcr.org/5559a9ed9.pdf https://reliefweb.int/sites/reliefweb.int/files/resources/JAM%20Report.pdf 25 (accessed 24 June 2022)
UNICEF 'Child displacement' Report https://data.unicef.org/topic/child-migration-anddisplacement/displacement/ (accessed 26 May 2021)
UNICEF USA 'Child refugees and migrants' https://www.unicefusa.org/mission/emergencies/child-refugees-and-migrants (accessed 1 June 2020)

CHAPTER 13

Refugees' and Asylum Seekers' Access to the Right to Work in Kenya: Barriers and Prospects

Julie Lugulu and Ferd Moyomba

1 Introduction

The Eastern African region and the Horn of Africa host a huge number of refugees, internally displaced persons (IDPs), returnees and other persons of concern. Over the years, the numbers of refugees on the African continent have risen due to conflict and the failure of the host countries to find

J. Lugulu (✉)
Department of Public Law, Kabarak University, Nairobi, Kenya

Faculty of Law, Dullah Omar Institute for Constitutional Law, Governance and Human Rights, University of the Western Cape, Cape Town, South Africa

F. Moyomba
Department of Public Law, Mount Kenya University Parklands Law Campus, Nairobi, Kenya

Faculty of Law, University of Pretoria, Pretoria, South Africa

E. Durojaye et al. (eds.), *Realising Socio-Economic Rights of Refugees and Asylum Seekers in Africa*, Politics of Citizenship and Migration, https://doi.org/10.1007/978-3-031-16548-1_13

lasting solutions to protracted refugee situations in their territories.[1] The reasons for forced migration are varied and may include conflict, environmental factors and terrorism.[2] Geographically, Kenya shares borders with Somalia, Ethiopia, South Sudan, Uganda and Tanzania. All these countries, except Tanzania have generated thousands of refugee asylum seekers who fled to Kenya over varying periods.[3] Kenya hosts 508,033 refugees and asylum seekers, 84 per cent of which reside in refugee camps while the remaining 16 per cent reside in urban areas.[4] According to the United Nations High Commissioner for Refugees (UNHCR), the majority of the refugees and asylum seekers in Kenya are from Somalia and South Sudan.[5] Kenya's track record in hosting refugees is well-documented.[6] The Dadaab complex in Garissa County was once considered the world's largest refugee camp.[7] Consequently, Kenya has continued to be a haven for hundreds of thousands of refugees to date.[8]

Kenya had a welcoming attitude towards hosting refugees and asylum seekers in the 1960s due to the Pan-Africanist approach to migration which was common among African countries after colonisation. During this period, refugees and asylum seekers enjoyed basic human rights including freedom of movement and access to employment and they

[1] African Commission on Human and People's Rights 'Declaration by the Special Rapporteur on Refugees, Asylum Seekers, Displaced Persons and Migrants in Africa on the occasion of the World Refugee Day, 2017' https://www.achpr.org/news/viewdetail?id=32 (accessed 15 September 2021).

[2] DS Schmidt, L Kimathi & MO Omondi 'Researching refugees and forced migration in Eastern and Horn of Africa: Introducing the issues' in DS Schmidt, L Kimathi & MO Omondi (eds) *Refugees and forced migration in the Horn and Eastern Africa: Trends, challenges and opportunities* (2019) 5. See further Declaration by the Special Rapporteur (n 1).

[3] UNHCR & World Bank 'Understanding the socioeconomic conditions of refugees in Kalobeyei, Kenya: Results from the 2018 Kalobeyei Socioeconomic Profiling Survey' (2020) https://www.unhcr.org/ke/wp-content/uploads/sites/2/2020/04/Kalobeyei_Socioeconomic-Report-1.pdf (accessed 19 April 2021).

[4] See The UN Refugee Agency 'Figures at a glance' https://www.unhcr.org/ke/figures-at-a-glance (accessed 19 April 2021).

[5] As above.

[6] M Sharpe *The regional law of refugee protection in Africa* (2018) 42. See further, Schmidt, Kimathi & Omondi (n 2) 9.

[7] UNHCR Africa 'Dadaab – World's biggest refugee camp 20 years old' (21 February 2012) https://www.unhcr.org/news/makingdifference/2012/2/4f439dbb9/dadaab-worlds-biggest-refugee-camp-20-years-old.html (accessed 19 April 2021).

[8] UNHCR & World Bank (n 3).

eventually integrated into the Kenyan society. A mass influx of refugees from Somalia and Sudan in 2011 shifted the Kenyan government's attitude towards refugees and asylum seekers.[9] Presently, the country is experiencing 'hosting fatigue' manifested by the adoption of an encampment policy which requires refugees to reside in designated areas.[10] As stated earlier 84 per cent of refugees reside in the refugee camps. Consequently, their access to the right to work and other human rights are limited.[11] In *Kituo Cha Sheria and 8 others v Attorney General*, the High Court of Kenya held that the encampment policy restricted refugees' access to the labour market, increased dependency on the state, and lowered the dignity of refugees and asylum seekers.[12]

The fundamental change in the treatment of refugees and asylum seekers in Kenya evidenced by the adoption of the encampment policy is discriminatory because it limits access to socio-economic rights and other human rights, which everyone is entitled to under the Constitution of Kenya, 2010 (Constitution). Tendayi argues that xenophobic discrimination occurs when a hosting state denies refugees and asylum seekers access to human rights and only allows members who are deemed to belong to a certain community, to enjoy the rights.[13] In this regard, refugees and asylum seekers are perceived not to belong, thus their enjoyment of human rights is limited.

This chapter examines whether refugees and asylum seekers in Kenya have access to the right to work, the challenges they face when accessing this right and prospects in accessing the right to work. It proceeds as follows: Part 2 defines a refugee and an asylum seeker under international, regional and domestic law; Part 3 examines the Refugee Status Determination (RSD) process; Part 4 examines the refugee protection and asylum seekers' enjoyment of human rights; Part 5 highlights the legal framework on socio-economic rights for refugees and asylum seekers in Kenya; Part 6 examines the barriers to accessing the right to work for

[9] A Maina 'Development of refugee law in Kenya' https://www.rckkenya.org/development-of-refugee-law-in-kenya/ (accessed 30 March 2022).

[10] See sec 31(1) of the Refugees Act, 2021.

[11] See N Omata 'Refugee livelihoods: A comparative analysis of Nairobi and Kakuma Camp in Kenya' (2021) 45 *Disasters* 865.

[12] [2013] eKLR.

[13] E Tendayi 'Race, refugees and international law' in C Costello, M Foster & J McAdam (eds) *The Oxford handbook of international refugee law* (2021) 47.

refugees and asylum seekers in Kenya; Part 7 highlights best practices from other jurisdictions which Kenya can draw from; and Part 8 provides concluding remarks and recommendations.

2 Definition of a Refugee and an Asylum Seeker

At the international level, article 1(A)(2) of the Convention Relating to the Status of Refugees (1951 Refugee Convention) defines a 'refugee' as an individual who fled their country of nationality due to a well-founded fear of persecution because of their race, religion, nationality, political opinion or membership of a particular social group. The aforementioned article further extends the definition of a refugee to a person who does not have a nationality, but is outside their place of habitual residence due to fear of persecution and is unable to return due to such fear.[14] Therefore, the term 'refugee' applies to a person who has fled his or her country and is unable to return due to that fear of being persecuted based on their race, religion, nationality, political opinion or membership to a particular social group. Similarly, a person without a nationality[15] and who is outside his or her place of habitual residence due to a fear of persecution is also recognised as a stateless person and is entitled to refugee protection.[16] Any person who satisfies the definition of a refugee as provided for under the 1951 Refugee Convention is eligible for refugee protection in terms of the 1951 Refugee Convention and the 1967 Protocol relating to the Status of Refugees (1967 Refugee Protocol).[17]

At the regional level, the 1969 OAU Convention adopts article 1(A) of the 1951 Refugee Convention and further expands the definition of refugees to include persons 'who have left their habitual place of residence to seek refuge outside their country of origin due to external aggression, occupation, foreign domination or events seriously disturbing public

[14] The UN Refugee Agency 'Refugee status determination' https://www.unhcr.org/ke/refugee-status-determination (accessed 13 March 2021).

[15] Article 1(1) of the UN General Assembly, Convention Relating to the Status of Stateless Persons, 28 September 1954, United Nations, Treaty Series, vol 360, p 117 defines a stateless person as an individual who is not considered as a national of any country in accordance with its laws.

[16] M Foster & H Lambert *International refugee law and protection of stateless persons* (2019) 2.

[17] UN General Assembly, Protocol Relating to the Status of Refugees, 31 January 1967, United Nations, Treaty Series, vol 606, p 267. AC Helton 'What is refugee protection?' in N Steiner, M Gibney & Gil Loescher (eds) *Problems of protection: The UNHCR, refugees, and human rights* (2003) 20.

order'.[18] Article 1(2) of the 1969 OAU Convention further broadens the scope of persons who could be considered refugees, beyond the provisions of the 1951 Refugee Convention. Consequently, article 1(2) of the 1969 OAU provides for refugee protection to more groups of people who could otherwise not have enjoyed the protection under the 1951 Refugee Convention. It is, however, unclear whether the 1969 OAU Convention applies to asylum seekers in Africa who come from outside the African continent. The assumption is that the 1969 OAU Convention applies to any person who meets the threshold requirements provided in article 1(2) of the 1969 OAU Convention. Its scope is thus not limited to refugees in Africa.[19] It is noteworthy that refugees and asylum seekers in Africa may claim protection and enjoyment of human rights, as enshrined in the Banjul Charter, which recognise the freedom of movement, their residence and the right to seek asylum in another country in the event of persecution.[20]

At the domestic level, section 3(1)(a) of the Refugees Act 10 of 2021 (Refugees Act) defines a 'refugee' as a person who has fled their country of nationality to seek protection in Kenya due to a well-founded fear of persecution based on their race, religion, nationality, belonging or political opinion. Further, the Refugees Act expands the meaning of refugees to include stateless persons or persons without nationality who are outside their country of habitual residence due to their fear of persecution based on their race, religion, nationality or belonging to a national group or due to their political opinion and are unable to return to their country of habitual residence due to such fear.[21]

A refugee is a person with a nationality or a stateless person outside their country of origin or habitual residence due to a well-founded fear of persecution based on his or her race, religion, nationality or belonging and is unable to return to their country of origin or place of habitual residence due to such fear. A person may also fit the definition of a refugee, if they are fleeing their country of origin to seek refuge across an international border due the effects of a natural disaster.[22]

[18] See art 1(2) of the OAU, Convention Governing the Specific Aspects of Refugee Problems in Africa (OAU Convention), 10 September 1969, 1001 UNTS 45. See further M Zard, C Beyani & A Odinkalu 'Refugees and the African Commission of Human and Peoples' Rights' https://docs.escr-net.org/usr_doc/Zard_article.pdf (accessed 15 October 2021).

[19] Sharpe (n 6) 42.

[20] Article 12(1) and (3) of the OAU, African Charter on Human and Peoples' Rights (Banjul Charter), 27 June 1981, CAB/LEG/67/3 rev 5, 21 ILM 58 (1982).

[21] See sec 3(1)(b) of the Refugees Act, 2021.

[22] L Madokoro *Elusive refuge: Chinese migrants in the Cold War* (2016) 3.

While the 1951 Refugee Convention clearly defines who a refugee is, it fails to explicitly provide for the definition of an asylum seeker. The 1969 OAU Convention and the Banjul Charter recognise the right of a person to seek asylum in another country in the event of persecution.[23]

The Refugees Act defines an 'asylum seeker' as a 'person seeking refugee status in accordance with the Act'.[24] Based on this definition, an asylum seeker is a person who has fled his or her country of origin seeking international protection in another country, but whose application for refugee asylum is yet to be confirmed. Resultantly, while an asylum seeker seeks protection in another territory and mainly enjoys the right to remain in the host country without expulsion, a refugee is entitled to more rights than the right to remain in the host country.[25] The aforementioned difference stems from the fact that an asylum seeker is in the process of seeking asylum through a formal application process and he/she awaits the outcome of that application, while a refugee has successfully undergone a formal RSD process and has been granted legal recognition as a refugee and has thus been conferred additional rights.[26] It is noteworthy, that the Refugees Act distinguishes between asylum seekers and refugees through the definition of the terms and the rights accorded to them.[27] The subsequent section discusses the RSD process in Kenya.

3 The RSD Process in Kenya

The RSD process determines whether or not an asylum seeker meets the definition of a refugee under section 3 of the Refugees Act.[28] The asylum seeker seeks protection through a formal application for asylum.[29] The ability to submit an application for determination through the RSD process is recognised as a fundamental right accorded to asylum seekers.[30] It

[23] Article 12(1) and (3) of the Banjul Charter.

[24] See sec 2 of the Refugees Act.

[25] C d'Orsi *Asylum-seeker and refugee protection in sub-Saharan Africa: The peregrination of a persecuted human being in search of a safe haven* (2016) 5.

[26] D'Orsi (n 25) 6.

[27] See secs 28 and 29 of the Refugees Act.

[28] Sec 3 of the Refugees Act.

[29] The UN Refugee Agency 'Asylum seekers' https://www.unhcr.org/ke/asylum-seekers (accessed 13 March 2021). See further, J Phillips 'Asylum seekers and refugees what are the facts' (14 January 2011) https://www.aph.gov.au/binaries/library/pubs/bn/sp/asylumfacts.pdf (accessed 13 March 2021). S Kneebone *Introduction: Refugees and asylum seekers in the international context – Rights and realities* (2009) 20.

[30] See art 1(6) of the 1969 OAU Convention.

is a vital procedure since it determines whether or not the applicant legally qualifies to be recognised as a refugee and it is from the recognition as a 'refugee' that successful applicants may access social, economic and other rights.

The RSD is conducted by the Kenyan Government through the Department of Refugee Services (DRS) with the support of the UNHCR.[31] The DRS is responsible for all administrative matters concerning asylum seekers and refugees in Kenya.[32] Further, the DRS is responsible for the reception, registration and issuance of documentation to refugees.[33]

While conducting RSD in Kenya, an RSD officer will consider the 1951 Refugee Convention and its extended mandate in the 1967 Refugee Protocol, the 1969 OAU Convention, the Refugees Act and the Refugee Regulations, 2009 to determine whether an asylum seeker deserves to be protected as a refugee in Kenya. The RSD process begins when an asylum seeker registers their asylum claim application at any of the DRS Refugee Reception and Registration offices located in Dadaab, Kakuma, Nairobi, Nakuru, Eldoret and Mombasa.[34] The applicants are screened before being formally registered as asylum seekers and issued with an asylum seeker pass. An asylum seeker pass is an identification document issued by the Kenyan government to confirm the registration as an asylum seeker in Kenya pending the completion of the RSD process.

Currently all asylum seekers (except those from South Sudan)[35] must undergo the RSD interview to ascertain the eligibility of their protection claim. The outcome of the interview can either be the recognition of the applicant's refugee status or the rejection of their asylum application. Applicants whose refugee asylum application is rejected may appeal to the Refugee Status Appeal Committee (RSAC) and further appeal to the High Court of Kenya.[36] Until a final decision is reached, the applicants' status remains that of an asylum seeker.[37]

[31] The UN Refugee Agency 'Eligibility/Refugee Status Determination (RSD)' https://help.unhcr.org/kenya/kakuma/refugee-status-determination (accessed 13 March 2021).

[32] See sec 7 of the Refugees Act.

[33] The UN Refugee Agency (n 31).

[34] See sec 12 of the Refugees Act, 2021. UNHCR 'Applying for asylum in Kenya' https://help.unhcr.org/kenya/applying-for-asylum-in-kenya/ (accessed 13 March 2021).

[35] Asylum seekers from South Sudan are exempted from the RSD process because they have been granted prima facie refugee status.

[36] See sec 14 of the Refugees Act, 2021.

[37] Sec 2 of the Refugees Act.

As a result of the influx of asylum seekers, the RSD process in Kenya is here associated with long delays. In the past, the RSD process took between six months and two years on average. The Refugees Act provides strict timelines for the RSD process and appeals.[38] Without documentation, asylum seekers face challenges in accessing socio-economic rights and other human rights. It is the applicants' duty to prove their eligibility to be granted refugee status. They must meet all the requirements before their status can be confirmed.[39] The applicant may submit documentary evidence or present witnesses' testimonies to support their claim for refugee status.[40] If the documentary evidence is unavailable, the testimony of the applicant together with information from the applicant's Country of Origin (COO), may establish the applicants' eligibility for refugee status.[41] Once the RSD process is concluded, the RSD officer assesses the refugee asylum claim and may conduct further research to make a fair determination. The RSD officer will recommend either that the applicant be granted or denied refugee status.[42] Once this process is completed, the refugee asylum application is forwarded to the Commissioner of Refugee Affairs who communicates the decision to the applicant within specified timelines.[43] An asylum seeker who is successful in this process is then legally recognised as a refugee.[44] The Cabinet Secretary in charge of Refugee Affairs, on recommendation by the Refugee Advisory Committee, may declare any class of persons to be prima facie refugees and may amend or revoke such declaration at any time.[45] Prima facie refugees are excluded from a rigorous RSD process and are usually accorded refugee status upon completion of the standard refugee asylum claim registration process and after their origin has been verified.[46]

For a long time, asylum seekers from South Sudan and South and Central Somalia were considered prima facie refugees in Kenya.[47] This has

[38] See sec 11, 12 & 13 of the Refugees Act.

[39] See sec 22 of the Refugees Regulations, 2009.

[40] See sec 25(2) of the Kenya Refugee Regulations.

[41] See sec 22 of the Kenyan Refugees Regulations.

[42] See sec 29 of the Kenyan Refugees Regulations.

[43] See sec 29 (2) and (3) of the Kenyan Refugees Regulations.

[44] See sec 3 of the Refugees Act.

[45] See sec 3(2) of the Refugees Act, 2021.

[46] See sec 3(1)–(2) of the Refugees Act, 2021. See H Goitom 'Refugee law and policy in selected countries: Kenya' The Law Library of Congress (March 2016) 201 https://www.loc.gov/law/help/refugee-law/refugee-law-and-policy.pdf' (accessed 19 March 2021).

[47] Library of Congress (n 46).

changed since the status was revoked for asylum seekers from South and Central Somali. Only persons from South Sudan are still regarded as prima facie refugees.[48] The next section examines refugees' and asylum seekers' enjoyment of human rights.

4 Refugees' and Asylum Seekers' Enjoyment of Human Rights

Human rights are inherent to all human beings.[49] These rights are universal, inalienable, indivisible, interdependent and interrelated.[50] The universal nature of human rights is captured in article 1 of the Universal Declaration of Human Rights (UDHR) which states that, '[a]ll human beings are born free and equal in dignity and rights'. Hence, asylum seekers and refugees are entitled to human rights and fundamental freedoms.[51] Protection of asylum seekers and refugees must be seen in the broader context of the protection of human rights.[52]

Traditionally, the field of refugee law was applied in a vacuum. Refugee law focused on persons who had fled their country of origin or place of habitual residence due to fear of persecution and sought asylum across international borders, while human rights law dealt with human rights violations perpetrated by states upon its nationals.[53]

Presently, the fields of refugee and human rights law are interdependent because when asylum seekers flee their countries or place of habitual residence, they rely on the 1951 Refugee Convention, the 1969 Convention, Banjul Charter, human rights instruments and the domestic legislation of

[48] Human Rights Watch 'Kenya: Protect Somalis facing conflict, abuses, drought' (23 March 2017) https://www.hrw.org/news/2017/03/23/kenya-protect-somalis-facing-conflict-abuses-drought (accessed 20 April 2021).

[49] United Nations Human Rights OHCHR 'What are human rights?' https://www.ohchr.org/en/what-are-human-rights (accessed 15 April 2021). See further, J Donelly *Universal human rights in theory and practice* (2003) 8.

[50] M Foster *International refugee law and socio-economic rights: Refuge from deprivation* (2009) 165.

[51] J Hathaway *The rights of refugees under international law* (2010) 154. See further Refworld 'Fact Sheet 20: Human rights and refugees' https://www.refworld.org/pdfid/4794773f0.pdf (accessed 13 March 2021).

[52] As above.

[53] B Ibhawoh 'Defining persecution and protection: The cultural relativism debate and the rights of refugees' in N Steiner, M Gibney & G Loescher *Problems of protection: The UNHCR, refugees, and human rights* (2003) 61.

the host country for refugee protection. As a result, refugee protection includes the application of refugee law and human rights law. In that regard, Kenya has ratified the 1951 Refugee Convention, 1967 Protocol relating to the Status of Refugees (1967 Refugee Protocol), 1969 OAU Convention and the Banjul Charter. At the national level, Kenya has enacted the Constitution of Kenya, 2010 (Kenyan Constitution), the Refugees Act and the Refugee (Reception, Registration and Adjudication) Regulations of 2009 (Refugee Regulations).[54] These international, regional and domestic legal instruments form part of legal refugees' and asylum seekers' protection in Kenya. Once an asylum seeker flees their country of origin or place of habitual residence and satisfies the definition of a refugee, the host state has an obligation to provide refugee protection and grant the refugee access to human rights in accordance with the 1951 Refugee Convention, the 1969 OAU Convention, other human rights treaties and domestic legislation.[55] The next section examines the legal framework for socio-economic rights for refugees and asylum seekers in Kenya.

5 Legal Frameworks for SERs of Refugees and Asylum Seekers in Kenya

The legal status of refugees and asylum seekers in Kenya is dealt with in section 28 of the Refugee Act which provides for the rights and duties of refugees and asylum seekers. Section 28 provides, 'Every refugee and asylum seeker in Kenya shall be entitled to; (a) the duties contained in the UN Convention, its Protocol and the OAU Convention; Therefore, the 1951 Refugee Convention obliges Kenya as states party to provide lawfully residing refugees with socio-economic rights of wage-earning employment, housing, public education and social security'.[56]

In addition, the Kenyan Constitution provides for socio-economic rights in article 43 which states as follows

[54] At the time of writing this chapter, The Refugee Act 2006 had been repealed and replaced by the Refugees Act 2021, it is noteworthy that the Cabinet Secretary in charge of Refugees is in the process of drafting new Refugee Regulations.

[55] Helton (n 17) 21. See also GS Goodwin-Gill 'The international law of refugee protection' in EF Qasmiyeh et al. (eds) *The Oxford handbook of refugee and forced migration studies* (2014) 5.

[56] Articles 17, 18, 21–24 of the Refugee Convention.

1. Every person has the right-

   (a) to the highest attainable standard of health, which includes the right to health care services, including reproductive health care; (b) to accessible and adequate housing, and to reasonable standards of sanitation; (c) to be free from hunger, and to have adequate food of acceptable quality; (d) to clean and safe water in adequate quantities; (e) to social security; (f) to education.

The aim of the above provision is to ensure access to socio-economic rights of persons who had been denied these rights in the past.[57] The provisions mentioned above indicate that refugees and asylum seekers in Kenya have the right to healthcare, adequate housing, reasonable standards of sanitation, adequate food, clean and safe water, social security and to education. While the above section has set out the socio-economic rights that refugees and asylum seekers are entitled to in Kenya, the next subsection provides an in-depth discussion of refugees' and asylum seekers' right to work in Kenya.

5.1 *The Right to Work of Asylum Seekers and Refugees in Kenya*

Every person has a right to work. This right is enshrined in the UDHR (article 23), CERD (article 5(e)(i)),[58] CEDAW (article 11(a)),[59] the CRPD (article 27),[60] the International Convention on the Protection of the Rights of All Migrant Workers and Members of Their Families (article 52)[61] and the ICESR (article 6).[62] Articles 17, 18 and 19 of the 1951 Refugee Convention recognise the right to work of lawfully residing refu-

[57] J Gitiri 'Progressive Nature of Social and Economic Rights in Kenya: a Delayed Promise?' 6 *Constitutional Review* 135. See also R Bwana 'Progressive Realization of Socio-Economic Rights: Nonsense on Stilts?' (15 December 2021) https://doi.org/10.2139/ssrn.3986266 (accessed 13 March 2022).

[58] International Convention on the Elimination of All Forms of Racial Discrimination (n 61).

[59] Convention of Elimination of Discrimination of All Forms of Discrimination Against Women (n 60).

[60] UN General Assembly, Convention on the Rights of Persons with Disabilities: resolution/adopted by the General Assembly, 24 January 2007, A/RES/61/106.

[61] UN General Assembly, International Convention on the Protection of the Rights of All Migrant Workers and Members of their Families, 18 December 1990, A/RES/45/158.

[62] N 59.

gees. Kenya has ratified the CERD, CEDAW, CRPD, ICESR and the 1951 Refugee Convention, and therefore has an obligation to fulfil every person's right to work including the right of refugees and asylum seekers. In Kenya the right to work is provided for under the Kenyan Constitution and the Refugees Act.

5.1.1 The Kenyan Constitution

The Kenyan Constitution recognises everyone's right to fair labour practices.[63] Every worker has a right to a fair remuneration and reasonable working conditions.[64] The use of the word 'everyone' includes refugees and asylum seekers, who have the right to fair labour practices. 'Worker' is defined as those who depend on an economic relationship with an employer.[65] The intent of the drafters of this provision was to promote fair labour relations between the employer and their employees and to ensure fair remuneration and reasonable working conditions.[66]

5.1.2 The Refugees Act

The Refugees Act recognises the right of refugees to engage individually or as a group in gainful employment or to practise a profession or trade if they hold qualifications recognised by competent authorities in Kenya.[67] This Act recognises refugees' right to engage in wage earning employment individually or as a group, the right to self-employment and also to practise a liberal profession if the person possesses the requisite documents that are recognised by competent authorities in Kenya. Consequently, the Refugees Act provides for refugees' right to work and earn a livelihood in Kenya.

It is noteworthy that the 1951 Refugee Convention only grants socio-economic rights to refugees who reside lawfully within the territory of a contracting state. The term 'lawfully residing refugees' is interpreted to mean individuals in the host country who are permitted to be within its territory. However, this does not include persons in transit or who are in the territory for a specified duration. More importantly, the term includes asylum seekers whose status has not been determined yet, or who are in

[63] See art 43(1) of the Kenyan Constitution, 2010.

[64] See art 41(2)(a) and (b) of the Kenyan Constitution, 2010.

[65] Lumumba & Franceschi (n 74) 195.

[66] MK Mbondenyi & JO Ambani *The New Constitutional Law of Kenya: Principles, government and human rights* (2012) 87.

[67] See sec 28(5) of the Refugees Act, 2021.

the process of appealing the outcome of the RSD process.[68] Since asylum seekers are regarded as lawfully residing in the host country, the issue that arises is whether they have the right to work. This question was addressed in *Minister of Home Affairs v Watchenuka*. The issue which arose in this case was whether the first respondent could access the right to seek employment while awaiting the outcome of the RSD process. The Supreme Court of Appeal of South Africa affirmed that asylum seekers have the right to work pending the outcome of their RSD and emphasised that this right is part of human dignity which is inherent in all individuals including non-nationals.[69] The question which arises is whether or not asylum seekers enjoy the right to work in Kenya.

It seems that lawfully residing refugees in Kenya can enjoy the right to wage earning employment, housing, public education and social security in terms of articles 22, 23 and 24 of the 1951 Refugee Convention. However, the Refugee Act only extends the right to work to refugees and it fails to acknowledge asylum seekers' right to work in Kenya. It seems that asylum seekers are not allowed to work in Kenya because they are not mentioned in relation to the enjoyment of this right in section 28(5) of the Refugee Act. It is unjustifiable for asylum seekers to be denied access to the labour market. In granting them access to the labour market, asylum seekers become independent while contributing to the economy. In *Kituo Cha Sheria & 8 others*[70] it was recognised that the rights outlined in the Bill of Rights in the Constitution apply to all persons residing in Kenya including refugees and asylum seekers.[71]

5.1.3 Progressive Realisation of Socio-Economic Rights in Kenya

The previous section has shown the extent to which refugees and asylum seekers enjoy socio-economic rights in Kenya. The enjoyment of socio-economic rights by refugees and asylum seekers is important because it helps them to survive in the country of asylum.[72] States parties to the ICESR have an obligation to take steps to ensure that they progressively realise socio-economic rights.[73] 'Progressive realisation' means that states,

[68] J Hathaway *The rights of refugees under international law* (2021) 809.

[69] *The Minister of Home Affairs v Watchenuka* [2004] 1 All SA 21 (SCA).

[70] N 12.

[71] See sec 31(3) of the Kenyan Constitution, 2010.

[72] R Lal 'Social and economic rights of refugees under international legal framework: An appraisal' (2018) 58 *Indian Journal of International Law* 467.

[73] Article 2(1) of the ICESR.

while taking into consideration available resources, should take measures to realise socio-economic rights over time. The full realisation of socio-economic rights cannot be achieved over a short period of time.[74] Therefore, this provision was not meant for states to use as a defence when they fail to realise socio-economic rights.[75]

Article 2(3) of the ICESR provides that '[d]eveloping countries with regard to human rights and their national economy, may determine to what extent they would guarantee economic rights ... to non-nationals... to progressively realize economic, social and cultural rights' to the extent of the limits of their resources. States have the obligation to fulfil socio-economic rights progressively or over time.[76] Resultantly, developing countries have an obligation to realise the socio-economic rights of non-nationals which include refugees and asylum seekers in accordance with their available resources over time.

Article 21(2) of the Kenyan Constitution obligates the state to take 'legislative and administrative measures' with the aim of improving standards progressively to ensure that every person in Kenya has access to socio-economic rights. In Matthew *Okwanda v Minister of Health and Medical Services & 3 others*, the Court held that the state has obligations to progressively realise socio-economic rights and to show that it is taking steps to actualise these rights. [77] Similarly, in *Mitu- Bell Welfare Society* versus *Kenya Airports Authority*, the Supreme Court of Kenya held that Kenya has an obligation to take concrete measures to achieve the realisation of the right to housing. The Supreme Court indicated that while the realisation of this right depends on the availability of land and resources, the state has an obligation to prove that it lacks resources to fulfil its obligation. [78] The state must be seen to be taking steps to ensure the progres-

[74] L Chenwi 'Unpacking "progressive realisation", its relation to resources, minimum core and reasonableness, and some methodological considerations for assessing compliance' (2013) 46 *De Jure Law Journal* 742. See also, PLO Lumumba & L Franceschi *The Constitution of Kenya, 2010: An introductory commentary* (2014) 203.

[75] The East African Centre for Human Rights 'A compendium on economic and social rights cases under the Constitution of Kenya, 2010' https://eachrights.or.ke/wp-content/uploads/2020/07/A_Compendium_On_Economic_And_Social_Rights_Cases_Under_The_Constitution_Of_Kenya_2010.pdf (accessed 15 April 2021).

[76] Hathaway (n 51) 470.

[77] *Mathew Okwanda v Minister of Health and Medical Services & 3 others* [2013] eKLR. See also, MMM v the Permanent Secretary, Ministry of Education and 20 others [2013] eKLR.

[78] *Mitu-Bell Welfare Society v Kenya Airports Authority & 2 others; Initiative for Strategic Litigation in Africa* (Amicus Curiae) (Petition 3 of 2018) [2021].

sive realisation of the right to education too. In *Satrose Ayuma and 11 others v Registered Trustee of the Kenya Railways Staff Retirement Benefits Scheme and three others*, the Court affirmed that socio-economic rights are not aspirational and that the government of Kenya needs to be seen to take steps towards their realisation.

From the above cases, it is evident that Kenya has an obligation to take measures towards the progressive realisation of socio-economic rights for all persons in Kenya including refugees and asylum seekers. The next sub-section addresses the barriers to refugees' and asylum seekers' access to the right to work in Kenya.

6 Barriers to Refugees' and Asylum Seekers' Access to the Right to Work in Kenya

It is important to note that the right to work for asylum seekers and refugees has not been realised fully in most developing and developed countries, due to the assumption that the fulfilment of the right would enhance their integration into the host countries, displace nationals from the labour market and attract more asylum seekers.[79] As a developing country, Kenya may find it difficult to strike a balance between fulfilling international obligations by allowing asylum seekers and refugees the right to work, with its national responsibilities of fulfilling its own citizens' right to work.[80] Evidently, the Refugees Act fails to expressly recognise asylum seekers' right to work, but it acknowledges the right to be enjoyed by refugees. While the right to work is provided for under the Kenyan Constitution and the Refugees Act, asylum seekers and refugees face barriers which impede their enjoyment of the right to work.

Refugees residing in refugee camps have limited access to work opportunities and to acquiring formal employment.[81] Kenya's encampment policy discourages refugees and asylum seekers from residing in urban areas. While the Citizenship and Immigration Act, 2011 allows refugees to apply for a Class M permit at no cost to enable them to access the right to work, in reality, it is difficult for refugees to acquire work permits due to

[79] P Mathew *Reworking the relationship between asylum and employment* (2012) 39.

[80] Hathaway (n 82) 925.

[81] S Carciotto & C d'Orsi 'Access to socio-economic rights for refugees: A comparison across six African countries' *The Scalabrini Institute for Human Mobility in Africa* (March 2017) https://sihma.org.za/reports/Final_report.pdf (accessed 4 April 2022).

stringent conditions that must be met before the issuance of permits.[82] Consequently, their only real option is to accept low-paying informal jobs.[83] Although Kenya is a party to the ICESR and the 1951 Refugee Convention which provides for the right to work for asylum seekers and refugees, few refugees have accessed this right. This predisposes them to exploitation.[84]

Kenya strictly applies the encampment policy which requires asylum seekers and refugees to reside in designated areas. Approximately 84 per cent of refugees reside in refugee camps which are located in remote areas. To access urban centres, refugees are required to obtain movement passes, which are valid for one month only. While the Refugees Act recognises the right of refugees to work, in reality, their freedom of movement is a barrier to realising the right to work. To compound the issue, work permits are rarely issued to refugees and asylum seekers. This limits their access to wage earning employment. In *Kituo Cha Sheria*, the Court held that the policy of encampment restricts access to gainful employment. Although freedom of movement is a civil and political right, human rights are interconnected. Consequently, without exercising their freedom of movement, refugees' right to work is undermined and results in an overreliance on the state, the UNCHR and its partners.

A refugee voiced concerns over the lengthy RSD process which hinders their access to the right to work as follows, 'How can I access a work permit when the law states that I require a refugee certificate but this certificate takes five years to get? What will I do in the meantime?'[85] As discussed earlier, the RSD process is lengthy and subject to delays. According to a UNHCR report, several months lapse before an asylum seeker receives a decision on his or her asylum application.[86] During that period, asylum

[82] Refugee Consortium of Kenya 'Refugees and asylum seekers lament limited access to work in Kenya' https://www.rckkenya.org/refugees-and-asylum-seekers-lament-limited-access-to-work-permits-in-kenya/ (accessed 9 April 2022).

[83] Carciotto & D'Orsi (n 104).

[84] Reliefweb 'Consultancy to support refugees' inclusion into NSSF "Haba Haba" products for workers in the informal community' https://reliefweb.int/job/3835552/consultancy-support-refugees-inclusion-nssf-haba-haba-product-workers-informal-economy (accessed 9 April 2022).

[85] Refugee Consortium of Kenya (n 82).

[86] The UN Refugee Agency 'What happens after I apply?' https://help.unhcr.org/kenya/applying-for-asylum-in-kenya/what-happens-after-i-apply/ (accessed 8 March 2022).

seekers are unable to apply for the Class M work permit, because they lack the requisite refugee identification documents to apply for it. The inability to legally access work opportunities is a violation of the right to work as envisaged by the drafters of the 1951 Refugee Convention.

The right to work of asylum seekers and refugees in Kenya is also undermined by the lack of commitment, consistency or goodwill by the government in ensuring the realisation of this right.[87] Moreover, Kenya lacks a designated policy to guide the implementation and realisation of the right to work of refugees and asylum seekers.

While the Refugees Act recognises the right to work of refugees, the application and issuance of a Class M work permit is a prerequisite. In theory, refugees can be issued with Class M permits at no cost to find employment, practise liberal professions or become self-employed.[88] In practice, however, 84 per cent of refugees reside in refugee camps located in remote areas. This is a barrier to their right to work. In addition, the Citizenship and Immigration Act, 2011 poses another obstacle to their right to work as it requires foreigner nationals who apply for the work permit to demonstrate that they have unique skills or that the job they are applying for cannot be done by ordinary Kenyans. This legal provision is a major barrier to the refugees' right to work and it leaves the majority of them with little option but to resort to the informal sector for employment.[89] While this section has addressed the challenges to refugees' and asylum seekers' right to work in Kenya, the next section examines good practices from Uganda, Sudan and Chad, which Kenya could draw lessons from.

[87] Refugees International 'New research suggests Kenyan Government isn't doing enough to support economic inclusion of refugees' https://www.refugeesinternational.org/reports/2021/11/16/new-research-suggests-kenyan-government-isnt-doing-enough-to-support-economic-inclusion-of-refugees (accessed 8 March 2022).

[88] Department of Immigration Services 'Application for Permit Class M: (Refugees:KEP/M)' https://fns.immigration.go.ke/infopack/permits/classM/ (accessed 8 April 2022).

[89] See S Konzolo 'An overview of refugee status determination and the rights of refugees in Kenya: The protection envisaged under the 2006 Refugees Act' Paper prepared for Refugee Studies Centre Workshop on Refugee Status Determination and Rights in Southern and East Africa https://www.rsc.ox.ac.uk/files/files-1/dp-rsd-kenya-2010.pdf (accessed 14 September 2021).

7 Good Practices from Uganda, Sudan and Chad

Kenya can borrow good practices from countries like Uganda, Sudan and Chad who host large numbers of refugees and asylum seekers. These countries protect refugees' and asylum seekers' right to work by promoting the enjoyment of the right to work among refugees and asylum seekers. In Uganda, refugees can access the right to work and to employment opportunities upon their recognition as refugees. They can engage in agriculture, industry, handicrafts, commerce and engage in liberal professions.[90]

While Sudan's Asylum (Organization) Act, 2014 allows refugees to work[91] in any field except national security and national intelligence,[92] there was a disparity between the law and practice. In reality it was difficult for refugees to obtain work permits. However, the UNHCR entered into an agreement with Kassala state and the Kassala Ministry of Finance, to allow refugees in Eastern Sudan to be issued with work permits to enable them to work.[93] Consequently, many refugees have been granted work permits and have access to the labour market which allows them to integrate into the community and to contribute to the Sudanese economy.

Chad hosts huge numbers of refugees who are mainly from Sudan and the Central African Republic. Chad adopted an asylum law which enhances the protection of refugees by granting them freedom of movement and allowing them to work upon attaining the requisite documentation.[94] This provision has enabled several refugees to sustain themselves.[95]

[90] Sec 29(4)–(6) Uganda Refugee Act, 2006.

[91] See sec 13(2) of the Asylum (Organization) Act, 2014.

[92] See sec 18(1) of the Asylum (Organization) Act.

[93] The L Pattison & N Brass 'UNHCR signs agreement to grant work permits for 30,000 refugees in East Sudan' UN Refugee Agency (2 October 2013) https://www.unhcr.org/news/makingdifference/2013/10/524bec189/unhcr-signs-agreement-grant-work--permits-30000-refugees-east-sudan.html#:~:text=Although%20Sudan's%20Asylum%20Act%20allows,issued%20with%20the%20required%20documentation (accessed 8 April 2022).

[94] United States Committee for Refugees and Immigrants *World Refugee Survey 2008 – Chad* (19 June 2008) https://www.refworld.org/docid/485f50c98a.html (accessed 8 April 2022).

[95] See sec 18(8) of the Refugees Amendment Act, 2017.

8 Conclusion and Recommendations

In conclusion, Kenya's encampment policy has resulted in 84 per cent of refugees and asylum seekers residing in designated areas, which restricts their freedom of movement and in turn prevents the full realisation of the right to work. The high percentage of lawfully residing refugees in designated areas indicates a prima facie breach of Kenya's obligation to fully promote, fulfil and protect the right to work of refugees and asylum seekers. It also suggests that Kenya is yet to progressively realise the right to work for refugees and asylum seekers. Kenya could borrow best practices on the rights of refugees and asylum seekers to work from Uganda, Sudan and Chad. Kenya should allow lawfully residing refugees, which also includes asylum seekers, to realise their right to work, as a way of protecting their human dignity while promoting self-reliance.

While the Refugees Act provides refugees with the right to work, there is a lack of full implementation of this right. This is manifested by the lack of work permits amongst most refugees and asylum seekers. In fulfilling its obligation in respect of the right to wage earning employment of refugees and asylum seekers, Kenya has a duty to enforce socio-economic rights which include the right to work of refugees and asylum seekers. Kenya could fulfil this obligation by, first, lifting the encampment policy which will in turn promote freedom of movement and promote the refugees' and asylum seekers' access to the labour market. Secondly, Kenya could implement the right to work by ensuring that refugees and asylum seekers can easily obtain work permits. Thirdly, Kenya could prevent lengthy delays in the RSD process which constitutes a barrier to allowing asylum seekers to apply for work permits. Finally, Kenya can draft policies to implement their realisation of the right to work of refugees and asylum seekers. In doing so, Kenya will be progressively realising the right to work in respect of lawfully residing refugees.

Bibliography

Books

D'Orsi, C *Asylum seeker and refugee protection in sub-Saharan Africa: The peregrination of a persecuted human being in search of a safe haven* (Routledge 2016)

Chapters in Books

Edwards, A 'Article 17' in Zimmermann, A (ed) *The 1951 Convention relating to the Status of Refugees and its 1967 Protocol: A Commentary* (Oxford University Press 2011)

Donelly, J. (2003) *Universal Human Rights in theory and practice* (pp 8) Cornell University Press.

Foster, M., & Lambert, H, (2019) *International Refugee Law and Protection of Stateless Persons* (pp 2) Oxford University Press.

Foster, M. (2009) *International Refugee Law and Socio-Economic Rights: Refuge from Deprivation* (pp 165) Cambridge University Press.

Hathaway, J. (2021) *The Rights of Refugees under International Law* (pp 173) Cambridge University Press.

Helton, A.C., (2003). What Is Refugee Protection? In Gibney M, & Loescher G (Eds.), *Problems of Protection The UNHCR, Refugees, and Human Rights* (pp 20) Routledge.

Ibhawoh, B, (2003). Defining Persecution and Protection the Cultural Relativism Debate and The Rights of Refugees In Gibney. M, & Loescher G (Eds.), *Problems of Protection The UNHCR, Refugees, and Human Rights* (pp 20) Routledge.

Kneebone, S. (2019) 'Introduction: Refugees and Asylum Seekers in the International Context – Rights and Realities'. In S Kneebone, (pp 20)

Lumumba, P.L.O, & Franceschi, L, (2014). *The Constitution of Kenya, 2010: An Introductory Commentary* (pp 195) Strathmore University Press.

Madokoro, L, (2016). *Elusive Refuge: Chinese Migrants in the Cold War* (pp 3). Harvard.

Mathew, P. (2012) '*Reworking the Relationship between Asylum and Employment*' (pp 39) Routledge.

Mbondenyi, M.K & Ambani, J.O. (2012). *The New Constitutional Law of Kenya. Principles, Government and Human Rights* (Law Africa).

Qasmiyeh, E.F., Loescher, G., Long, K & Sigona, N. (2014). The Oxford Handbook of Refugee and Forced Migration Studies. In G.S Goodwin-Gill (ed), The *International Law of Refugee Protection*' (pp 5) Oxford University Press.

Schmidt, D.S & Omondi M.O. (2019). 'Refugees and Forced Migration in the Horn and Eastern Africa: Trends, Challenges and Opportunities'. In D. S Schmidt & M.O (Eds.), *Researching Refugees and Forced Migration in Eastern and Horn of Africa Introducing the issues* (pp.9) Springer International Publishing.

Sharpe, M. (2018).*The Regional law of Refugee Protection in Africa*'(pp 42) Oxford University Press.

Tendayi, E (2021). Race, Refugees and International Law. In Costello C, Foster M & MacAdam J (Eds.), *The Oxford Handbook of International Refugee Law* (pp 47). Oxford University Press. https://doi.org/10.1093/law/9780198848639.001.

Journal Articles

Chenwi, L 'Unpacking "progressive realization", its relation to resources, minimum core and reasonableness, and some methodological considerations for assessing compliance' (2013) 46 *De Jure Law Journal* 742.

Lal, R.(2018). Social and Economic rights of refugees under international legal framework: an appraisal *Indian Journal of International Law* 472 58(3): 467-488.

Mathew, P, et al. (2010). The Michigan Guidelines on the Right to Work 31 *Michigan Journal of International Law* 299.

Omata, N. (2021). Refugee livelihoods: a comparative analysis of Nairobi and Kakuma camp in Kenya 45 (4) *Disasters* 865-886.

Legislation

Constitution of the Republic of Kenya, 2010
Kenyan Citizenship and Immigration Act, 2011
Kenya Refugees Regulations, 2009
Refugees Act 10 of 2021
Refugees Act, 1998
The Asylum (Organization) Act, 2014
The Refugees Amendment Act, 2017
Uganda Refugee Act, 2006

Case Law

Petition 19 of 2013 consolidated with Petition 115 of 2013.

The Minister of Home Affairs and two others v Watchenuka and another 10/2003

Mathew Okwanda v Minister of Health and Medical Services & 3 others [2013] eKLR.

Mitu-Bell Welfare Society v Kenya Airports Authority & 2 others; Initiative for Strategic Litigation in Africa (Amicus Curiae) (Petition 3 of 2018) [2021]

MMM v the Permanent Secretary, Ministry of Education and 20 others [2013] eKLR

International Conventions

African (Banjul) Charter on Human and People's Rights, article 12(1) & (3), (Adopted 27 June 1981, OAU Doc. CAB/LEG/67/3 rev. 5, 21 I.L.M. 58 (1982), entered into force 21 October 1986).
Convention on the Elimination of All Forms of Racial Discrimination
Convention relating to the Status of Refugees art 17-24 & 30
Convention relating to the Status of Stateless Persons
Convention of Elimination of Discrimination of All Forms of Discrimination against Women
Convention on the Rights of Persons with Disabilities resolution/adopted by the General Assembly A/RES/61/106 24 January 2007.
International Covenant on Economic, Social and Cultural Rights Adopted and opened for signature, ratification and accession by General Assembly resolution 2200A (XXI) of 16 December 1966 entry into force 3 January 1976
International Convention on the Protection of the Rights of All Migrant Workers and Members of Their Families Adopted by General Assembly resolution 45/158 of 18 December 1990
ICESR Adopted and opened for signature, ratification and accession by General Assembly resolution 2200A (XXI) of 16 December 1966 entry into force 3 January 1976
Organization of African Unity Convention Governing the Specific Aspects of Refugee Problems in Africa Adopted 10 September 1969, Entered into force 20 June 1974,1001 UNTS 45
Universal Declaration of Human Rights

Internet Sources

African Commission on Human and People's Rights, 'Declaration by the Special Rapporteur on Refugees, Asylum seekers, Displaced Persons and Migrants in Africa on the occasion of the World Refugee Day', 2017 https://www.achpr.org/news/viewdetail?id=32 (accessed 15 September 2021).
Carciotto, S, et al. 'Access to Socio-Economic Rights for Refugees: A Comparison Across Six African Countries' The Scalabrini Institute for Human Mobility in Africa March 2017, https://sihma.org.za/reports/Final_report.pdf (accessed 4 April 2022).
Department of Immigration Services 'Application for Permit Class M' (Refugees:KEP/M) https://fns.immigration.go.ke/infopack/permits/classM/ (accessed 8 April 2022).
Historical background of ESCR, https://www.cesr.org/sites/default/files/ESCR%20-%20A%20guide%20to%20the%20legal%20framework.pdf (accessed 15 April 2021).

Human Rights Watch 'Kenya Protect Somalis Facing Conflict abuses and Drought' https://www.hrw.org/news/2017/03/23/kenya-protect-somalis-facing-conflict-abuses-drought accessed (accessed on 20 April 2021).

Maina, A, 'Development of Refugee Law in Kenya' https://www.rckkenya.org/development-of-refugee-law-in-kenya/ (accessed 30 March 2022).

Refworld 'Fact Sheet No. 20, Human Rights and Refugees,' https://www.refworld.org/pdfid/4794773f0.pdf (accessed 13 March 2021).

Refugee Consortium of Kenya 'Refugees and Asylum Seekers lament limited access to work in Kenya' https://www.rckkenya.org/refugees-and-asylum-seekers-lament-limited-access-to-work-permits-in-kenya/ (accessed 9 April 2022).

Reliefweb 'Consultancy to support refugees' inclusion into NSSF "HabaHaba" products for workers in the informal community' https://reliefweb.int/job/3835552/consultancy-support-refugees-inclusion-nssf-haba-haba-product-workers-informal-economy (accessed 9 April 2022).

The East African Centre for Human Rights 'A compendium on economic and social rights cases under the Constitution of Kenya, 2010', https://eachrights.or.ke/wp-content/uploads/2020/07/A_Compendium_On_Economic_And_Social_Rights_Cases_Under_The_Constitution_Of_Kenya_2010.pdf (accessed 15 April 2021).

The UN Refugee Agency 'Rapid Phone surveys in Kenya show disproportionately negative impact on refugees' https://www.unhcr.org/blogs/rapid-phone-surveys-in-kenya-show-disproportionately-negative-impact-on-refugees/ (accessed 8 April 2022a).

The UN Refugee Agency 'UNHCR signs agreement to grant work permits for 30,000 refugees in East Sudan' https://www.unhcr.org/news/makingdifference/2013/10/524bec189/unhcr-signs-agreement-grant-work-permits-30000-refugees-east-sudan.html#:~:text=Although%20Sudan's%20Asylum%20Act%20allows,issued%20with%20the%20required%20documentation (accessed 8 April 2022b).

The UN Refugee Agency 'Figures at a glance' https://www.unhcr.org/ke/figures-at-a-glance(accessed 19 April 2021a).

The United Nation Refugee Agency 'Asylum seekers', https://www.unhcr.org/ke/asylum-seekers (accessed 13 March 2021). See further, Phillips J 'Asylum seekers and refugees what are the facts', https://www.aph.gov.au/binaries/library/pubs/bn/sp/asylumfacts.pdf (accessed 13 March 2021).

The UN Refugee Agency 'Eligibility/Refugee Status Determination (RSD)', https://help.unhcr.org/kenya/kakuma/refugee-status-determination (accessed on 13 March 2021b).

The Law Library of Congress 'Refugee Law and Policy: Kenya' https://www.loc.gov/law/help/refugee-law/refugee-law-and-policy.pdf (accessed on 19 March 2021).

The UN Refugee Agency 'Refugee Status Determination', https://www.unhcr.org/ke/refugee-status-determination (accessed 13 March 2021c)
United Nation High Commission for Refugees, 'Understanding the Socioeconomic Conditions of Refugees in Kalobeyei, Kenya Results from the 2018 Kalobeyei Socioeconomic Profiling Survey', https://www.unhcr.org/ke/wp-content/uploads/sites/2/2020/04/Kalobeyei_Socioeconomic-Report-1.pdf (accessed 19 April 2021a).
UNHCR 'Dadaab- World's biggest refugee camp 20 years old', https://www.unhcr.org/news/makingdifference/2012/2/4f439dbb9/dadaab-worlds-biggest-refugee-camp-20-years-old.html (accessed 19 April 2021a).
UNHCR 'Understanding the Socioeconomic Conditions of Refugees in Kalobeyei, Kenya Results from the 2018 Kalobeyei Socioeconomic Profiling Survey', https://www.unhcr.org/ke/wp-content/uploads/sites/2/2020/04/Kalobeyei_Socioeconomic-Report-1.pdf (accessed 19 April 2021b).
UNHCR 'Applying for asylum in Kenya', https://help.unhcr.org/kenya/applying-for-asylum-in-kenya/ (accessed on 13 March 2021c).
United Nations Human Rights 'What are human Rights', https://www.ohchr.org/en/issues/pages/whatarehumanrights.aspx (accessed 15 April 2021).
United Nations Population Fund 'Human rights are universal and religious cultural or ethnic background', https://www.unfpa.org/pcm/node/9206#:~:text=Human%20rights%20are%20universal%20and,religious%2C%20cultural%20or%20ethnic%20background (accessed 13 March 2021).
United Nations Human Rights Office of the High Commissioner 'Economic, Social and Cultural Rights' https://www.ohchr.org/EN/Issues/ESCR/Pages/ESCRIndex.aspx (accessed on 18 April 2021).
United Nation High Commission for Refugees, 'Understanding the Socioeconomic Conditions of Refugees in Kalobeyei, Kenya Results from the 2018 Kalobeyei Socioeconomic Profiling Survey', https://www.unhcr.org/ke/wpcontent/uploads/sites/2/2020/04/Kalobeyei_Socioeconomic-Report-1.pdf (accessed 19 April 2021b).
United States Committee for Refugees and Immigrants 'World Refugee Survey 2008 – Chad' 19 June 2008 https://www.refworld.org/docid/485f50c98a.html (accessed 8 April 2022).
Zard M, Beyani C & Odinkalu 'A Refugees and the African Commission of Human and People's Rights' https://docs.escr-net.org/usr_doc/Zard_article.pdf (accessed 15 October 2021).

CHAPTER 14

From De Jure to De Facto? Realising the Socio-Economic Rights of Refugees in Malawi

Angela Nkatha Mutema

1 Introduction

By their nature, socio-economic rights are empowerment rights because they allow vulnerable and marginalised individuals and groups to use the law to satisfy their essential socio-economic needs.[1] These rights enable individuals to hold governments accountable for their development.[2] As a

[1] M Pieterse 'Resuscitating socio-economic rights: Constitutional entitlements to health-care services' (2006) 22 *South African Journal on Human Rights* 473 at 477.
[2] *Mazibuko v City of Johannesburg* 2010 (4) SA 1 (CC) para 59.

A. N. Mutema (✉)
School of Law, Jomo Kenyatta University of Agriculture and Technology, Nairobi, Kenya
e-mail: amutema@jkuat.ac.ke

E. Durojaye et al. (eds.), *Realising Socio-Economic Rights of Refugees and Asylum Seekers in Africa*, Politics of Citizenship and Migration, https://doi.org/10.1007/978-3-031-16548-1_14

consequence, the fulfilment of the social and economic rights of individuals leads to the development of their full potential in all spheres of life.[3]

Statistics from the United Nations High Commission for Refugees (UNHCR) indicate that as of 31 August 2021, Malawi is home to 51,415 refugees and asylum seekers.[4] The main camp for refugees is Dzaleka refugee camp, which is located 25 miles north of Lilongwe, the capital city of Malawi.[5] This camp, initially designed for 10,000 people, is congested with over 51,415 persons—a serious health risk during the Covid-19 pandemic.[6] (The impact of Covid-19 will be addressed in a later section of the chapter.) This camp was built 25 years ago to accommodate the refugees who fled from conflict in Burundi, Rwanda and the Democratic Republic of the Congo.[7]

The Malawian government announced through its Homeland Security Minister, that refugees and asylum seekers who had left Dzaleka camp should return to the camp within 14 days or face eviction.[8] Without specifying the details, the Minister stated that the refugees and asylum seekers posed a security threat.[9] It was reported in the media that some refugees stated that their economic activities enabled them to ensure that their families benefitted from the enjoyment of better education and health services.[10] This media report requires an evaluation of the normative and jurisprudential sphere on the rights of refugees and asylum seekers in Malawi. The need to understand this sphere stems from the overcrowding in the refugee camp and the need to give effect to refugees' and asylum seekers' socio-economic rights in Malawi.

In international law, a refugee is entitled to all the rights as provided for in the Convention Relating to the Status of Refugees (UN Refugee

[3] S Liebenberg & B Goldblatt 'The interrelationship between equality and socioeconomic rights under South Africa's transformative Constitution' (2007) 23 *South African Journal on Human Rights* 335 at 337.

[4] Reliefweb 'Malawi: UNHCR Fact Sheet, August 2021' (2021) https://bit.ly/3dwdPCF (accessed 9 December 2021).

[5] Reliefweb (n 4).

[6] Reliefweb (n 4).

[7] B Kunchezera 'Return to the refugee camp: Malawi orders thousands back to "congested" Dzaleka' *The Guardian* 25 November 2021 https://bit.ly/3pYSYOf (accessed 9 December 2021).

[8] L Masina 'Malawi orders all refugees back into camp within 14 days' *VOA News* 17 April 2021 https://bit.ly/3oBGpIW (accessed 9 December 2021).

[9] Masina (n 8).

[10] Masina (n 8).

Convention).[11] Socio-economic rights include the right to religion and religious education,[12] public education,[13] health[14] and housing.[15] This position is reiterated by other regional instruments such as the Convention Governing the Specific Aspects of Refugee Problems in Africa (OAU Convention).[16]

Based on the preceding summary, this chapter provides a critical discussion of the position of socio-economic rights in Malawi in a chronological order of international, regional and national law. Further, a critique of the courts' approach to socio-economic rights is provided. Subsequently, suggestions on the way forward are made, a conclusion is reached and recommendations are offered.

2 The Position of International Law in Malawi's Legal Context

The Constitution of 1994 as amended in 2017 is the supreme law of the land, and provides various positions regarding the application of international law. The Constitution recognises that customary international law is applicable. This is based on the provision which states that the Republic of Malawi is a sovereign state with rights and obligations under the Law of Nations.[17] This is supported by the marginal notes to the section which provides that customary international law is an interpretational aid to the Constitution. The use of marginal notes is not novel in the interpretation of statutes. Earlier jurisprudence from the English common law suggests that marginal notes are simply catchwords that offer a glimpse into the content of the provision in question. In *Chandler v DPP*, Lord Reid stated the following

[11] UN General Assembly, Convention Relating to the Status of Refugees, 28 July 1951, United Nations, Treaty Series, vol 189, p 137, acceded to the Convention on 10 December 1989.

[12] Article 4 of the UN Refugee Convention.

[13] Article 22 of the UN Refugee Convention.

[14] Article 23 of the UN Refugee Convention.

[15] Article 21 of the UN Refugee Convention.

[16] Article 8(2) of the OAU, Convention Governing the Specific Aspects of Refugee Problems in Africa (OAU Convention), 10 September 1969, 1001 UNTS 45 https://bit.ly/3dCwX1P (accessed 9 December 2021).

[17] Section 1 of the Constitution of Malawi, 1994.

> In my view, side notes cannot be used as an aid to construction. They are mere catchwords and I have never heard of it being supposed in recent times that an amendment to alter a side note could be proposed in [either] House of Parliament [sic]. Side notes in the original Bill are inserted by the draftsman. During the passage of the Bill through its various stages, amendment to it or other reasons may make it desirable to alter a side note. In that event I have reason to believe that alteration is made by the appropriate officer of the House no doubt in consultation with the draftsman. So side notes cannot be said to be enacted in the same sense as the long title or any part of the body of the Act.[18]

Some jurisdictions provide for the position of marginal notes in statutes. For instance, in Canada, the Interpretation Act provides that

> Marginal notes and references to former enactments that appear after the end of a section or other division in an enactment form no part of the enactment, but are inserted for convenience of reference only.[19]

This position is informed by the fact that marginal notes are not specifically discussed in Parliament and are perhaps merely the practicalities of drafting and seeing legislation to its passage. Following this, the question that arises is whether the weight attached to the marginal note leads to the interpretation of a given provision. It is argued that the weight attached depends on the effect of the marginal note on the provision.[20] In the instant provision, the marginal notes in the Malawian Constitution point to the fact that marginal notes may be used to aid the interpretation of the Constitution, provided they touch on the content and context of the provision. On this basis, it is important to look at other provisions that deal with international law in the Constitution. For instance, the Constitution gives guidelines on the use of international law regarding its interpretation by courts of law. The relevant provision states that '[i]n interpreting the provisions of this Constitution a court of law shall – c. where applicable, have regard to current norms of public international law and comparable foreign case law'.[21]

[18] *Chandler v DPP* [1964] AC 763, at 789–790.

[19] Chapters 1–21, sec 14 of the Interpretation Act, 1985 (Canada).

[20] For more on the use of marginal notes, please see BH Simamba 'Should marginal notes be used in the interpretation of legislation?' (2005) 26 *Statute Law Review* 125.

[21] Sec 11(2) of the Constitution.

The abovementioned provision makes international law one of the guides to the interpretation of the Constitution. Another look at the marginal notes of the above-noted provision indicates that the international law referred to includes customary international law and international law. The use of international law in Malawi is also evident in the principles of national policy as contained in the Constitution that call for the use of international law in governance. The relevant section provides

> 13. Principles of national policy
>
> The State shall actively promote the welfare and development of the people of Malawi by progressively adopting and implementing policies and legislation aimed at achieving the following goals—
>
> ....
>
> k. To govern in accordance with the law of nations and the rule of law and actively support the further development thereof in regional and international affairs.[22]

The above provision is an indication that international law is very central to the governance structures and the promotion and protection of human rights provided in the Constitution. This is further accentuated by the requirement that the derogation from the rights provided for under the Malawian Constitution and international law is prohibited and only allowed in the following two instances:

> (4), ... during a state of emergency within the meaning of this section and to the extent that—
>
> a. such derogation is consistent with the obligations of Malawi under international law; and
>
> b. in the case of—
>
> i. war or threat of war, it is strictly required to prevent the lives of defensive combatants and civilians as well as legitimate military objectives from being placed in direct jeopardy; or
>
> ii. a widespread natural disaster, it is strictly required for the protection and relief of those people and facilities whether in or outside the disaster area.[23]

[22] Section 13(k) of the Constitution.

[23] Section 45(4)(a) & (b) of the Constitution.

Despite the above permitted derogation, it is imperative to reiterate the applicability of international law in Malawi. In this regard, the question is whether a provision to this effect is provided for in the *grundnorm*. Section 211 of the Constitution underscores this important role as far as it (international law), reinforces three critical aspects. The first critical aspect is the applicability of international agreements concluded after the commencement of the Constitution.[24] The second is the binding nature of international agreements concluded before the commencement of the Constitution[25]; the third critical aspect is the applicability of customary international law that is consistent with the Constitution and Acts of Parliament.[26] Accordingly, the preceding discussion indicates that international law in various covenants and conventions forms part of the laws of Malawi.[27] These international laws are critical to the discussion at hand as they have provisions that touch on socio-economic rights of refugees. The various instruments will be discussed later in this chapter.

The Constitution provides for equality and freedom from discrimination.[28] In this regard, the Constitution provides that any form of discrimination against persons is prohibited and that all persons are, under any law, guaranteed equal and effective protection against discrimination on the grounds of race, colour, sex, language, religion, nationality, ethnic or social origin, disability, property, birth or other status.[29] This is further amplified by the requirement that no restrictions or limitations may be placed on the exercise of any rights and freedoms in the Constitution, unless they are prescribed by law, which is reasonable, recognised by international human rights standards and necessary in an open and democratic society.[30] To give effect to the enjoyment of socio-economic rights, it is only prudent that the right to movement is guaranteed. However, while this is guaranteed under the Constitution and common law, there is a

[24] Section 211(1) of the Constitution.

[25] Section 211(2) of the Constitution.

[26] Section 211(3) of the Constitution.

[27] Some of the instruments ratified by Malawi include, the UN General Assembly, International Covenant on Civil and Political Rights, 16 December 1966, United Nations, Treaty Series, vol 999, p 171; UN General Assembly, International Covenant on Economic, Social and Cultural Rights, 16 December 1966, United Nations, Treaty Series, vol 993, p 3; The OAU Convention; and the UN General Assembly, Convention on the Rights of the Child, 20 November 1989, United Nations, Treaty Series, vol 1577, p 3.

[28] Sections 13, 20, 24 and 31 of the Constitution.

[29] Section 20(1) of the Constitution.

[30] Section 44(2) of the Constitution.

caveat to this position. The Refugee Act of Malawi provides that any person granted refugee status under this Act shall be subject to the laws of Malawi, jurisdiction of courts in Malawi and to all measures taken for the maintenance of public order.[31]

Consequently, it is interesting to establish how the courts have navigated this provision and reconciled it with the position in the Constitution.

3 The Legal Status of Socio-Economic Rights of Refugees in National Law

Malawi has ratified various international human rights instruments that are crucial to the enjoyment of human rights. These include: the UN Refugee Convention[32]; the International Covenant on Civil and Political Rights (ICCPR)[33]; the International Covenant on Economic, Social and Cultural Rights (ICESCR)[34]; the Convention on the Rights of the Child (CRC)[35]; the Convention on the Elimination of all Forms of Discrimination against Women (CEDAW)[36]; the OAU Convention on Specific Aspects of Refugees in Africa[37]; the African Charter on Human and Peoples' Rights (Banjul Charter)[38]; and the African Charter on the Rights and Welfare of the Child.[39] As indicated earlier, international law is applicable in Malawi as a source of law and as an interpretation tool for national legislation.[40] The Constitution of the Republic of Malawi provides for the enjoyment of socio-economic rights. This is evident in section 30 which states that

[31] Section 9 of the Refugee Act, 1989.

[32] N 11.

[33] N 27.

[34] N 27.

[35] N 27.

[36] UN General Assembly, Convention on the Elimination of All Forms of Discrimination Against Women, 18 December 1979, United Nations, Treaty Series, vol 1249, p 13.

[37] N 16.

[38] OAU, African Charter on Human and Peoples' Rights (Banjul Charter), 27 June 1981, CAB/LEG/67/3 rev. 5, 21 ILM 58 (1982).

[39] OAU, African Charter on the Rights and Welfare of the Child, 11 July 1990, CAB/LEG/24.9/49 (1990).

[40] LD Mvula 'Refugee status determination and rights in Malawi' A paper presented at the Refugee Studies Centre Workshop Discussion on RSD and Rights in Southern and East Africa (2010) https://www.rsc.ox.ac.uk/files/files-1/dp-rsd-malawi-2010.pdf (accessed 23 May 2022).

> [a]ll persons and peoples have a right to development and therefore to the enjoyment of economic, social, cultural and political development and women, children and the disabled in particular shall be given special consideration in the application of this right.[41]

Furthermore the section provides that

> [t]he state shall take all necessary measures for the realisation of the right to development. Such measures shall include, amongst other things, equality of opportunity for all in their access to basic resources, education, health services, food, shelter, employment and infrastructure.[42]

In addition, the Constitution provides that '[t]he state has a responsibility to respect the right to development and to justify its policies in accordance with this responsibility'.[43] According to the Constitution, the Malawian government is obligated to respect socio-economic rights guaranteed in the Bill of Rights. Despite the inadequacy of this protection, there are specific sections of the Constitution which are informative in this regard. According to section 15(1), the government has a duty to 'respect' and 'uphold' all rights in the Bill of Rights. Furthermore, where a court finds that constitutional rights or freedoms have been unlawfully denied or violated, it is empowered to make any orders that are necessary and appropriate to secure the enjoyment of the impugned constitutional rights.[44] Scholars opined that the Constitution provides an avenue for protecting various socio-economic rights even if they are not expressly recognised in the Malawian Constitution.[45] As has been shown above, the limited recognition of all the socio-economic rights (that would inevitably and positively affect the refugees' enjoyment of various rights) is remedied by the Directive Principles of National Policy in section 13 of the Constitution.[46] These Principles place a mandate on the state to actively promote the welfare and development of the people of Malawi by progressively adopting

[41] Section 30(1) of the Constitution.

[42] Section 30(2) of the Constitution.

[43] Section 30(4) of the Constitution.

[44] Section 46(3) of the Constitution.

[45] DM Chirwa 'A full loaf is better than half: The constitutional protection of economic, social and cultural rights in Malawi' (2005) 49 *Journal of African Law* 224.

[46] Section 13 of the Constitution. S Gloppen & FE Kanyongolo 'Courts and the poor in Malawi: Economic marginalisation, vulnerability, and the law' (2007) 5 *International journal of Constitutional Law* 258.

and implementing policies and legislation that provide for gender equality, the enjoyment of the right to education and health.[47]

Malawi has specific legislation to deal with refugees. The Refugee Act of 1989 provides for the control and administration of refugees.[48] It incorporates the two definitions of a refugee as per the UN Refugee Convention and the OAU Convention.[49] This shows a wider complementary role of both conventions. However, due to the reservations that Malawi placed on the UN Refugee Convention, it has greatly affected the application of all the provisions of the Refugee Act.[50] It is also argued that the government's stance is based on the need to ameliorate the pressure of the rights and freedom of refugees and asylum seekers.[51] The Refugee Act places an obligation on a refugee to subject him or herself to laws/measures regarding the maintenance of public order.[52] While this provision is not problematic per se, it creates an unnecessary burden on the refugee (in civil cases) to prove certain facts that pertain to steps taken to maintain public order. The danger with this approach is the possibility of extending this obligation so that a refugee is required to prove his innocence instead of the state proving his guilt. From a procedural perspective, the Refugee Act prohibits the refoulement of refugees.[53] Similarly, the Act also allows refugees and asylum seekers to enter the country and present themselves before a competent officer within 24 hours of their entry or within such longer period as the competent officer may consider acceptable in the circumstances.

4 Progressive Realisation of Socio-Economic Rights and Challenges Regarding Refugees

'Progressive realisation', a concept with its basis in international human rights instruments, informs the state's obligation to respect, protect and fulfil the realisation of human rights. As noted in the foregoing section, Malawi has ratified various international human rights instruments that are crucial to the enjoyment of human rights. It is required that Malawi

[47] Section 13(c) & (f) of the Constitution.
[48] Long title to the Refugee Act 1989 of Malawi.
[49] Section 2 of the Refugee Act.
[50] Mvula (n 40).
[51] As above.
[52] Section 9 of the Refugee Act.
[53] As above.

strives to realise the 'fulfilment and improvement in the enjoyment of socio-economic rights to the maximum extent possible, even in the face of resource constraints'.[54] The Committee on Economic, Social and Cultural Rights (CESCR) recommends that a state uses 'all appropriate means, including particularly the adoption of legislative measures' to realise the enjoyment of socio-economic rights in its territory.[55]

From a normative perspective, various indicators that point to the enablement of progressive realisation are evident in several provisions. First, the constitutional recognition of the responsibility of the state to use the necessary measures to realise many socio-economic rights such as education, health services, food, shelter, employment and infrastructure, is important.[56] Secondly, the acknowledgement of the responsibility to use the constitutional recognition of the right to development and to ensure it informs adequate national policies, shows that the enjoyment of socio-economic rights is a condition precedent to the policies that Malawi adopts.[57] In addition, despite the existence of specific legislation to deal with refugees, existing reservations by the state to the UN Refugee Convention affect the progressive realisation of the socio-economic rights of refugees.[58] Further, the government's restriction of the rights and freedoms of the citizens stifles the erstwhile progressive realisation of socio-economic rights of refugees in Malawi.

As previously mentioned, scholars have alluded to the fact that the Constitution provides an avenue for protecting various socio-economic rights even if they are not expressly recognised in the Malawian Constitution.[59] As has been shown above, the limited recognition of all the socio-economic rights (that would inevitably and positively affect the refugees' enjoyment of various rights) is remedied by the Directive

[54] Chenwi, L. (2013). Unpacking "progressive realisation", its relation to resources, minimum core and reasonableness, and some methodological considerations for assessing compliance. De Jure, 46(3), 742–769, 743. See also Fukuda-Parr, Lawson-Remer & Randolph "Measuring the Progressive Realization of Human Rights Obligations: An Index of Economic and Social Rights Fulfilment" (2008) Department of Economics Working Paper Series 22 (University of Connecticut) 7.

[55] UN Committee on Economic, Social and Cultural Rights (CESCR), General Comment 3: The Nature of States Parties' Obligations, 14 December 1990, UN Doc E/1991/23 (1990), para 3.

[56] Section 30(2) of the Constitution.

[57] Section 30(4) of the Constitution. See also secs 15(1) and 46(3) of the Constitution.

[58] See foregoing section on the status of socio-economic rights (SERs) in Malawi.

[59] Chirwa (n 45) 224.

Principles of National Policy in section 13 of the Constitution.[60] To reiterate, they place a mandate on the state to actively promote the welfare and development of the people of Malawi by progressively adopting and implementing policies and legislation that provide for gender equality, the enjoyment of the right to education and health.[61]

Chirwa points out that the rights which are not adequately protected include the right to the highest attainable standard of health, the right to water, the right to education, the right to food, the right to social security and the right to housing.[62] He argues that Malawi is not alone in treating these rights in this manner. There are other states that afford the same (or worse) treatment to these rights and this is evidenced in a number of constitutions of African countries. Some give limited protection to these rights in constitutional directives and/or principles of state policy rather than in the Bill of Rights.[63] The author affirms that the adequacy of the Constitution to protect socio-economic rights depends on laws, policies and their implementation by the government.[64]

Maluwa contends that Malawi moved at a snail's pace in formulating a well-defined refugee policy following its independence, largely because of the opportunistic ambivalence of Malawi's regional politics. One may argue that considering political developments such as the amendment to the Constitution and the growing refugee population in the country, Malawi finally adopted the Refugee Act.[65] The challenge of how to deal with a mass influx of refugees within the meaning of the Refugee Convention, however, still remains.[66] There is some degree of consistency

[60] See (n 46) above.

[61] Section 13(c) & (f) of the Constitution.

[62] Chirwa (n 45).

[63] Chirwa (n 45) 24.

[64] This is against the backdrop that the inadequacy of the protection of socio-economic rights was amplified before the adoption of the 1994 Constitution. See GS Pindano 'Justiciability of socio-economic rights under the Constitution of Malawi: Unbundling the right to development' (2020) 7 *Journal of Law, Society and Development* 1.

[65] T Maluwa 'The domestic implementation of international refugee law: Brief note on Malawi's Refugee Act of 1989' (1991) 3 *International Journal of Refugee Law* 503.

[66] For instance, if one considers the principle of non-refoulement, the use of mass or group determination of refugee status can and should be made. Section 7(3) of the Refugee Act of Malawi specifically provides for this procedure, where the Minister 'may, by notice published in the Gazette, direct that, with respect to any group of foreign nationals specified in the notice, seeking refugee status in Malawi, the Committee shall apply such group determination procedures as may be prescribed. The challenge is in the willingness by the Minister to exercise the discretion to direct the grant of refugee status'.

in the law that ensures that both legal and illegal immigrants may stay in Malawi pending the determination of their refugee status. An application of section 10(4) of the Refugee Convention shows that persons who enter Malawi illegally for the purpose of seeking asylum are protected against expulsion or refoulement, provided they report to a competent officer within 24 hours of such entry or subject to acceptable circumstances.[67]

Malawi's reservation that denies refugees the right to work and at a bare minimum fend for their families, does not only have ripple effect in the denial of socio-economic rights, but also on the right to life, and dignity of an individual as provided for in Malawi's Constitution.[68] It is reported that this restriction on the refugee's right to work stifles emerging refugee enterprises.[69] For instance, the restriction on the sale of food or other aid to meet the needs or to raise capital for other activities, limits the economic abilities of refugees in the host communities. This creates an unfortunate opportunity by the locals to exploit refugees, which may inhibit the enjoyment of their socio-economic rights.

Malawi instituted a lockdown to reduce the spread of the pandemic on 20 March 2020 following the confirmation of the first confirmed coronavirus case on 2 April 2020.[70] The rights that were most affected included education, health and work.[71] The schools were closed to mitigate the spread of the pandemic. Online education for learners was available for all the learners especially those in rural areas.[72]

[67] The yardstick for measuring the status of protection is the extent to which such persons are not denied socio-economic services due to their status as refugees.

[68] KK Wilson 'Enhancing refugees' own food acquisition strategies' (1992) 5 *Journal of Refugee Studies* 226.

[69] KB Wilson, DR Cammack & F Shumba 'Mozambicans in Malawi: A Study of aid, livelihood and development' Refugee Studies Programme, Oxford and World Food Programme, Rome (1989).

[70] GW Mzumara et al. 'The health policy response to COVID-19 in Malawi' (2021) 6 *BMJ Global Health* e006035.

[71] Mzumara et al. (n 70) 1.

[72] The UNHCR attempted to find solutions through the development of education low-tech solutions like the distribution of solar radios in Malawi for children and youth who do not have access to internet. OCHA's Inter-Agency Standing Committee partners developed low-tech solutions such as the distribution of solar radios in Malawi, Mali and Malaysia and no-tech solutions such as home learning kits in South Sudan and Uganda for children and youth who do not have access to internet. See Save the Children et al. 'Roundtable on Refugee Education: Meeting our Promises on Refugee Education during COVID-19 – Outcome Paper) 7 https://resource-centre-uploads.s3.amazonaws.com/uploads/refugee_education_roundtable_discussion_outcomes_paper.pdf (accessed 1 June 2022).

Access to healthcare was also affected as the government re-aligned its priorities to cater for the treatment of Covid-19 patients and subsequent vaccinations.[73] It is reported that the right to work was greatly affected. Refugees who relied on humanitarian organisations for the provision of food, could only be fed when such organisations were allowed access to Dzaleka camp.[74]

There are some discernible lessons which may be taken from Malawi's approach to the pandemic. First, it used a multi-sectoral approach to address health and socio-economic aspects of the Covid-19 pandemic. This process successfully increased the Covid-19 testing capacity but did not equally benefit all persons in Malawi. Refugees in particular were deprived of benefitting equally.[75] Secondly, the consequences of the response policies led to the use of online learning—a situation that disadvantaged the vulnerable communities like refugees.[76] Thirdly, there was a glaring gap in the provision of health services as Malawi's public health system did not have adequate frameworks to support the citizens and refugees in terms of surveillance, infrastructure and health information systems.[77] Consequently, the pandemic exacerbated the various challenges that Malawi faced concerning socio-economic rights.

A look at the courts' approach follows.

5 Courts' Approach to the Enjoyment of Socio-Economic Rights by Refugees

From the outset, it must be noted that access to reported cases on the issue at hand is limited as it may not be widely publicised. Four cases were available from an online source[78] and a quick overview of the cases

[73] Mzumara et al. (n 70) 1.

[74] J Barchfield 'Pandemic deepens hunger for displaced people the world over' *UNHCR* 21 March 2021 https://www.unhcr.org/news/stories/2021/3/6062fe334/pandemic-deepens-hunger-displaced-people-world.html (accessed 27 June 2022).

[75] Mzumara et al. (n 70) 1.

[76] As above.

[77] As above.

[78] MalawiLii (2022) Search results https://malawilii.org/search?search_api_fulltext=refugee&op=Submit&f%5B0%5D=content_type%3Ajudgment (accessed 1 February 2022).

indicated that all four decisions were from the High Courts of the Republic.[79] However, two of the decisions neither referred to any contextual issues concerning refugees nor issues of socio-economic rights and were therefore excluded.[80] Consequently, the other two cases—*Ex parte Nsabimana* (2006)[81] and *Jones v Refugee Committee* (2005), form the focus of this section of the chapter as discussed below.[82] These two cases were applications and not fully fledged suits. This means that some intricate engagements of the facts and law might not be addressed aptly to highlight the issues at hand.

5.1 Ex parte Nsabimana *(2006)*

In *Ex parte Nsabimana*, the respondent state (The government of Malawi) issued an order on 6 February 2006 that all refugees and asylum seekers residing outside Dzaleka and Luwani camps (as their designated camps), should return to these camps. The Court reproduced the respondent's directive which stated

> **NOTICE TO ALL ASYLUM SEEKERS AND REFUGEES**
> All asylum seekers and refugees residing outside Dzaleka and Luwani refugees camps are being ordered to return to camp, in Dowa and Neno districts respectively, the designated places of residence for all asylum seekers and refugees. The government of Malawi has, however, observed that some asylum seekers and refugees have settled elsewhere without any authorization. All asylum seekers and refugees are therefore, ordered to return to camp by 28th February, 2006. Those that were issued with identity cards must go to Dzaleka camp and those that were not issued with the same must go to Luwani camp. Signed

[79] The decisions include: *State v The President of Malawi & Ors. ex parte Mponda, Soko & Ors* (Judicial Review 13 of 2020) [2020] MWHC 6 (7 April 2020); *State (oao Lin Xiaoxiao & Ors) v The Director General – Immigration and Citizenship Services* (Judicial Review 19 of 2020) [2020] MWHC 5 (3 April 2020); *Ex Parte Nsabimana & Ors.; S v the Department of Poverty and Disaster Management Affairs & Anor.* (19 of 2006) [2008] MWHC 79 (16 April 2008); and *In the matter of Section 10(5) of the Refugees Act (Cap 11.04) of the Laws of Malawi; Jones & Ors. v Refugee Committee* (Misc Civil Cause 313 of 2005) [2005] MWHC 24 (28 December 2005).

[80] These are: *State v The President of Malawi* (n 79); *State v The Director General – Immigration and Citizenship Services* (n 79).

[81] N 79.

[82] N 79.

Dr. M.D NOWA PHIRI.
COMMISSIONER FOR REFUGEES IN MALAWI.[83]

The applicants requested the Court to review the decision of the respondent.[84] The applicants averred that the decision by the executive was unlawful and unconstitutional, and sought that the order be quashed.

The applicant, Frodovard Nsabimana, claimed that he was granted authority and issued an identity card by an office of the respondent to reside in urban areas. He added that he was aware of refugees residing outside the camps in Malawi for up to ten years, and as such, the applicant stated that the requirement that the respondent afforded 22 days for the refugees to return to the designated camp, was insufficient as he had both property and children who were at school.[85] The government argued that the permission to reside outside of the refugee camp had been granted on medical, educational and other related grounds.[86] The challenge that the Court faced was while the facts related to the need for a review of the decision, the judicial review proceedings hinged on the decision-making process rather than on an examination of the merits or demerits of the case.[87] As a result, the Court considered whether or not the applicant(s) had an opportunity to be heard or were fairly treated considering the circumstances as a whole. Various issues were raised in the application, including whether the applicant had a sufficient interest in the matter and whether the applicant had a permit authorising him to reside outside the camp. Other issues were whether the order was discriminatory and in breach of sections 20(1) and 44(2) of the Constitution, and whether the order violated article 26 of the Refugee Convention to which Malawi is a signatory.

A further issue raised in the application concerned the possession of a permit that authorised the applicant to reside outside the camp. It is interesting that the state had different narratives concerning the position of a permit. While one position was that a permit was granted to enable the applicant to stay outside the camp, another indicates that one of the stakeholders, the World Food Programme (WFP), required the applicant to

[83] *Ex Parte Nsabimana*, 2.

[84] As above.

[85] As above.

[86] As above.

[87] The Court alluded to the fact that it looked at whether the rules of natural justice on fairness were observed as stated in *Chief Constable of North Wales Police* vs *Evans* (1982) 3 ALL ER 141.

have a permit, so as to avoid giving him food rations. The permit (or ID, according to the government) is issued by the Government of Malawi to refugees under the Refugee Convention and the 1998 Malawi Refugee Act to facilitate all administrative formalities regarding their protection. This led to different interpretations of the ownership of the permit. While it was understood that the permit gave the applicant the authority to reside outside the camps and fend for himself on the one hand, it was also considered a simple document for administrative purposes on the other.

The Court looked at the format of the permit granted by the respondent to the applicant which stated

> Accordingly, you are authorized to reside away from Dzaleka Refugee Camp on the following terms: Acquisition of Temporary Employment Permit: Your employer UN (International Criminal Tribunal for Rwanda) to apply on your behalf to the Immigration Department for the Permit within three months. New Location Area 49 Township, Lilongwe city. Duration: From 24th February, 2006 to 22nd February, 2007. Grounds for Relocation Employment with Arusha Tribunal as Defence Team Investigator required to operate from urban setting. This permit is subject to replacement and renewal at the end of the duration of its validity.
>
> Yours faithfully
>
> Signed....

Furthermore, the specific purposes for the grant of the permit to the applicant was to reside outside the camp, to be able to work in Area 49 in Lilongwe. While the applicant applied for the permit, there was no evidence to show that such permission was eventually granted to reside outside the camp. The Court found that being a holder of a permit was not an indication of permission to reside outside the camp, unless he applied and obtained an employment permit.

It is argued in the context of this chapter, that this process presents various impediments to the enjoyment of socio-economic rights by refugees especially in instances where various administrative delays affect the final enjoyment of the rights of a refugee. This may be contrasted with the position in South Africa, where upon receipt of an application of recognition of refugee status, the applicant is granted a permit that allows him or her to study and work.[88] This is further cemented by the fact that refugees are integrated into the South African community.[89]

Another critical issue worth mentioning was the Court's perspective on the constitutionality of the order. The Court considered the existence of possible discriminatory practices against refugees due to their status. This occurred as a result of the contention that the order was discriminatory and in breach of sections 20(1) and 44(2) of the Constitution. The Court, in considering the issue, stated that it was the duty of an individual refugee/asylum seeker to prove by means of documentation the existence of a permit. Subsequently, it found that the order was not discriminatory or a hindrance to the right to movement or its limitations thereof. While this position is appreciated, the effect of this finding on socio-economic rights was not envisaged by the Court. The limitation on movement affected the right to education and health among other rights. The Court interestingly stated

> [T]he Government of the Republic of Malawi reserves its right to designate the place or places of residence of the refugees and to restrict their movements whenever consideration of national security or public order so require.[90]

The application of the principle of non-discrimination to the enjoyment of all right is important to uphold the rights of refugees in Malawi. This principle is also essential to the state's obligation to progressively realise socio-economic rights. Hence the Court should have given greater consideration to the immediate impact that its decision regarding the purpose and existence of refugees' permits would have on the realisation of other rights of refugees.[91]

The Constitution's recognition of the application of international law in Malawi did not enjoy prominence in deciding upon the plight of refugees who had to go back to Dzaleka Camp. It is contended that although the Court had to make a ruling on the facts, it should have engaged more

[88] These are some of the notable features that the South African regime accords to refugees and asylum seekers, such as the right to education and work. C Kavuro 'Housing and integrating refugees: South African exclusionary approach' (2019) 40 *Orbiter* 75.

[89] South Africa's Refugee Act 130 of 1998.

[90] *Ex Parte Nsabimana*, 2.

[91] As above.

with the international law principles applicable to Malawi.[92] The consideration of international law principles calls for the application of international refugee law.[93] International refugee law, for instance, may be applied through the use of both constitutional and statutory law, policy documents and principles of national policy.[94]

Furthermore, as mentioned earlier, it would have been useful to evaluate the effect of the Court's decision on the enjoyment of socio-economic rights of refugees. It is argued that the implementation of this decision places refugees who were able to enhance their enjoyment of socio-economic rights in a predicament.[95] They would be forced to be refouled to other frontiers where they may face persecution due to this decision.

In addition, the Court should have at least considered the minimum core obligation as a guiding factor in the enjoyment of socio-economic rights.[96] The Court ought to have reiterated the duty on the state to take all steps to ensure the enjoyment of all rights by refugees.

5.2 **Jones v Refugee Committee** *(2005)*

In *Jones v Refugee Committee*, the plaintiffs sought judicial review of the Refugee Committee's revocation of their refugee status and order of deportation.[97] It should be noted that the implementation of the decision would affect the enjoyment of socio-economic rights by refugees as per the Court's findings that are highlighted hereafter.[98] The Court hinted that the defendant ought to have referred to guidance from international law such as the Refugee Convention and its 1967 Protocol.[99] At the core of its discussion, the Court referred to the principle of non-refoulment, a position that was not considered in *Ex parte Nsabimana*. The Court stated that

[92] Section 11(2) of the Constitution.

[93] *Ex Parte Nsabimana*, 2.

[94] Section 13(k) of the Constitution.

[95] Consequently, the better quality socio-economic services that are outside Dzaleka camp are out of reach.

[96] *Ex Parte Nsabimana & Ors*, generally.

[97] *Jones v Refugee Committee.*

[98] *Jones v Refugee Committee.*

[99] UN Refugee Convention.

> Article 32 of the Convention, 1951 ... states that the contracting States shall not expel a refugee lawfully in their territory save on ground of national security or public order.[100]

The Court found that because the plaintiffs posed a significant threat to national security and public order in Malawi due to their unregulated movements,[101] they were properly stripped of their refugee status and repatriated to Mozambique. Unlike the position in *Ex parte Nsabimana*, the Court in *Jones* made an informed decision that engaged various principles of international law such as non-refoulement. It is thus argued that, although the decision to repatriate the refugees was upheld, this was an informed decision that drew from both national and international jurisprudence.[102]

This decision, was a departure from the approach in *Ex parte Nsabimana* as it recognised the place of international refugee law principles in deciding cases affecting refugees' rights. The Court engaged applicable international law principles in Malawi.[103] It also engaged with the principle of non-refoulement but balanced it in the context of national security.[104] Without delving into the merits or demerits of the case, the fact that this was a more nuanced decision is worth noting. Just like in *Ex parte Nsabimana*, however, the Court did not engage the use of the minimum core obligation as a guiding factor in the enjoyment of socio-economic rights.[105]

5.3 Way Forward

The government's position on refugees and asylum seekers is characterised by minimal engagement with the issue of the protection of refugee rights excluding socio-economic rights,[106] promoting national security and the use of the encampment policy.[107] This position has been reiterated by the

100 *Jones v Refugee Committee.*

101 As above.

102 A close application of the socio-economic rights of refugees in international and regional law would have led to a different outcome.

103 Section 11(2) of the Constitution.

104 As above.

105 *Ex parte Nsabimana*, 10.

106 Chirwa (n 45) 224.

107 Section 11(2) of the Constitution.

court decisions above. Since there are very few readily accessible court decisions available on the issue at hand, it is possible that there may be unreported cases in which the courts have engaged with the issues raised in this chapter, but that are inaccessible. Considering this limitation, this analysis raises academic debate and highlights the need for further research on these issues. In the interim, the Courts have upheld the government's approach to the balancing of civil and political rights (other than the socio-economic rights) at the expense of matters of national security and the encampment policies. It may be argued that the existence of a derogation clause in the Constitution offers the government an opportunity to deviate from its obligations under the Refugee Convention.

Consequently, an enunciation of such matters is required, which calls for a deliberate effort that places refugees at the centre of any interventions developed. This would require the posing of the 'Malawian refugee question' in addition to the general 'refugee question'.[108] This entails the use of a human rights approach that deals with the enjoyment of socio-economic rights by refugees as the central aspect of every initiative that emphasises the enjoyment of the rights of refugees.[109]

6 Conclusion

Malawi provides for the application of international law under its Constitution using both express and implied provisions as seen. This is affirmed by its ratification of various international instruments, and national legislation on the protection of refugees. With regard to socio-economic rights, Malawi is a signatory to instructional instruments such as the ICESCR, that calls on the state to take on various measures in the realm of legislative, administrative, financial, educational and social engagements to realise the enjoyment of socio-economic rights.[110] Further, various international and regional instruments, place a duty on the state to engage the normative guidance these instruments, such as the progressive and immediate realisation of socio-economic rights of refugees. These legal principles are echoed by various sections of the Constitution, as discussed above.

[108] See E Durojaye & O Oluduro 'The African Commission on Human and People's Rights and the woman question' (2016) 24 *Feminist Legal Studies* 315.

[109] Durojaye & Oluduro (n 108) 315.

[110] Paras 5 and 7 of CESCR General Comment 3.

It has also been noted that the courts have to a great extent upheld the position of the government in the use of the encampment policy, which emphasises the promotion and protection of civil and political rights rather than socio-economic rights. In turn, these decisions have greatly affected the enjoyment of socio-economic rights of refugees in Malawi. As a consequence, it is argued that there has been a minimal use of international principles in the decisions affecting the enjoyment of socio-economic rights of refugees generally. Therefore, it is proposed that a deliberate effort be made which adopts a human rights-based approach, to ensure that the 'Malawian refugee' and his or her corresponding rights are at the centre of any interventions.

Bibliography

Journal Articles

Chirwa, DM 'A full loaf is better than half: The constitutional protection of economic, social and cultural rights in Malawi' (2005) 49 *Journal of African Law* 224

Chenwi, L 'Unpacking "progressive realisation", its relation to resources, minimum core and reasonableness, and some methodological considerations for assessing compliance' (2013) 46(3) *De Jure*,742.

Durojaye, E & Oluduro, O 'The African Commission on Human and People's Rights and the woman question' (2016) 24 *Feminist Legal Studies* 315

Fukuda-Parr, Lawson-Remer & Randolph "Measuring the Progressive Realization of Human Rights Obligations: An Index of Economic and Social Rights Fulfilment" (2008) Department of Economics Working Paper Series 22 (University of Connecticut) 7.

Gloppen, S & Kanyongolo, FE 'Courts and the poor in Malawi: Economic marginalisation, vulnerability, and the law' (2007) 5 *International Journal of Constitutional Law* 258

Kavuro, C 'Housing and integrating refugees: South African exclusionary approach' (2019) 40 *Orbiter* 75

Liebenberg, S & Goldblatt, B 'The interrelationship between equality and socio-economic rights under South Africa's transformative Constitution' (2007) 23 *South African Journal on Human Rights* 335

Maluwa, T 'The domestic implementation of international refugee law: Brief note on Malawi's Refugee Act of 1989' (1991) 3 *International Journal of Refugee Law* 503

Mzumara, GW; Chawani, M; Sakala, M; Mwandira, L; Phiri, E; Milanzi, E & Tam, PYI 'The health policy response to COVID-19 in Malawi' (2021) 6 *BMJ Global Health* e006035

Pieterse, M 'Resuscitating socio-economic rights: Constitutional entitlements to healthcare services' (2006) 22 *South African Journal on Human Rights* 473

Pindano, GS 'Justiciability of socio-economic rights under the Constitution of Malawi: Unbundling the right to development' (2020) 7 *Journal of Law, Society and Development* 1

Simamba, BH 'Should marginal notes be used in the interpretation of legislation?' (2005) 26 *Statute Law Review* 125

Wilson, KK 'Enhancing refugees' own food acquisition strategies' (1992) 5 *Journal of Refugee Studies* 226

Wilson, KB; Cammack, DR & Shumba, F 'Mozambicans in Malawi: A Study of aid, livelihood and development' Refugee Studies Programme, Oxford and World Food Programme, Rome (1989) **This should be cited as Report (Kindly add a section for Report)**

Case Law

Chandler v DPP [1964] AC 763.

Chief Constable of North Wales Police vs Evans (1982) 3 ALL ER 141

Ex Parte Nsabimana; S v the Department of Poverty and Disaster Management Affairs (19 of 2006) [2008] MWHC 79 (16 April 2008)

In the matter of Section 10(5) of the Refugees Act (Cap 11.04) of the Laws of Malawi; Jones v Refugee Committee (Misc Civil Cause 313 of 2005) [2005] MWHC 24 (28 December 2005)

Mazibuko v City of Johannesburg 2010 (4) SA 1 (CC)

State v The Director General - Immigration and Citizenship Services (Judicial Review 19 of 2020) [2020] MWHC 5 (3 April 2020)

State v The President of Malawi. Ex parte Mponda, Soko (Judicial Review 13 of 2020) [2020] MWHC 6 (7 April 2020)

Legislation

Constitution of the Republic of Malawi 1994 with Amendments through 2017

Interpretation Act, 1985 (Canada)

Refugee Act 130 of 1998 (South Africa)

Refugee Act, 1989 (Malawi)

AU Documents

OAU, African Charter on Human and Peoples' Rights (Banjul Charter), 27 June 1981, CAB/LEG/67/3 rev. 5, 21 ILM 58 (1982)

OAU, African Charter on the Rights and Welfare of the Child, 11 July 1990, CAB/LEG/24.9/49 (1990)

OAU, Convention Governing the Specific Aspects of Refugee Problems in Africa (OAU Convention), 10 September 1969, 1001 UNTS 45

UN Documents

UN Committee on Economic, Social and Cultural Rights (CESCR), General Comment 3: The Nature of States Parties' Obligations (Art 2, Para 1, of the Covenant), 14 December 1990, UN Doc E/1991/23 (1990)

UN General Assembly, Convention on the Elimination of All Forms of Discrimination Against Women, 18 December 1979, United Nations, Treaty Series, vol 1249, p 13

UN General Assembly, Convention on the Rights of the Child, 20 November 1989, United Nations, Treaty Series, vol 1577, p 3

UN General Assembly, Convention Relating to the Status of Refugees, 28 July 1951, United Nations, Treaty Series, vol 189, p 137

UN General Assembly, International Covenant on Civil and Political Rights, 16 December 1966, United Nations, Treaty Series, vol 999, p 171

UN General Assembly, International Covenant on Economic, Social and Cultural Rights, 16 December 1966, United Nations, Treaty Series, vol 993, p 3

Internet Sources

Barchfield, J 'Pandemic deepens hunger for displaced people the world over' UNHCR 21 March 2021 https://www.unhcr.org/news/stories/2021/3/6062fe334/pandemic-deepens-hunger-displaced-people-world.html (accessed 27 June 2022)

Kunchezera, B (2021) 'Return to the refugee camp: Malawi orders thousands back to "congested" Dzaleka' *The Guardian* 25 November 2021 https://bit.ly/3pYSYOf (accessed 9 December 2021)

MalawiLii (2022) Search results https://malawilii.org/search?search_api_fulltext=refugee&op=Submit&f%5B0%5D=content_type%3Ajudgment (accessed 9 December 2021)

Masina, L 'Malawi orders all refugees back into camp within 14 days' *VOA News* 17 April 2021 https://bit.ly/3oBGpIW (accessed 9 December 2021)

Mvula, LD (2010) 'Refugee status determination and rights in Malawi' A paper presented at the Refugee Studies Centre Workshop Discussion on RSD and Rights in Southern and East Africa (2010) https://www.rsc.ox.ac.uk/files/files-1/dp-rsd-malawi-2010.pdf (accessed 23 May 2022)

Reliefweb 'Malawi: UNHCR Fact Sheet, August 2021' (2021) https://bit.ly/3dwdPCF (accessed 9 December 2021)

Save the Children et al. 'Roundtable on Refugee Education: Meeting our Promises on Refugee Education during COVID-19–Outcome Paper' 7 https://resource-centre-uploads.s3.amazonaws.com/uploads/refugee_education_roundtable_discussion_outcomes_paper.pdf (accessed 1 June 2022)

UN Refugee Agency 'States parties, including reservations and declarations, to the 1951 Refugee Convention' https://www.unhcr.org/5d9ed32b4, (accessed 31 May 2022)

CHAPTER 15

Realising the Socio-Economic Rights of Refugees and Asylum Seekers in Africa: The Nigerian Situation

Olubayo Oluduro and St. Emmanuel Ayooluwa

1 Introduction

Since time immemorial, violations of the integrity of the person, communal violence, ethno-religious crises, political persecution and various abuses of human rights have forced people to flee their country. Likewise, revolutionary technological developments in transportation and communications have led to the mass movement of people, goods and information across frontiers throughout the twentieth century, but not all human

O. Oluduro (✉) • St. E. Ayooluwa
Faculty of Law, Adekunle Ajasin University,
Akungba-Akoko, Ondo State, Nigeria
e-mail: olubayo.oluduro@aaua.edu.ng; simon.stemmanuel@aaua.edu.ng

E. Durojaye et al. (eds.), *Realising Socio-Economic Rights of Refugees and Asylum Seekers in Africa*, Politics of Citizenship and Migration, https://doi.org/10.1007/978-3-031-16548-1_15

movements of the century have been voluntary.[1] Contemporary technology has also led to the development of weapons of mass destruction, which caused violence to become the greatest factor to instigate involuntary departures and exoduses of people from their countries of origin.[2] In modern times, some African countries either produce or host refugees and asylum seekers. This is premised on the fact that the continent is inundated with natural disasters, civil wars, ethno-religious crises, communal clashes and colossal abuses of human rights. Since attaining independence from Great Britain on 1 October 1960, Nigeria has witnessed arrivals of refugees from neighbouring African countries, such as Chad, Liberia and Sierra Leone.[3]

The protracted Boko Haram insurgency in Northeast Nigeria has caused a great humanitarian catastrophe in the Lake Chad basin region. The insurgency has been the major cause of displacement and refugee crises in the countries within the region. In January 2021, there were 2,922,133 internally displaced persons (IDPs) due to the sectarian insurgency in Nigeria, Niger, Cameroon and Chad.[4] In addition, there are 304,966 Nigerian refugees in Niger, Cameroon and Chad.[5] However, given the scope of this chapter, the focus will be on refugees and asylum seekers in Nigeria and the realisation of some of their pertinent socio-economic rights regarding their survival. This is premised on the fact that persons displaced whether by violence or natural causes become refugees once they cross an international border into another country to seek refuge.[6]

The Nigerian refugee and asylum situation is characterised by Cameroonian refugees and asylum seekers, who fled their country as a result of deadly conflict between Cameroonian security forces and

[1] Office of the High Commissioner for Human Rights (OCHR) 'Fact Sheet 20: Human rights and refugees' 2 https://www.ohchr.org/Documents/Publications/FactSheet20en.pdf (accessed 22 February 2021).

[2] OCHR (n 1) 2.

[3] RC Chhangani & PK Chhangani 'Refugee definition and the law in Nigeria' (2011) 53 *Journal of the Indian Law Institute* 34.

[4] United Nations High Commissioner for Refugees (UNHCR) 'Operational Portal Regional Response – Nigeria situation' https://data2.unhcr.org/en/situations/nigeriasituation (accessed 22 February 2021). The country breakdown of this figure is as follows: Nigeria: 2,144,135; Chad: 336,124; Cameroon: 321,886; and Niger: 119,988.

[5] UNHCR (n 4). The country breakdown of this figure is as follows: Niger: 171,013; Cameroon: 117,826; and Chad: 16,127.

[6] UNHCR 'What is a refugee?' https://www.unhcr.org/what-is-a-refugee.html (accessed 22 February 2021).

separatist fighters seeking independence for the mainly English-speaking Southwest and Northwest regions,[7] under the name Ambazonia Republic.[8] The crisis was elicited by protests and strikes by teachers and lawyers in 2016 over the increasing influence of French on their education and legal systems.[9] According to Ajakaye, English-speakers complain they are being marginalised and excluded from top civil service jobs, forced to use French in public institutions and schools, and to use the French-Cameroon legal system in courts.[10]

The Internal Displacement Monitoring Centre (IDMC), a Norwegian Refugee Council outfit, based in Geneva, reported in its 2020 Global Report on Internal Displacement (GRID), that the deteriorating security situation in Anglophone Cameroon, increased in the Northwest and Southwest regions, and also spilled over into West and Littoral regions in 2019.[11] Cameroonian asylum seekers began fleeing the violence and entered Nigeria since 1 October 2017.[12] A female Cameroonian refugee in Calabar reportedly narrated that on 7 October 2017 at about 3 pm 'a helicopter loaded with government forces landed in Daddi village in Akwaya, Manyu division. Everyone in sight was shot and killed'.[13] In addition, she stated that her father was killed, and her husband arrested and detained in a prison in Buea.[14]

[7] L Unah 'Cameroon refugees struggle to cope with life of need in Nigeria' *Al Jazeera* 8 March 2020 https://www.aljazeera.com/features/2020/3/8/cameroon-refugees-struggle-to-cope-with-life-of-need-in-nigeria (accessed 22 February 2021).

[8] Y Akinwale 'Heartbreaking tales of Southern Cameroonian refugees in Nigeria' *ICIR Nigeria* 6 February 2021 https://www.icirnigeria.org/heartbreaking-tales-of-southern-cameroonian-refugees-in-nigeria/ (accessed 22 February 2021).

[9] 'Cameroon teachers, lawyers strike in battle for English' *Al Jazeera* 5 December 2016 https://www.aljazeera.com/news/2016/12/5/cameroon-teachers-lawyers-strike-in--battle-for-english (accessed 22 February 2021).

[10] R Ajakaye 'UN blasts Nigeria over return of Cameroon separatists' *AA* 1 February 2018 https://www.aa.com.tr/en/africa/un-blasts-nigeria-over-return-of-cameroon-separatists/1052118 (accessed 22 February 2021).

[11] Internal Displacement Monitoring Centre (IDMC) 'Global Report on Internal Displacement: GRID 2020' (April 2020) 17 https://www.internal-displacement.org/sites/default/files/publications/documents/2020-IDMC-GRID.pdf (accessed 22 February 2021).

[12] 'Cameroonians pour into Nigeria, stretching scant resources – UN refugee agency' *UN News* 20 March 2018 https://news.un.org/en/story/2018/03/1005372 (accessed 22 February 2021).

[13] Akinwale (n 8).

[14] As above.

Attacks and raids on villages in Southern Cameroon by military personnel have intensified since the 2018 election, when President Paul Biya won another re-election, which is his seventh term in office.[15] After the re-election, the Southern Cameroonian refugees in Nigeria continues to multiply daily as the crisis persists.[16] In addition, many more are running away from their homes as government forces keep arresting dissidents and setting villages ablaze.[17]

Killings in the Anglophone regions intensified and escalated ahead of parliamentary and municipal elections in February 2020.[18] Amnesty International confirmed killings of villagers by the army and burning of more than 50 houses in Babubock and neighbouring villages of Bangem in the Southwest around 14 January 2020.[19] Armed dissenters were also reported to have committed serious crimes, such as killings, abductions and extortions. Consequently, civilians are trapped in a spiral of violence.[20] On 7 January 2020, the armed dissenters burnt the Elections Cameroon (ELECAM) office in Misaje commune, Donga Mantung division in the Northwest region, to reiterate their earlier decision not to participate in the legislative and municipal council elections scheduled for 9 February 2020.[21] Furthermore, it was reported that at least 21 people, including 14 children, were deliberately killed by government forces in Ngarbuh village in the Northwest region on 14 February 2020.[22]

According to Craig, the protracted conflict has killed at least 4000 civilians in the Anglophone region.[23] It is pertinent to mention that this figure exceeds that of Cameroon's far north region where Boko Haram has been waging an insurgency since 2014.[24] Refugees fleeing the violence were

[15] As above.

[16] As above.

[17] As above.

[18] Amnesty International 'Cameroon: Rise in killings in Anglophone regions ahead of parliamentary elections' (6 February 2020) https://www.amnesty.org/en/latest/news/2020/02/cameroon-rise-in-killings-in-anglophone-regions/ (accessed 22 February 2021).

[19] As above.

[20] As above.

[21] ACAPS 'Cameroon: Escalation of the Anglophone crisis' (21 January 2020) 1 https://reliefweb.int/sites/reliefweb.int/files/resources/20200121_acaps_short_note_escalation_of_the_anglophone_crisis_cameroon_0.pdf (accessed 22 February 2021).

[22] Unah (n 7).

[23] J Craig 'Violence in Cameroon's Anglophone crisis takes high civilian toll' *Al Jazeera* 1 April 2021 https://www.aljazeera.com/news/2021/4/1/violence-in-cameroon-anglophone-crisis-takes-high-civilian-toll (accessed 11 April 2021).

[24] As above.

reported to have trekked across the savannah and forests to reach Nigeria and some arrived across the border with gunshot wounds.[25]

According to the United Nations High Commissioner for Refugees (UNHCR), the arrival of Cameroonian refugees in Nigeria has since presented a new dimension to the already complex humanitarian situation in Nigeria.[26] Out of the more than 26.3 million refugees in the world,[27] available statistics reveal that there are over 65,486 registered Cameroonian refugees in Nigeria, out of which 52,374 have been biometrically verified as in March 2021.[28] These refugees are spread across Akwa-Ibom, Benue, Cross River and Taraba States.[29] Thousands of these refugees are living in resettlement camps and most of them struggle to access food, healthcare services, shelter, education, water and sanitation facilities.[30]

It is pertinent to mention at this point that although there are other refugee and asylum-seeking nationalities in Nigeria such as people from the Central African Republic (CAR), Democratic Republic of Congo (DRC) and Chad, refugees and asylum seekers from Cameroon are in the majority and still top the list of these vulnerable groups of people.[31] Hence, the scope and focus of this chapter is on Cameroonian refugees and asylum seekers.

[25] UNHCR 'More Cameroonian refugees flee to Nigeria, bringing total arrivals close to 60,000 mark' (13 February 2020) https://www.unhcr.org/news/press/2020/2/5e452d2b4/cameroonian-refugees-flee-nigeria-bringing-total-arrivals-close-60000-mark.html (accessed 1 April 2021).

[26] UNHCR Nigeria 'Cameroon refugees overview' (January 2021) https://reliefweb.int/sites/reliefweb.int/files/resources/UNHCR%20Nigeria%20-%20Cameroonian%20Refugees%20Registration%20Dashboard%20January%202021.pdf (accessed 1 April 2021).

[27] UNHCR 'Refugee data finder' https://www.unhcr.org/refugee-statistics/ (accessed 11 April 2021).

[28] UNHCR 'Cameroon refugees overview' (March 2021) https://reporting.unhcr.org/sites/default/files/UNHCR%20Nigeria%20-%20Cameroonian%20Refugees%20Overview%20-%20March%202021.pdf (accessed 26 April 2021).

[29] UNHCR 'Operational update: Cameroonian refugees in Nigeria' (6 March 2021) https://data2.unhcr.org/en/documents/download/86242 (accessed 26 April 2021). The breakdown by states is as follows: Cross River—37,719; Taraba—16,541; Benue—9961; Akwa Ibom—1215 and others—50. See UNHCR (n 30).

[30] L Unah 'Cameroonian refugees in daily struggle for survival in Nigeria' *TRT World* 23 April 2019 https://www.trtworld.com/magazine/cameroonian-refugees-in-daily-struggle--for-survival-in-nigeria-26106 (accessed 1 April 2021).

[31] UNHCR, Nigeria 'Refugees and asylum seekers in Nigeria as of 28 February 2021' https://reliefweb.int/sites/reliefweb.int/files/resources/UNHCR%20Nigeria%20-%20Population%20Statistics%20February%202021.pdf (accessed 1 April 2021).

For this chapter, it is apposite to distinguish between a 'refugee and an asylum seeker'. A 'refugee' is someone who has left his or her country of origin and is unable or unwilling to return because of a serious threat to his or her life or freedom,[32] and has been recognised as a refugee under the 1951 United Nations Convention relating to the Status of Refugees (UN Convention). The UN Convention defines a 'refugee' as any person who

> [A]s a result of events occurring before 1 January 1951 and owing to well-founded fear of being persecuted for reasons of race, religion, nationality, membership of a particular social group or political opinion, is outside the country of his nationality and is unable or, owing to such fear, is unwilling to avail himself of the protection of that country; or who, not having a nationality and being outside the country of his former habitual residence as a result of such events, is unable or, owing to such fear, is unwilling to return to it.[33]

It is submitted that this definition is not comprehensive enough. However, the 1967 Protocol relating to the Status of Refugees provides a better definition of who a refugee is. In support of this submission, the UNHCR states that

> Initially, the 1951 Convention was more or less limited to protecting European refugees in the aftermath of World War II, but the 1967 Protocol expanded its scope as the problem of displacement spread around the world.[34]

The Protocol defines a refugee as follows:

> For the purpose of the present Protocol, the term 'refugee' shall, except as regards the application of paragraph 3 of this article, mean any person within the definition of article I of the Convention as if the words 'As a result of events occurring before 1 January 1951 and...' and the words '...as a result of such events', in article 1 A (2) were omitted.[35]

[32] F Nicholson & J Kumin *A guide to international refugee protection and building state asylum systems: Handbook for parliamentarians N° 27* Inter-Parliamentary Union and the United Nations High Commissioner for Refugees (2017) 17.

[33] Article 1(2).

[34] UN General Assembly, Protocol Relating to the Status of Refugees, 31 January 1967, United Nations, Treaty Series, vol 606, p 267. See UNHCR 'The 1951 Convention and its 1967 Protocol' (September 2011) 1 https://www.refworld.org/pdfid/4ec4a7f02.pdf (accessed 25 February 2021).

[35] Article 1(2).

Though this description does not explicitly describe a refugee, it expands the applicability of the UN Convention and also obliterates the geographical and time limitations, which originally limited the Convention to persons who became refugees due to events occurring in Europe before 1 January 1951. Despite this advantage over the UN Convention, the definition of refugees adopted in the Protocol did not cover people who became refugees as a result of civil wars, decolonisation, demarcation and new states.

Under the African regional level, the Organisation of African Unity (OAU) Convention Governing the Specific Aspects of Refugee Problems in Africa (OAU Convention) definition of a refugee is pragmatic, wider and contains an additional provision, which caters for the peculiarities of Africa and also clearly distinguishes it from the UN Convention.[36] According to Chatham House, while under pressure from Geneva, the OAU adopted the 1951 definition of refugee but broadened it to accommodate the social reality of refugees in Africa at a time of decolonisation and national liberation.[37]

An asylum seeker is someone who is seeking international protection but whose claim for refugee status has not yet been determined.[38] There is no international instrument that defines asylum. Article 14 of the Universal Declaration of Human Rights 1948,[39] provides that 'Everyone has the right to seek and to enjoy in other countries asylum from persecution'. However, article 1 of the UN Declaration on Territorial Asylum 1967, states that

[36] OAU, Convention Governing the Specific Aspects of Refugee Problems in Africa (OAU Convention), 10 September 1969, 1001 UNTS 45. Article 1(2) of the African Convention provides that: 'The term "refugee" shall also apply to every person who, owing to external aggression, occupation, foreign domination or events seriously disturbing public order in either part or the whole of his country of origin or nationality, is compelled to leave his place of habitual residence in order to seek refuge in another place outside his country of origin or nationality'.

[37] Chatham House 'The Refugees Convention: Why not scrap it?' (20 October 2005) https://www.chathamhouse.org/sites/default/files/public/Research/International%20 Law/ilp201005.pdf (accessed 25 February 2021).

[38] J Phillips 'Asylum seekers and refugees: What are the facts?' (14 January 2011) 2 https://www.aph.gov.au/binaries/library/pubs/bn/sp/asylumfacts.pdf (accessed 25 February 2021).

[39] UN General Assembly, Universal Declaration of Human Rights, 10 December 1948, 217 A (III).

> [a]sylum granted by a State, in the exercise of its sovereignty, to persons entitled to invoke Article 14 of the Universal Declaration of Human Rights … shall be respected by all other States.[40]

While not every asylum seeker will be recognised as a refugee, every refugee is originally an asylum seeker.[41] Part 3 of this chapter will examine and discuss the realisation of the socio-economic rights of Cameroonian refugees and asylum seekers. The rights to food and water will be specifically focused on. The next part will discuss the legal regime on the protection of these vulnerable people.

2 The Legal Regime on the Protection of Refugees and Asylum Seekers in Nigeria

Although states have been granting protection to individuals and groups fleeing persecution for centuries, the modern regime for the protection of refugees is the outcome of the second half of the twentieth century.[42] Like international human rights law, modern refugee law has its origins in the outcome of World War II as well as the refugee crises of the interwar years that preceded it.[43] Consequently, there exists a legal framework of international law and standards that protects refugees and asylum seekers. Since the international and regional norms on the rights of refugees and asylum seekers are discussed elsewhere in this book, we shall only provide a brief reference to these norms to avoid repetition. The first attempt to protect refugees and asylum seekers at the international level was made with the support of the League of Nations.

[40] Article 1(1) of the UN General Assembly, Declaration on Territorial Asylum, 14 December 1967, A/RES/2312(XXII).

[41] Amnesty International 'What's the difference between a refugee and an asylum seeker?' https://www.amnesty.org.au/refugee-and-an-asylum-seeker-difference/ (accessed 1 April 2021).

[42] International Justice Resource Center (IJRC) 'Asylum and the rights of refugees' https://ijrcenter.org/refugee-law/ (accessed 25 February 2021).

[43] As above.

The 1951 UN Convention[44] and its 1967 Protocol[45] are the principal instruments for the protection of refugees. It is pertinent to mention that Nigeria acceded to the Convention and its Optional Protocol on 23 October 1967 and 2 May 1968 respectively.[46] By acceding to these instruments, Nigeria has a legal obligation and duty to grant Cameroonian refugees and asylum seekers equal treatment to that enjoyed by citizens.

The legal framework for protecting refugees and asylum seekers in Nigeria includes the Universal Declaration of Human Rights (Universal Declaration) 1948.[47]

The United Nations Convention against Torture and other Cruel, Inhuman or Degrading Treatment or Punishment (UNCAT) 1984 is also a legal instrument for the protection of refugees and asylum seekers.[48] The UN Convention on the Rights of the Child (CRC) 1989 is a similar instrument.[49]

The inadequacies in the UN Convention approach were exposed at the regional level.[50] Regional instruments in Africa are instrumental in ensuring that refugees or asylum seekers are given adequate protection regarding their status at the national level.[51] This is premised on the fact that the evolution of the international regime for the protection of refugees and asylum seekers did not initially concern Africa, but dealt with the problems

[44] This is the principal international legal instrument for the protection of refugees because it defines who qualifies as refugee in art 1. In addition, it provides for the rights of refugees, principle of non-refoulment and states' obligations in protecting refugees.

[45] The Protocol is an autonomous refugee instrument and can be ratified separately without prior accession to the UN Convention.

[46] UNHCR 'States parties to the 1951 Convention relating to the Status of Refugees and the 1967 Protocol' https://www.unhcr.org/protect/PROTECTION/3b73b0d63.pdf 3 (accessed 1 April 2021).

[47] UN General Assembly, Convention Against Torture and Other Cruel, Inhuman or Degrading Treatment or Punishment, 10 December 1984, United Nations, Treaty Series, vol 1465, p 85. Article 14(1) provides that everyone has the right to seek and to enjoy in other countries asylum from persecution.

[48] Article 3(1) provides that no state party shall expel, return (refouler) or extradite a person to another state where there are substantial grounds for believing that he would be in danger of being subjected to torture.

[49] UN General Assembly, Convention on the Rights of the Child, 20 November 1989, United Nations, Treaty Series, vol 1577, p 3. See Article 22 of the Convention.

[50] Chatham House (n 37).

[51] EC Muma 'The principle of non-refoulement and the obligations of the United Nations in ensuring the accountability of states toward refugee protection: Lessons from Nigeria and Cameroon' (2018) *RAIS Conference Proceedings* (2018) 346 at 348.

that existed in Europe before 1951.[52] Eze states that even when the international regime was extended to Africa by the 1967 Protocol, it still fell short of dealing with the problems of Africa.[53]

At the African regional level, the principal legal framework is the OAU Convention. The OAU Convention was among the first to give a measure of normative content to the discretionary competence of states to grant asylum by virtue of article II. Regional human rights instruments that guarantee the protection of refugees and asylum seekers are the African Charter on Human and Peoples' Rights (Banjul Charter) 1981[54] and the African Charter on the Rights and Welfare of the Child (ACRWC) 1990.[55]

Domestic protection of Cameroonian refugees and asylum seekers is guaranteed under the National Commission for Refugees Act, 1989 (NCRA).[56] It is noteworthy that Nigeria ratified both the UN Convention with its Optional Protocol and the OAU Convention through the enactment of the NCRA. The NCRA provides a broader definition of a 'refugee' by combining the definitions of the UN and OAU Conventions.[57] In addition, NCRA provides the legal and institutional framework for refugee management in the country,[58] and sets out the guidelines for

[52] OC Eze 'The Convention Governing the Specific Aspects of Refugee Problems in Africa' in AA Yusuf & F Ouguergouz (eds) *The African Union: Legal and institutional framework* (2015) 496.

[53] As above.

[54] OAU, African Charter on Human and Peoples' Rights (Banjul Charter), 27 June 1981, CAB/LEG/67/3 rev. 5, 21 ILM 58 (1982). Adopted through the Resolution the Draft African Charter on Human and Peoples' Rights, 24–27 June 1981, OAU Doc AHG/Dft. Res.55 (entered into force on 21 October 1986). The ACHPR was incorporated into Nigeria's domestic legislation and it came into effect on 17 March 1983. It is now contained in the African Charter on Human and Peoples' Rights (Ratification and Enforcement) Act, Cap. A9, Laws of the Federation of Nigeria, 2004 thereby giving it force of law in the country. Article 12(3) provides that every individual shall have the right, when persecuted, to seek and obtain asylum in other countries in accordance with laws of those countries and international conventions.

[55] Article 23 contains a similar provision with art 22 of the UN Convention on the Rights of the Child (CRC).

[56] Cap N21, Laws of the Federation of Nigeria 2004.

[57] Section 20(1) provides that for the purposes of this Act, etc, a person shall be considered a refugee if he falls within the definition provided by: (a) Article I of the 1951 United Nations Convention set out in the First Schedule to this Act; (b) Article 1 of the 1967 Protocol Relating to the Status of Refugee, set out in the Second Schedule to this Act; (c) Article I of the 1969 Organisation of African Unity Convention Governing the Specific Aspects of Refugee Problems in Africa, set out in the Third Schedule to this Act.

[58] See secs 2–7.

application[59] and determination of refugee status in Nigeria.[60] The NCRA prohibits the expulsion or return of refugees whether they entered or are present in the country legally or illegally.[61] Consequently, the UN Convention, OAU Convention and NCRA are the three major instruments which guarantee the right of Cameroonian refugees to seek asylum and to qualify for refugee status in Nigeria. Furthermore, the legal framework for the protection of refugees and asylum seekers in Nigeria is consistent with international and regional norms.

According to Eze, the United Nations system, especially through the United Nations High Commissioner for Refugees (UNHCR), supplemented by the OAU Convention, fills some of the gaps associated with African refugees and complements state efforts in cases where asylum has been granted.[62] Having discussed the legal framework for the protection of Cameroonian refugees and asylum seekers in Nigeria, the discussion will now turn to the socio-economic challenges of this vulnerable group.

3 Socio-Economic Rights Challenges of Refugees and Asylum Seekers in Nigeria

Asylum seekers and refugees are entitled to all the rights and fundamental freedoms that are indicated in international human rights instruments. It follows therefore that their protection must be seen in the broader context of the protection of human rights.[63]

According to Rehman, political, racial, religious, economic and environmental cataclysms during the twentieth century and at the start of the new millennium highlight the importance of refugee law for human rights law.[64] International human rights law provides fundamental and basic rights to people in a country, whether they are citizens or not. However, the rights of both categories of persons cannot be absolute and they cannot be the same. Unlike other refugee treaties, the UN Convention comprises a range of provisions relating to refugees' socio-economic rights such as the right to housing.[65] It follows therefore that

[59] Section 8.
[60] Section 12.
[61] Sections 1(1), (3) & (4).
[62] Eze (n 52) 495.
[63] OCHR (n 1) 6.
[64] J Rehman *International human rights law* 2nd ed (2010) 641.
[65] Article 21.

the protection of the socio-economic rights of Cameroonian refugees and asylum seekers is a legally binding obligation on Nigeria and not just an issue of humanitarian assistance. In addition, socio-economic rights are based on the ideas of equality and guaranteed access to essential social and economic goods, services and opportunities.[66] Despite the non-provision of socio-economic rights in other refugee treaties, discussions in this section pertaining to the rights to health and food will use analogies from other human rights instruments. It is against this backdrop that pertinent socio-economic rights problems which Nigeria associates with the presence of Cameroonian refugees and asylum seekers will be discussed next.

The UNHCR in fulfilling its mandate, plays an important role in the protection of the socio-economic rights of Cameroonian refugees and asylum seekers in Nigeria. To improve the COVID-19 response to refugees, the UNHCR built an isolation centre at the General Hospital Adikpo, Benue State, and furnished it with medical equipment, furniture and supplies, including beds, mattresses, bedside lockers, pulse oximeters, infra-red thermometers, bedsheets, medical scrubs/shoes, digital blood pressure apparatus and drug trolleys.[67] In February 2021, the UNHCR also provided approximately 8000 refugees with cash for food in Ikyogen, Adagom and Ukende Refugee Settlements in Benue and Cross River States.[68] However, there is still the challenge of insufficient livelihood opportunities, which has resulted in negative coping mechanisms, lack of drugs at the health centres, no healthcare for uninsured refugees and lack of ambulances to transport critically ill refugees to the health facilities. These challenges as they pertain to the right to health will be discussed. In addition, the associated adequate standard of living, rights to food, shelter and water, sanitation and hygiene (WASH) will also be discussed briefly.

[66] Council of Europe 'The evolution of human rights' https://www.coe.int/en/web/compass/the-evolution-of-human-rights (accessed 22 February 2021).

[67] UNHCR 'Operational update: Cameroonian refugees in Nigeria' (2 February 2021) https://reliefweb.int/sites/reliefweb.int/files/resources/Operational%20Update%20Cameroonian%20Refugees%20in%20Nigeria%20February%202021.pdf (accessed 1 April 2021).

[68] As above.

3.1 *Right to Health*

An 'adequate standard of living' means that everyone including refugees and asylum seekers shall have a right to the highest attainable standard of health, especially in terms of health services. The right to health forms part of the guarantees provided under international human rights instruments that Nigeria is a signatory to. The UDHR,[69] International Convention on Economic, Social and Cultural Rights (ICESCR)[70] and UNCRC are relevant instruments in this regard.[71] Other international and regional human rights instruments such as the Convention on the Elimination of all Forms of Discrimination against Women (CEDAW) 1979[72] and the Banjul Charter[73] also guarantee the right to health of refugees and asylum seekers and impose obligations on states to implement this right. Consequently, Cameroonian refugees and asylum seekers are entitled to essential medical services and sanitation.

Although, an Economic, Social, Cultural Right (ESCR), the right to health is recognised under section 17(3)(c) of the 1999 Nigerian Constitution, which makes it a non-justiciable right. Despite the fact that the right to health is not a justiciable right in Nigeria,[74] the Federal High Court in the case of *Sunday Akinyemi v Attorney General of the Federation*,[75] linked the right to health to the right to life which is a justiciable right. Idris J stated, inter alia, that there is no doubt that life is the ultimate measure of all things, and for that reason, the right to life is undisputedly the

[69] Article 25(1).

[70] UN General Assembly, International Covenant on Economic, Social and Cultural Rights, 16 December 1966, UNTS vol 933, p 3. See art 12(1). Nigeria ratified this instrument on 29 July 1993.

[71] Article 24(1). Nigeria ratified this instrument on 19 April 1991.

[72] UN General Assembly, Convention on the Elimination of All Forms of Discrimination Against Women, 18 December 1979, UNTS vol 1249, p 13. See arts 12(1) & (2).

[73] Article 16(1) & (2).

[74] This is premised on the fact that it is contained in Chapter II provisions on Fundamental Objectives and Directive Principles of State Policy of the Constitution of the Federal Republic of Nigeria, 1999 (as amended). By virtue of sec 6(6)(c) of the Constitution, it is not justiciable. In the case of *Femi Falana v Attorney-General of the Federation* (Suit FHC/IKJ/CS/M59/10), the Federal High Court dismissed an application to secure the right of the applicant to life and health. The Applicant had requested the court to declare an act as unconstitutional where senior civil servants had access to medical treatment abroad, but junior civil servants were not granted such medical treatments. It was the view of the court that section 17 of the Constitution which guarantees the right to health is not justiciable.

[75] Suit FHC/L/CS/925/2011.

most fundamental of all liberties. Without the right to life, no other right can be enjoyed. The UN Committee on Economic, Social and Cultural Rights in its General Comment 14 also linked the right to health to other rights such as the rights to life, dignity and non-discrimination.[76] Furthermore, the African Commission on Human and Peoples' Rights in *Purohit & Moore v The Gambia*[77] held that

> Enjoyment of the human right to health as it is widely known is vital to all aspects of a person's life and well-being, and is crucial to the realisation of all the other fundamental human rights and freedoms. This right includes the right to health facilities, access to goods and services to be guaranteed to all without discrimination of any kind.

According to Eide, the term 'right to health' is ambiguous because there is no human right to be healthy.[78] Due to risky behaviours, genetics, accidents and other factors, it is not within the capacity of states to ensure that everyone lives a full and lengthy life.[79] Eide argues that it is envisaged under international human rights law that everyone shall have a right to the highest attainable standard of health. People should be entitled to what is attainable in terms of the individual's potential, the social and environmental conditions affecting the health of the individual and in terms of health services.[80] Consequently, in the chapter based on Eide's contention, the term 'right to health', means the right to the highest attainable standard of health. Nigeria's healthcare system has always experienced certain negativities, with different healthcare establishments having their peculiar problems.[81] The arrival of Cameroonian refugees and asylum seekers in the country further challenges the already-struggling healthcare system, which is not intended to meet the needs of displaced

[76] UN Committee on Economic, Social and Cultural Rights (CESCR), General Comment 14: The Right to the Highest Attainable Standard of Health (Art 12 of the Covenant), 11 August 2000, UN Doc E/C.12/2000/4 (2000) para 8.

[77] (Communication 241/2001) [2003] ACHPR 49 (29 May 2003) para 80.

[78] A Eide 'Adequate standard of living' in D Moeckli et al. (eds) *International human rights law* (2010) 243.

[79] As above.

[80] As above.

[81] M Abdullahi, L Cheri & AI Chikaji 'The implication of Boko Haram insurgency on healthcare service delivery in Bornu State, Nigeria' (2017) 3 *Ilorin Journal of Administration and Development, University of Ilorin* 1 at 5.

populations.[82] Hence, the healthcare system is overburdened, with a shortage of supplies, and it is inadequately prepared for potential disease outbreaks.[83]

Healthcare remains an issue of concern among Cameroonian refugees and asylum seekers. Having fled and considering the reasons for their flight, Cameroonian asylum seekers often arrive in Nigeria, traumatised, in need of medical treatment, and without any cash or other means of survival. The UNHCR, in its February 2021 operational update on Cameroonian refugees in Nigeria, reported that there were over 650 new arrivals in Sardauna Local Government Area (LGA), Taraba State and they are mostly women and children.[84] However, by March 2021, this figure rose to over 4000. This was within a period of one month.[85] These newly arrived asylum seekers fled from Nwa sub-division, Northwest Region of Cameroon, because of increasing violent clashes, which resulted in killings and the burning of houses. Consequently, their critical needs included healthcare and food.[86] In addition, the lack of medication and consumable medical supplies in all the primary health centres in Benue, Cross River and Taraba States, continues to affect the provision of basic healthcare services to refugees and locals.[87]

Pregnant Cameroonian refugees and asylum seekers reportedly slept on floors in halls and on mats in tents throughout their pregnancy and without attending an ante-natal clinic, due to a lack of adequate transportation to a nearby health facility.[88] They could not get mattresses from the Refugee Agency because '[mattresses are] given based on the family size' and '[it's] one mattress per a family of five and below, the rest are mats'.[89] As a result, 'some of the babies died; some died after delivery while some were stillbirths due to poor health care services at the settlement'.[90] It is submitted that this is a clear violation of the physical and mental health

[82] 'Improving access to health care for Cameroonian refugees in Nigeria' *FHI 360* 17 February2020https://www.fhi360.org/news/improving-access-health-care-cameroonian--refugees-nigeria (accessed 1 April 2021).

[83] As above.

[84] UNHCR (n 67).

[85] UNHCR (n 29) 2.

[86] UNHCR (n 67) 2. See also UNHCR (n 29) 2 & 3.

[87] UNHCR (n 67) 4.

[88] Akinwale (n 8).

[89] As above.

[90] As above.

rights of these vulnerable Cameroonian women. Their health rights as guaranteed in human rights instruments such as the UDHR,[91] ACHPR,[92] CEDAW,[93] and Protocol to the African Charter on Human and Peoples' Rights on the Rights of Women in Africa (Maputo Protocol) were violated.[94] At the domestic level, it is a violation of the provisions of the Constitution of the Federal Republic of Nigeria 1999 (as amended) which guarantees that Nigeria shall direct its policy towards ensuring that there are adequate medical and health facilities for all persons.[95]

It was reported that at Adagom-3, a settlement for more than 500 refugees in Ogoja, Cross River State, asylum seekers did not receive essential health-related items such as mosquito nets.[96] In addition, most asylum seekers had to drink water from streams, ponds and other unsafe sources, because of inadequate or dysfunctional drinking water facilities.[97]

It was further stated that apart from not having access to clean water, fewer than 25 per cent of Cameroonian asylum seekers received essential relief items such as clothing, blankets and plastic sheeting.[98] In confirming these statements, Unah also reported that a refugee complained that there is barely water to bathe in.[99] The UNHCR states that the main gap in the WASH sector remains the inadequate water supply in the refugee settlements. This is despite the construction and rehabilitation of over 15 boreholes and hand dug wells by UNHCR. These efforts are insufficient and will merely meet about 20 per cent of refugees' water need.[100] In addition, other WASH challenges are inadequate latrine and bathing facilities within refugee settlements.[101]

The right to sexual and reproductive health is another important right, which is of significant concern and it is germane to the protection of

[91] Article 25.

[92] Article 16(1).

[93] Articles 12(1) and 14(2)(b).

[94] AU, Protocol to the African Charter on Human and Peoples' Rights on the Rights of Women in Africa, 11 July 2003. See art 14(2)(a) and (b).

[95] Section 17(3)(d).

[96] Unah (n 7).

[97] UN News (n 12).

[98] MA Awel 'Over 20,000 Cameroon refugees registered in Nigeria' *AA* 20 March 2018 https://www.aa.com.tr/en/africa/over-20-000-cameroon-refugees-registered-in-nigeria-/1094559# (accessed 1 April 2021).

[99] Unah (n 7).

[100] UNHCR (n 29) 3.

[101] As above.

Cameroonian refugees and asylum seekers. These vulnerable groups of persons are susceptible to sexual exploitation and violence. In the year 2020, in Benue, a large number of Cameroonian refugees were victims of sexual assaults and rape and in Taraba, 43 per cent of reported cases were sexual assaults and rape, which occurred more frequently than other physical assaults.[102]

3.2 Right to Food

Another major socio-economic rights challenge faced by Cameroonian refugees is the lack of adequate food. The right to food forms one of the guarantees provided for under the 1999 Nigerian Constitution[103] and ICESCR.[104] According to Eide, human beings do not live by bread alone and without food there is no life. Furthermore food that is not nutritious may render human beings prone to ill-health and could shorten their lifespans.[105] Oluduro in support of Eide's position, states that the right to food and the right to life are intertwined and interdependent and without the right to food, all other rights will be meaningless.[106] He argues further that whether one speaks of human rights or basic human needs, the right to food is the most basic of all.[107]

The provision of food is one of the most urgent needs of vulnerable groups in Nigeria. The neglect or violation of the right to food is probably the most serious global human rights issue as it affects a substantial number of people whose rights are not ensured.[108] Cameroonian refugees and asylum seekers in Nigeria are a case in point. They live in deplorable conditions in Nigeria and the traditional breadwinners (usually the females) have little food to feed their families. Many have had to carry bricks to earn money (at a rate of 20 Naira per brick) to supplement the relief which

[102] DD Sasu, Violence towards Cameroonian refugees in Nigeria 2020, by state, Statista, 12 December 2022, at Nigeria: violence toward refugees from Cameroon | Statista (accessed 2 March 2023).

[103] Section 16(2)(d) provides that the state shall direct its policy towards ensuring that suitable and adequate food are provided for all citizens.

[104] Article 11.

[105] Eide (n 78) 237.

[106] O Oluduro *Oil exploration and human rights violations in Nigeria's oil producing communities* (2014) 244.

[107] As above.

[108] Eide (n 78) 237.

agencies provided to them.[109] In March 2018, a video[110] and photo[111] emerged online which showed how Cameroonian refugees in Abande, Benue State, survive by eating elephant grass, which is pounded before it is cooked.

Cameroonian refugees and asylum seekers are more dependent on food assistance, because they have limited access to land even where land is available and they are disconnected from their normal means of income. Most refugees and asylum seekers used to receive cash-based interventions (CBI) of ₦7200 naira per month from the UNHCR to cover their food and basic needs.[112] The UNHCR reports that 7965 individuals from 1766 refugee families received cash for food in Ikyogen, Adagom and Ukende settlements in Benue and Cross River States.[113] This figure increased to 27,000 refugees across the aforementioned settlements in March 2021.[114] The UNHCR stated that over 34,000 refugees have received the cash for food in 2021.[115]

The cash for food has, however, been reduced to ₦4600 naira,[116] with more deductions anticipated and there have been occasional delays in receiving the payments.[117] According to Glory Tiku, an 18-year-old, Cameroonian refugee, before the CBI is paid, she borrows money to feed and take care of her four-month-old baby as her monthly payment

[109] ARA Shaban 'Condition of Cameroonian refugees in Nigeria worries top UNHCR official' *Africa News* 31 March 2018 https://www.africanews.com/2018/03/31/condition-of-cameroonian-refugees-in-nigeria-worries-top-unhcr-official// (accessed 25 February 2021).

[110] Twitter post by E Mpimbaza on 27 March 2018 https://twitter.com/BethMpimbaza/status/978603534395564032?ref_src=twsrc%5Etfw%7Ctwcamp%5Etweetembed%7Ctwterm%5E978603534395564032%7Ctwgr%5E%7Ctwcon%5Es1_&ref_url=https%3A%2F%2Fwww.africanews.com%2F2018%2F03%2F31%2Fcondition-of-cameroonian-refugees-in-nigeria-worries-top-unhcr-official%2F (accessed 25 February 2021).

[111] Twitter post by Antonio Jose Canhandula on 29 March 2018 https://twitter.com/kanyandulajose/status/979229810500259840?ref_src=twsrc%5Etfw%7Ctwcamp%5Etweetembed%7Ctwterm%5E979229810500259840%7Ctwgr%5E%7Ctwcon%5Es1_&ref_url=https%3A%2F%2Fwww.africanews.com%2F2018%2F03%2F31%2Fcondition-of-cameroonian-refugees-in-nigeria-worries-top-unhcr-official%2F (accessed 25 February 2021).

[112] Unah (n 7).

[113] UNHCR (n 67) 3.

[114] UNHCR (n 29) 4.

[115] UNHCR (n 29) 5.

[116] Unah (n 7).

[117] UNHCR 'Cameroon Situation Update/Nigeria Operation' https://data2.unhcr.org/en/documents/details/84103 (accessed 22 February 2021).

is not enough to feed herself and her baby.[118] The Cameroonian asylum seekers' situation regarding food is dire. It was reported that 95 per cent of them had food for only three days.[119] It is pertinent to mention that some Cameroonian refugees residing in host communities in Cross River State are unable to receive their CBIs because they cannot afford to spend up to ₦3000 naira ($8) to travel to Ogoja where the money is disbursed.[120]

The UNHCR has indicated that refugees continue to cross the borders into and out of Cameroon to search for food and livelihood opportunities to sustain their families. This is caused by the increased prices of basic food commodities in refugee populated areas. There has been an average 30 per cent increment on essential food commodities since early 2020. The increase is attributed to the COVID-19 pandemic.[121] In addition, the UNHCR states that despite the substantial increase in the prices of food the amount of cash for food granted to refugees is less than in the past as a result of funding constraints.[122] Since the advent of the COVID-19 pandemic, refugees and asylum seekers have been faced with a myriad of challenges in Nigeria. They have experienced the loss of daily wages and livelihoods and have had to endure psychosocial hardship. In a press release on 14 May 2020, the UN High Commissioner for Refugees (UNHCR) stressed that

> COVID-19 is not just a physical health crisis, but it is now also triggering a mental health crisis. While many refugees ... are remarkably resilient and can move forward despite having experienced violence or persecution firsthand, their capacities to cope are now being stretched to the limit.[123]

It is pertinent to state that the lack of adequate food has resulted in 'negative coping mechanisms including alcohol abuse and survival sex

[118] Unah (n 7).
[119] UN News (n 12).
[120] Unah (n 7).
[121] UNHCR (n 67) 3.
[122] UNHCR (n 29).
[123] Cited in UN Refugee Agency (UNHCR) 'Socio-Economic Impact Assessment of COVID-19: Pandemic among persons of concern in Nigeria' (July 2020) 6 file:///C:/Users/User/Downloads/Report%20on%20Assessment%20of%20Socio-Economic%20Impact%20of%20COVID-19%20on%20PoCs_19082020.pdf (accessed 28 June 2022).

[being] reported among youth and women-headed households'.[124] According to the UNHCR, Cameroonian women and girls face high risks of Sexual and Gender Based Violence (SGBV). They suffer such violence when they flee their home country and in their asylum country. As a result, teenage pregnancies, early marriage and rape are prevalent amongst them. The refugee agency attributes the SGBV to the outbreak of hostilities, lack of food and non-food assistance, lack of livelihood opportunities, inadequate and overcrowded accommodation, and insufficient resources to meet their basic needs.[125]

It must be emphasised that states are the principal duty bearers and under an obligation to fulfil, respect and protect all human rights of individuals in their territories and who are subject to their jurisdictions.[126] Consequently, Nigeria has an obligation to provide adequate healthcare and food to Cameroonian refugees and asylum seekers, and to eliminate acute malnutrition amongst them. This is explicitly provided for in the ICESCR by virtue of article 2(3), which states that:

> Developing countries, with due regard to human rights and their national economy, may determine to what extent they would guarantee the economic rights recognised in the present Covenant to non-nationals. It is submitted that non-nationals as mentioned in this provision include refugees and asylum seekers.

4 Legal Status of Socio-Economic Rights and an Appraisal of Case Law on Socio-Economic Rights of Refugees and Asylum Seekers in Nigeria

Socio-economic rights as contained in chapter II of the Constitution of the Federal Republic of Nigeria 1999 (as amended) are non-justiciable in the courts in Nigeria by virtue of section 6(6)(c) of the 1999 Constitution. In *Archbishop Anthony Okogie v. AG Lagos State*,[127] the Court held that

[124] UNHCR (n 29) 3.

[125] As above.

[126] OS Ekundayo 'The legal protection of children's right to free and compulsory primary education in Nigeria: Problems and prospects' PhD Thesis, University of London, 2015 at 19.

[127] (1981) 2 NCLR 337 at 350.

> …While Section 13 of the Constitution makes it a duty and responsibility of the judiciary among other organs of government to conform to and apply the provisions of Chapter II, section 6 (6) (c) of the same constitution makes it clear that no court has jurisdiction to pronounce any decision as to whether any organ of government has acted or is acting in conformity with the Fundamental Objectives and Directive Principles of State Policy. It is clear therefore that section 13 has not made chapter II of the Constitution justiciable…,

Despite the Court's finding, socio-economic rights can be enforced if they are subsumed under the fundamental human rights which are guaranteed under Chapter IV of the 1999 Constitution. This may be achieved by applying the principle of progressive realisation through judicial interpretation as utilised in terms of the Indian model. India is known for applying the integrative approach to ensure that violations of socio-economic rights can be remedied due to their relationship with civil and political rights.[128]

The progressive realisation principle as contained in article 2(1) ICESCR, appears to be based on the understanding that all socio-economic rights will not be realised within a short period of time.[129] States parties are therefore required to take appropriate steps, within the limits of available resources, to fully realise socio-economic rights in line with Article 2(1) and 11(1) of the ICESCR. According to Chenwi:

> …The progressive realisation qualification requires a state to strive towards fulfilment and improvement in the enjoyment of socio-economic rights to the maximum extent possible, even in the face of resource constraints…[130]

Available data suggest that there is a dearth of case law on the socio-economic rights to health and food of Cameroonian and other refugees and asylum seekers. This may be as a result of the non-enforceability of socio-economic rights, which are provided for in Chapter II of the 1999

[128] S Ibe, 'Beyond justiciability: Realising the promise of socio-economic rights in Nigeria' (2007) 7 *African Human Rights Law Journal* 225–248 at 226.

[129] E Idornigie-Pearce, *Realisation of Socio-Economic Rights in Nigeria: A Comparative Study*, being a PhD Thesis Submitted to Canterbury Christ Church University 2022, p.19.

[130] L Chenwi 'Unpacking "progressive realisation", its relation to resources, minimum core and reasonableness, and some methodological considerations for assessing compliance"' *De Jure* (2013) 742–769 at 743.

Constitution of the Federal Republic of Nigeria, as Fundamental Objectives and Directive Principles of State Policy, because of the retrogressive non-justiciability clause contained in section 6(6)(c).[131] It is trite that courts give effect to the aforementioned provision in a statute over and above a preceding provision.[132] Nigerian courts gave effect to section 6(6)(c) of the Constitution in addition to positive decisions regarding section 13 in cases which related to fundamental objectives. As a result, Nigerians and foreign nationals within Nigeria are denied socio-economic rights such as the rights to health[133] and food[134] as contained in Chapter II because they are progressive rights that cannot be enforced by the courts.

According to Govindjee and Taiwo, the rights which are categorised as 'Fundamental Objectives and Directive Principles of State Policy' in Nigeria, are amongst the most essential rights for any society, because they give meaning to other rights guaranteed in the Constitution, hence their non-recognition erode the strength of the remaining fundamental rights.[135] Thus, it is submitted that there is an indirect protection of the socio-economic rights to health and food of Cameroonian and other refugees and asylum seekers through the interdependence, indivisibility and interrelatedness of the right to life, freedom from degrading treatment and protection of the child.

Notwithstanding the non-justiciability of socio-economic rights in the 1999 Nigerian Constitution, Nigeria has been found to be in breach of its obligations in respect of these rights in a plethora of cases. In *Socio-Economic Rights and Accountability Project (SERAP) v Federal Republic of Nigeria*,[136] the applicant brought an application alleging that the defendant violated the rights to health, adequate standard of

[131] This section provides that the judicial powers vested in courts shall not except as otherwise provided by this Constitution, extend to any issue or question as to whether any act or omission by any authority or person or as to whether any law or any judicial decision is in conformity with the Fundamental Objectives and Directive Principles of State Policy set out in Chapter II of this Constitution.

[132] See *N.P.A S. F v Fasel Service Ltd* (2001) 17 NWLR (Pt 742) 261 at 284.

[133] Section 17(3)(d) of the 1999 Constitution of the Federal Republic of Nigeria.

[134] Section 16(2)(d) of the 1999 Constitution of the Federal Republic of Nigeria.

[135] A Govindjee & EA Taiwo 'Justiciability and enforceability of the fundamental objectives and directive principles in Nigeria: Lessons from South Africa and India' (2011) 7 *Nigerian Bar Journal* 65 at 90–91.

[136] ECW/CCJ/JUD/18/12.

living and the rights to economic and social development of the people of the Niger Delta. It was also alleged that the defendant failed to enact and implement laws and regulations to protect the environment and prevent pollution. The Economic Community of West African States (ECOWAS) Community Court of Justice held that socio-economic rights were justiciable before the court and that Nigeria was in breach of the obligation to ensure a healthy environment under article 24 of the ACHPR. It further held that Nigeria has violated articles 1 and 24 of the ACHPR. It is submitted that based on this judgment, Cameroonian and other refugees and asylum seekers can assert their claim for the enforcement of their rights to an adequate standard of living of health and food.

In *Registered Trustees of the Socio-Economic and Accountability Project (SERAP) v Federal Republic of Nigeria and Universal Basic Education Commission*,[137] there was an application to the ECOWAS Community Court for the enforcement of the right to education guaranteed under the ACHPR. The second defendant contended, inter alia, that the educational objective of the first defendant contained in Chapter II of the 1999 Nigerian Constitution lies at the heart of the plaintiff's suit and that the provisions of that chapter are not justiciable. The ECOWAS Court dismissed the aforementioned objection and held that the application was directed at the enforcement of the right to education under article 17 of the ACHPR and not at a breach of the right to education contained under Chapter II of the 1999 Nigerian Constitution. Therefore, since the plaintiff's application was in pursuance of a right guaranteed by the ACHPR, the contention of the second defendant that the right to education is not justiciable as it falls within the directive principles of state policy, was rejected.[138]

A search for case law which deals with the socio-economic rights to health and food of Cameroonian refugees and asylum seekers, yielded a case concerning the extradition of 47 Cameroonian refugees and asylum seekers. *In casu*, the Abuja Judicial Division of the Federal High Court of Nigeria declared their arrest by Nigerian security forces and subsequent deportation to Cameroon as illegal and unconstitutional.[139] On Friday, 5 January 2018, Julius Sisiku Ayuk Tabe and 46 other activists of the

[137] ECW/CCJ/APP/0808.
[138] Paragraph 20.
[139] Amnesty International *Human rights in Africa: Review of 2019* (2020) 26.

pro-independence movement of Northwest and Southwest (Ambazonia) of Cameroon were arrested in Nigeria. They were extradited by the Government of Nigeria and back on Cameroon soil on 29 January 2018.[140] Before their extradition to Cameroon, they were detained in an underground cell at the headquarters of the Directorate Intelligence Agency in Abuja.[141]

Two cases were filed on behalf of the refugees. The first, by a group of human rights lawyers against the National Security Advisor and Attorney-General of the Federation, while the second was filed by the deportees.[142] In the first case, Chikere, J in the Federal High Court, in exercising its jurisdiction under section 251(1)(i) of the Nigerian Constitution, found that the arrest on 7 January 2018 and subsequent detention of the academics was illegal and unconstitutional.[143] In respect of the second case, the Court also ruled that the deportation on 26 January 2018 was illegal and violated the deportees' rights as guaranteed by the Nigerian Constitution.[144] According to Fatunde

> On the issue of their illegal arrest and detention, the judge ordered the state to pay damages of NGN5 million (US$13,800) to each detainee 'as general and aggravated damages for illegal violation of their fundamental rights to life, dignity of person, fair hearing, HEALTH, freedom of movement and freedom of association'. On the issue of their deportation, the court ordered the state to pay damages of NGN200,000.[145]

[140] MN Mbe 'Human rights issues in Cameroon in the case of the independentists arrested in Nigeria and extradited to Cameroon' (21 October 2019) https://papers.ssrn.com/sol3/papers.cfm?abstract_id=3472963 (accessed 22 February 2021). It is submitted that this is a violation of the principle of non-refoulment, which is the cornerstone of international refugee law and explicitly provides that refugees and asylum seekers should not be extradited to a country where they could be persecuted.

[141] 'Court declares detention, deportation of Cameroonian refugees illegal' *Channels Television* 2 March 2019 https://www.channelstv.com/2019/03/02/court-declares-detention-deportation-of-cameroonian-refugees-illegal/ (accessed 22 February 2021).

[142] T Fatunde 'Academics hail court rulings on deported lecturers' *University World News* 13 March 2019 https://www.universityworldnews.com/post.php?story=20190313082701764 (accessed 22 February 2021).

[143] As above.

[144] As above.

[145] As above.

This case though bordering mostly on civil liberties and fundamental freedoms, is relevant by analogy to this chapter because the judgment recognised the right to health of the Cameroonian refugees.

5 Recommendations on How to Strengthen the Protection of Socio-Economic Rights of Refugees and Asylum Seekers in Nigeria

In the preceding sections, this chapter examined the refugee situation in Nigeria. The Cameroonian refugee situation in Nigeria is a typical illustration of the interdependence of the international community in protecting the socio-economic rights of vulnerable groups such as refugees and asylum seekers in Africa. It shows how the problems of one country can have immediate consequences for another country.

This chapter illustrates that the realisation of the socio-economic rights to health and food is an urgent need faced by Cameroonian refugees and asylum seekers. The fulfilment of socio-economic rights is necessary for the full participation of Cameroonian refugees and asylum seekers in the Nigerian society. This is especially true about the adequate standard of living, rights to health and food. Due to these rights, material necessities for a dignified life, essential for human dignity is guaranteed to Cameroonian refugees and asylum seekers. A lack of these rights is condescending as demonstrated in this chapter. The rights to health and food of Cameroonian asylum seekers and refugees' should therefore be respected before, during and post the asylum-seeking process. By ratifying the UN and AU conventions, Nigeria agreed to protect Cameroonian refugees and asylum seekers in her territory and under her jurisdiction. Such protection should be in accordance with the provisions of these instruments, and consistent with international human rights obligations.[146] In addition, Nigeria is obligated under international law to take a variety of measures to ensure that the socio-economic rights to health and food of everyone including people with

[146] See art 2(1)(b) of the United Nations, Vienna Convention on the Law of Treaties, 23 May 1969, United Nations, Treaty Series, vol 1155, p 331, which provides that: 'ratification', 'acceptance', 'approval' and 'accession' mean in each case the international act so named whereby a state establishes on the international plane its consent to be bound by a treaty.

special needs, and particularly vulnerable groups such as Cameroonian refugees and asylum seekers are protected.[147]

There can be no doubt that the Nigerian government has assisted Cameroonian refugees and asylum seekers in some respects, such as by the allocation of land to the UNHCR for the construction of shelters to ensure the safety, security and self-reliance of refugees.[148] Furthermore, from March 2018, the Federal Government of Nigeria granted a two-year Temporary Protection Status to Cameroonians who seek asylum in Nigeria.[149] In addition to the efforts of the Nigerian government, the UNHCR and other humanitarian actors have been providing protection and life-saving assistance to refugees with the limited available resources.[150] However, it is submitted that more still needs to be done to protect the rights to health and food of Cameroonian refugees and asylum seekers, and to help them rebuild their lives.

The following recommendations are imperative. It is recommended that adequate judicial protection of the socio-economic rights to health and food of Cameroonian and other refugees and asylum seekers should be ensured. The various judicial organs at the national, sub-regional and regional levels have important roles to play in strengthening the protection of these socio-economic rights in Nigeria. Although, the jurisprudence of the ECOWAS Community Court of Justice (ECCJ) in respect of social and economic rights is commendable, much is still required from

[147] These measures include adopting appropriate measures but not limited to legislative measures towards the realisation of socio-economic rights; provision of remedies in legislative texts; introducing policies relevant for the realisation of socio-economic rights; adopting targeted, effective and low-cost programmes to protect the most at risk (refugees and asylum seekers inclusive), even in instances of limited resources. In addition, it is pertinent to mention that although the ICESCR lays out the general obligation of progressive achievement with respect to the rights enumerated in the Covenant, the UN CESCR and other authorities have identified that not every aspect of a particular right is subject to this progressive qualifier. The UN CESCR has in some of its General Comments indicated certain elements of provisions that are 'capable of immediate application by judicial and other organs in many national legal systems'. See further, International Commission of Jurists 'State obligations stemming from international law' https://www.icj.org/chapter-2-esc-rights-under--international-law-and-the-role-of-judicial-and-quasi-judicial-bodies-2/2-3-identifying-breaches-of-international-obligations-of-states-pertaining-to-esc-rights/2-3-1-state-obligations-stemming-from-international-law/ (accessed 22 February 2021).

[148] UN News (n 12).

[149] UNHCR 'Protection strategy for Cameroonian refugees in Nigeria 2018–2019' 3 https://data2.unhcr.org/en/documents/download/68381(accessed 22 February 2021).

[150] As above.

the courts and its Nigerian, regional and international counterparts. This is premised on the fact that the decisions of these judicial organs will contribute to the consistent and sound interpretation and application of protection standards. Judicial decisions will also help to bridge shortfalls in cases where political, administrative and legislative processes may be weak and insufficient.

It is also highly recommended that the African Court on Human and Peoples' Rights should be obligated to accept individual complaints from Cameroonian and other refugees and asylum seekers, without the declaration of acceptance or recognition of the Court's competence by affected states parties. This can be achieved with the amendment of the Protocol to the African Charter on Human and Peoples' Rights Establishing the African Court on Human and Peoples' Rights 1998 and by deleting article 34(6) of the Protocol.[151]

The jurisdiction of the African Court on Human and Peoples' Rights will complement national courts. This recommendation is based on the fact that the enforcement procedures of the ICCPR and ICESCR are at the level of committee reports and recommendations. Consequently, Cameroonian and other refugees and asylum seekers cannot fully benefit from the direct enforcement of these human rights instruments.

In addition to the recommendation on adequate judicial protection of refugees and asylum seekers in Nigeria, it is also recommended that the government should ensure that there are adequate provisions on non-judicial mechanisms for their protection. This recommendation stems from the fact that Nigerian courts, due to large caseloads and dockets, may not have the requisite expertise and mandate to analyse the protection system and to make recommendations. The inclusion of non-judicial measures will allow for the concentration on the adequacy, integrity, quality and coordination of the protection availed to Cameroonian and other refugees and asylum within the country. Consequently, the National Human Rights Commission (NHRC) should be empowered to receive complaints from Cameroonian and other refugees and asylum seekers about the protection of socio-economic rights to health and food and to make recommendations on how to improve their protection. The role of the NHRC in protecting the rights to health and food of this vulnerable group of people can be actualised through:

[151] Entered into force in 2004.

1. monitoring and reporting on the Nigerian government's implementation of national legislation and compliance with international treaty obligations in respect of refugees and asylum seekers;
2. receiving complaints from the UNHCR and other relevant organisations about violations of the rights to health and food of Cameroonian and other refugees and asylum seekers;
3. assisting the Nigerian government to draft policies and plans of action to address refugee situations; and
4. networking with the Cameroonian National Commission on Human Rights and Freedoms and other NHRCs in other countries.

The choice of the NHRC as a non-judicial mechanism is premised on its independence, credibility, commitment to human rights and ability to act on individual complaints.

Cameroonian refugee children should be able to benefit from the national child protection provided by the Child Rights Act to promote and protect their rights to health and food. The Nigerian government should also increase the financial and human resources allocated to the National Commission for Refugees, Migrants and Internally Displaced Persons (NCFRMI) to ensure the progressive realisation of the rights to health and food of asylum seekers and refugees.

Nigeria, as a developing country, cannot protect the rights to health and food of Cameroonian refugees and asylum seekers on its own as it has to contend with several serious problems such as the Boko Haram insurgency, banditry, internal displacement and economic recession. Accordingly, there is a need for international cooperation, solidarity and burden sharing to improve the protection of refugees and asylum seekers in the country. This can be achieved through interventions by developed countries. Interventions may include the provision of financial assistance and technical support.

In conclusion, it is suggested that a political solution be found for the crisis in Cameroon so that Cameroonian refugees and asylum seekers can safely and voluntarily return home. Failure to find a political situation will aggravate the safe return of Cameroonian refugees and asylum seekers.

At the beginning of January 2020, the Cameroonian government concluded an arrangement with Nigeria for the return of 700 repented separatists, refugees, and asylum seekers by the end of February 2020, but this was not achieved.[152] It is submitted that the continuous escalation of the Anglophone crisis will stop the return of Cameroonian refugees and asylum seekers from Nigeria.

Bibliography

Books

GS Goodwin-Gill and J McAdam *The refugee in International Law* (2007).

O Oluduro, *Oil exploration and human rights violations in Nigeria's oil producing communities* (2014).

R Rehman *International human rights law* 2nd ed (London: Longman Pub Group, 2010)

Chapters in Books

A Eide 'Adequate standard of living' in Moeckli, D; Shah, S, Sivakumaran, S Harris, DJ (eds) *International human rights law* (Oxford University Press 2010)

ML Uwais 'Fundamental objectives and directive principles of state policy in modern constitution: Possibilities and prospects' in CC Nweze (ed) *Justice in the Judicial Process: Essays in Honour of Honourable Justice Eugene Ubaezeonu, JCA* (2002)

OC Eze, 'The Convention Governing the Specific Aspects of Refugee Problems in Africa' in Abdulqawi A. Yusuf &Fatsah Ouguergouz (eds) *The African Union: Legal and Institutional Framework* (2015).

Journal Articles

A Govindjee & EA Taiwo 'Justiciability and enforceability of the fundamental objectives and directive principles in Nigeria: Lessons from South Africa and India' (2011) 7 *Nigerian Bar Journal* 65

L Chenwi 'Unpacking "progressive realisation", its relation to resources, minimum core and reasonableness, and some methodological considerations for assessing compliance' *De Jure* (2013) 742

LW Holborn 'The League of Nations and the Refugee Problem' (1939) 203 *The Annals of the American Academy of Political and Social Science.*

M Abdullahi, L Cheri & AI Chikaji, 'The implication of boko haram insurgency on healthcare service delivery in Bornu State, Nigeria' (2017) 3(1) *Ilorin Journal of Administration and Development, University of Ilorin.*

RC Chhangani and PK Chhangani 'Refugee definition and the law in Nigeria' (2011) 53 (1) *Journal of the Indian Law Institute.*

152 ACAPS (n 21).

S Ibe, 'Beyond justiciability: Realising the promise of socio-economic rights in Nigeria' (2007) 7 *African Human Rights Law Journal* 225

T Clark and F Crepeau 'Mainstreaming Refugee Rights - The 1951 Refugee Convention and International Human Rights Law' (1999) 17 (4) *Netherlands Quarterly of Human Rights.*

Theses

E Idornigie-Pearce, *Realisation of Socio-Economic Rights in Nigeria: A Comparative Study*, being a PhD Thesis Submitted to Canterbury Christ Church University 2022

OS Ekundayo 'The legal protection of children's right to free and compulsory primary education in Nigeria: problems and prospects' PhD Thesis, University of London, 2015.

Reports

Amnesty International *Human rights in Africa: Review of 2019* (2020a)

EC Muma, 'The Principle of Non-Refoulement and the Obligations of the United Nations in Ensuring the Accountability of States toward Refugee Protection: Lessons from Nigeria and Cameroon' (2018) *RAIS Conference Proceedings*

F Nicholson and J Kumin, *A guide to international refugee protection and building state asylum systems: Handbook for parliamentarians N° 27*, Inter-Parliamentary Union and the United Nations High Commissioner for Refugees, 2017.

Case Law

Adan v Secretary of State for the Home Department [1998] 2 WLR 702

Femi Falana v Attorney-General of the Federation (Suit N0. FHC/IKJ/CS/M59/10)

N.P.A S. F v Fasel Service Ltd (2001) 17 NWLR (Pt. 742) 261

Purohit & Moore v The Gambia (Communication No. 241/2001) [2003] ACHPR 49

Registered Trustees of the Socio-Economic and Accountability Project (SERAP) v Federal

Republic of Nigeria and Universal Basic Education Commission ECW/CCJ/APP/0808.

Socio-Economic Rights and Accountability Project (SERAP) v Federal Republic of Nigeria ECW/CCJ/JUD/18/12.

Sunday Akinyemi v Attorney General of the Federation & Anor. Suit N0. FHC/L/CS/925/2011.

Legislation

Constitution of the Federal Republic of Nigeria, 1999 (as amended) Cap. C23, Laws of the Federation of Nigeria 2004

AU Documents

OAU, African Charter on Human and Peoples' Rights (Banjul Charter), 27 June 1981, CAB/LEG/67/3 rev. 5, 21 ILM 58 (1982)

OAU, African Charter on the Rights and Welfare of the Child, 11 July 1990, CAB/LEG/24.9/49 (1990)

Organization of African Unity (OAU) Convention Governing the Specific Aspects of Refugee Problems in Africa, 1969.

Protocol to the African Charter on Human and Peoples' Rights on the Rights of Women in Africa (Maputo Protocol).

UN Documents

General Resolution establishing the Human Rights Council (2006), GA Res 60/251 (3 April 2006)

International Convention on Economic, Social and Cultural Rights, 1966.

National Commission for Refugees, etc. Act 1989, Cap. N21, Laws of the Federation of Nigeria 2004.

New York Optional Protocol relating to the Status of Refugees 1967.

UN General Assembly, Convention on the Elimination of All Forms of Discrimination Against Women, 18 December 1979, United Nations, Treaty Series, vol 1249

United Nations, *Compilation of International Instruments* (Vol. 1, First Part, 1993).

United Nations Committee on Economic, Social and Cultural Rights (CESCR), 'The Right to the Highest Attainable Standard of Health' (CESCR General Comment 14) UN Doc E/C/12/2000/

United Nations Convention against Torture and other Cruel, Inhuman or Degrading Treatment or Punishment (UNCAT) 1984.

United Nations Convention on the Rights of the Child (CRC) 1989

United Nations Convention relating to the Status of Refugees 1951

Universal Declaration of Human Rights (Universal Declaration) 1948

Vienna Convention on the Law of Treaties 1969.

Vienna Declaration and Programme of Action, A/CONF.157/23 (25 June 1993).

World Summit Outcome Document, GA Res 60/1/ (24 October 2005).

Internet Sources

ACAPS 'Cameroon: Escalation of the Anglophone crisis' (21 January 2020) https://reliefweb.int/sites/reliefweb.int/files/resources/20200121_acaps_short_note_escalation_of_the_anglophone_crisis_cameroon_0.pdf (accessed 22 February 2021)

Amnesty International 'Cameroon: Rise in killings in Anglophone regions ahead of parliamentary elections' (6 February 2020b) https://www.amnesty.org/en/latest/news/2020/02/cameroon-rise-in-killings-in-anglophone-regions/ (accessed 22 February 2021)

Amnesty International 'What's the difference between a refugee and an asylum Seeker?' https://www.amnesty.org.au/refugee-and-an-asylum-seeker-difference/ (accessed 1 April 2021)

'Cameroon teachers, lawyers strike in battle for English' *Al Jazeera* 5 December 2016 https://www.aljazeera.com/news/2016/12/5/cameroon-teachers-lawyers-strike-in-battle-for-english (accessed 22 February 2021)

Chatham House 'The Refugees Convention: why not scrap it?' (20 October 2005) https://www.chathamhouse.org/sites/default/files/public/Research/International%20Law/ilp201005.pdf (accessed 25 February 2021)

'Court declares detention, deportation of Cameroonian refugees illegal' *Channels Television* 2 March 2019 https://www.channelstv.com/2019/03/02/court-declares-detention-deportation-of-cameroonian-refugees-illegal/ (accessed 22 February 2021)

Shaban, ARA 'Condition of Cameroonian refugees in Nigeria worries top UNHCR official' *Africa News* 31 March 2018 https://www.africanews.com/2018/03/31/condition-of-cameroonian-refugees-in-nigeria-worries-top-unhcr-official// (accessed 25 February 2021)

Twitter post by Antonio Jose Canhandula on 29 March 2018 https://twitter.com/kanyandulajose/status/979229810500259840?ref_src=twsrc%5Etfw%7Ctwcamp%5Etweetembed%7Ctwterm%5E979229810500259840%7Ctwgr%5E%7Ctwcon%5Es1_&ref_url=https%3A%2F%2Fwww.africanews.com%2F2018%2F03%2F31%2Fcondition-of-cameroonian-refugees-in-nigeria-worries-top-unhcr-official%2F (accessed 25 February 2021)

Council of Europe, 'The Evolution of Human Rights' https://www.coe.int/en/web/compass/the-evolution-of-human-rights (accessed 22 February 2021).

DD Sasu, Violence towards Cameroonian refugees in Nigeria 2020, by state, Statista, 12 December 2022, at Nigeria: violence toward refugees from Cameroon | Statista

E Mpimbaza 27 March 2018, https://twitter.com/BethMpimbaza/status/978603534395564032?ref_src=twsrc%5Etfw%7Ctwcamp%5Etweetembed%7Ctwterm%5E978603534395564032%7Ctwgr%5E%7Ctwcon%5Es1_&ref_url=https%3A%2F%2Fwww.africanews.com%2F2018%2F03%2F31%2Fcondition-of-cameroonian-refugees-in-nigeria-worries-top-unhcr-official%2F (accessed 25 February 2021).

FHI 360 'Improving access to health care for Cameroonian refugees in Nigeria' 17 February 2020, https://www.fhi360.org/news/improving-access-health-care-cameroonian-refugees-nigeria (accessed 1 April 2021).

Internal Displacement Monitoring Centre (IDMC) 'Global Report on Internal Displacement: GRID 2020' (April 2020) 17. https://www.internal-displacement.org/sites/default/files/publications/documents/2020-IDMC-GRID.pdf (accessed 22 February 2021).

International Commission of Jurists 'State obligations stemming from international law' https://www.icj.org/chapter-2-esc-rights-under-international-law-and-the-role-of-judicial-and-quasi-judicial-bodies-2/2-3-identifying-breaches-of-international-obligations-of-states-pertaining-to-esc-rights/2-3-1-state-obligations-stemming-from-international-law/ (accessed 22 February 2021).

International Justice Resource Center (IJRC) 'Asylum and the Rights of Refugees', https://ijrcenter.org/refugee-law/ (accessed 25 February 2021).

J Craig, 'Violence in Cameroon's Anglophone crisis takes high civilian toll' 1 April 2021, https://www.aljazeera.com/news/2021/4/1/violence-in-cameroon-anglophone-crisis-takes-high-civilian-toll (accessed 11 April 2021).

J Phillips 'Asylum seekers and refugees: what are the facts?' 14 January 2011, 2. https://www.aph.gov.au/binaries/library/pubs/bn/sp/asylumfacts.pdf (accessed 25 February 2021).

L Unah, 'Cameroonian refugees in daily struggle for survival in Nigeria' 23 April 2019. https://www.trtworld.com/magazine/cameroonian-refugees-in-daily-struggle-for-survival-in-nigeria-26106 (accessed 1 April 2021).

L Unah 'Cameroon refugees struggle to cope with life of need in Nigeria' 8 March 2020. https://www.aljazeera.com/features/2020/3/8/cameroon-refugees-struggle-to-cope-with-life-of-need-in-nigeria (accessed 22 February 2021).

MA Awel 'Over 20,000 Cameroon refugees registered in Nigeria' 20 March 2018, https://www.aa.com.tr/en/africa/over-20-000-cameroon-refugees-registered-in-nigeria-/1094559# (accessed 1 April 2021).

Merriam-Webster 'The Origin of Refugee' https://www.merriam-webster.com/words-at-play/origin-and-meaning-of-refugee (accessed 1 April 2021).

MN Mbe 'Human rights issues in Cameroon in the case of the independentists arrested in Nigeria and extradited to Cameroon' 21 October, 2019, https://papers.ssrn.com/sol3/papers.cfm?abstract_id=3472963 (accessed 22 February 2021).

Office of the High Commissioner for Human Rights (OCHR) 'Fact Sheet No.20, Human Rights and Refugees' 2. https://www.ohchr.org/Documents/Publications/FactSheet20en.pdf (accessed 22 February 2021).

R Ajakaye 'UN blasts Nigeria over return of Cameroon separatists' 1 February 2018. https://www.aa.com.tr/en/africa/un-blasts-nigeria-over-return-of-cameroon-separatists/1052118 (accessed 22 February 2021).

T Fatunde 'Academics hail court rulings on deported lecturers' 13 March 2019. https://www.universityworldnews.com/post.php?story=20190313082701764 (accessed 22 February 2021).

United Nations High Commissioner for Refugees (UNHCR) 'Cameroon Refugees Overview' March 2021, https://reporting.unhcr.org/sites/default/files/UNHCR%20Nigeria%20-%20Cameroonian%20Refugees%20Overview%20-%20March%202021.pdf (accessed 26 April 2021).

UNHCR 'Cameroon Situation Update/Nigeria Operation' https://data2.unhcr.org/en/documents/details/84103 (accessed 22 February 2021a).

UNHCR 'More Cameroonian refugees flee to Nigeria, bringing total arrivals close to 60,000 mark' 13 February 2020, https://www.unhcr.org/news/press/2020/2/5e452d2b4/cameroonian-refugees-flee-nigeria-bringing-total-arrivals-close-60000-mark.html (accessed 1 April 2021).

UNHCR 'Operational Portal Regional Response-Nigeria Situation' https://data2.unhcr.org/en/situations/nigeriasituation (accessed 22 February 2021b).

UNHCR, 'Operational Update: Cameroonian Refugees in Nigeria', 2. February 2021c, https://reliefweb.int/sites/reliefweb.int/files/resources/Operational%20Update%20Cameroonian%20Refugees%20in%20Nigeria%20February%202021.pdf (accessed 1 April 2021).

UNHCR 'Operational Update: Cameroonian Refugees in Nigeria' 6. March 2021d, https://data2.unhcr.org/en/documents/download/86242 (accessed 26 April 2021). UNHCR 'Refugee Data Finder' https://www.unhcr.org/refugee-statistics/ (accessed 11 April 2021).

UNHCR 'Protection strategy for Cameroonian refugees in Nigeria 2018–2019' 10. https://data2.unhcr.org/en/documents/download/68381 (accessed 22 February 2021e).

UNHCR, 'Refugees and Asylum Seekers in Nigeria as of 28 February 2021' https://reliefweb.int/sites/reliefweb.int/files/resources/UNHCR%20Nigeria%20-%20Population%20Statistics%20February%202021.pdf (accessed 1 April 2021f).

UNHCR, 'States Parties to the 1951 Convention relating to the Status of Refugees and the 1967 Protocol', https://www.unhcr.org/protect/PROTECTION/3b73b0d63.pdf 3 (accessed 1 April 2021g).

UNHCR 'The 1951 Convention and its 1967 Protocol' September 2011, 1. https://www.refworld.org/pdfid/4ec4a7f02.pdf(accessed 25 February 2021).

UNHCR 'The Refugee Convention at 50' 2 July 2001, https://www.unhcr.org/news/editorial/2001/7/3b4c06f0d/refugee-convention-50.html#:~:text=After%20more%20than%20three%20weeks,to%20the%20Status%20of%20Refugees. (accessed 1 April 2021).

UNHCR 'What is a refugee?' https://www.unhcr.org/what-is-a-refugee.html (accessed 22 February 2021h).

UNHCR Nigeria, 'Cameroon Refugees Overview', January 2021, https://reliefweb.int/sites/reliefweb.int/files/resources/UNHCR%20Nigeria%20-%20Cameroonian%20Refugees%20Registration%20Dashboard%20January%202021.pdf (accessed 1 April 2021).
UN News 'Cameroonians pour into Nigeria, stretching scant resources – UN refugee agency' 20 March 2018. https://news.un.org/en/story/2018/03/1005372 (accessed 22 February 2021).
UN Refugee Agency (UNHCR), Socio-Economic Impact Assessment of COVID-19 Pandemic Among Persons of Concern in Nigeria, July 2020, p.6 at file:///C:/Users/OLUDURO/Downloads/Report%20on%20Assessment%20of%20Socio-Economic%20Impact%20of%20COVID-19%20on%20PoCs_19082020.pdf
Y Akinwale 'Heartbreaking tales of Southern Cameroonian refugees in Nigeria' 6 February 2021. https://www.icirnigeria.org/heartbreaking-tales-of-southern-cameroonian-refugees-in-nigeria/ (accessed 22 February 2021).

Index[1]

[1] Note: Page numbers followed by 'n' refer to notes.

E. Durojaye et al. (eds.), *Realising Socio-Economic Rights of Refugees and Asylum Seekers in Africa*, Politics of Citizenship and Migration, https://doi.org/10.1007/978-3-031-16548-1

SPRINGER NATURE

GPSR Compliance

The European Union's (EU) General Product Safety Regulation (GPSR) is a set of rules that requires consumer products to be safe and our obligations to ensure this.

If you have any concerns about our products, you can contact us on ProductSafety@springernature.com

In case Publisher is established outside the EU, the EU authorized representative is:

Springer Nature Customer Service Center GmbH
Europaplatz 3
69115 Heidelberg, Germany

FSC
www.fsc.org
MIX
Papier | Fördert gute Waldnutzung
FSC® C083411

Kolibri 360 GmbH
Ferdinand-Jühlke-Straße 7
99095 Erfurt, Deutschland
produktsicherheit@kolibri360.de